Reimagining Liberal Education

ALSO AVAILABLE FROM BLOOMSBURY

Reimagining Liberal Education

Affiliation and Inquiry in Democratic Schooling

HANAN A. ALEXANDER

Bloomsbury Academic
An imprint of Bloomsbury Publishing Plc

B L O O M S B U R Y
NEW YORK • LONDON • NEW DELHI • SYDNEY

Bloomsbury Academic

An imprint of Bloomsbury Publishing Plc

1385 Broadway	50 Bedford Square
New York	London
NY 10018	WC1B 3DP
USA	UK

www.bloomsbury.com

BLOOMSBURY and the Diana logo are trademarks of Bloomsbury Publishing Plc

First published 2015

© Hanan A. Alexander, 2015

British Library Cataloguing-in-Publication Data
A catalogue record for this book is available from the British Library.

ISBN: HB: 978-1-4411-2243-8
PB: 978-1-4411-6764-4
ePDF: 978-1-4411-8344-6
ePub: 978-1-4411-6158-1

Library of Congress Cataloging-in-Publication Data
A catalogue record for this book is available from the Library of Congress

Typeset by Integra Software Services Pvt. Ltd.
Printed and bound in the United States of America

This book is dedicated to the legacy of my parents
Fran and Ernie Alexander
who taught by example that
a life well lived is devoted to caring for others.
May my father's memory live on as a blessing

זכר צדיק לברכה

and may my mother continue to enjoy many healthy and happy years

שתבדל לחיים ארוכים.

And to my friend and colleague
Ilan Gur-Ze'ev
who taught by example that
a life well lived engages the other in loving dialogue.
May Ilan's memory live on as a blessing

יהי זכרו ברוך.

CONTENTS

ACKNOWLEDGMENTS

This book articulates a perspective on education that, while rooted in the experiences of my youth, reached maturity after I took up a professorship in philosophy of education at the University of Haifa in 1999. With the exception of the first chapter, which was penned during my graduate school years, and the introduction and penultimate chapter which were written for this volume, it consists of essays first published subsequent to the completion of *Reclaiming Goodness* (which was written on a 1997 study leave in Haifa and published in 2001), revised and updated for republication here.

I am grateful to the University of Haifa for excellent conditions that made this work possible, especially to its Education Deans and Rectors during the period in which the essays were written: Professors Ruth Linn, Ofra Mayseless, Lily Orland-Barak, Yossi Ben-Artzi, and David Faraggi. I am also grateful to the benefactors of the Center for Jewish Education, which I have headed since coming to the University, Ruth Ziegler of the Ziegler Family Trust and Mark Lainer of the Mark and Eli Lainer Family Foundation, for their ongoing support over these many years. Additionally, I would like to thank the organizations and funders mentioned here that made study leaves possible at the University of Cambridge in 2003 and the University of California, Berkeley, from 2008 to 2010. I would also like to express my gratitude to the many students, friends, and colleagues mentioned who offered comments, criticism, advice, and counsel that helped to sharpen my arguments; to my friend and editor Michele Waldinger who has now assisted me with a third book with professionalism and good humor; and to my editor at Continuum/Bloomsbury, David Barker, for his patience and guidance. And of course I am thankful to the publishers listed here for permission to reproduce essays in revised forms that were originally published under their imprimatur.

An earlier version of Chapter One was first published in *Religious Education* 76, no. 3 (1981): 307–20. Chapter Two is a revised version of an essay originally published in *Journal of Philosophy of Education* 40, no. 2 (2006): 205–22. I am grateful to the students in my seminar on Methodological Issues in Education Research at the University of Haifa, where some of these ideas were first presented, to Professor Denis Phillips of Stanford University for pointing out the importance of Dewey's thought to the historical sketch presented here, and to Professors Rivka Eisikovits of the University of Haifa and David Bridges of Cambridge University for comments on the manuscript.

An earlier version of Chapter Three was published under the title "Aesthetic Inquiry in Education: Community, Transcendence, and the Meaning of Pedagogy," in *Journal of Aesthetic Education* 37, no. 2 (2003): 1–18. It also appeared in Hebrew as "Mehkar Esteti Behinuh," in *Mesorot Vezeramim Bemehkar Haeihuti*, edited by Naama Sabar, 229–56, Tel Aviv: Z'mora Betan, 2000. I am grateful to Professor Naama Sabar Ben-Yehoshua of Tel Aviv University for inviting me to contribute that essay to her collection and for helpful comments and criticism.

Chapter Four first appeared as "Traditions of Inquiry in Education: Engaging the Paradigms of Educational Research," in *The Springer Companion to Educational Research*, eds M. Peters and A. Reid, 13–25 (The Hague: Springer, 2013). I am thankful to Alan Reid of the University of South Australia for useful comments and to Richard Pring of Oxford University for writing a response to the piece in that volume.

Chapter Five first appeared as "Education in Ideology," *Journal of Moral Education* 34, no. 1 (2005): 1–18. I am grateful to Professor Yossi Yona of Ben Gurion University, Professor David Carr of the University of Edinburgh, and other members of the Philosophy of Education Society of Great Britain for helpful comments and criticism on this paper.

Chapter Six first appeared as "Literacy and Citizenship: Tradition, Reason, and Critique in Democratic Education," in *Philosophy of Education in the Era of Globalization*, eds Y. Raley and G. Preyer, 30–50 (New York: Routledge, 2010). I am grateful to the American Israel Cooperative Enterprise and the Richard and Rhoda Goldman Foundation for a Visiting Professorship at the University of California, Berkeley, during the 2008–2010 academic years; to Professor P. David Pearson, then Dean of the Berkeley Graduate School Education (GSE), for exceptional conditions that made writing this chapter possible; to students in my graduate seminar on citizenship education at Cal; and to Professor Jabari Mahiri, then chair of the GSE's Division of Language, Society, and Culture, for helpful comments and suggestions.

Chapter Seven first appeared as "What Is Common About Common Schooling: Rational Autonomy and Moral Agency in Liberal Democratic Education," *Journal of Philosophy of Education* 41, no. 4 (2007): 609–24. It also appeared in *The Common School and the Comprehensive Ideal*, eds M. Halstead and G. Haydon, 108–23 (Oxford: Blackwell Publishers, 2008). I am grateful to Professor Paul Standish of the Institute of Education, University of London, for his encouragement and helpful comments.

Chapter Eight first appeared in *Theory and Research in Education* 3, no. 3 (2005): 343–69. I am grateful to anonymous reviewers, to Professor Randall Curran of the Universities of Rochester and Birmingham, and to participants in the 2005 meeting of the Philosophy of Education Society of Great Britain for helpful comments and suggestions.

The ninth chapter first appeared as "Moral Education and Liberal Democracy: Spirituality, Community, and Character in an Open Society," *Educational Theory* 53, no. 4 (2004): 367–87. I am grateful to Nicholas C. Burbules, the blind reviewers of this paper, and Professor Lynn Bosetti, then of the University of Calgary, for helpful comments and criticism, to the late Terence H. McLaughlin of the Universities of London and Cambridge for many valuable conversations, to Drs. Rebecca Nye and Rosalind Paul of the Center for Advanced Religious and Theological Studies in the Cambridge University Faculty of Divinity, and to the Master and Fellows of St. Edmund's College, Cambridge, for a Visiting Fellowship that afforded an extraordinarily supportive and congenial environment in which to work out these ideas.

Chapter Ten first appeared as "Autonomy, Faith, and Reason: McLaughlin and Callan on Religious Initiation," in *Faith in Education: A Tribute to Terence McLaughlin*, ed G. Haydon, 27–45 (London: Institute of Education, University of London, 2009). I am grateful to Dr. Graham Haydon of the Institute of Education, University of London, for helpful comments and suggestions.

Chapter Twelve first appeared as "Spirituality, Morality, and Criticism in Education: A Response to Kevin Gary," in *Studies in Philosophy and Education* 25, no. 4 (2006): 327–34. I am grateful to Dr. Kevin Gary for his generous review of *Reclaiming Goodness* in that volume of *Studies of Philosophy of Education*, 325–26, entitled "Spirituality, Critical Thinking, and the Desire for What Is Infinite," and for organizing a symposium at the 2009 annual meeting of the Philosophy of Education Society in San Francisco at which I presented Chapter Eleven, "To the Truth, Roughly Speaking."

I owe a profound debt to my wife and life partner Shelley, and to our three children Aliza, Yehuda, and Yonina, who traveled with me across the globe so that I could accept the position at Haifa. Although my job provided comparatively excellent objective conditions for immigration, the subjective experience was far more complex. It involved working and going to school in an unfamiliar environment, communicating in a second language, and living in a culture very different in many respects from our American origins.

I met Ilan Gur Ze'ev almost immediately upon my arrival as a visiting professor at the University of Haifa in 1996. We became fast friends, discussing the challenges of philosophy of education and Israeli society in the hallways of the Faculty of Education and during lunches that we shared on a regular basis. At first glance, it was an unlikely duo, since I was a lifelong Zionist who trained as an analytic philosopher with little tolerance for critical social theory and he a highly identified post-Zionist critic of Israeli education. But we were both skeptical of the philosophical traditions in which we were educated, and Ilan's exceptional capacity for dialogue and collegiality made it an easy partnership. It was my great privilege to work closely with Ilan as the philosophers in Haifa's Faculty of Education for close to two decades. Together we established the Israel Philosophy of Education Society and the Haifa Philosophy of Education Forum, planned many conferences and joint projects, and taught many students. From Ilan I learned a deep respect for the traditions of critical social theory in which he wrote—neo-Marxism, postmodernism, and critical pedagogy—and I recall with pride how he embraced philosophical analysis in one of the last lectures he gave at the University. Ilan's untimely passing in 2012 was a profound loss to the international philosophy of education community, to the academic community in Israel, to the University of Haifa, to his loving father, wife, and children, and to me personally. Our many conversations had a profound influence on this volume, and it is with deep respect and warm affection that I dedicate it in part to him.

If the philosophical project described here reached something of a zenith in Haifa, Israel, it began in a Berkeley, California, family many years ago. I acquired my deep identification with the Jewish People from my father, Ernie Alexander, and my love of Israel from my mom, Fran Alexander. But I learned from both of my parents a profound respect for difference rooted in the belief that the obligation to care for one another as human beings who are all children of God is the most meaningful message of our heritage. It is this dual legacy of robust commitment to a particular inheritance, on the one hand, and deep respect for difference, on the other, that I have endeavored to explore in these pages. My dad of blessed memory passed away in 2007, but my mom continues to head our family with wisdom and unbelievable energy in the spirit that guided their loving partnership for 63 years. It is to my father's memory and to the legacy he shared with my mom, which together they passed on to their children and grandchildren, that this book is also dedicated.

Introduction

Over the past many decades there has been a flight from normative discourse in education grounded in philosophical, theological, ethical, or political traditions, from systematic, thoughtful, and careful deliberations concerning the highest ideals to which schools ought to aspire. Witness the decline in the number of university teaching positions in the philosophy of education around the world today, the alarm aroused at any mention of a connection between religion and education, or the confusion in many multicultural societies concerning what values to transmit to children across the generations. In the effort to become more scientific, more tough- than tender-minded, as William James once put it, to base findings on hard empirical data, to offer clear and cogent justifications of new and innovative research methodologies, and even to enhance the rigor with which we conduct philosophical discourse, educational scholarship has too often become overly focused on the more technical aspects of teaching and learning while losing sight of the purposes it should seek to attain.[1] I have long sought to reverse this trend by arguing that cultivation of transcendental concepts of the good through initiation into dynamic traditions prepared to engage alternative points of view is a high ideal of schooling in diverse democratic societies.

This book reflects an intellectual journey of many years, in which I have endeavored to understand the role of robust affiliations and perspectives—grounded in faith, culture, language, gender, race, ethics, or politics—in the education of citizens in open, pluralistic, liberal democratic societies, and the relation of these affiliations to inquiry, both about the processes and institutions by means of which such an education is conducted and within particular subject-matter disciplines that comprise its content and pedagogy. The concern for inquiry refers to the challenges of maintaining a rigorous, open, and broadly critical stance, given a robust affiliation with particular ways of life, toward both the academic study of education and the examination and teaching of substantive content. Addressing tensions between affiliation and inquiry in democratic schooling entails a contribution to the long-standing philosophical and theological conversation about the proper relation between faith and reason in the context of contemporary educational research, policy, and practice.

Like many other pursuits, this book is a product of the circumstances into which I was born and have chosen to live my life. I was raised in the middle of the post-World War II baby boom, in hyper liberal Berkeley, California, by the children of Eastern European Jewish immigrants to the United States, who were seeking to reclaim their own ethnic and religious heritage amidst an ever-increasing openness to new ideas and alternative lifestyles. It was an idyllic time to be a child, or at least so it seemed to me. The economy was growing, schools were mostly safe (at least for the middle and upwardly mobile classes), and we were allowed to roam freely, with little fear of danger, to explore opportunities of which our parents, not to mention our grandparents, could never have dreamed. Other than my father's service in the American army during the war, our family escaped the devastation of Jewish life in Europe, and we felt fully accepted as Jews in a mostly gentile land. But as tolerant as our friends and teachers may have been of difference, and of those who pushed the boundaries of accepted norms, they offered little guidance to us concerning how to choose among the many new paths with which our contemporaries were experimenting. And they were often nonplussed, even impatient, when we sought to ground our choices in a return to the traditions of our ancestors rather than relying solely on untested innovations focused primarily on a tenuous present or an uncharted future. In the Berkeley of my youth, I often felt that people were tolerant of every proposition so long as it was perceived to be as liberal as they were. Paradoxically, although a general atmosphere of tolerance appeared to prevail, the curriculum to which we were exposed both inside and outside of the classroom was anything but accepting of difference. The students were lily white, the holidays were mostly Christian, and our studies reflected the "one best system" described so eloquently by historian David Tyack, in which belief in the objectivity of the natural and human sciences and in the neutrality of the American melting pot prevailed.[2]

My decision to complement my studies in philosophy with an intensive education in my own heritage and to pursue a career on two tracks, one focusing on philosophy of education and the other on Jewish learning, was a direct outgrowth of a personal struggle shared by many with particular religious or cultural commitments to distinguish ourselves from the tendency toward homogeneity that characterizes so many liberal democracies and to find our own way amidst societies that appear to be more accepting of nonaligned secularism than of abiding commitment to ancestral traditions. I began my career at the American Jewish University in Los Angeles, where I headed an undergraduate college featuring a core curriculum in Jewish and Western civilization and prepared educators to teach in faith schools, while I was also teaching philosophy of education at UCLA. The tremendous disparity between the resources available for educational research concerning the public sector versus those devoted to so-called nonpublic matters such as faith and spirituality, and the difficulty of creating an intellectual dialogue between the two in a single institution, left me with a feeling of great unease.

My decision to continue this dual-track career in an Israeli institution of higher learning was motivated by the realization that Israel offers a unique opportunity to integrate the pursuit of educational philosophy in general with a concern for the transmission and transformation of one culture in particular, shared with the majority of citizens and lived in the public as well as the private domains. In a democratic and Jewish state it is possible to explore education in the Jewish heritage in much of its variety as part of a state-sponsored system, which requires not only the reinterpretation of one particular tradition in light of the demands of democracy but also a reassessment of democratic values in consideration of that ancient inheritance.

Yet upon my arrival at the University of Haifa in 1999, I was confronted with an increasing opposition both by a minority of intellectuals within Israel and a growing number abroad to the very idea that any account of Jewish collective identity, cultural or religious, is reconcilable with democracy, however conceived. They argued that addressing the rights of Israel's Palestinian minority, who are citizens of Israel and not part of any Palestinian state that may emerge in the West Bank and Gaza, requires Israel to sever its Jewish connection and become a neutral "state for all of its citizens." This solidified in me the sense that lingered from the experiences of my youth and early career that we require a new approach to liberalism as it impacts the study and practice of education that celebrates particularity and distinctiveness in ways that recognize the rights of both majority and minority cultures while enhancing the individual capacity for intelligent choice, personal freedom, and respect for difference required in democratic regimes.

It was perfectly natural then that my first publication outlined the contours of a research program that explores the role of much more robust forms of affiliation than those tolerated by my Berkeley compatriots those many years ago, which in turn raises hard questions about the very idea that tough-minded inquiry, both about and within education in open, pluralistic, democratic societies, can ever be truly neutral concerning questions about how one ought to live. This research program reached a milestone with the publication of *Reclaiming Goodness* in 2001, soon after my arrival in Haifa.[3] I argued there that democratic education should aim to inspire a spiritual quest in which students seek self-definition in the context of learning communities that are committed to higher goods—"higher" but not "highest" goods since any putative vision of goodness might be later transcended by a better one—and willing to engage in dialogue with alternative perspectives.[4]

For the most part this volume brings together essays that were published after *Reclaiming Goodness*, in a revised form that emphasizes the flow of a common argument. I introduce them with an updated version of that very first essay that set me on this intellectual path. They develop a number of innovative concepts around which I ask the reader to reimagine liberal education in order to make greater room for people like myself—committed at once to the values of an ancient tradition on the one hand and to open, pluralistic, liberal democracy on the other. Each essay marks a phase in my intellectual development by considering the consequences of this thesis for one of three different aspects of educational thought and practice: (1) the history and philosophy of educational research; (2) education for citizenship and its basis in political theory; and (3) moral, spiritual, and religious education in the democratic curriculum.

I call the search for transcendent visions of human flourishing that are open to engagement with alternative views a quest for *intelligent spirituality*[5] and the process by which one learns to be different by identifying with such a vision while respecting the differences of others, the *pedagogy of difference*.[6] I refer to the political dimension of this view as *liberal communitarianism*,[7] which is tied closely to Isaiah Berlin's diversity liberalism,[8] and to its broader philosophical and epistemological perspective as *transcendental pragmatism*.[9] The path to developing these concepts was not chronological. Concerns for methodology and epistemology overlapped with those of spirituality, ethics, politics, and pedagogy, such that I would move back and forth from work on one topic to another. For the purposes of this volume, however, I have organized them conceptually. To sharpen the meaning and significance of these themes and clarify how they are organized in the structure of the book, I will spell out here in greater detail the problem that I seek to address by bringing these essays together, the method that they employ, and the combined argument that they make in addressing that problem when taken as a whole.

The problem of the book

The penchant for tough-mindedness in education is tied to the idea that there is a view from nowhere grounded in one or another account of reason that is neutral with respect to decisions about what to believe and how to behave. James put rationalism on the tender side of his dichotomy, by which he meant an idealistic and optimistic intellectual temperament devoted to free will and a principled, if too often monist and dogmatic, form of religious or spiritual transcendentalism, such as the neo-Hegelian absolutists of his day.[10] But there is another, more tough-minded, account of reason, of the sort reappraised by Michael Oakeshott in his well-known critique of rationalism in politics.[11] It descends from Immanuel Kant's response to David Hume's devastating assessment of Francis Bacon's empiricism in the *Critique of Pure Reason* and travels through August Comte's scientific positivism to the logical positivism of the Vienna circle and into early analytic philosophy. It also descends from John Locke's *Second Treatise* and Kant's *Critique of Practical Reason* to John Stuart Mill's *On Liberty* and John Rawls's *A Theory of Justice* and *Political Liberalism*. Attraction to this sort of tough-minded rationalism tied closely to naïve empiricism has long lingered in political, social, and educational thought, motivated in part by the desire to prove that the human sciences can be every bit as hardheaded as their counterparts in the natural sciences, even though many of the key theories of logical positivism have been subjected to hard criticism after the latter Wittgenstein by the likes of William Sellars, W. V. O. Quine, and Donald Davidson, and its counterparts in ethics and politics were reassessed by the likes of Oakeshott and Berlin. This more skeptical and irreligious rational temperament professes pluralism, at least in theory (though, as the Berkeley of my youth appears to suggest, it may be less pluralistic than it professes to be), and tends toward materialism, pessimism, and fatalism.[12]

This idea of rationality as rigorously neutral has long held sway in many influential traditions of thought, grounded in what Richard Rorty called Philosophy with a capital *P* that seeks final answers to questions about the nature of truth and goodness.[13] It impacts epistemology, thinking about the nature of knowledge and the difference between truth and falsehood. It also reverberates in politics, thinking about the nature of a good society and the requirements of citizenship, as well as in ethics and religion, approaches to what it means to be a good person and to live a good life. Through discussions about what is true and what is good, this penchant for rational neutrality enters into much thinking about the nature of education, the students in its charge, the professionals in its employ, the aspirations it should pursue, the content it should transmit, the ways it should do so, and the discourses it should use to justify, deliberate, and reflect on all of the above. The problem is that few of us believe in neutrality any longer because it cannot be demonstrated without presupposing what it sets out to prove.[14]

This book is about education without neutrality. I call this view of education liberal because it holds that open, pluralistic, liberal democracy offers the best account available of how to share a life with others, especially when such a life seeks a middle course between extreme forms of comprehensive and diversity liberalism, the one prioritizing a rational account of individual autonomy at the expense of plurality and the other pluralism to the exclusion of the individual. An account of the appropriate relation between the requirements of democratic citizenship for the individual, on the one hand, and those of diverse traditions that seek to live with one another across difference, on the other, is essential for any genuinely liberal understanding of education. Conceiving such an account, along with defending substantive views of what schools should seek to achieve, is an important task of educational thought that has been forfeited by many educationalists enamored with the neutrality of reason.

That it is not possible to base what we believe or how we behave on neutral criteria is of no mere philosophical or educational interest alone. Two of the most pressing dilemmas facing open, pluralistic, liberal democracies today are bound up with this idea. One has to do with the compatibility of key liberal values such as mutual respect and peaceful coexistence with serious faith, cultural, or national commitments, and the other with the relation both within and across national divides between domains conceived as common or public and those thought to be particular or private. Many influential liberal theories address these dilemmas by maintaining that the democratic commons should remain essentially indifferent to religious and other so-called nonpublic commitments that lie within the province of either particular communities or personal preference. However, this approach fails to resolve these dilemmas because it leads to at least three additional difficulties. It too often endorses a distorted, even intolerant, picture of faith and other traditions as necessarily crazy, dogmatic, or divisive, a representation that limits our ability to identify those seeking to live in peace with others who are different. It also encourages opponents of liberalism, especially critical social theorists, to look for hidden power relations beneath the guise of neutrality, which tends to exacerbate not ameliorate social conflict. Finally, it embraces a picture of personal autonomy that is overly centered on the self, rather than also engrossed in a received tradition or the needs of others. Such an approach can become so open to everything that one loses the ability to commit to anything at all.

Consider Robert Nash's self-description in his book on teaching about religion in American schools and colleges, *Faith, Hype, and Clarity*, which is fairly typical of how many educational theorists today address these sorts of dilemmas:

> I am an existential agnostic, a "seeker," who has yet to foreclose on the major religious questions that continue to intrigue me to this day. I have been greatly influenced by…existential theologians…however, I remain unconvinced that the peculiar "transcendental" solutions to the existential problems they so powerfully define are able to touch my life in any meaningful way…. I have become a postmodern skeptic on most matters, including religious; although paradoxically I have strong, virtually insatiable, metaphysical curiosities. I do not believe that there can ever be a final or definitive religious meaning for everyone, never a "master [religious] narrative" binding on each of us, because reality is endlessly interpretable and always a product of our unique historical and cultural conditionings…. Though, I must confess that I worry about the political authoritarianism and moral and epistemological nihilism that seem to accompany much postmodern thinking today.[15]

Nash expresses appropriate concern for the epistemological, moral, and political problems and paradoxes inherent in religious dogmatism on the one hand and postmodern nihilism on the other. Under these conditions, however, other than skepticism itself what can we possibly be justified in teaching our children in schools, why should they believe anything we ask them to consider, and how can we explain the methods we use to systematically examine the pedagogies used for doing so? Without the presumption of rational neutrality, the curriculum of common schools in liberal democracies and the methodologies for studying them appear to be in crisis.[16] Liberal educators are unsure about the knowledge and values that ought to be transmitted across the generations and educational researchers continue to be at war over the methods that are most appropriate for systematically examining the processes and institutions that purport to do so. But how is it possible to initiate into one particular normative tradition in a pluralistic society, or to prefer one approach to research over another, without fostering discord among opposing points of view, or to educate for peaceful coexistence among rival perspectives within a common civil society, or across national or epistemological divides, given that there exist no neutral criteria to adjudicate between them?

The method of the book

Philosophers have long been concerned with questions of this kind. How, they ask, is one thing possible, supposing certain other conflicting or contradictory things? How is it possible for us to have free will, for example, supposing that all actions are causally determined, or for evil to be possible, given the existence of an omnipotent omniscient good God? Addressing these sorts of questions requires what Robert Nozick has called a philosophical explanation, which articulates deeper principles that can remove the apparent conflict and put one's beliefs in alignment.[17] This book proposes just such a deeper or reconciled understanding of the relation between affiliation and inquiry—faith and reason—in democratic schooling than is currently available, between competing normative philosophies and traditions of inquiry based in rival theological, ethical, political, or epistemological traditions and the ground on which they might meet in the education of citizens for open, pluralistic, liberal democratic societies.

This requires a renewed and nuanced attempt at reconciling old and new ideas that appear to clash with one another, such as intelligence and spirituality, individualism and communitarianism, or pragmatism and transcendentalism. To accomplish this we need to consider the "practical cash value" of an idea, to use James's famous expression, set at work within the stream of one's experience[18]; we need to look "away from first things, principles, categories, and supposed necessities" and "towards last things, fruits, consequences, facts."[19] Although we may have abandoned the chimera of neutrality, many of us are nevertheless dissatisfied with the false dichotomy between tough- and tender-mindedness, between hardheaded reliance on rationalism and empiricism on the one hand and softhearted concern for meaning and understanding on the other. "We have a hankering for the good on both sides of the line"[20]; we want to combine "the scientific loyalty to facts" with the "old confidence in human values ... whether of the religious or romantic type."[21] We are dissatisfied with a misleading dualism that places empiricism and irreligious anti-transcendentalism on the one side of a divide, while on the other side recognizes as genuinely religious or spiritual only dogmatic traditions that are "out of all definite touch with concrete facts and joys and sorrows." In this view, "ideas (which themselves are part of our experience) become true just in so far as they help us to get into satisfactory relation with other parts of our experience."[22]

In this pragmatic sense, the term "transcendence" suggests that some ideas may be judged at least provisionally to be higher than others and so used as normative criteria for assessment, even though they are not final or highest ideals that are immune from criticism based on subsequent experience. James understood that in order to adequately consider our world on the basis of "last things," what Dewey called "ends-in-view," we require a robust account of those goods that, while themselves encountered in experience, can nonetheless serve as criteria for judging the worth of other experiences, even if those goods may originate in mystical, religious, spiritual, or transcendental traditions. This in contrast to other pragmatists, such as Dewey, who embraced a naïve faith in the ability of individual growth to serve as the final criterion against which to judge the satisfaction of an idea,[23] and Rorty, who held that even growth cannot overcome the radical consequences of this perspective.[24] As James put it once again:

> If there is any life that is really better we should lead, and if there is any idea which, if believed in would help us to lead that life, then it would be really *better for us* to believe that idea, *unless, indeed, belief in it incidentally clashed with other greater vital benefit* .... If theological ideas should do this, if the notion of God should prove to do it, how could pragmatism possibly deny God's existence? She could see no meaning in treating as "not true" a notion that was so pragmatically successful. What other kind of truth could there be, for her, than all of this agreement with concrete reality.[25]

The discourse of this book is philosophical, then, in the broad analytic sense of the term, especially considering the pragmatic turn of several influential latter-day analysts, using methods of conceptual analysis to unwrap the meaning of language, logical analysis to clarify the coherence of arguments, and dialectical analysis to consider how to balance ideas that are in tension with one another. This said, I am passionate about using these intellectual tools to address normative questions of value and meaning that were once eschewed by analytic philosophy in education, and following the likes of Berlin[26] and Alasdair MacIntyre,[27] I appreciate that analyzing concepts and arguments requires first understanding them within the historical contexts in which they were formulated.

Additionally, unlike the analytic tradition in which I was trained, it is my view that philosophy of education can do more than the mere elimination of confusions in language and logic. With Kurt Lewin I believe that "there is nothing so practical as a good theory."[28] Curriculum and schooling in the West today are plagued by the absence of such integrated theories, owing in part to difficulties with many of the views mentioned here. The task, however, is not the creation of some new grand theory, a la sociologists Talcott Parsons or C. Wright Mills.[29] Early analytic philosophers of education such as Richard Peters were right to be suspicious of the perils of such grandiose pretentions.[30] Rather, the task is to develop what Robert Merton called "integrated theories of the middle range" for education in open, pluralistic, liberal democratic societies.[31] This book offers but one effort at conceiving philosophically such an interconnected group of middle-range theories that integrate Joseph Schwab's concern for society, subject matter, teaching, students, and field data, with no pretense of comprehensiveness.[32]

The argument of the book

This book reimagines the justification, substance, process, and study of education in open, pluralistic, liberal democratic societies, in the absence of a neutral account of reason. Liberal education under these conditions entails initiation into a transcendental vision of the good embodied in a dynamic heritage that is willing to engage rival accounts of the truth and different visions of how best to live, not exposure to weak personalized cultures or indoctrination into dogmatic traditions closed to alternatives. One can acquire the capacity to make independent choices given that we can never stand outside of the lives we lead by learning to be different and to respect the difference of others. This requires an understanding of the traditions to which one is heir or with which one chooses to affiliate that is open to exposure and critique according to traditions other than one's own.[33]

I say reimagine because the task as I have understood it requires reinterpreting ancient metaphors for envisaging the purposes and possibilities of education in light of current circumstances, as an illustration at least of how dynamic traditions that are open to dialogue with rival perspectives can learn from one another. The metaphors I have in mind hark back to the philosophical rationality of Aristotle on the one hand and the religious tradition of the Hebrew Bible on the other; and the reinterpretation to which I refer entails rereading each of these views independently of one another in ways that eschew absolutism and then recrafting the long-standing relation between them accordingly. Following Aristotle, this reinterpretation distinguishes between *Phronesis*, practical wisdom grounded in tradition, and *Sophia*, theoretical knowledge grounded in reason.[34] The former addresses ethical and political questions concerning the lives we ought to lead and the ways communities should be organized to foster them. The latter is focused on teleological and causal reasoning that considers the purposes of events in the world and how they influence one another. However, unlike Aristotle and in keeping with Oakeshott, the view offered here prioritizes tradition over reason—Phronesis over Sophia—rather than the other way around.[35] This requires a robust form of pluralism that presupposes, at least as a regulative principle, a higher good beyond the boundaries of our various perspectives, the possibility and substance of which can only be perceived from within the confines of those very boundaries.

Aristotle thought that reason was built into the metaphysical structure of the universe. The very possibility of one thing being caused by another presupposes a first cause, he reasoned, the existence of which only makes sense if the very purpose of existence itself is inherently rational. In accord with his teacher Plato, Aristotle understood this concept of transcendent reason to be absolute, singular, and unchanging.[36] The twelfth-century rabbi and poet Yehuda Halevy called this "the god of the philosophers,"[37] the godhead of Greek philosophy that medieval scholastic philosophers such as Mohammed Al Farabi, Moses Maimonides, and Thomas Aquinas sought to reconcile with the God of religious revelation.[38] Human flourishing was to be found, in Aristotle's view, by employing this teleological form of reasoning to discover the golden mean, a midway between extremes, so as to understand and enact the wisdom of divine rationality in human society. In principle this account of transcendence could be expressed and preserved by means of a variety of customs and ceremonies in different political cultures, provided they adhered to the ultimate authority of absolute transcendental reason. Hence, Aristotle's politics permitted a nascent and truncated form of pluralism, which made possible a modicum of tolerance among Muslim, Jewish, and Christian medieval religious philosophies. But at the end of the day, reason dominated faith in this view, rather than the two engaging one another in dialogue.

This marriage between Greek rationalism and monotheistic faith crumbled under the weight of modern skepticism, which revealed a variety of fallacies in Aristotle's theological metaphysics. When Hume employed the same skepticism to show that the consequences of scientific empiricism were merely contingent, not necessary,[39] Kant awoke from his dogmatic slumber to argue that empiricism only makes sense when coupled with the assumption that causation is built into the rational structure of consciousness, not things-in-themselves.[40] This entailed a new philosophical idea of God as the beginning and end of reason and a new universal religion, within the limits of reason alone.[41] This religion of reason sought to subjugate all other faith traditions. Despite their professed belief in pluralism, it also became the underlying faith commitment of comprehensive liberals and the price of entry into liberal society.

Yet, as G. W. F. Hegel famously pointed out in critique of Kant, there is no way to justify any account of reason a priori, outside the bounds of some concrete tradition of practice rooted in history, culture, and language, without presupposing the very sort of a priori reason in question.[42] This calls for a reassessment of the relation between theory and practice, following pragmatists such as James and Dewey, such that we formulate theories to resolve problems felt in practical experience. However, as Quine would have it, we can only formulate what counts as a need and what it would mean to meet it, or a problem and what it might mean to solve it, within the context of a web of belief.[43] Oakeshott argued that these webs are embedded in traditions of practice that are always historically, culturally, and linguistically contingent.[44]

It follows that faith and rational traditions—those that call for affiliation and those that insist upon the rigors of critical inquiry—belong on a more equal footing than has heretofore been allowed by most philosophical accounts of the relation between them. Indeed, ethics preceded epistemology, since the moral independence required for democratic citizenship necessitates first that one learns to receive a tradition of practice engaged with others before seeking to assert one's rational autonomy.[45] Hence, both the study and practice of liberal education require initiation into traditions of primary inheritance along with exposure to alternative viewpoints; the one makes possible the construction of coherent ethical and epistemic identities from within a particular orientation and the other the criticism of that viewpoint from an outsider's perspective. A person thus learns to ground moral and methodological choices in particular ethical orientations while considering the contributions of alternative points of view, including the possibility of a life path other than the one in which one was raised, and to complement one research tradition with insights from another.

The structure of the book

The book is organized into five parts. The first part consists of a Prologue with a chapter arguing for a transcendent dimension to education. The three central parts contain chapters addressing each of the themes mentioned earlier: the history and philosophy of educational research, education for citizenship and its basis in political theory, and moral, spiritual, and religious education in the democratic curriculum. The last part is an Epilogue with two chapters responding to critics. The reader with a special interest in any one of these fields may find it useful to skip directly to the relevant section. However, I have weaved these essays into a single volume because I believe that together they tell a coherent story about the study and practice of liberal education as a whole. That story begins with new thinking about educational research, because it is through methods of inquiry that we conceive the very nature of pedagogy. It then moves to a face of liberalism not often considered in education, because it is the liberal state that sets the concrete conditions for how we put pedagogy into practice. It concludes by considering the consequences of this alternative view of liberalism for education in faith and morals, because these are what today's democratic schooling needs most. Each part is preceded by a brief introduction that pulls the various threads of this story together.

Part One, "Prologue," contains the first chapter, "Schools Without Faith," which states the problem of the book: In the absence of empirical, rational, or utilitarian neutrality, how can liberal education be reconceived? It argues that humans are endowed with a transcendental imagination—a propensity to interpret their environments in light of ultimate ideas—which when left undeveloped can lead to serious problems for liberal societies, nihilism and narcissism on the one hand and dogmatism on the other. The task of liberal education is the cultivation of this propensity within the context of dynamic traditions open to engagement with rival perspectives.[46]

Part Two, "Transcendental Pragmatism in Educational Research," considers over the next three chapters how both quantitative and qualitative epistemologies have contributed to the flight from philosophy, theology, ethics, and politics in educational research and practice by assuming the possibility of an empirical or rational view from nowhere. Contra this view I argue that testing the merits of an idea against practical experience requires an account of what it means to be meritorious, which is only possible in the context of a transcendent vision of the good.

The flight from normative discourse in education is tied to the rise of empirical research in educational policy and practice. Hence, Chapter Two, "A View from Somewhere," begins by examining the epistemological debate between quantitative and qualitative methodologies in social and educational research. One aspect of the qualitative critique of quantitative research concerns the fact that in its quest for certainty the latter eschews normative concerns that the former presumably takes into account. However, I ask why we should believe the subjective perceptions of qualitative participant-observers altogether given the concern for objectivity in the behavioral and social sciences, and I critique the most common answer to this question within the social and educational research community. This answer posits the existence of two (or more) equally legitimate epistemological paradigms—positivism and constructivism, the one adhering to a stronger and the other a weaker concept of empirical neutrality. I call this the dual- (or multiple-) epistemology thesis. The chapter offers an alternative to this thesis—transcendental pragmatism—that places a priority in all educational research, both quantitative and qualitative, on understanding the purposes and meanings that humans attribute to educational practices. Only within the context of a transcendent view from somewhere can we make sense of research findings altogether, qualitative as well as quantitative. The empirical turn in educational policy and practice heightens rather than mitigates the need for normative discourse.[47]

How then is it possible to conceive educational practice and inquiry in ways that take seriously this need for a normative view from somewhere? Chapter Three, "Aesthetic Inquiry in Education," addresses this question by offering an account of education rooted in artistic imagination. I reshuffle the relation between science, art, and ethics by challenging two influential dogmas of social and educational research: that there exists a clear disjunction between the cognitive and affective domains and that truth, beauty, and goodness are radically independent of one another. This leads to a fresh look not only at the practice, appreciation, and assessment of pedagogy, but also at the sorts of inquiry that can fruitfully inform its performance, which constitutes an alternative to both the positivist and the constructivist epistemologies of the dual-epistemology thesis. Assessing whether or to what extent a particular example of pedagogy is worthy of praise, for example, only makes sense in the context of an articulate and defensible concept of what counts as praiseworthy, which entails an engagement with normative considerations in the form of intelligent spirituality, the search for a better version of ourselves in the context of communities with visions of a higher good.[48]

Chapter Four, "Traditions of Inquiry in Education," examines the dual-epistemology thesis and the two dogmas of educational research outlined in the previous two chapters from the perspective of Oakeshott's critique of rationalism in the study of human conduct.[49] Contrary to the positivist view that causal explanation based on randomized experimentation is the highest standard of knowledge, I argue that when it comes to the study of human subjects, even statistical generalizations depend upon a prior form of qualitative understanding that relates to the meanings and purposes that humans attribute to their conduct. Identity is constructed out of the contingent historical traditions by means of which humans engage the world. Learning to make intelligent choices concerning how to define oneself within the context of such traditions is what education is all about. The systematic study of how this is accomplished should lead us toward, not away from, substantive engagement with the values of those traditions.[50]

But how can engagement of this kind be accomplished in open, pluralistic, liberal societies without falling prey to excessive indoctrination; indeed how should we conceive the very nature of those societies and the schools that serve them? Part Three, "Pedagogy of Difference and the Other Face of Liberalism," addresses these issues by exploring the sort of initiation into dynamic and rival traditions intelligent spirituality requires. To this end I draw on the political philosophies of Berlin and Oakeshott and the communitarian critique of comprehensive liberalism developed by Michael Sandel, Charles Taylor, and Michael Walzer to elaborate an account of the sort of democracy that this pedagogy demands.[51] William Galston refers to this as "diversity," as opposed to "autonomy," liberalism, although as explained in the Epilogue and Chapter Eleven, I embrace a "weaker" version of this approach than Galston that prefers dynamic to dogmatic traditions—dynamic traditions that are open to engagement with alternative points of view.[52] John Gray refers to positions of this kind as the other face of liberalism, and Rorty has noted some of the affinities between these alternative accounts of liberalism and various interpretations of pragmatism. I call this view *liberal communitarianism*.[53]

If both the process and study of education require engagement with substantive visions of a transcendental good, does it not follow that this will always entail some form of indoctrination that undermines the very critical spirit inherent in the concept of education? Chapter Five, "Education in Ideology," addresses this concern by examining the difference between inculcation in moral or ethical and amoral or nonethical ideologies. The former are conducive to education in open societies and require initiation into dynamic traditions; the latter entail indoctrination in closed societies that prefer dogmatic traditions. To ensure that education in ideology remains open and not closed requires a *pedagogy of difference* dedicated to the sort of transcendental ethics discussed earlier, which involves exposure to alternative traditions in addition to initiation into a particular point of view.[54]

How then ought we to conceive the political community in which an education inspired by the pedagogy of difference can transpire? Chapter Six, "Literacy and the Education of Citizens," considers this question by exploring initiation into dynamic traditions from the perspective of the three prevailing political theories: civic republicanism, comprehensive liberalism, and critical social theory. None of these meets the demands of open, pluralistic societies, however—the former because it is too parochial and the others because they are too universal. A version of diversity liberalism is the preferred political theory for liberal education nurtured by pedagogies of difference, I argue, based on Berlin's robust pluralism and Oakeshott's critique of rationalism in politics. Grounded in value pluralism associated with Gray's other face of liberalism, this theory suggests that the task of liberalism should be to discover a modus vivendi for rival and incommensurable cultures to live together in a common civil society, rather than to impose liberal toleration as a universal ideal.[55]

What should be the character of the schools that serve such a diverse society? This is the query addressed in Chapter Seven, "What Is Common about Common Schools?" In this chapter I ask whether initiation into dynamic traditions of the sort discussed here is best accomplished in the common schools of liberal democracies that promote a neutral account of rational autonomy characteristic of comprehensive liberalism; or, alternatively, whether this might be equally or even more effectively achieved in schools that endorse particular faith or national traditions that promote a more robust account of human agency. I put faith schools or those that emphasize particular cultural, national, or linguistic traditions on equal footing with common schools in liberal democracies, provided those schools engage students with dynamic traditions that respect different points of view and are open to dialogue with rival perspectives.[56]

Part Four of the book, "Intelligent Spirituality in the Curriculum," explores the contours of transcendental pragmatism and liberal communitarianism by examining what it would mean to design a curriculum that emphasizes instruction in intelligent spirituality through pedagogies of difference and how such a curriculum compares to other theories of moral education and religious initiation in open, pluralistic, liberal democracies.

Chapter Eight, "Human Agency and the Curriculum," argues that several leading theories of curriculum undermine the sort of human agency necessary for initiation into dynamic ethical traditions, including the technological curriculum of Ralph Tyler, the academic curriculum of Joseph Schwab, the aesthetic curriculum of Elliot Eisner, and the radical curriculum of Michael Apple. The chapter concludes by discussing how these theories might be adapted to education in liberal society from a liberal communitarian perspective by means of pedagogies of difference.[57]

Chapter Nine, "Moral Education and Liberal Democracy," contends that the sort of robust identities associated with intelligent spirituality is a desideratum of liberal democracy in the form of what Terence McLaughlin and Mark Halstead have called an "expansive" approach to character education. I argue that this approach is preferable in liberal democracies to Lawrence Kohlberg's cognitive developmentalism, Nel Noddings's ethic of care, and Peter McLaren's critical pedagogy, and that liberal communitarianism is the most desirable formulation of diversity liberalism. The chapter concludes with a discussion of the sorts of practical wisdom required for such an approach to character education.[58]

In Chapter Ten, "Religious Initiation in Liberal Democracy," I apply the foregoing analysis to religious education by way of a well-known dispute between McLaughlin and Eamonn Callan over the liberal rights of parents to raise their children in particular religions.[59] I take McLaughlin's side by clarifying what he meant by "autonomy via faith," a special case of what I call *human agency*, as opposed to Callan's "autonomy via reason." The former entails a capacity to receive another person or tradition into oneself and is consistent with a liberal communitarian account of diversity liberalism; the latter involves assertion of self on the basis of rational rights and leans toward autonomy liberalism.[60]

The book concludes with Part Five, which is an Epilogue containing two chapters. Chapter Eleven, entitled, "To the Truth, Roughly Speaking," develops a nuanced account of the liberal communitarian view of diversity liberalism by situating my response to Callan in the context of McLaughlin's later work on liberalism and citizenship education. In addition to examining McLaughlin's notion of "openness with roots," the chapter distinguishes between strong and weak diversity liberalism.[61] The former was embraced by Galston and entails a limited conception of the common good across difference that tolerates dogmatic traditions closed to dialogue with rival views.[62] The latter, which is McLaughlin's position as well as my own, seeks a greater balance between common and particular conceptions of the good.

Chapter Twelve responds to Kevin Gary's generous review of *Reclaiming Goodness* by considering two main concerns: that I tend to conflate spirituality and morality and that I am not sufficiently sensitive to tensions between spirituality and critical thinking. I note that Gary has not taken adequate account of the distinction between deontological morality and aretaic ethics, in the first instance, and between the Aristotelian notions of *Sophia* and *Phronesis*, or pure reason and practical wisdom, in the second. While the spiritual quest may be distinguished from morality in the deontological sense, its interest in exploring worthwhile living is precisely the concern of ethics in the aretaic sense. Hence, there is nothing spurious about linking spirituality to critical thinking in a teleological sense, grounded in the practical wisdom of aretaic ethics. On the contrary, without the ability to evaluate whether life choices are worthwhile, it would be impossible to make sense of what it could mean to live a purposeful life. This is why the concepts of education and spirituality are so closely intertwined.

Conclusion

The view that emerges from these essays has profound consequences for the justification, substance, process, and study of education for open, pluralistic, liberal democracies, in reference to both common visions of the good across difference and particular cultural traditions. It speaks to the opportunities as well as limitations in faith as well as common schooling; to education in majority as well as minority cultures; to the powerful significance of languages, cultural customs, public ceremonies, religious rituals, and the arts, in addition to the more conventional rational disciplines in the curriculum; to the preparation of teachers and school leaders as well as educational policy makers, analysts, and researchers; and to the ways we assess educational personnel, school programs, and student achievement. It teaches that diverse democracies require citizens who can ground their commitments in particular heritages while accepting those whose perspectives and life paths are different from their own; and that to accept the other one must know oneself, but to know oneself one must also accept the other.

PART ONE

Prologue

The first chapter of this volume, unlike those that follow, was written long before the publication of *Reclaiming Goodness*. In fact, it is an updated version of an essay that was my first published article. I include it here because in many respects that early publication set the stage for the intellectual project that followed, of which *Reclaiming Goodness* was but a way station, albeit an important one. The chapter argues that human beings are endowed with a need and propensity to organize their lives around working assumptions preserved and transmitted across the generations in the form of liberating myths. I call this propensity the *transcendental imagination* and the forms in which we seek to express this imagination the *spiritual quest*. When left unexercised, I argue, this imagination can have serious negative consequences for schooling in open, pluralistic, liberal democratic societies. This is too often the case in today's schools, which is why I propose that we reimagine the study, practice, and content of education for those societies.

This chapter also illustrates William James's extraordinary influence on my work, a fact of which I was more or less unaware until my friend and colleague, sociologist Philip Wexler, pointed this out to me a few years ago when I described to him my transcendental interpretation of pragmatism. I had read James as an undergraduate while I was a visiting student at the Hebrew University of Jerusalem, and I recall how impressed I was at the time by the clarity of his prose and the cogency of his arguments, especially as regards matters of faith. But I lost sight of him by the time I got to graduate school, probably due to John Dewey's dominance in American philosophy of education and the impact on my thinking of my doctoral mentor Denis Phillips, who saw a great affinity between Dewey's philosophy of science and that of the British postpositivist Karl Popper. I have even referred to myself from time to time as a pragmatist with stronger religious sentiments who is less suspicious of tradition than is Dewey, not paying attention to the fact that this position quite nicely describes James as well; and I wrote *Reclaiming Goodness* in part as a corrective to ambivalence toward religion and spirituality among educational philosophers of a pragmatic and postpositivist bent. At Wexler's urging I reread James, only to discover not only the lingering impact of his thought on mine, in particular on what I have come to call the transcendental imagination, but also on my concern with the primacy of ethics and teleology over epistemology, what James called "last" instead of "first" things, and on the form of dialectic reasoning I so often employ in seeking a middle course between tough- and tender-mindedness.

Due to its early composition, some of the references in the chapter may appear a bit dated, being from the middle of the last century, although their continued relevance today never fails to impress me. Additionally, the argument may occasionally suffer from the exuberance of youth. I wrote the piece soon after the Jonestown massacre in 1978, in which a cult leader brought about a mass suicide of 918 of his followers. I had moved to New York from San Francisco at the time to begin rabbinic studies and was haunted by the symbolism of the fact that, prior to its move to Guyana, the People's Temple founded by cult leader Jim Jones had taken up residence in what was once a beautiful San Francisco synagogue. Nevertheless, in this new version I have endeavored to moderate and strengthen the argument, recapture James's influence, and add additional references that set the stage for the chapters that follow.

CHAPTER ONE

Schools Without Faith

Introduction

Many liberal societies today appear ambivalent about the importance of human spirituality and transcendent goodness, offering too little guidance to the young (and old) as to how to direct the powerful inner passions of humankind toward a meaningful and valuable life. These societies seem concerned more with the makeup than with the meaning of reality, with appearance above ethical substance, with cause and effect before significance and purpose, with validity of arguments prior to their moral consequences. Although the empirical turn so crucial to democracy has doubtless led to many important scientific discoveries, it may have also brought in its wake a loss of faith in the possibility of higher values to guide our actions and lofty ideals to pass along to our children, at least according to one narrow interpretation of this turn.

This chapter explores the role of faith in the schools of open, pluralistic, liberal democratic societies. It is divided into five sections. In the first section, I explore the human need and propensity to order life in terms of transcendental ideals often expressed in terms of liberating myths. I call this the *transcendental imagination*. In the second section, I discuss how this need has been systematically excluded from the development and curriculum of modern schooling. The third section considers the assumptions that have led to this exclusion, and the fourth section addresses the consequences of these assumptions for the spiritual lives of students. The fifth and final section reiterates the central challenge of this book in response to this spiritual malaise: What would it mean to reimagine liberal education so as to engage rather than avoid this transcendental imagination?

I argue that we have succeeded so well in diminishing the influence of particular transcendent beliefs and spiritual practices from modern schooling, especially in the common schools of liberal democracies, in providing a "dispassionate," "objective," "scientific," "value-free" education, that our success is contributing to our demise. This trend is as evident in the prevailing methodologies of educational research as it is in civic education and curriculum thought. But when put into practice, dispassionate neutrality too often comes to mean that no institution is worth defending and no idea of ultimate significance. With no conception of things sacred, we can communicate neither a social vision nor a sense of purpose to our youth. If education is to accomplish anything, it must accomplish this; and although schools should not be blamed for social ills that stem from far beyond their walls, they can often play an important role in addressing those ills.

The transcendental imagination

In order to understand the role of faith and in turn values in the school, we must first deal with their roles in human life more generally.

People need order to live. Without it, the world is nothing but meaningless particles of sense perception, chaos. We must overcome chaos if we are to think, learn, remember, eat—indeed, if we are to be at all. We achieve order by organizing or interpreting our perceptions. That is, we sense which perceptions are most striking, vivid, real, or important and accept that they are *truly real* by virtue of their vividness or obviousness. Students of religion refer to experiences of such vividness as hierophany, or manifestations of the sacred.[1] William James called these faith assumptions genuine hypotheses, options that are live as opposed to dead, forced instead of avoidable, and momentous rather than trivial.[2] We make our way through the "whirling snow and blinding mist" of life by choosing assumptions of this kind, argued James, establishing norms and practices that provide social stability, physical safety, and answers to basic questions of existence: Why am I here? What am I to live for? How ought I to live?[3]

Historically, people have tended to express that which they perceive as ultimately important or truly real in religious terms. Our fundamental presumptions become sacred. This is especially pronounced in archaic or traditional societies. Ancient gods always have to do with creating realities with which people must live. The order constructed from our perceptions of the sacred is often expressed in terms of myth. Myths relate sacred history. They tell how things began; how, through the intervention of trans-human powers, reality came into existence, be it the whole of reality, the cosmos, or only fragments of reality—an island, a species of plant, a particular kind of human behavior, an institution. As depictions of the source of reality, myths become paradigmatic or exemplary. We attempt to repeat them and live according to their basic messages. They express the norms that govern our lives.[4]

Though especially prevalent among traditional societies, the appeal to the sacred and the propensity for myth is also found in our own age.[5] Thomas Jefferson's conviction that we have a divinely ordained right to life, liberty, and the pursuit of happiness, for example, though penned over two hundred years ago to justify among the most significant political revolutions of modern times, still rings true for many of us today. Consider also how the Exodus narrative became a model for so many modern struggles for political liberty and social equality.[6] Even the basic principle of science that states that one event may be caused by another is, according to the philosopher David Hume, a culturally engrained assumption that we make out of psychological necessity.[7]

Humankind is endowed, in other words, with what Richard Rubenstein called a religious imagination, with the ability of self-orientation not by merely accepting that which is perceived, but by molding the environment according to what we accept as essential, fundamental, ultimately significant.[8] Given that this imagination may not necessarily be tethered to a particular religious tradition, indeed some interpretations of religion can even hamper this process, I have taken to calling this propensity for self-orientation a transcendental rather than merely a religious imagination, and the yearning for narratives, myths, and customs to express it, a spiritual quest.[9] Contemporary curriculum theorist Dwayne Huebner called it "the lure of the transcendent."[10] And political theorist Alexis de Tocqueville already noted in his nineteenth-century observations on American democracy that this "taste for the infinite and love of what is immortal" is not "the offspring of some caprice of the will," but "embedded" in human nature.[11] It is through the transcendental imagination, through myth, that we orient ourselves in a disordered world to live meaningful lives grounded in values that we can discuss with one another and pass along to our children.

James described this phenomenon as follows in his pioneering study, *Varieties of Religious Experience*:

> The individual, so far as he suffers from his wrongness and criticizes it … identifies his real being with the … higher part of himself…. He becomes conscious that this higher part is coterminous and continuous with a MORE of this same quality, which is operative in the universe outside of him….
>
> Is such a "more" merely our own notion, or does it really exist? If so, in what shape does it exist?
>
> It is in answering these questions that the various theologies perform their theoretical work…. They all agree that the "more" really exists; though some of them hold it to exist in the shape of a personal god or gods, while others are satisfied to conceive it as a stream of ideal tendency embedded in the eternal structure of the world. They all agree, moreover, that it acts as well as exists and that something really is effected for the better when you throw your life into its hands.[12]

According to religion scholar Kees Bolle, this need and propensity for transcendence has a liberating quality. In his study of myth and mysticism, *The Freedom of Man in Myth*, Bolle discussed how myth frees humankind by ordering and reordering existence. Just as the artist requires the structure of tradition to free talents in order to reach beyond the creations of the past, humans need such a structure to free talents for living meaningfully in a potentially painful and chaotic world. Properly conceived, the transcendental experience is a liberating one—liberation from chaos to order, from the uncivilized to the cultured.[13] James concurred:

> If religion is to mean anything definite for us, it seems to me that we ought to take its meaning as this added dimension of emotion, this enthusiastic temper of espousal, in regard where morality strictly so called can at best bow its head and acquiesce. It ought to mean nothing short of this new reach for freedom for us, with the struggle over, the keynote of the universe sounding in our ears and everlasting possession spread before our eyes.[14]

The transcendental imagination not only liberates us to create meaningful order out of a chaotic environment; it also contributes to the ways in which we think about that order. In the spirit of Lev Vygotsky, who explored the relation between culture and the physiology of the brain, educational psychologists Manuel Ramirez and Alfredo Castaneda examined the relation between cultural context and cognitive styles. According to Ramirez and Castaneda, industrial and postindustrial societies prefer an analytic style of thought focused on the incontrovertible conclusions of necessary logic, whereas traditional societies prefer an existential style of thought attuned to human relations.[15] In a well-known distinction, sociologist Ferdinand Tonnies referred to these contemporary industrial and postindustrial societies as "Gesellschaften" and to traditional communities as "Gemeinschaften"; Emile Durkheim called them "mechanical versus organic communities."[16] If our experience of the ultimately important is at the heart of social order, the transcendental imagination is a deciding factor in cognitive style. We apparently need myth not only to live meaningfully, but also to think sensibly in ways that tie our ability to reason to our very humanity.

Additionally, psychotherapist and Holocaust survivor Victor Frankl argued that the sort of purpose and meaning inherent in this transcendental capacity are essential to a normal or balanced psychological makeup. It was because of such a sense of purpose that he and many cohorts survived the atrocities of Auschwitz without succumbing to emotional imbalance, and it was for lack of a clear conception of purpose that many of his disturbed patients found their way to emotional disorder.[17] Lacking this sense of self-orientation within what James called a "healthy minded" attitude that provides purpose and direction to life, we can come to suffer from a certain "sickness of the soul," according to which "back of everything there is the great specter of universal death," and which engenders the question: "Can things whose end is always dust and disappointment be the real goods which our souls require?"[18]

What happens, then, to a society that has become ambivalent about, sometimes even resistant to, transcendence? What becomes of generations educated in schools that are uncomfortable with any reference to things sacred or spiritual? Might they come to suffer from such a sickness of the soul? In his essay, "The Impoverished Mind," Elliot Eisner argued that if we can speak of the human mind as composed of a multiplicity of potentialities, and if the aim of education is to provide opportunities to develop them, then any available potential left untouched can be compared to a muscle left to atrophy.[19] If myth lies at the root of the human culture, then the atrophy of the transcendental imagination in the hearts and minds of our youth may be serious indeed. For lack of spiritual sophistication could lead to a decline in social cohesion, a social pathology brought about by a lessening of ability to think and communicate about human values, indeed about our shared humanity altogether. The mass suicide at Jonestown in 1978 was an early hint of such a problem. The rise of radical Islamic fundamentalism around the world over the past several decades, even among the best educated Muslims, may constitute a more recent and pressing example.

Let us turn, then, to the development, structure, and content of schooling as it emerged in the industrial and later postindustrial world. We will see that as an agent of technology, the school has too often come to ignore the transcendental dimension of existence by replacing historic faith traditions with a narrow account of rationality and a naïve approach to empiricism.

The desacralization of schooling

Family was the main agent of socialization in traditional, premodern societies. The educational problem was simply that of reproducing in the young the values, habits, and skills of older generations. Industrialization brought with it a number of complications. S. N. Eisenstadt argued that age group identification is a natural by-product of a nonkinship universalistic orientation. When the individual replaces the clan as the focus of identity, the family ceases to be a primary source of values. Parents can no longer serve as ideal models, for each must find one's own path. Thus, the ethnic group stops serving as locus of ultimate loyalty. Loyalties must be redefined and new models sought out. It makes perfect sense to associate with those with whom one shares the most. Age, then, is the most natural universalistic principle of social division.[20]

Eisenstadt also explained how the technological need for professionalization and specialization and the related redistribution of labor from family to individual added to the downfall of the family as the basic educational institution. No longer could the child be expected to follow the family economic pursuits.[21] No longer could the family supply economic needs or professional preparation for the society at large.[22]

Finally, the rapid rate of technological development and consequent rapid social change made it impossible for parents to instruct their children in specialized professional fields. Society cannot afford for adults to shape their children in their own image. Parents are often obsolescent in their skills (not to mention their ideas and values), trained for jobs that are passing out of existence, and, thus, unable to transmit the accumulated social knowledge.[23] Witness today's digital revolution, in which children who have access to these technologies are far ahead of their parents' abilities to access and manipulate them.

Schools as we know them, then, are products of the industrial revolution. Raymond E. Callahan discussed one example of how this process transpired in early twentieth-century America, during which the decision-making apparatus of educational institutions came to be made for what might be called technological reasons.[24] It seems that in the early part of the last century, business leaders attempted to adopt the methodologies prevalent in the physical and life sciences of the day in order to systematize operations, increase efficiency, and hence, maximize profit. The most prominent such development was by Frederick W. Taylor. Callahan stated:

> In the flood of enthusiasm, an attempt was made to apply the principles of scientific management to many aspects of American life, including the army and navy, the legal profession, the home, the family, the household, the Church, and last but not least, to education.[25]

Scientific efficiency became the panacea for American administrators. Decisions regarding class size, teacher–student ratios, standards of achievement, and the like were made not for educational reasons, but for reasons of businesslike efficiency. The goal was to produce as many degreed individuals using the lowest possible budget and the most efficient methods available.

It is not only school administration that has been industrialized; the classroom and curriculum have as well. Henry M. Levin has described how the school is merely a model of the industrial workplace. The teacher is the boss figure who assigns work (not learning) to students according to her own whim, as well as the guidelines established by her superiors. The classroom is supervised by a principal-executive who is responsible to still higher executives, on up the corporate ladder to the Board of Directors—the school board. Moreover, it is assumed that students must receive an extrinsic reward for their labors in school because, after all, learning is not fun but work. Fun time is reserved for after school hours— after work—when the teacher-boss no longer holds any sway over student behavior.[26]

The curriculum followed suit in the move to industrialize. Not only has curriculum planning and construction been molded into a technologically efficient endeavor, but, especially during the second half of the twentieth century, schools entered the space race and later the digital revolution, emphasizing math, science, and technological skills.[27] I can myself recall how it was the math and physics students who were always thought to be the brightest in my high school during the 1960s. They received the new buildings, the fancy equipment, and most importantly, the college scholarships. Anyone can study history, my fellow students would say, but to study math one must really be smart.

The age of curriculum as technology arrived with techniques serving as not only the content but also the method of instruction. Computers can teach more efficiently than humans, it was argued. Education packets are sold that attempt to obliterate individual differences among teachers, creating a consistently reliable system of reading instruction. Indeed, the very notion behind instructional or behavioral objectives is to manipulate the classroom variables in a scientific manner in order to reproduce predictable results.[28]

There can be little doubt, then, that our present educational system is intimately tied to a growing technological social order, an order whose watchword too often entails an unsophisticated account of science. As Theodore Rozak put it long before computers came to dominate our lives as they do today, "The technological society in which those who govern justify themselves by appeal to scientific forms of knowledge, and beyond science, there is no appeal."[29]

Narrow rationalism and naïve empiricism

Our current epoch is not devoid of myth altogether. Rather it too often replaces the myths of various religious and spiritual traditions with a new set of working assumptions. Narrow accounts of science and technology come to serve this sacred function, as a court of ultimate appeal. Let us examine the working assumptions of this contemporary myth, then, in order to ask whether a narrowly conceived empiricism can, indeed, order existence in a sufficiently meaningful fashion to justify being the focal point of the school curriculum.

First, it is often assumed that to discover truth and not be deceived, one must maintain a skeptical perspective. We must believe neither what we read nor what we hear unless it is substantiated by evidence. In the classical formulation of Rene Descartes, this assumption can be stated as follows:

… to never accept anything as true if I did not know clearly that it was so; that is, carefully avoid prejudice and jumping to conclusions, and to include nothing in my judgments apart from whatever appeared so clearly and distinctly to my mind that I had no opportunity to cast doubt on it.[30]

A second assumption has to do with what counts as evidence for truth. In the technological world we are willing to admit as true only that which can be sensed by our five senses. Moreover, the sensation must be shared, or in principle, sharable. Others must be able to repeat our experience with the same observed results. Nothing that is perceived by the individual inner being then can be counted as truth. In the words of John Locke:

> Let us, then, suppose the mind to be, as we say, white paper void of all characters without any ideas: How comes it to be furnished? …Whence has it all the materials of reason and knowledge? To this I answer in one word, from EXPERIENCE. In that all our knowledge and from that it ultimately derives itself.[31]

Third, it is commonly accepted, particularly in the United States, that ideas, programs, institutions, and the like are best judged according to their results. Americans tend to think in pragmatic terms and are most often interested in what James referred to as the "cash value" of ideas.[32] However, the term has too often come to be taken literally, as seen in the recent movements to evaluate all educational success in terms of a limited set of standards, rather than metaphorically as it was intended, referring to teleological ends, such as transcendental ideals or conceptions of the good life and society.

Fourth, we often look to formal logic as the classical model for truth formulation. If an idea is "logical," then we see it as true. The most extreme version of this is found in Alfred Tarski's epic semantic conception of truth, in which he argues that absolute certainty is found only within formal languages of which empirical statements can only achieve informal approximations.[33]

Fifth, we believe that to reach truth or an approximation of truth requires an "objective," dispassionate method that prevents the personal feelings of the investigator from perverting the road to certainty. In the words of Max Weber:

> It is one thing to state facts, to determine mathematical or logical relations or the internal structure of cultural values, while it is another thing to answer questions of the value of culture and individual contents and the question of how one should act in the cultural community and in political associations. These are quite heterogeneous problems. If he (the university instructor) asks further why he should not deal with both types of problems in the lecture room the answer is: because the prophet and the demagogue do not belong in the academic platform.[34]

From this it follows that we make a sharp distinction between facts and values and accept as true only the proven facts. Values are a matter of personal preference. It also follows that facts, once proven, are of universal significance. Truth is true forever and in any equivalent formulation. Thus, we limit our statements, endlessly attempting to weed out any point that makes them false, excluding any circumstances in which they will not apply. These, then, are our last two assumptions.

The reflection of these working assumptions in today's schools can be seen in the very technological development and structuring of schools previously described. Mass education has been moved out of the family and community, which traditionally served as sources of values, and moved into the public arena of the state. No longer does the parent represent the moral paradigm—some even argue that parents should refrain from transmitting a vision of the good across the generations for fear of impinging on the autonomy of their children[35]; rather the classroom represents the economic paradigm. George Spindler has argued that in traditional societies the purpose of intentional education was not vocational training but rather to transmit the essence of culture, the ultimately important, the holy.[36] The contemporary technological school does offer such a message. Work and economic sustenance are the ultimate values. It is the material world, the observable world, the world of objective fact that is truly real. Beyond what we can see or measure, there is no truth. The educator is no longer a paradigm of the moral life. He is a business manager.

More strikingly, neutrality and value freedom have even made their way into moral education. The mid-twentieth-century authors of "value clarification" and theories of "moral development" claimed that it is not the job of the educator to "impose" his or her value systems but to enable students to learn according to their level of cognitive development and to help them develop further along the moral development scale.[37] Despite numerous efforts to promote a variety of approaches to character education, not much appears to have changed in the mass education of many liberal societies.[38] The teacher is expected always to be dispassionate and objective. "It is not you personally, Jimmy," we can hear her say, "I would have punished anyone who threw spitballs the same way." The teacher becomes not a model of love but one of dispassion and distance.

Finally, we evaluate our students, their teachers, and schools on the basis of measurable results. It matters little to the college admissions committee or to the advocates of standardized assessment of teachers what processes went on within Mr. Smith's high school so long as his grades and psychometric scores are competitive. "I don't care about the problems," I once heard a parent complain. "I want to *see* results."

These are but a few ways in which a technological outlook has affected life in our classrooms. Has this been a movement that provides meaning in the lives of children helping them to see order and purpose in life, or has industrialization of school limited the intellectual horizons of our youth? Has the technological school as it emerged over the last century liberated with illuminating understanding or has it become a drudgery wrought with arbitrariness and futility?

A spiritual malaise

In his classic examination of American education, *Life in Classrooms*, Phillip Jackson describes four overlapping studies that address this question conducted during the middle of the last century.[39] The studies represent a cross section of socioeconomic groups—the broad mainstream of American students of the day. He summarizes one such study in a way that seems to capture key findings that they all share: Although "girls have more positive feeling toward school than do boys," and "a quick reading of these results would lead to the conclusion that most students like school. It is equally valid to conclude that somewhere between one-third and one-half of the students have their doubts about the matter."[40] He continues:

> If we believe the statistics they would seem to indicate that one child in five or six students in every average-sized classroom feels a sufficient amount of discomfort to complain about it given the opportunity. If this figure were the same in all grades and all geographic regions (a big "if" to be sure!) it would mean that when we talk about the child who does not like school we are discussing a problem of some seven million students in our elementary schools alone. Certainly not a number that can be easily dismissed.[41]

These negative findings may be especially pronounced when considering lower socioeconomic classes of the same period. In a dramatic description of a slum school in Harlem, Gerry Rosenfeld describes the sense of futility felt by students and the arbitrary nature of classroom life. He quotes young Thomas, a student at Harlem School in the 1960s:

> When you're a kid, everything has some kind of special meaning. I always could find something to do, even if it was doing nothing. But going to school was something else. School stunk. I hated school and all its teachers. I hated the crispy look of the teacher and draggy long hours they took out of my life from nine to three thirty. I dug being outside no matter what kind of weather. Only chumps worked and studied.... Always ended up the same way. I got up and went to school. But I didn't always stay there.... It was like escaping from a kind of prison.[42]

Of course, the urban school has long been wrought with problems far beyond the meaningfulness of a scientific worldview. In his book *The Uncommitted*, Kenneth Keniston described the problems and frustrations of alienated youth of the 1960s. A segment of the school population seemed to be distant and estranged, without a sense of clear positive values, frustrated by the "impossibility of certainty." Although these are certainly on the fringes of the youth society, Keniston argues: "the major themes in the lives of these alienated youth are but extreme reactions to pressures that affect all young Americans."[43]

Perhaps the most troubling aspect of these findings is that, here too, not much appears to have changed. If anything, the situation has worsened. Extreme expressions of narcissism and nihilism on the one hand and violent forms of fundamentalism and xenophobia on the other are becoming increasingly attractive to graduates of these schools around the world, with effects even more devastating than the mass suicide at Jonestown that first motivated me to offer this analysis. Among the perpetrators of the atrocities of 9/11 or bombings in the subways of London or Madrid, for example, were people who were educated in the common schools of liberal societies.

Peter McLaren's *Life in Schools* offers a more recent account than that of Jackson of the experience of American students, grounded in critical pedagogy:

> Today's students have inherited an age in which liberty and democracy are in retreat. Ironically, existing criticisms of schooling and the agenda for educational reform themselves constitute part of the retreat. On the one hand, neoconservatives have defined the school as an adjunct of the labor market, couching their analysis in the technocratic language of human capital theory. On the other hand, liberals have provided a more comprehensive critique of schooling, but so far been incapable of addressing the major problems that schools face within a … divided society.[44]

Critical social theorists such as McLaren contend that this alienation is best explained by an unequal distribution of power; inequities in the allocation of economic, cultural, intellectual, linguistic, and other resources; oppression based on race, ethnicity, nationality, gender, religion, sexual orientation; and more. McLaren attributes the disenchantment of young people in school to classical Marxist analysis based on class. He writes:

> It is becoming clear that the consequences of schooling are dependent on the social class of the child. Radical educators argue that the structural constraints that characterize schooling and the wider society reinforce inegalitarian stratification—that schools are reduced to credentializing mechanisms, protected enclaves that favor the more affluent. The "best" schools nurture cocoons of yuppie larvae, facilitating entry of certain students into more privileged locations in the labor market; the worst simply lock the doors to those privileged locations for students already disproportionately disadvantaged. In all, the schools constitute a loaded social lottery in which the dice fall in favor of those who already have money and power.[45]

The consequent alienation does not affect oppressed classes alone—minorities, immigrants, women, the poor—"middle-class, suburban youth are also caught in a dilemma," coming of age in a stagnating economy and brought up in a televised and digitalized "world of self-interest and greed based on the principle that commodities buy happiness."[46] Following Ralph Larkin, McLaren sees this student alienation as twofold, "from adult society wherein lies the power, and from each other as invidious competition and mobility undercut authenticity and understanding of each other."[47]

Combating these inequities in schooling and the consequent feelings of helplessness and despair, argues McLaren, requires fostering a form of critical consciousness that empowers students to treat the so-called knowledge they are taught in school with suspicion, since they are but expressions of oppressive ideologies of the ruling economic elites:

> These students do not recognize their own self-repression and suppression by the dominant society, and in our vitiated learning environments they are not provided with the requisite theoretical constructs to help them understand why they feel as badly as they do. Because teachers lack a critical pedagogy, these students are not provided with the ability to think critically, a skill that would enable them to better understand why their lives have been reduced to feelings of meaninglessness, randomness, and alienation, and why the dominant culture tries to accommodate them to the paucity of their lives.[48]

I will have much to say in what follows about the importance of a critical perspective and how it might be fostered, but I for one find this sort of analysis formulaic and unsatisfying. First consider the internal contradictions that it so often entails—if all knowledge claims are suspect because they are the product of uneven power relations, the claims of critical social theory are also suspect. Then there is the confusion of explanation with justification, allowing ostensibly liberating ends to justify, not merely explain, almost any means. But most dramatically, many of those who are attracted to the most virulent and violent forms of religious extremism today are not necessarily oppressed minorities at all. As McLaren admits, they fit the profile of Jackson's middle-class majority. Even if one argues that these youngsters have awakened with anger to the sorts of oppression to which they have been complicit as a result of their privileged upbringing, this cannot account for conversion to a religious fanaticism so extreme that it seeks to force its own faith on others by means of violence, even against innocent bystanders.

Those of a comprehensive liberal bent might suggest that the source of this alienation stems from another source altogether, the denial of autonomy to students at home and at school by an excessively heteronomous culture that imposes its expectations upon them. Harry Brighouse put this position as follows:

Education should aim at enabling people to lead flourishing lives, and the argument that education should facilitate autonomy depends on the idea that autonomy plays an important role in enabling people to live flourishing lives.... For someone actually to flourish, they have to identify with the life they are leading. They have to live it from the inside, as it were.... They must at the very least, not experience their way of life as being at odds with their most fundamental experiences, interests, and desires.[49]

In this view, students may be attracted to extreme religion because they are alienated, unable to live the lives they have been offered at home and in school from the inside. This prevents them from flourishing. Although I strongly agree that moral independence is an essential aim of education, I find the argument that students tend to be alienated for lack of autonomy as unconvincing as is the explanation of the social critics. Were young people seeking more autonomy why would they choose life paths so heavily laced with heteronomy, in which they give themselves over to forms of authority over which they have no control whatsoever?

Others might complain that data upon which I have based the claim that contemporary schooling yields alienation among too many of its graduates is merely impressionistic; it lacks scientific rigor. I will also have a good deal to say about the requirements of meritorious educational scholarship in chapters that follow, since finding our way out of this morass entails fresh ways of thinking about teaching and learning, and one can always strengthen the rigor of social research. However, some of the consequences of the malaise I have been discussing are so public and dramatic—for example, the rise of religious terrorism perpetrated by young adults who hail from middle-class common school education— that they cannot be easily discounted by withdrawing to the nuances of academic discourse, which under these circumstances has the feeling of medieval scholastics debating the number of angels that can dance on the head of a pin.

No, there is more to this malaise than an awakening against oppression or a lack of autonomy, and we avoid it at our peril by retreating to debates over research methodology. Jackson was careful to remind us not to make too much of the sporadic data that he was able to pull together, and I should likewise be cautious not to overstate my case. There are to be sure many different and overlapping explanations for the sorts of dissatisfaction with schooling reported over many years by students. Yet, it is hard to avoid the conclusion that at least one such explanation is tied to the fact that the schooling these youngsters receive initiates them into assumptions about the nature of knowledge that are so severely limiting that they are left to their own devices when choosing a path to fill their lives with meaning and purpose. Indeed, with few criteria if any to distinguish between the strengths and weaknesses of the alternative conceptions of a worthwhile life or good society, they are left confused as to what it might possibly mean to be satisfied with school altogether.

Eisner argued that allowing a narrow view of science and technology to dominate our conceptions of knowledge to be taught in school diminishes the abilities of children to experience and express much about the world in which they live.[50] Perhaps the most important limitation placed on the minds of youth by this narrow view is the marginalization of transcendence, religious experience, and spiritual practice from schools. For some this can lead to alienation and meaninglessness in the technological framework both inside the school and beyond. For others it may mean that the technological worldview so often taught in school is the very cause of the urban decay and oppression with which they live every day. For most, however, it means a lack of contact with and control over those aspects of life that cannot be rationalized or explained. This leaves students with no means of coping with the unknowable or ineffable, with the primal assumptions upon which culture is based and the experiences that might lead one to change them.

Though the assumptions of a narrow rationalism and a naïve empiricism have become sacred in our schools, they differ markedly from historical religious expressions of things sacred, for the religion of science and technology has become in too many instances one of antireligion—which has led some people of faith by way of response to embrace extremely antimodern interpretations of the traditions to which they are heir. The values of narrow rationalism and naïve empiricism deny the truth of any values; they desacralize the cosmos and demystify our world. In the words of Mircea Eliade:

> Modern man's "private mythologies"—his dreams, reveries, fantasies, and so on—never rise to the ontological status of myths...(they) do not transform a particular situation that is paradigmatic. In the same way, modern man's anxieties, his experience in dream or imagination, although "religious" from the point of view of form, do not... make part of a "Weltanschauung" and provide the basis for a system of behavior.[51]

The myth of narrow rationalism and naïve empiricism is really no myth at all, at least not in the robust sense in which Eliade uses the term. As a system of neutral "value-free" values, it provides little guidance for action, no answers to the basic questions of existence. It leaves parents and educators alike at bay as to what to transmit across the generations concerning the purpose and meaning of human life. While this leaves young people open to a variety of life paths, which enhances their opportunities to exercise personal autonomy in choosing among them, some of these paths may be less than wholesome, and this orientation offers few criteria to assess which may be the most promising to pursue. Therefore the exercise of choice is more arbitrary than considered, leaving youngsters open to overtures from extreme forms of religious fundamentalism and cult-like organizations that are little concerned, if at all, with their well-being. The problem has been put most dramatically by one rabbi when talking with the son of congregants regarding the son's participation in one of the popular local cults. The rabbi said, "They want your soul. All that they are interested in is your soul." The young man responded, "At least someone is interested in my soul."[52]

The problem of pluralism

Yet the problem remains: How can we take the transcendental imagination seriously in the schools of a pluralistic society, when it is so often expressed in terms of particular cultures and faith traditions? How is faith to play a role in school without allowing a particular religion to impose itself upon children of differing backgrounds? Can a transcendental dimension to education be expressed without violating the separation between religion and state or the moral independence of the child? Can it be embraced in the school without indoctrination? Can faith-based education be justified in liberal theory? Can it leave room for a common good across difference, in addition to fostering distinctive visions of the good? The answers to these questions are far from simple, and much will be said in what follows about ways we might respond to them. It is appropriate at this juncture, however, to conclude this chapter with some preliminary observations.

First, it must be emphasized that no argument has been made here against the positive attributes of science and consequent technological developments. I have focused rather on what happens when a caricature of science and technology is taken to an exclusionary extreme. Since the publication of Thomas Kuhn's *The Structure of Scientific Revolutions*, it has become increasingly clear that "science" consists of a plurality of competing descriptive theories regarding phenomena of our experience.[53] When claims are made in the name of science to exclusive knowledge, as is the case, for example, among certain accounts of scientific positivism,[54] a new scientistic dogma emerges that is no different than the medieval dogmas rejected by Descartes. To rekindle the transcendental imagination is not to replace science but scientism, which is a popular corruption of the intentions of professional scientists.

Second, we must recall that spiritual traditions in general and religions in particular tend to be particularistic. Myths speak to particular people about particular events in their lives and the lives of their families and ancestors. But, if we are to have a truly pluralistic society, there must be room for a variety of such particular perspectives and educational space to learn about them. The notion that religion must be kept out of schools has often stemmed as much from the desire of ethnic minorities not to be forced to succumb to the religious practices of majority cultures, as from a desire to separate religion from state. But learning about and participating in particular traditions does not have to come at the expense of tolerance and respect for others who are different, regardless of their position or influence. There should be exploration of traditions other than one's own. Indeed exposure to alternative religious and spiritual traditions can shed light on one's own spiritual practice through studying the practices of others, in addition to promoting mutual respect among schoolmates of different backgrounds.

Third, if we are to sustain the advantages of a scientific point of view while searching for traditional roots, we must maintain a balance between both perspectives and strive to find points of interaction as well as contradiction. Thus, there seems to be a place in school curricula not only for education in philosophical and religious traditions but also for a more academic approach to study of religion. The study of comparative religions from an "objective" or "distant" perspective over the last century has shed much light on the relations between various religious traditions as well as between religion and science.

Many problems remain that are addressed in the chapters that follow. How is such a formidable area of content to be forced into an already crowded curriculum? If the school itself is a product of the technology-dominated society, can it house traditional study of religious source? What of those parents and students who see no need for study of this sort—is it to be imposed upon students as a requirement? Can the study of religion and spirituality be made meaningful and relevant to students' lives? How can a critical attitude be fostered to mitigate problematic consequences of engaging the transcendental imagination—for example, the arousal of religious passions or of ancient superstitions or hatreds? How are we to systematically examine educational programs designed in this spirit, explain how they function, understand how teachers and students experience them, assess their effectiveness, and evaluate their outcomes; and how can scholarship of this kind be used to improve practice?[55]

There is often a fine line between the passions of religious or spiritual genius and those of ascetic or fundamentalist extremism or even insanity, between our capacities to lead wholesome, healthy, and fulfilling lives, on the one hand, and our desire to fully engage our transcendental imaginations, on the other. "Even more perhaps than other geniuses," wrote James, "religious leaders have been subject to abnormal psychological visitations."[56] Yet, we would be hard put to call the world's great religious and spiritual traditions insanity. It is through the rigors of spiritual practice and intellectual engagement, of ritual observance and scholarly interpretations, of traditional structures and creative innovations that religious and spiritual institutions provide avenues for expressing human passions for the transcendent, on the one hand, while teaching us to exercise control over them, on the other. This is why I have argued for a renewed emphasis in the schools on the traditions of centuries and not the cults of today. Engaging the transcendental experience is full of tensions, and including it in our school curricula is not without perils. Still, the alternatives, as suggested by a tendency toward rootless openness, on the one hand, and the rising tide of radical fundamentalisms, on the other, may be far more frightening.

PART TWO

Transcendental Pragmatism in Educational Research

This part brings together three essays in which I have tried to understand what it means to employ the most rigorous scholarly tools available to study social and educational institutions, given that there is no objective *view from nowhere*. Consequently, we are required to take a stand, to view the subjects of our inquiries *from somewhere*, to begin our research programs based on working assumptions of some kind or another. James entertained the possibility that these sorts of scholarly assumptions have a good deal in common with the faith assumptions we choose to guide our lives, the aesthetic values we use to express our most basic feelings and desires, and the significant ideals that ought to inspire teachers and students in schools. Upon close examination, they may look quite different than the narrow rational and naïve empiricist assumptions previously outlined here, because they are to be found in the contingent histories and languages of concrete traditions and cultures. What might alternative assumptions of this sort look like? According to what criteria should we formulate and evaluate them? How do they fit into commonly accepted accounts of quantitative and qualitative research in education, and in what ways might they prove useful to educational practitioners and policy makers?

Although the essays upon which these chapters are based were published decades after "Schools Without Faith," they reflect an epistemological curiosity about the nature of subject-matter knowledge to be engaged in schools and the sort of curriculum and pedagogic knowledge needed to engage it that originated before I penned that essay while still a graduate student. If the knowledge through which we conceive the content and process of education is modeled in the ideal case after the mechanics of causation and correlation alone, I wondered, how could the curricula and pedagogies we design to engage that content reflect anything other than mere technique? Addressing this sort of question, I came to understand, requires the rigors of history and philosophy of science, a discipline associated closely with Karl Popper, applied in this instance to the study of education. It requires, so to say, an inquiry into the history and philosophy of educational research, with special attention to the debate over quantitative versus qualitative methodologies. It was on this subject that I wrote my doctoral dissertation more than twenty-five years ago under the tutelage of Denis Phillips.

The purpose of including this sort of inquiry here, however, is not merely to serve as what John Locke once called an under-laborer of the educational sciences, explaining the logic of inquiry to researchers who actually collect and analyze data, though this is a valuable undertaking in its own right. Rather, the purpose of this sort of investigation is also, and perhaps more importantly, to offer a window into how we have come to conceive education altogether, and through that window to create an opportunity for critically examining those conceptions in order to imagine more promising alternatives. Critiquing matters of this kind from a pragmatic perspective, especially the sort of transcendental pragmatism I advocate in what follows, requires that the logic of inquiry be viewed in its historical context, employing what Richard Rorty called philosophy with a small p, so as to consider the extent to which particular theories of inquiry address key problems presented in contemporary experience. In this instance the problem of greatest concern is the atrophying of our individual and collective capacities to engage the transcendental imagination. It is to the assessment of key issues in the history and philosophy of educational research in light of this spiritual malaise, then, that we now turn.

CHAPTER TWO

A View from Somewhere

Introduction

For some time now educational researchers have puzzled over the question: How can the subjective perceptions of single participant-observers in particular cases found in qualitative inquiry yield knowledge worthy of the name, given the concern for objectivity and generalizability inherent in the positivist approach to social and behavioral science?[1] This is a dialectical question of the form, "How is one thing possible given certain other contradictory or conflicting things?" As mentioned previously, questions of this kind require a philosophical explanation that articulates deeper principles that can remove the apparent conflict and put one's beliefs in alignment.[2]

Perhaps the most common explanation offered in response to this question among educational researchers argues that qualitative inquiry such as phenomenology and ethnography is grounded in constructivism, an alternative epistemology to the positivist orientation associated with quantitative research.[3] According to this account, positivism is not the only epistemological game in town. We can distinguish at least two conceptions of knowledge, one that aims to discover and explain relations between dependent and independent variables and another that strives to understand human experiences, norms, and purposes.[4] To buttress this approach, some authors refer to Thomas Kuhn's notion of a scientific research paradigm,[5] suggesting that qualitative inquiry constitutes a new paradigm in social and educational research that is as intellectually legitimate as the quantitative paradigm.[6]

I shall refer to this as the dual- (or plural-) epistemology thesis. Its chief advantage is that in the so-called methodology wars between quantitative and qualitative methods, this thesis allows for a strategy of mutual appeasement that enables the two orientations to coexist in the professions of social and educational research. Nevertheless, this explanation of the viability of both qualitative and quantitative research methods suffers from a number of serious flaws.[7]

In this chapter, I offer an alternative to the dual-epistemology thesis that avoids these difficulties. I argue that something like John Dewey's pragmatism may offer a promising way out of the false dichotomies that have so often characterized this debate.[8] However, with William James I acknowledge that avoiding the quagmires of self-defeating relativism to which pragmatism too often succumbs requires appeal to a limited conception of transcendence—higher ideals that are not dependent upon but that govern human activities within space and time—though tied more closely to what Aristotle called practical wisdom than to the sort of abstract theory or pure reason with which ideas of this kind have often been associated. Acknowledging the futility of what Thomas Nagel called "the view from nowhere"—a completely neutral account of objective reality—requires admitting the possibility of a view from somewhere, even if we cannot come to agreement concerning where that view is from or what vantage point it allows.[9] I call this alternative, rather provocatively, *transcendental pragmatism.*[10]

The chapter is divided into five sections. In the first section, I discuss the reemergence of the so-called methodology wars between quantitative and qualitative methods in the educational research community. Next, I consider some of the difficulties with the dual-epistemology thesis as a basis for resolving tensions between the warring camps, along with some of the historical debates that led me to search for an alternative. The fourth section lays out that alternative, and the final section addresses some of its consequence for educational research.

New skirmishes in the methodology wars

The question of how it is possible to believe the findings of qualitative inquiry, given concerns for causal explanation and generalization, gained prominence in the educational research community in the last part of the twentieth century. In the United States, researchers such as Egon Guba, Yvonna Lincoln, Robert Stake, Michael Patton, and Elliot Eisner questioned some of the central assumptions of the positivist orientation against which their emerging interest in qualitative methods was being judged.[11] Interest in this question became more acute as critical social theorists in education gained prominence, such as Henry Giroux, Stanly Aronowitz, Peter McLaren, Michael Apple, and Thomas Popkewitz. They challenged the very possibility that knowledge in education (or elsewhere) could be distinguished from power and ideology, not only the ways in which positivist educational researchers collect and analyze data.[12]

After a quarter century of methodology wars, in which positivists and antipositivists of different stripes attempted to expose and defeat one another's assumptions, it appeared for a time as though educational researchers had reached a truce that allowed different camps to tolerate, if not also respect, each other's positions, based at least in part on the doctrine of dual epistemology. That truce was broken, however, in 2001 when an act of the US Congress entitled "No Child Left Behind" endorsed randomized controlled experimentation as the so-called "gold standard" of research methodologies. The research branch of the US Department of Education consequently allocated federal funds to support experimental research such as randomized field trials almost exclusively, or in a few instances quasi-experimental approaches such as regression discontinuity methods.[13] The political environment in Washington during the period that led up to this endorsement was characterized by social conservatism and concern about the poor quality of much educational research. It prompted many interested parties in the US educational research community to call upon the National Research Council (NRC) of the National Academy of Sciences to establish an independent group to, as one commentator put it, "jump the Congressional gun, and offer a less narrow and more reasoned account … of what it is to be 'rigorously scientific.' "[14] The NRC report, which on this account was careful to recognize the academic respectability of a variety of disciplines in educational research, including, for example, educational anthropology and ethnography, offered the following six criteria as "guiding principles" for a "healthy community" of scientific researchers. Scientific research should

(i) Pose significant questions that can be investigated empirically; (ii) Link research to relevant theory; (iii) Use methods that permit direct investigation of questions; (iv) Provide a coherent and explicit chain of reasoning; (v) Yield findings that replicate, and generalize across studies; and (vi) Disclose research data and methods to enable and encourage professional scrutiny and critique.[15]

Yet, as a number of critics point out,[16] the NRC report does not veer as far as its advocates claimed from the narrow empiricist path set by the revival of what another commentator called "experimentism" in educational research.[17] For example, it continues to hold up replication and generalization as standards against which most, if not all, educational research ought to be judged. Some critics point out that the NRC report does not take sufficient account of the epistemological differences between research that seeks to discover causal explanation for purposes of prediction and control, on the one hand, and that which pursues purposive (or intentional) explanation and hermeneutic understanding, on the other.[18] Other commentators offer various forms of pragmatism or postpositivism as an alternative to the scientific positivism inherent in the preference for randomized experiments.[19]

One can only wonder why this debate has reemerged in the educational research community with such vehemence. There are surely many social and political influences that can account for the acrimony and intensity of the discussion. But there are philosophical issues involved here as well, including weaknesses in the doctrine upon which the truce in the methodology wars was, at least in part, founded. For the dual-epistemology thesis never adequately addressed the question of how it is possible to embrace the findings of research grounded in a qualitative orientation given the empiricist demand for randomization and generalizability, or, conversely, how quantitative results can be meaningful given the hermeneutic critique of positivism and postpositivism.

Dual epistemology and its discontents

One difficulty with the dual-epistemology thesis is that it tends toward a self-refuting form of relativism that hinders the systematic assessment of merit in social and educational research. Each paradigm has its own assumptions, according to this view, and it is unreasonable to criticize one on the basis of the other. It follows that the only criteria that can be used to evaluate any specific application of a research paradigm are internal; and if an orientation does not prize logical consistency, for example, there is no way to call it to account. As R. Burke Johnson and Anthony Onwuegbuzie wrote recently, "When it comes to research quality, it is not the case that anyone's opinion about quality is just as good as the next person's, because some people have no training or expertise or even interest in research."[20]

A second problem with dual epistemology is that it tends to discourage mixing qualitative and quantitative methods in single studies by encouraging epistemological and methodological purism among both qualitative and quantitative researchers. However, an increasing number of researchers are looking to integrate quantitative and qualitative methods in mixed research designs.[21] These designs "attempt to legitimate the use of multiple approaches in answering research questions, rather than restricting or constraining researchers' choices." This form of research is expansive, inclusive, and pluralistic, suggesting that researchers may select their methods eclectically, in accordance with the research question being asked.[22]

The third problem with this orientation concerns its interpretation of Kuhn's concept of scientific research paradigms. Setting aside the fact that Kuhn did not hold that scientific paradigms exist in the social or behavioral sciences—a belief probably linked to his positivist past—if the advent of qualitative inquiry is a scientific revolution a la Kuhn, it cannot leave our attitude toward the previous paradigm—positivist social science—unaffected. On Kuhn's view, the new paradigm ought to replace the old one, as Copernican supplanted Ptolemaic astronomy, by accounting for data that were previously unexplained. Alternatively the new paradigm should enable us to view the old one in a new light, as Einstein's relativity thesis contextualized the meaning of Newtonian mechanics.[23]

Fourth, the qualitative revolution in social and educational research raised hard questions concerning the coherence of such positivist notions as social laws that are generalizable across historical, cultural, or linguistic contexts; behavioral facts independent of ethical values or political ideology; or valid and reliable measures that meaningfully capture the dynamic flow of human discourse.[24] Yet, many dual-epistemology devotees continue to check for possible errors in qualitative descriptions using softer versions of these very criteria, such as consensual validity, structural corroboration, and referential adequacy, or trustworthiness, authenticity, and accountability.[25] This presents qualitative inquiry as a weak form of empiricism, when according to the constructivists it is grounded in an entirely different and, to their minds, more compelling account of the very nature of knowledge itself. Although some have also recognized that standards of this kind are unduly influenced by positivism and misrepresent qualitative inquiry as a weak form of empiricism,[26] few have acknowledged the impact of these criticisms on how we ought to view measurement-based research in its own right, as well as how it ought to connect to emergent trends in qualitative inquiry.[27]

In contrast to the methodological purism mentioned earlier, one consequence of this weak empirical attitude is a tendency to embrace forms of eclecticism that do not take adequate account of conceptual and epistemological differences between alternative accounts of the research process. For instance, Madhabi Chatterji refers to longitudinal studies of class size that involve randomized field trials in a large number of elementary schools to show that evaluation conditions violate the assumptions of textbook field experiments, and so require a mixture of qualitative and quantitative methods. It is difficult for researchers to properly manipulate independent variables (IV) in such cases, since they are "rarely, if ever, single, discrete, narrowly scripted and easily identifiable" conditions in field settings.

In most studies of "class-size reduction," the definition of the IV becomes complicated by the presence or absence of volunteers, para-professionals, teacher interns, or other teachers who along with regular teachers in the classroom, provide different degrees of instructional support to a given number of students. This alters the ratio of instructional staff to pupils and the operational definition of the field "treatment" condition. Often field treatment conditions may vary across classrooms and schools studied, and sometimes, even in the same classroom at different times of the day. Without adequate documentation of these *qualitative variables* (emphasis in the original), the effects are hard to interpret, let alone replicate.[28]

No doubt some form of observation would be useful in such cases to assist evaluators in developing empirically valid operational definitions of class size and teacher–student ratios. However, as we shall see subsequently, the very idea of a "qualitative variable," the identification of which can assist in the proper manipulation of "quantitative variables," misconstrues the heart of qualitative inquiry, which aims to understand the meanings and purposes of human activity, not the causes of human behavior. More importantly, this example underestimates the conceptual difficulties inherent in randomized field testing, even when its weaknesses are overcome by the addition of supplemental methodologies.

For the qualitative revolution in educational research joins a philosophical debate unresolved since David Hume challenged the very idea of causal explanation and undermined the modern departure from conceptions of knowledge descendent from Plato and Aristotle.[29] Of the responses to Hume, two have been especially influential, and both are problematic. One followed Immanuel Kant in understanding knowledge as a rational approximation of reality grounded in universal cognitive structures.[30] This approach leaves the methods of empirical science intact, but vests their epistemological authority in the structure of mind. On this view, knowledge is objective, universal, and generalizable. Positivists and postpositivists have generally taken this route. The other response followed G. W. F. Hegel in challenging Kant and reviving Platonic and Aristotelian transcendentalism.[31] In this view, knowledge is contextual, subjective, and particular—a product of embodied agents living in concrete historical and linguistic communities. Phenomenologists and hermeneutic theorists have generally followed this path.[32]

Positivism is probably the most influential movement to apply the principles of empiricism, developed originally by the likes of Francis Bacon and John Locke to transform the study of nature, to the investigations of people and societies.[33] It did so, however, with a certain naiveté about the possibility of resolving the Humean predicament by means of the emerging statistical sciences. Recall that Hume argued that we can never know in an apodictic or indubitable sense that empirical consequences "$C_i \ldots C_n$" will necessarily follow from initial conditions "$I_i \ldots I_n$," but only that at best they may probably follow. Our acceptance of so-called scientific laws based on such notions as cause and effect, Hume concluded, is more a matter of psychological need and cultural custom than epistemological warrant.[34] Yet even the exact extent of this probability cannot be measured, since we have no way of accurately judging the number of possible cases in which these conditions or consequences might apply.[35]

Karl Popper responded to Hume's critique by claiming that we may not be able to verify that consequences "$C_i \ldots C_n$" follow from initial conditions "$I_i \ldots I_n$," but we can say with certainty when this is not the case. Falsification should replace verification, therefore, as the primary aim of science.[36]

This view, which became known as postpositivism, has become especially influential in educational research,[37] but it turns out to be overstated. Popper's disciple Imre Lakatos pointed out that scientific researchers do not falsify single statements or even more complex theories one at a time. Rather they extend the core assumptions of larger research programs, until such time as there is sufficient evidence to contravene those assumptions, which are then rejected for a new core and concomitant program of research.[38] In other words, scientific research programs may vary according to the judgments of distinct knowing subjects. The threat that this sort of subjective judgment poses to the objectivity of scientific knowledge may be offset by appeal to an intersubjective community of researchers that decides when to abandon one research program for another. However, at the end of the day, postpositivism does not succeed in salvaging the objectivity of scientific knowledge from Hume's critique.

Edmund Husserl may have offered the clearest account of the epistemological underpinnings of what later became known as constructivism. If there ever was a paradigm shift in the history of epistemology that sought to replace its predecessor it was this.[39] Husserl argued that empiricism got off to a false start at the outset, when Rene Descartes challenged the veracity of his very existence; perhaps life is a mere dream or grand deception.[40] Husserl objected to the comprehensiveness of Descartes's famous response, "I think therefore I exist." That someone doubts his own reality, Husserl reasoned, shows only the existence of a questioning subject, not of a person with a physical presence. We can only know indubitably that which presents itself within consciousness, concluded Husserl; we can say nothing at all with certainty about life beyond our own thoughts and experiences. To achieve knowledge that cannot be doubted, a new science called "phenomenology" would need to bracket all references to reality outside of consciousness, and focus our attention on life as it is experienced internally.[41] Unfortunately, Husserl's brackets leave the questioning subject alone in her own solipsistic universe, since Husserl allows no reference whatsoever to anything other than that which presents itself in consciousness.

Not only does phenomenology bracket objective reality, it embraces Friedrich Nietzsche's critique of every other form of external transcendence as well, leaving for analysis only that constructed within consciousness.[42] But if ideals independent of consciousness are ruled out of court as well as objects, then there is nothing independent of the self to which one could possibly appeal as a criterion for judging the merit of a phenomenological depiction. Narcissism and nihilism must necessarily result. Of course, like the postpositivists, Husserl and his disciples do refer to intersubjective tests for phenomenological studies.[43] Yet given the ontological isolation that follows from Husserl's critique of Descartes, it is hard to know what such an intersubjectivity could possibly mean, since the only subjects that can be accounted for within this orientation are those that present themselves in consciousness, and there is no way of knowing, according to Husserl's account, whether these other subjects exist beyond the self.

An alternative: Transcendental pragmatism

How, then, might we conceive deeper principles that can explain how it is possible to believe qualitative descriptions in the face of the demands of positivism or to embrace experimental results given the phenomenological critique? To answer we require an account of inquiry that is pluralistic in that it allows for different methods to coexist, but that also defines the conditions under which it makes sense to speak of them as agents of some notion of truth. This was essentially Kant's project in which he followed an interpretation of Aristotle that emphasized theory over practice, although not without acknowledging a deep connection between the two.

Aristotle distinguished between the practical wisdom suitable for understanding how personal and political affairs ought to be conducted, *Phronesis*, and theories about how the world works, *Sophia*. Phronesis consists of ethical and civic virtues required for living a good life and creating a just society. Though alluding to higher ideals, the virtues are always expressed in terms of local cultures and customs. Sophia, on the other hand, attempts to grasp physical and metaphysical reality by means of two sorts of reasoning—*techne*, designed to reveal what he called the efficient or mechanical causes of events, and *episteme*, which focuses on teleological or final causes. Efficient causes precede events, "pushing" them into being as it were, by disrupting or intervening in a state of affairs in a random or chance manner. Teleological causes, on the other hand, "pull" an event toward a natural or intrinsic state, one that is part of the very design of things. Since events cannot be explained without reference to a larger order in which they are set, the whole possesses a greater degree of reality than the parts. Teleological explanations are more fundamental than mechanical explanations, in Aristotle's view, because they tie physical to metaphysical reality.[44]

Perhaps the problems with both postpositivism and phenomenology originate in just such a naïve distinction between theory and practice—description and prescription—that cannot withstand criticism. It was American pragmatism, Dewey's in particular, that emphasized the incoherence of the theory–practice distinction. An opponent of what he called "false dualisms," Dewey avoided a harsh dichotomy between the inner lives of human beings and a so-called "objective" reality that exists outside of them. However, rather than expressing his views in the terms of German idealism, he chose what has sometimes been called a naïve naturalism. What exists, on Dewey's view, are not objects but events, which like Heidegger's notion of "Being" entail the interaction between organisms and their environments.[45] Dewey called the amalgamation of these events experience. All inquiry, whether in the natural or human sciences, is about resolving problems that present themselves in experience. We confront a problem, formulate a hypothesis about how to address it, and test out our hypothesis in experience to see if it works. A hypothesis is said to be true, on this view, not if it corresponds to an uncritical conception of external reality, but rather only if it resolves the dilemma or difficulty for which it was formulated. Inquiry, then, is a practice designed to solve problems encountered in experience.[46] Practice, not theory, is the driving force of all scientific endeavors; or to reverse the motto attributed to social psychologist Kurt Lewin that there is nothing so practical as a good theory, in Dewey's view there is nothing so theoretical as intelligent practice.[47]

Whatever the merits of this position, however, one cannot avoid its tendency toward radical relativism or subjectivism. How, one might ask, is it possible to decipher the degree to which one account of events is better than another, since each person brings her own conception of what it might mean to solve the problem at hand? An answer may be found by applying Aristotle's analysis of efficient and final causes to this Deweyan synthesis of theory with practice, at least as it appears in the human sciences.

Charles Taylor argues that even if some behaviors can be explained by statistical laws over which actors can exercise no influence, many if not most human activity is governed by norms or purposes over which people can exercise control. If one wants to understand why someone took an umbrella from the umbrella stand today, when he failed to do so yesterday, or covers or uncovers his head when entering a house of worship, one must inquire into the norms that govern the culture in which that person lives and the reasons why he chooses to behave in this way and not that. Humans are purposeful beings; and to understand their actions we are compelled to reference teleological explanations that articulate the purposes that move people to act. Although many such purposes are imminent in existence or experience, such as the desire to fit in with a particular group, or to please (or displease) one's family, or to meet basic needs for survival, they will always be subordinate to higher ideals, such as friendship, loyalty, solidarity, respect, or the sanctity of life. Taylor calls these ideals strong values.[48] In short, to recall James's formulation, when it comes to understanding human activity at least, we need to consider "last" before "first" things, ethical and political ends concerning the worthwhile life and the just society before epistemological foundations relating to objectivity and subjectivity.[49]

But how can ethical and political ideals serve as a basis for criticism in educational research when they are often contested? One answer lies in the fact that the very idea of critique implies standards of assessment grounded in competing traditions or conceptions of the good. Of course, some traditions embrace ideals dogmatically. They are resistant to changing circumstances, counterarguments, or contrary experience. They also tend to discourage independent ideas and choices and understand human behavior as under the control or authority of an external agent or force. Traditions of this kind often appear to provide clear ethical standards against which to judge social policies and programs. But in fact, these dogmatic standards tend to undermine a key condition for ethical discussions or debates to be meaningful altogether—that within reasonable limits, people are the agents of their own beliefs, behaviors, and desires. Only if we can effect a change in these matters does it make any sense at all to call upon us to do so. But if I am the agent of my own actions, then it follows that it must be possible for me to be wrong about even my most fundamental commitments. Were this not the case, if I was right, for example, because it is in my very nature to be correct, then it would be my nature, not me, choosing my commitments. For ideals to be ethical, in other words, they *must* be fallible. Ethical traditions that provide genuine standards of assessment must therefore be dynamic not dogmatic, embracing ideas that represent the best available formulation of the good, at least as we are given to understand it for now, but assuming that there could always be a better way or a more compelling perspective.[50]

Viewed in this light, knowledge—at least in education—is always the possession of an embodied agent, constrained by language, culture, and history, who grasps, albeit imperfectly, the contours of an entity or the meaning of an idea that transcends—exists independently or outside of—his or her limited experience. And this requires—as a regulative principle—the existence of ideals beyond our own contextualized experience, whose ultimate content remains shrouded in culture, history, language, and tradition. To recognize the futility of a view from nowhere we must acknowledge the possibility of a view from somewhere.

Contrary to the "No Child Left Behind" legislation, it would appear that before we can decipher what might count as a significant causal link in education we must first unwrap the meanings, identify the purposes, or grasp the concepts embedded in traditions created by historical communities; devise new ways to extend or understand those traditions; and even occasionally create new traditions of understanding altogether.[51] Knowledge of the human condition, in short, is first qualitative in nature—and to the extent that measurement comes into play, it is for the sake of making more precise the qualities that we seek to clarify, understand, and distinguish.

Such a view, as Plato long ago observed, is mediated through the logic of illustration rather than generalization that communicates enduring truths by means of discursive descriptions and nondiscursive symbols.[52] We understand and create meaning out of experience—in other words, through examples communicated in narratives, allegories, and parables. However, in contrast to Plato for whom illustrations facilitate communication of absolute truth,[53] the position emerging here suggests that concrete cases are a good but imperfect means to articulate very limited understandings of what we can only assume lies beyond our complete grasp.[54] Truth is conceived in this view not as correspondence to objective reality, or as serving some theoretical function or purpose, but in the way descriptions embody and enable us to grasp the nuanced and dynamic form of transcendent ideals,[55] the capacity of texts, symbols, and stories to capture the contours of feelings in forms. Viewed from this perspective, even a large, random statistical sample is but an extended and elaborate case that outlines the conceptual shape of experiences common to a significant population of people.[56]

Consider intelligence testing, among the paradigm cases of measurement-based research in the behavioral and social sciences. Walter Feinberg has demonstrated the degree to which tests of this kind reflect strong socioeconomic, cultural, and linguistic biases, rather than the capacities of a given cognitive structure. In other words, these sorts of tests actually measure the degree to which a person has the ability to realize certain cultural, social, or ethical ideals. Though ideals about an aspect of human flourishing, the constructs measured by tests of this kind are by no means absolute or unchanging. On the contrary, the very contextualization of these measures brought about by critiques such as Feinberg's has itself led to reevaluation of views about the personal qualities that enable scholastic, educational, or social achievement, which in turn entails a reassessment of the sorts of societies in which one should want to live and what it could mean to prosper in those societies.[57]

Some consequences for educational research

At least three consequences for educational research emerging from the analysis in this chapter deserve emphasis. First, all educational research entails a philosophical dimension involving substantive ethics and the analysis of educational aims and aspirations. Not only does the proper interpretation of causation and correlation in the human sciences depend upon understanding human purposes and intentions as part of the social and cultural norms, values, and ideals that govern people's lives, but we can only acquire this sort of understanding from the vantage point of our own aims and aspirations. Hence, educational research worthy of the name can only be properly conducted within the context of explicit and adequately defended visions of the good in which nondogmatic norms, values, and ideals are articulated to govern policies, practices, and pedagogies. The tendency within contemporary schools of education in leading universities around the world to diminish the presence of properly trained philosophers in favor of so-called hard-nosed empirical researchers specializing in randomized field testing therefore poses a serious threat to the quality of scholarship conducted within those institutions and to the standards according to which educational practitioners and policy makers are prepared to embark on their professional careers. The very idea promulgated in the wake of "No Child Left Behind" that standards in education are first and foremost quantitative misses the essential point of a standard altogether, which is to gauge the quality of a practice, to assess whether or to what degree an activity has been performed in a manner that should be deemed meritorious. But to understand what counts as more or less meritorious, one must first possess a concept of what it means for an activity to be worthwhile, which is precisely the job of an adequately defended vision of the good.

Second, randomized field experimentation cannot be a "gold standard" of educational research, since the very search for correlations and causal explanations in the human sciences depends upon prior understanding of the relevant teleological explanations that address the reasons why people choose to behave as they do, the purposes they hope to achieve, the norms they follow, and the ideals they embody. Indeed, since most forms of qualitative inquiry seek to understand human purposes and intentions, they can stand on their own without any reference to power relations or the relationships between quantitative variables. The same, however, cannot be said for positivist social inquiry or for critical social theory, both of which must be appropriately situated in an account of the relevant social norms and ideals in order to be properly understood. In this sense, quantitative and critical studies in education require in the nature of the case what has come to be called mixed methods, since qualitative understanding is required to make sense of them. On the other hand, though qualitative studies may often benefit from the integration of various forms of measurement or radical criticism, depending of course on the research question involved, making sense of them does not necessarily depend upon correlations, causes, or power relations.

Finally, norms, values, and ideals are best understood by analyzing concrete cases. Correlation and causation can add nuance and precision, but the search for abstract covering laws does not constitute the most appropriate approach to understanding human purposes and intentions. The logic of illustration, in other words, is prior to the logic of generalization in the study of human activity; and it is a category mistake of the first order to understand illustration as a form of weak empiricism by reference to such irrelevant concepts as reliability, validity, and generalizability. Illustration is rather more like coming to understand a nuanced use of language or a fine point of law than a statistical regularity. Language and law are best grasped by means of a limited number of clear and detailed cases that illuminate practices and principles that can be applied in a host of circumstances well beyond their confines. To be sure, these cases can be and often are combined with tests and measures or radical analysis in a variety of useful ways to assist in learning a language or in convincing a judge or jury to apply the law in certain ways under particular circumstances. But to communicate in a language or interpret the law one must first understand the practices and principles that govern their use. So too in the study of education; correlations, causes, and radical criticism may assist in improving the practice of a particular pedagogy or in convincing policy makers to think about current circumstances in new and innovative ways, but to achieve these ends there is no substitute for understanding the norms, values, and ideals of the culture that seeks to transmit itself across the generations within the context of the aims and aspirations of a clear and defensible concept of the good.

This account may be a disappointment to those whose preferred epistemology seeks control on the basis of explanation and prediction. But the fact that we can sometimes predict does not authorize us to control, and in all events we control much less than the positivists may have once supposed. It follows that we should be wary about what we think inquiry enables us to predict, since what we take to be true or right today may turn out to be false or troubled tomorrow. Inquiry at its best endows us with insights to better control ourselves, not generalizations to more efficiently dominate others; and the surest path to self-governance lies in reaffirming Socrates's realization that genuine wisdom begins with the recognition of how little we really know.

CHAPTER THREE

Aesthetic Inquiry in Education

Introduction

What does it mean to understand education as an art, to conceive inquiry in education aesthetically, or to assess pedagogy artistically? Answers to these queries are often grounded in John Dewey's naïve pragmatism, neo-Marxist critical theory, or postmodern skepticism that fall prey to many paradoxes of radical relativism and extreme subjectivism.[1] This chapter offers an alternative account of education as an art and inquiry in education as an aesthetic endeavor grounded in the sort of transcendental pragmatism previously developed here that avoids these difficulties.

I begin by examining the emergence of aesthetic inquiry in education in the context of the larger qualitative revolution in educational research. The struggle to justify the qualitative turn in educational thought was initially framed in terms of two influential doctrines: that cognition and affect, on the one hand, and truth, beauty, and goodness, on the other, can be clearly distinguished from one another. Qualitative methods were conceived as an alternative research paradigm, a cognitive endeavor aimed at discovering a form of knowledge no less valid and reliable than that produced by quantitative methodologies.[2] This way of framing the discussion led to the dichotomizing of positivist and constructivist epistemologies (discussed in the previous chapter), one embracing absolutism, objectivism, and rationalism, the other relativism, subjectivism, and romanticism. As we saw, this approach succeeded in pointing to some serious flaws in the prevailing positivist account of social research, yet it left qualitative inquiry dependent on versions of epistemological relativism and subjectivism that philosophers of knowledge have shown to be incoherent.[3]

Conceiving of pedagogy in aesthetic terms challenges the prevailing positivist epistemology on a deeper level because it questions the accepted distinctions between thinking and feeling and between truth, beauty, and goodness. If art can be conceived as a form of cognitive inquiry in addition to affective expression, then the appreciation and assessment of education as art requires a reshuffling of our very conception of the relations between science, art, and ethics, and in turn a reimagining of how we view education, not merely a new research paradigm or alternative epistemology.

These concepts can be reconceived to avoid the paradoxes of radical relativism and extreme subjectivism if we recognize with Iris Murdoch that sovereignty belongs to communal conceptions of a transcendent good. Educational arts empower people to express, appreciate, and critique collective conceptions of goodness, and artistic criticism of pedagogy celebrates a sacred dimension in educational thought and practice.[4] This approach occasions a fresh look not only at practice, appreciation, and assessment of pedagogy but also at the very meaning of the concept of education and the sorts of inquiry that can fruitfully inform its practice.

Two dogmas of educational research

Two dogmas have dominated educational research since the middle of the last century: the idea that there exists a clear disjunction between the cognitive and affective domains; and the supposed radical independence from one another of truth, beauty, and goodness.[5] According to a popular view rooted in these doctrines, the search for truth is a cognitive affair governed by science, while ethics and the arts are tied to the emotions and the humanities. Inquiry into the former is objective—reliability depends on method not researcher—and into the latter, subjective—results can vary according to interpreter. In this attitude, the cognitive domain dominates the public arena through the influence and prestige of science and measurement.[6]

Until the middle 1970s, behavioral and social research in education expressed these dichotomies in the distinction made between quantitative and qualitative research. The former was thought to be scientific and objective, the latter, humanistic and subjective. As qualitative inquiry came into its own in the 1980s, its proponents sought justification and legitimization in accord with cognitive dominance.[7] First, they argued that qualitative research methods had checks against error as rigorous as its quantitative counterparts.[8] Later, the cognitive domain was redefined as neither objective nor subjective, but relative and intersubjective.[9]

Qualitative inquiry was argued to be a viable alternative research paradigm, uniquely suited to documenting intersubjectivity.[10] This account of qualitative inquiry left the distinctions between cognition and affect and between truth, beauty, and goodness intact. Instead, it critiqued the objectivism inherent in positivist thinking by articulating and defending alternative forms of socially constructed knowledge.[11]

This new sort of inquiry became known as naturalistic.[12] It considers fleeting social occasions in natural settings, altered only minimally by the intrusion of participant-observers, in contrast to experimental research that manipulates behavioral variables in order to examine the statistical relations between them.[13] According to this "paradigm," qualitative methods seek to describe and understand the reasons and meanings that influenced social activity, rather than to explain, predict, and control behavior by means of random selection, comparison groups, and instruments of measurement.[14]

The researcher's eyes and ears become the primary tools for collecting qualitative data, by means of participant observation, interviewing key informants, and examining printed documents and other cultural artifacts. The data are then edited into thick descriptions of social occasions with as much neutrality as allowed by the fact that we can only see through our own eyes and hear with our own ears.[15] To limit observer bias, alternative data sources, observer viewpoints, theoretical perspectives, and research methodologies are compared in a process called triangulation. By examining a single phenomenon from multiple perspectives, we discover the intersubjective "validity" of an account—the degree to which it is confirmed within alternative subjective perspectives.[16]

Approaches to qualitative inquiry share these methods of data collection. However, at least three naturalistic perspectives can be distinguished concerning what is done with this data. Phenomenology explores the structure of experience with consciousness.[17] It grew from Edmund Husserl and Alfred Schutz.[18] Ethnography articulates public but often unstated social norms and can be best understood in terms articulated by George Mead and to a lesser degree Ludwig Wittgenstein.[19] Finally, the arts capture the dynamic form of social events in symbolic language, behaviors, sounds, and artifacts. Aesthetic concepts have been adapted to educational research by reference to Dewey, Suzanne Langer, and Nelson Goodman.[20]

Although sometimes blurred in practice, these different attitudes lead to divergent approaches to the interpretation of qualitative data. Phenomenologists often employ empathy or self-projection to grasp how someone experiences a particular event, while ethnographers might be more likely to analyze the interrelations between publicly observable rituals, symbols, and concepts.[21] Artists and art critics, on the other hand, not only describe what they experience; they create virtual experiences in language, space, time, or sound so that others can grasp what they perceive directly, through encountering a new work of art.

All three approaches to qualitative inquiry expanded our conceptions of what is "out there" to be studied. But phenomenology and ethnography hue closer to the purely cognitive account of knowledge than does artistic inquiry by embracing the view that social "things"—however ephemeral— exist to be comprehended and interpreted by the mind. These ephemeral "things" may reside within consciousness—an arena within our inner lives much more vast than the limited domain of the "thinking subject." Or they may exist implicitly in our public social lives, but they are "there"; and alternative methods of social inquiry—new research paradigms—are required to understand them.

The epistemological relativism implicit in this view has often been grounded in the skepticism of critical theory or postmodernism.[22] Laurel Richardson writes, for example:

> The postmodernist context of doubt distrusts all methods equally. No method has a privileged status. The superiority of "science" over "literature"—or from another vantage point, "literature" over "science"—is challenged. But a postmodern position does allow us to know "something" without claiming to know everything. Having a partial, local, historical knowledge is still knowing.[23]

But this view falls prey to well-known paradoxes of radical relativism and extreme subjectivism.[24] For example, if all methods are to be doubted by virtue of their association with power relations, what of the postmodern method that privileges skepticism; should not it too be subject to doubt? However, if postmodern skepticism is suspect in its own right, then does it not follow that some methods are in fact better than others? If the postmodern skeptic is right, in other words, then he is wrong, and if wrong, then right. The result of this sort of thinking is not multiple ways of knowing, but the impossibility of any coherent sort of knowledge altogether.

A more dramatic departure challenged the cognitive–affective split altogether. The arts are not merely expressions of feeling, according to this view, nor are the sciences purely cognitive, rather "the growth of cognition is…inseparable from the education of emotions."[25] Artists express cognitive perceptions, not only feelings. Their symbolic representations give shape to new ways of seeing, hearing, and understanding the external world, not only to the dynamic form of inner life.[26] Similarly, science entails not only truth-preserving methods of discovery and justification, but also gives voice to significant feelings such as the "joy of verification" and the "feeling of surprise," and "does not forbid use of feeling in exploration and discovery, the impetus of inspiration and curiosity, or the cues given by excitement over intriguing problems and promising hypotheses."[27]

The arts are distinct from the sciences, then, by virtue of their approaches to symbolic representation, not the degree to which they engage cognition or emotion. According to Goodman, symbolic "density, repleteness, and exemplification are earmarks of the aesthetic; articulateness, attenuation, and denotation are earmarks of the non-aesthetic."[28] Langer called the latter discursive and the former nondiscursive symbolic form.[29]

The arts, like the sciences, entail methods of inquiry resulting in knowledge.[30] However, this is not an independent aesthetic form of knowledge, but rather a transformation of what it means to know something altogether. Inquiry is not merely about grasping meanings that already exist in a world that lies "outside" of us. It is also, and perhaps primarily, about creating new meanings for a world as yet unseen. The "known" is not a mere given that stands over against us. We construct and reconstruct—interpret and reinterpret, create and recreate—it as our thoughts and feelings come into relation with that which is entirely other. Parker Palmer wrote, "The myth of objectivity, which depends on the radical separation of the knower and the known, has been declared bankrupt.... We now see that to know something is to have a living relationship with it—influencing and being influenced by the object known."[31] Philip Phenix and Dwayne Huebner called this sense of otherness "transcendence"; and Martin Buber dubbed the process of meeting the other "dialogue."[32] The excellence of both process and product is to be judged in terms of the artistic and scientific traditions in which the encounter with transcendence is formulated.[33]

The tendency of phenomenology and ethnography to preserve cognitive dominance and of artistic inquiry to go beyond it is evident in the task of interpretation in each orientation. Anthropologists distinguish between the insider (or *emic*) and the outsider (or *etic*) perspectives.[34] Although the participant-observer experiences cultural events with her whole being, both phenomenology and ethnography use that experience as data to translate an insider into an outsider perspective by means of cognitive processes resulting in discursive description.

Artistic inquiry, on the other hand, blurs the distinction between these perspectives. As in other forms of qualitative description, the artistic observer enables an outsider to view an event from the inside. Yet, this insider view is not that of a participant in the culture, but rather that of the aesthetic researcher herself. Nor is the depiction a mere reflection of the participant's experience. Rather, it is a virtual reality created nondiscursively by a whole, thinking-feeling person using metaphoric language, symbolic behavior, or virtual shapes, sounds, or movement.

Additionally, hermeneutic theorists distinguish between *exegesis* and *eisegesis*. The former process interprets a text by "drawing out" the meanings that lie within it, taking into account the intentions of the author and the context in which it was written.[35] The latter process permits us to read new meanings "into" a text that may have not been intended by the author or understood by readers in the context for which it was written.[36] Phenomenology and ethnography strive to interpret experience as we might read a text from an exegetical perspective—drawing out what is already there. The "describing subject" (the knower) is distinguished from that which is described (the known); and it is the mind (the cognitive dimension of inner life) that constructs the interpretation.

In addition to embracing this exegetical view, however, the creation and criticism of art also enables us to read experience eisegetically—teaching us to see and hear that which had not been previously seen or heard. Artistic inquiry not only expresses well-worn thoughts and feelings; it fosters the discovery of new ideas and emotions through the engagement of a whole thinking-feeling person in the artistic discipline in which an aesthetic form is created. The result is a reeducation of perception.[37]

The privileged position of science may be questioned by this aesthetic view, but the second dogma of educational research—the thesis that truth, beauty, and goodness are radically independent—is not challenged with sufficient clarity. Some argue that knowledge actually begins with aesthetic discovery because art seeks to give nondiscursive expression to inchoate experiences that become routinized and conceptualized within various scientific disciplines. This is often accomplished through symbolic form and metaphoric expression. Immanuel Kant called this the "origin" of reason.[38] Others replaced the supremacy of science with that of art. According to Paul Feyerabend, for example, science is a distinct and elaborate form of poetry, and history is a peculiar sort of storytelling.[39] This may collapse scientific inquiry into the arts, but it also reelevates the cognitive domain, replacing science as the guardian of truth with art. "Beauty is truth, and truth beauty," as John Keats would have it[40]; but the good remains the province of pure subjective emotion, while the new aesthetic guardian of truth offers too few criteria to distinguish it from falsehood.

Without a defensible concept of transcendence, artistic and other forms of inquiry cannot be extricated from the quagmires of radical relativism and extreme subjectivism. We need not only to dismantle the duality of facts and feelings, but also to reintegrate the pursuits of truth, beauty, and goodness; debunking the first dogma depends upon discrediting the second. This requires a synthesizing principle: the concept of goodness. Neither science nor art is to be privileged. All inquiry, in several crucial respects, involves ethics. Sovereignty, to use Murdoch's felicitous phrase, belongs to the good.[41]

The sovereignty of goodness

For the most part, we humans live in communities with conceptions of how life is to be lived. We can distinguish between ideological and ethical conceptions of life.[42] Ideologies, in the Marxist and neo-Marxist sense, express the interests of those in power. They tend to be mechanical, deterministic, and instrumental and to lead to unintelligent behavior and indoctrination. On this account there is no difference between truth, beauty, and goodness, because they are all determined by ideology. This does not allow for free inquiry or genuine discovery, since all that there is to "know" is already present in the ideological concern to protect power interests.[43]

This position leads to a radical constructivism in which there is no knowledge, only ideology. All that we claim to "know" is a reflection of interests. Truth, like beauty, is constructed in the radical sense that no external reality or internal structures of consciousness influence what we believe to be true.[44] The sole determining force in the construction of consciousness is the social distribution of power.[45] On the Marxist and neo-Marxist ideological model, truth, beauty, and goodness are not independent of one another because everything is tied to the unrelenting logic of history that cannot be undone. This leaves little room for free agency, ethics, or democracy or for education.[46] Symbolic expression in this context entails not innovation, but articulation of that which is permitted by the ruling ideology. This purely reproductive or mimetic stance—as is found in many examples of socialist realism—can never generate art in the fullest sense. Murdoch calls the resulting activity "bad art."[47]

Goodness, on the other hand, is dynamic and complex. It is associated with the intelligent behaviors and beliefs tied to education. It is first an ethical concept that distinguishes between positive and negative value. For this sort of distinction to make sense, we must assume that people possess free agency, intelligence, and fallibility. Without free agency and fallibility, negative values could never be actualized, so they could not be distinguished from the positive; and without intelligence the difference between good and bad could not be comprehended. No particular articulation of the good can claim preeminence, therefore, since all people—and all communities—are fallible, and another's conception could turn out to be better than my own. Goodness is also holistic—it envisages the whole, pragmatic (it is expressed in terms of virtues that can be seen in the lives and characters of exemplary persons) and synthetic (it can be integrated with other ethical visions accepting the conditions of freedom, intelligence, and fallibility).[48]

There are, of course, nonethical goods such as good food, good art, good taste, and good scholarship. Yet, if J. J. C. Smart is correct, that goodness "has something to do with commendation or approval or answering certain purposes," then it is a teleological concept that subjugates various goods to higher intrinsic purposes.[49] What counts as "commendable," or worthy of "approval," or attentive to a particular "purpose," depends on what we mean by something being more or less valuable; and the meaning of value terms can only be deciphered in relation to concepts of the good that, in the end, derive from what communities or traditions cherish most.[50] Accordingly, all goods are ultimately subject to a higher good that is the source of their value. In this view, to blur the distinction among truth, beauty, and goodness—to argue that they are not fully independent domains—is not to say that they completely collapse into one another or that there are no differences among them. It is to say rather that they are *influenced* by a vision of the good, not *determined* by ideological interests.

The result is not radical constructivism, since truth is not relative to goodness in a strong sense, but rather *quasi-realism, weak objectivism*, or *soft relativism*.[51] To say that knowledge—truth—is socially constructed is to say that interpretations of reality are influenced, not determined, by the ethical visions through which researchers view the world.[52] And to say that beauty is in the eye of the beholder entails acknowledging the influence of collective ethical vision over how and what we see. What counts as "good science" or "good art"—one pursuing truth, the other beauty—is inexorably tied, therefore, to what counts as goodness according to particular traditions and communities.[53]

If we are not to fall prey to the quagmires of radical relativism or extreme subjectivism, however, there must be some sense in which goodness transcends individuals and communities, even if people disagree about its content or the forms in which it is expressed. Such a transcendent ideal is inherent in the very nature of consciousness. Built into our experiences of time, place, and value is the recognition that there is always another time, a broader place, and a better formulation of an idea. This is a source of hope and creativity because it leaves open the possibility that there is a better way.[54] It is also the origin of doubt, for to see the possibility of that which lies beyond, I must be willing to question that which lies at hand.[55] I, therefore, speak of transcendence as a higher—rather than an absolute or ultimate—good. However we conceive it, there could always be a better way.[56]

The pursuit of goodness, then, might properly be called a *spiritual* endeavor. Murdoch put it this way:

> Goodness is connected with the attempt to see the unself, to see and respond to the real world in light of a virtuous consciousness. This is the non-metaphysical meaning of the idea of transcendence to which philosophers have so consistently resorted.... "Good is a transcendent reality" means that virtue is the attempt to pierce the well of selfish consciousness and join the world as it really is.[57]

The assumption that there is a reality beyond experience that presents itself by way of consequences within experience is a regulative idea. It motivates us to strive to improve upon our current approximations, while at the same time serving as the ultimate end of inquiry—knowledge, as it were, the way it ought to be. Recognizing that every point of view is limited, and every framework fallible, regulates our belief in the value of our current perspective. Even our most basic beliefs and practices could turn out to be wrong.

The concept of a world outside of consciousness has ethical as well as theoretical significance. The world as it ought to be understood is not only the ideal that scientific reason strives to explain; it is the sort of existence that moral reasoning teaches us to emulate. This concept also has aesthetic significance as the "natural world" aesthetic imagination seeks to engage.[58] The ideals of science, art, and ethics turn out to be the same. Kant called them the "Noumenon" or the "Idea of God."[59] We construct truth and beauty through a meeting of consciousness and transcendence, which is influenced, but not determined, by collective visions of goodness. Ethics, in other words, precedes inquiry, scientific as well as aesthetic.[60]

Education as art

Charles Taylor maintains that human experience is layered. Mechanical behaviors and beliefs are those that require little or no investment of intelligence.[61] Our hearts beat; we learn to walk; we believe that the sun will rise tomorrow. These do not require drawing conclusions, forming intentions, attributing, or creating new meaning. We do or believe them because the mechanics of our world require this of us—breathing and pumping blood through our veins—or because we have become habituated to doing so—believing that the sun will rise or putting one foot in front of another. As mechanical behaviors and attitudes become increasingly complex we must learn to perform or adopt them. This process is often called training.

Greater complexity, however, requires the investment of intelligence. Taylor uses the term "action" or "activity" to denote intelligent behaviors that call for drawing a conclusion, forming an intention, achieving understanding, or conceiving a new creation. Beliefs, when they involve reasons or meanings, can also be intelligent. Like their mechanical counterparts, intelligent behaviors and beliefs are learned. We commonly call the process of facilitating this sort of learning, teaching. It usually requires prior training. We must learn the alphabet before we can read, spell before we can write poetry, add and subtract before proving the Pythagorean theorem, hold a pencil before drawing, and play scales before playing Mozart.[62]

Education can be understood as an accumulation of what is taught and learned. The task, however, is not to teach all conclusions, intentions, understandings, and designs, but only those that are worthwhile; and to have a sense of what is most worth learning requires a conception of the good. Education, therefore, involves initiation into the traditions of reason, morality, meaning, and creativity deemed most valuable within the context of particular concepts of the good, which are constituted at the level of entire communities.[63]

Another layer of educational experience, however, involves its relation to the culture or tradition into which it initiates. Teaching not only transmits old ideas; it creates new ones. It is associated not only with predetermined feelings and norms; it also creates new attitudes and practices. Teaching is generative, not merely reproductive. It recalls the past, but it also pushes the limits, criticizes, explores, examines.[64] In this respect education can be viewed as a creative or artistic activity. It draws on subject matter and a host of artistic traditions—drama, painting, calligraphy, poetry, music, dance—to explain and explore, transmit and transform. To view education from an aesthetic perspective is to understand it as the creation of learning materials, processes, programs, institutions, and experiences in various forms of symbolic representation to initiate people into visions of the good.

And these collective visions point to an ideal that lies beyond the symbols with which we conceive it, even though we have no way of envisaging that ideal other than by means of those very local symbols. Education can be understood, then, as "the lure of the transcendent...the protest against present forms that may be reformed and transformed...the consciousness that we live in time, pulled by the inexorable otherness that brings judgment and hope to forms of life which are but the vessels of present experience."[65] If the distinction between craft and fine art can withstand criticism, education might be viewed in the latter category.[66] Crafts or useful arts involve employing designs to achieve predetermined ends. Fine arts, on the other hand, not only reproduce symbolic forms for instrumental purposes; they explore, as well as express, that which we cherish most. They work at the boundaries of culture, expanding and testing our communal conceptions of the good. Education is the art, and perhaps sometimes also the craft, of initiating people into communities with visions of the good through study, practice, and celebration; and pedagogy the art of nurturing good people, not promoting or overcoming ideological interests.[67] As agents of the good, their value is intrinsic; and their symbolic beauty—density, repleteness, and exemplification—lies in the pedagogic activities through which goodness is explored and expanded.[68]

The appreciation of education

To appreciate education as art is to have a sense of the variety of symbolic forms of representation that are used to initiate people into visions of the good and to be able to distinguish between more and less meritorious examples of those symbolic forms.[69] The standards that one must comprehend to be capable of such appreciation derive from a community's vision of goodness. This is so, partly because education is a teleological enterprise aimed at the intrinsic purpose of promoting goodness and partly because all artistic expression ultimately embraces, redefines, or reacts against a communal concept of the good.

But artistic expression and inquiry grow from traditions tied to communities. To notice innovation in a particular painting or musical composition, its freshness must be gauged against the context in which it was created. Hence, artistic—like scientific, scholarly, or theoretical—merit will always be judged within a subcommunity with its own conceptions of goodness. To say that a work is beautiful, among its other meanings, entails that it is good art. Artistic and scientific communities enjoy complex relationships with ethical conceptions of goodness that govern the larger communities in which they reside. Sometimes they support, and other times they challenge, the values of these communities, pushing the limits of culture while exploring new ideas and ideals.

Communities of educators constitute one such subculture within the larger ethical communities they serve. And like other artistic and scholarly communities, they live at once in harmony and in tension with dominant ethical values. They seek to transmit, but also to transform, inherited conceptions of goodness. The aesthetic standards that inform appreciation of education as art, then, hail from a variety of communities. They come from the ethical community whose visions of the good are being transmitted within a particular institution. Additionally, they are taken from particular traditions of educational thought and practice such as progressive education, humanistic education, the child-centered movement, the structure of the disciplines movement, and the great books tradition.

Standards for the appreciation of education as art are also drawn from subject-matter disciplines in which particular content-specific pedagogies develop and from divergent interpretations of data within those disciplines.[70] They also can come from various arts and crafts that teachers draw upon to illustrate, enliven, explain, and entertain. Some teachers rely on dramatic arts in their teaching, others use creative bulletin boards, some can paint pictures with words, and others are wizards with media. Each of these arts and crafts has its own standards that can be drawn upon in the appreciation of educational creativity.

To appreciate education as art is to develop an understanding of the community in which an educational program is conducted, the educational communities whose ideas and ideals influence the program in question, subject-matter communities whose traditions are being explored within that program, and the artistic communities whose forms of expression are being used to engage in that exploration. Joseph Schwab called the amalgamation into curriculum of these traditions, standards, and crafts the "art of eclectic."[71] This sort of eclectic integration, he suggested, is the special gift of the educator. Elliot Eisner calls the understanding that is acquired through the cultivation of such pedagogic gifts "educational connoisseurship."[72]

Educational criticism

It is fruitful to view training from the perspectives of quantitative behavioral science. To understand teaching, which is more complex than training, we must look not only to the explanations of quantitative behavioral science, but also to lenses of qualitative inquiry, to understanding how people experience it and the cultural norms that govern it. Phenomenology offers an account of how students and teachers experience schooling in consciousness, while ethnography articulates unspoken public norms operating in classrooms.

To grasp education fully as an art, however, we need not only to explain and understand, but also to appreciate and assess the value of educational expression. In addition to being viewed exegetically, from positivist, phenomenological, and anthropological perspectives, education should also be grasped eisegetically, as a form of artistic inquiry in which new meanings are constantly being created and recreated.

If the appreciation of education can be conceived in terms of connoisseurship, its assessment and evaluation can be thought of as a form of art criticism. And if appreciation of education as art involves understanding educational processes, criticism of education as art means both translating that understanding into forms accessible to others and formulating judgments that are concerned with the educational merit of particular cases. Eisner discusses four aspects of educational criticism: the descriptive, the thematic, the interpretive, and the evaluative.[73]

The descriptive aspect

The criticism of education begins artistically. If artists see reality with heightened clarity and express what they see in nondiscursive forms that capture the imagination, art critics see works with similar clarity and present what they perceive in symbolic forms. The presentation of naturalistic data by the educational critic, then, does not involve the mere exegesis of norms or experiences; it involves eisegesis as well—the creation of a direct perception of a pedagogic work by using rich, metaphoric, symbolic language. The task is to create a new experience of the work in which light is thrown on a particular aspect of the reality that it presents to consciousness.

A good example of the descriptive phase of criticism can be found in Sarah Lawrence Lightfoot's notion of educational "portraiture," in which pictures of "good enough" high schools are painted in words to identify common themes among outstanding examples of educational institutions:

> The piecing together of the portrait has elements of puzzle building and quilt making. How does one fit the jagged, uneven pieces together? When the pieces were in place, what designs appear? A tapestry emerges, a textured piece with shapes and colors that create moments of interest and emphasis. Detailed stories are told in order to illuminate more general phenomena; a subtle nuance of voice or posture reveals a critical attitude…. Words are chosen that try to create sensations and evoke visions for the reader. It is a palpable form, highly textured.[74]

To ask about the "accuracy" or "reliability" of this sort of presentation of data is to ask the wrong sort of question. It is like asking about the accuracy or reliability of Mozart's *Requiem* or of the *Mona Lisa*. What we want to know of the critic's grasp of reality is whether it "rings true," whether it captures the "dynamic form" of something present in the experience of the whole. Langer explains how symbols capture the "dynamic form" of experience much as a dried riverbed conforms to the "shape" of the rapidly flowing river that once ran through it.[75] To ask whether or to what degree of merit a critic has enabled others to "see" a work is itself a task for criticism.

Eisner suggests three strategies for assessing the descriptive aspect of criticism: structural corroboration, consensual validation, and referential adequacy. The first asks whether the story that is woven hangs together. It questions not accuracy, but artistic holism. It seeks to understand whether the critic's rendition of the work represents an integrated whole. The second strategy, like the concept of triangulation, considers whether descriptive data is confirmed from a variety of perspectives. The third strategy inquires whether this data draws upon symbols and themes that were indeed present in the work itself. Adequacy asks whether the whole that is recreated by the critic is an entirely new creation, or whether it in fact captures some dimension of the work in question, allowing us to see it afresh.[76]

Egon G. Guba and Yvonna S. Lincoln have proposed two sorts of criteria for judging the merit of qualitative investigations that, while drawing more on social scientific than aesthetic metaphors, parallel Eisner's strategies to some degree.[77] First, they contend that a qualitative study should be trustworthy. This means that it should meet four conditions: First, a study must be credible. This assures a fit between participant and researcher perspectives. Second, it should also be transferable. It must provide enough data for comparison to other cases. Additionally, a study ought to be dependable. The researcher must insure that the process was logical, traceable, and documented. Finally, a study needs to be confirmable. Findings should be linked to data in readily discernible ways.[78]

Guba and Lincoln later recognized that trustworthiness hues closely to the positivist notions of internal and external validity, generalizability, and objectivity, so they advanced a second set of criteria concerning the authenticity of qualitative data that is more closely aligned with a constructivist epistemology. Authenticity criteria

are part of an inductive, grounded, and creative process that springs from immersion with naturalistic ontology, epistemology, and methodology (and the concomitant attempts to put those axioms and procedures into practice.... They are addressed largely to ethical and ideological problems...that increasingly concern those involved in social action and in the schooling process. In that sense, they are confluent with an increasing awareness of the ideology-boundaries of public life and the enculturation processes that serve to empower some social groups and classes and to impoverish others.[79]

According to this attitude, a study should meet five conditions. First, it should be fair. Differing respondent perspectives should be represented in an evenhanded way. Second, it should be ontologically authentic. Respondents' own constructions should be enhanced as a result of their participation in the study. Third, it ought to be educatively authentic. Participants in an inquiry should acquire a greater appreciation of themselves by engaging the views of others. Fourth, a study must also reflect catalytic authenticity. It should stimulate appropriate action. Finally, it needs to be tactically authentic by empowering participants to act.[80]

The thematic aspect

The descriptive aspect of educational criticism is accompanied by a thematic phase in which significant cultural and artistic tropes are identified, compared, and exposed for examination and exploration. Here writing takes on an important role as part of the inquiry process. We discover and refine these themes through the process of writing itself. Richardson put it this way:

> I write because I want to find something out. I write in order to learn something that I didn't know before I wrote it. I was taught, however, not to write until I knew what I wanted to say; until my points were organized and outlined.... The model has serious problems. It ignores the role of writing as a dynamic creative process.[81]

The interpretive aspect

In this dimension, the critic attempts to elucidate the meaning of the new insight that has been achieved by viewing the work in this way. To do so, the critic often turns to additional analogies found in theories of education, art, culture, or social science. In Eisner's words,

> In the interpretive aspect of criticism, ideas from the social sciences frequently come into play. These ideas form the conceptual maps that enable the educational critic to account for the events that have occurred and to predict some of their consequences.... The point here is not that there is one theory to be used to interpret the meaning of events within classrooms, but that there are a variety of theories. No one is interested in the facts by themselves, but rather in the facts interpreted.[82]

The evaluative aspect

The final aspect of educational criticism involves the assessment of value: Given this presentation and interpretation of the work, is it meritorious when assessed in terms of the various sorts of standards discussed above?

> To make such judgments requires...the application of educational criteria.... The truly competent educational critic...will be able to provide grounds for the value choices made while recognizing that others

might disagree with these choices. The grounding of such values not only requires knowledge of the history and philosophy of education; it also benefits from practical experience in the schools.[83]

When the critic assesses the "authenticity" of her data, discovers underlying themes through writing and rewriting, interprets an educational phenomenon according to some social scientific theory, or grounds her value judgments in educational history, philosophy, or practice, she gives voice to conceptions of good education embedded in the languages and communicative codes of the communities in which her interpretations and judgments are formulated. These in turn draw their normative bite— their evaluative authority—from an explicit or implicit vision of a higher good, from a communal sense of the sacred through which we engage a transcendent other.

Conclusion

Practicing, appreciating, and criticizing the educational arts preserve our collective spiritual heritages by reconceiving and reenvisaging them. This enables us "to see beyond appearances into the hidden realities of life— beyond facts into truth, beyond self interest into compassion, beyond our flagging energies and nagging desires into the love required to review the community of creation."[84] This insight empowers students and teachers to respond meaningfully to the new realities they face each day.

Despite his aversion to the arts, Plato held that beauty could be a starting point for the pursuit of goodness through what Murdoch called "images of the spiritual life."[85] Art, she wrote, "pierces the veil and gives sense to the notion of reality beyond appearances"; it is not "diversion or side issue, it is the most educational of all human activities and a place in which the nature of morality can be seen."[86] Artistic inquiry in education, then, is not a supplement to other forms of investigation and assessment; it lies at the very heart of pedagogic research. Through artistic educational inquiry we reeducate ourselves, reassessing pedagogies that speak to our highest priorities, redefining our most fundamental commitments, and reclaiming what we cherish most.

CHAPTER FOUR

Traditions of Inquiry in Education

Introduction

The study of education as an independent academic field began in the late nineteenth and early twentieth centuries in an effort to base teaching, school administration, and the curriculum on empirical findings.[1] It was part of a wider movement that promoted applying the methods of natural science that had become so successful during the two previous centuries to the study of mind and society. August Comte called it positivism to convey the belief that empirical science alone can verify positive statements about human beings and societies in addition to the natural world.[2] Teachers and administrators, who had previously been chosen on the basis of religious or political affiliations and who grounded their practice in theological traditions or political ideologies, could now be professionalized, according to supporters of this movement, through a rigorous training in the scientific principles of child development, human learning, or organizational management; and the curriculum could be constructed on a solid statistical foundation. Educational research on this view is an applied branch of developmental and behavioral psychology and, to a lesser extent, organizational sociology with scientific experimentation as the ideal mode of inquiry.[3]

As I pointed out previously, this perspective dominated educational research, especially in the United States, until the mid-twentieth century, when it came under attack on two fronts, one modeled after cultural anthropology and the humanities, especially literature and the arts,[4] and the other grounded in the radical social criticism of Karl Marx and his intellectual descendents.[5] Advocates of the former position called their methods qualitative and their approach to knowledge constructivist, in contrast to the penchant of the positivists for statistical generalizations of quantitative relationships between objects or events given in the world.[6] Proponents of the latter orientation referred to their view as critical, since it aimed to critique hidden power relations in ideological institutions such as schools in order to bring about a more equal or just distribution of resources in society.[7] To refer to these rival traditions of inquiry, opponents of positivism in education borrowed the term "research paradigm" from Thomas Kuhn's influential historical study of science, *The Structure of Scientific Revolutions*. They also adapted some of his observations about the emergence of new paradigms in the physical sciences to justify what they saw as innovations in educational research.[8]

This picture depicts fairly accurately more than a century of Anglo-American thinking about research in education. It sidesteps, however, the acrimonious debate known since the mid-1980s as the "methodology wars," in which the positivists and their qualitative and radical critics sought to defeat one another. It appeared for a time during the 1990s that the two camps had reached an accommodation. However, as discussed in Chapter Two, when in 2001 the US Congress declared "randomized controlled experimentation" to be the "gold standard" of educational research, the warring camps girded their loins for renewed combat. No doubt the primary catalyst for the renewal of hostilities can be found in No Child Left Behind's aggressive pro-positivism and overt disapproval of much qualitative and critical inquiry.[9] But we saw that the truce was also fragile. It masked deep and ancient philosophical differences over the nature of knowledge and human conduct by embracing problematic assumptions. The advocates of accommodation tended to view positivism in education naively as the standard against which other traditions of educational research are to be judged, to conceive constructivism as a form of weak empiricism that ignores the roots of qualitative inquiry in conceptions of knowledge that predate the rise of empiricism, to embrace hard and often incoherent forms of epistemological relativism as a path to coexistence between positivism and constructivism, and to pay insufficient attention to the potentially devastating impact of critical social theory on the very possibility of uninterested knowledge altogether upon which to base educational practice or policy.[10]

I criticized these assumptions in the two previous chapters under two separate headings: (1) "the dual- (or multiple-) epistemology thesis" and (2) "the two dogmas of educational research." The first heading refers to the idea that positivism and constructivism can be conceived as equally legitimate theories of knowledge.[11] The second relates to two common distinctions of contemporary educational thought between the cognitive and affective domains, on the one hand, and between facts and values or truth, beauty, and goodness, on the other.[12] In this chapter, I wish to elaborate on these objections by exploring their connection to Michael Oakeshott's distinction between technical and practical knowledge and his critique of rationalism in the study of human conduct. Oakeshott's view offers a useful conceptual framework within which to reformulate and expand upon my previous complaints and to clarify how we ought to think about the paradigms of educational research.[13] Contrary to the positivist view that causal explanation based on randomized experimentation is the highest standard of knowledge, I will argue that when it comes to the study of human subjects, including educational research, even statistical generalizations depend upon a prior form of qualitative understanding. The chapter will conclude by considering some consequences of this perspective, which I have dubbed "transcendental pragmatism," for the practice of inquiry in education.

Two concepts of knowledge

Oakeshott divided human life into two interrelated sorts of experiences. On the one side lies our encounter with the natural world of things, objects, events, and facts. These can be conceived technically in terms of unambiguous and mechanical rules, universal laws, statistical generalizations, correlational relationships, and causal explanations. On the other side, there is the world of performances and occurrences, which have meanings that can be interpreted in a variety of different ways. Although people possess bodies and live in the natural world, what distinguishes them from the rest of nature is that they also inhabit a self-created historical world of diverse cultures. These are comprised of performances and occurrences. The former are activities that disclose beliefs about the sort of people we choose to be, how we prefer to live with others, or the meanings that we attribute to the world around us; the latter entail events and experiences that we interpret in light of those beliefs. The stories we tell our children about who they are and where they come from involve performances, for example, while occurrences can be seen in historical or natural events to which we attribute meaning or from which our lives derive purpose, such as the birth of a nation or a child.[14]

   Accordingly, we can distinguish between two sorts of knowledge: one technical, focused on things, objects, and facts; the other practical, concerned with performances, occurrences, and meanings. Technical knowledge entails techniques required to properly engage in such human activities as natural science, the fine arts, or the governance of a good society. These can be formulated in propositions—rules, principles, directions, and maxims— that are found in manuals for cooking, driving, or scientific research. Practical knowledge, on the other hand, exists only in use and is shared or becomes common not by means of formulated doctrines, but through traditions of practice. "Technical knowledge can be learned from a book," wrote Oakeshott. "Much of it can be learned by heart, repeated by rote, and applied mechanically." It can, in short, "be both taught and learned in the simplest meanings of these words." Practical knowledge, on the other hand, "can be neither taught nor learned, but only imparted and acquired. It exists only in practice, and the only way to acquire it is by apprenticeship to a master—not because a master can teach it (he cannot), but because it can be acquired only by continuous contact with one who is perpetually practicing it."[15]

Following this way of thinking, Oakeshott differentiated behavior from conduct. Behavior is associated with the world of techniques and objects, with conditioning and reactions to circumstances, with that which can be observed about what a person does disconnected from what she thinks or feels or intends. Conduct, on the other hand, is situated in the world of practice and meaning. It relates to wants rather than needs, to active recollections not mere passive memories, thinking and believing not just doing, understanding and interpreting instead of only recording, creating and innovating rather than simply imitating. Behavior, in other words, is mechanical, bound either by natural or behavioral laws or by preestablished human rules. Conduct, on the other hand, is intelligent, subject to multiple interpretations and capable of generating new norms.[16]

Positivist research in education is an example of technical knowledge, since it is grounded in inflexible rational rules and focused primarily on observable human behavior. The ingredients of experimentation are intended to render a wholly mechanical account of how things, objects, facts, events, and behaviors are related to one another. Concepts such as valid and reliable measurement, treatment and control groups, random selection, pre- and posttesting, and dependent and independent variables are employed to induce universal laws or statistical generalizations from otherwise messy data stating that predictable consequences are necessarily or probably caused by defined events under given conditions. According to the so-called deductive-nomological account, scientific explanations are deduced from such laws or generalizations when the expected results follow particular instances of those initial conditions as anticipated.[17] Less rigorous research designs, such as quasi-experimentation, which contrasts treatment to unsystematic comparison rather than randomly selected control groups or nonexperimentation, which may forgo comparison groups altogether, can measure correlations between two events—how often they occur simultaneously—but not whether one is caused by another.[18]

Qualitative inquiry, on the other hand, aims to illuminate practical knowledge of human conduct by rendering an understanding of the rich variety of performances, occurrences, and meanings—manners, styles, tastes, customs, symbols, and stories—that are embedded in diverse, historically contingent, cultural traditions. Various sources of data— participant observation, in-depth interviews, and material culture—are collected and compared with others sources—additional observations, interviews, or artifacts—for purposes of corroboration (triangulation) to construct coherent depictions of performances that occur in particular natural settings.[19] These can then be interpreted according to one or more of several hermeneutic orientations: for example, phenomenologically, to give voice to the ways insiders experience the setting and the meanings they attribute to that experience; ethnographically, to offer an account of the social norms that govern the actors in that setting; or aesthetically, to assess the value of the events that transpired in that setting according to one or another standard of merit or to discover new meaning in them that might not have previously been conceived.[20]

Critical social knowledge is more technical than practical, in Oakeshott's view, despite the emphasis of many critical theorists on debunking the theory–practice dichotomy in favor of a nexus they call praxis.[21] Like positivism, critical social theory—from Marx through the neo-Marxists such as Max Horkheimer and Theodor Adorno to postmodern theorists such as Michel Foucault—is grounded in rigid rules, albeit different ones.[22] Positivist reasoning is inductive and deductive, while critical theory is dialectical and power related. Marxist philosopher Louis Althusser dubbed this the logic of the "conflictual sciences,"[23] and hermeneutic philosopher Paul Ricoeur called it the "hermeneutics of suspicion," which like Althusser he also associated with Sigmund Freud and the psychoanalytic tradition.[24] The ingredients of critical social theory are designed to reveal hidden conflicts that are believed to arise necessarily—mechanically—when power is distributed inequitably in a society. Concepts such as basic structure (means of production, alienation of labor, political economy, and socioeconomic status); superstructure (false consciousness, ideology, hegemony, power relations, and social interests); and poststructure (discourse analysis, deconstruction, postcolonialism, and postmodernism) are used either to hasten the inevitable revolution that will redistribute resources with utopian justice or to sensitize us to the sundry ways we dominate one another in order to lessen but not alleviate the unrelenting grip that inherited power relations hold over us.[25]

Although they are clearly distinct from one another, Oakeshott insisted, these technical and practical forms of knowledge are also inseparable. Many human activities such as the fine arts—painting, dancing, acting, poetry—require a high degree of technical knowledge. But this knowledge only acquires meaning in the context of concrete traditions of practice. What counts as great technique in one tradition may be scoffed at by another. The same can be said not only of crafts such as cooking and pottery making, but also of knowledge in the natural and social sciences. The techniques of psychoanalysis, to take but one example, have no meaning whatsoever when viewed from the perspective of experimental or behavioral psychology. To make sense, its rules and maxims must be embedded in a tradition of psychological and therapeutic practice. What is true for art, craft, science, and therapy is true for education as well, which involves the attainment of self-understanding by learning to see oneself in the mirror of historically contingent and culturally embedded traditions of practice. Nowhere, writes Oakeshott, "can technical knowledge be separated from practical knowledge, and nowhere can they be considered identical with one another or able to take the place of one another."[26]

The pursuit of knowledge and the study of education

In contrast to the idea that technical knowledge entails the standard against which other perspectives should be judged, the pursuit of knowledge on this view begins with acquiring an understanding of human conduct preserved in traditions of practice. This becomes apparent when we distinguish skills from abilities and information from judgment. Skills relate to our capacity to do or make something by means of behaviors. As complexity increases, however, and greater degrees of mental activity are required, the term "skills" is often replaced by "abilities," which exhibit characteristics associated with human conduct. The movement from skills to abilities can be detected by noting the sorts of knowledge that each entails. To the extent that skills require knowledge, it will typically take the form of technical information—inert facts often accepted without question or a process of inquiry. Information is bound by rule-like propositions and discovered by the application of mechanical formulas or techniques. Complex abilities, on the other hand, require partnering information with "judgment," the tacit ingredient of knowledge that cannot be specified in propositions.

Judgment cannot be itemized in the form of facts characteristic of information. It is concerned with the "how," not the "what," of knowledge, not in the sense of rules of inquiry—these can be conveyed as information—but in the sense that enables us to interpret that information, to decide upon its relevance, to recognize what rule to apply, and to discover what action to take where no rule is relevant. Judgment is not information of another sort, then, but what has sometimes been called the "art of inquiry," without which inquiry itself remains unintelligible. To be initiated into a mode of understanding such as history, philosophy, science, politics, or educational studies requires not merely that one has acquired the mechanical skill to recite information or apply rules of inquiry; one must have also mastered the ability—that is, acquired the judgment necessary—to understand and explain that information and those rules, to grasp their meanings, and even to generate new ideas by using the relevant language in fresh and original ways.[27]

Learning to inquire involves becoming a connoisseur of good judgment and proper conduct, not only a master of technical procedures and formulas. This requires an ability to comprehend and create meanings, not merely to recite facts or apply rules or principles. The one is accomplished implicitly, through apprenticeship to qualified mentors, the other by means of conditioning, training, and telling. Oakeshott explained that it is in learning to appreciate the significance of information that the real substance of an inheritance lies: to distinguish between the sorts of answers appropriate for different kinds of questions, to enjoy intellectual virtues such as curiosity, patience, honesty, exactness, industry, concentration, and doubt—in short, the ability to think. And this is not taught overtly by precept or through a separate subject matter in the school timetable or a university course of study. The arts of thinking are imparted unobtrusively in everything that appears in the curriculum, in a tone of voice or a gesture that accompanies instruction, in asides and oblique utterances[28]—in short, in the "intricacies" and "intimations" of a tradition or culture.[29] Even though they are independent and interdependent, therefore, the acquisition of technical knowledge presupposes prior practical knowledge that entails initiation into a tradition. Qualitative understanding is logically prior to causal explanation, not the other way around.

In this view, becoming educated entails initiation into a number of diverse conversations about how to understand and interpret the world in which we live; to appreciate a variety of literatures, not merely to speak the relevant languages; to master the subtle arts of argumentation from several perspectives, not only one or another partisan theory among a narrow array of possibilities. Schools or universities are themselves historic communities with their own customs and ways of life, places set apart from the world for the purpose of enabling students to engage the "intimations of excellence" that characterize these literatures, some of which may have never been encountered before, to promote satisfactions that might never have otherwise been imagined or wished for.[30] The study of education, in this view, cannot be reduced to the mere mechanics of instruction in inert facts and inflexible rules or the outcomes of policies designed to improve student achievement, reduce school violence, or produce some or other predetermined technical result; it requires an understanding of the cultural traditions in which these facts, rules, and policies are embedded and their values, aspirations, and conceptions of excellence. In short, qualitative understanding is no less a prerequisite for quantitative analysis in education than in other pursuits. Abstract rules cannot substitute for an appreciation of the hermeneutic subtleties embedded in the practices of teaching and learning. If there is a "gold standard" to educational research, it is surely not to be found in "randomized controlled experimentation."

Methodology wars and research paradigms in historical perspective

How then did it come to pass that nearly the opposite of what appears to be the case is accepted as common wisdom in many circles of educational and social research? Oakeshott attributes this to what he calls the fallacy of rationalism in politics or the false idea that human affairs can be adequately captured by means of abstract and rigid concepts, rules, or techniques such as those taught in empirical science and critical theory, which include not only inductive, deductive, and dialectical forms of reasoning but also skeptical methods for deconstructing social structures, power relations, and regimes of meaning. "Rationalism," in this view, asserts that practical knowledge is no knowledge at all; all knowledge is technical, the superiority of which lay in the appearance that it springs from ignorance and ends in certainty. But this is an illusion. Technical knowledge is never self-complete; it relies on presuppositions grounded in practice, without which the techniques of a particular field of inquiry make no sense.[31]

The problem with rationalism so conceived, Oakeshott contended, is that it confuses genuine knowledge of human affairs with half-truths torn from experience of the world that is normally recalled in the political traditions of a society. Worse, it attributes to those traditions, which are preeminently fluid, "the rigidity and fixity of character" that in fact belongs to the ideological principles born of arid technique.[32] This has two especially egregious consequences. First, it is incapable of addressing its own shortcomings, since the only body of knowledge capable of correcting its errors is rejected in advance, such that when one rationalist project fails it can only be replaced by another.[33] Second, a society that embraces rationalism of this kind will tend to prefer an exclusively technical form of education, grounded in the empiricism of Immanuel Kant and John Locke or the dialectical thinking of both left- and right-leaning Hegelians. The Rationalist believes that training in technical knowledge, not initiation into the moral and intellectual achievements of his society, is the only education worthwhile, "because he is moved by the faith that there is no knowledge, in the proper sense, except technical knowledge."[34]

The source of this fallacy, in Oakeshott's view, lies in the preoccupation with certainty found in the seventeenth-century epistemological writings of Francis Bacon and Rene Descartes, who held that scientific inquiry can be reduced to a set of "clear and apparent" rules that are indifferent to subject matter and that can be formulated as a precise set of directions; and it is no doubt the case that the privilege afforded positivist technique in the methodological debates in educational research can be traced back to these empiricist origins.[35] However, as I have intimated here, the methodology wars in education join a much older philosophical discussion about the very possibility of knowledge altogether in which the fixation on certainty and inflexible rules begins not with empiricism but with a more ancient form of transcendental rationalism.

Plato was among the first to question whether practical experience is a reliable source of knowledge. He argued that, instead, certainty could only be achieved by rationally abstracting essential forms from the material accidents of things experienced in practice. This resulted in the sort of rigid, monistic rationality characteristic of technical knowledge, although Plato's method was dialectical, not inductive or deductive, involving a process of conceptualization and critique; and his findings were transcendental, not empirical, abstracted from not based on experience.[36] To address the monism and rigidity of this approach, Aristotle distinguished abstract theory from practical wisdom; though, like his teacher, he privileged theory over practice. Aristotle's conception of theoretical knowledge included both efficient and teleological (purposive) causes. The former are mechanical, in the sense of technical knowledge, "pushing" antecedent events into being by means of random interventions. The latter, on the other hand, "pull" events toward a natural state inherent in the very rational design or meaning of things. Aristotle's practical wisdom consisted of the ethical and civic virtues required for a good life and just society that reflect the same rational ends as his teleological causes but expressed in local customs.[37] Thus, when skeptics such as Descartes challenged the rational metaphysics of Aristotle's final causes (in both theory and practice), efficient causes were all that was left, which led empiricists like Bacon to suggest that certainty was only possible when natural laws explain causal relations between objects mechanically.

What positivists often fail to recall, however, is that David Hume applied Cartesian skepticism to efficient causes just as others had done to final ends, pointing out that empirical laws are contingent, not necessary, since events may not turn out as expected. Our faith in causal reasoning is therefore more psychological and cultural than epistemological.[38] To this, Kant responded that the necessity of causation is built into the universal structure of mind, not things-in-themselves, by means of which both theoretical laws and practical duties can be discovered.[39] It was Kant's response to Hume that allowed positivists like Comte to remain sufficiently confident about causal reasoning as to extend its reach to the human sciences. However, once it is admitted that mind plays a role in the construction of knowledge, it is hard to deny that this structure is relative to history and culture, not universal. To salvage causation, Karl Popper argued that although Hume may have been right that it is impossible to verify the connection between a cause and an effect, it is possible to prove that connection false.[40] But as seen in Chapter Two, this turns out to be an exaggeration, since as Popper's disciple Imre Lakatos pointed out, empirical scientists do not falsify single statements or even more complex theories, but entire research programs; and whether a research program is progressing or degenerating depends to a considerable extent on the cultural initiation of a community of researchers.[41]

This may be why G. W. F. Hegel's epistemological thinking took an entirely different direction after Kant. Hegel abandoned the mechanical causes of empiricism altogether and revived the transcendental knowledge of Plato's dialectical and Aristotle's teleological reasoning. The purpose of inquiry in this view is to arrive at the rational end of history, not the universe, which entails absolute freedom expressed in a particular human culture. We progress toward this end when each generation critiques the ideas of its immediate ancestors.[42] Following Hegel, Marx accepted the idea that the purpose of inquiry is liberation, but argued that this could only be accomplished by critiquing oppressive ideologies used to rationalize the unequal distribution of economic and cultural resources within society. This became the basis for critical social theory.[43] Unfortunately, as Foucault maintained, it turns out that liberation from one false consciousness leads only to another.[44] Edmund Husserl, on the other hand, took this teleological thinking in yet another direction by suggesting that inquiry should seek to understand not the ultimate purpose of history, but the subjective intentions of individuals and the intersubjective ways people create society and culture. This became the basis for constructivism.[45] But without an ultimate metaphysical or historical end upon which to justify this line of reasoning, it becomes difficult to differentiate the intentions of the subjects of inquiry from those of the researchers seeking to understand them. In short, the romance of Western epistemology with certainty born of rational theory, whether empirical or teleological, appears to have reached a dead end.[46]

It was William James and John Dewey, among other pragmatists, who most emphatically returned to Aristotle's original distinction between theory and practice, but with an emphasis on the latter rather than the former.[47] This led a number of influential educationalists to justify qualitative inquiry as a methodological alternative to positivism in pragmatic terms. Dewey, however, was an epistemological monist; he viewed all inquiry as of a piece, applying a new universal logic of trial and error to address all problems experienced in interactions with our surroundings. Thus, when Kuhn historicized science by arguing that it progresses not by laying one fact on top of another like bricks, but by rejecting the ways in which data and methods are conceived in one research paradigm for a new one, it was appealing to rely on this idea in justifying methodological pluralism in the study of education and other human institutions, even if Kuhn himself had not abandoned positivism sufficiently to see social and educational research as other than preparadigmatic. On the other hand, like James, Oakeshott was a methodological and value pluralist who believed in multiple modes of understanding grounded in diverse practical traditions.[48] He sided with Hume in holding that the rational theories are but technical abridgements of cultural practices. Meaning is a contingent human achievement enacted in history, according to this view, not an expression of universal reason given in the structure of the universe a la Aristotle or mind a la Kant or history a la Hegel or class a la Marx or consciousness a la Husserl; and mechanical causes acquire meaning from—they do not drive—the practical traditions in which they are embedded.

The dogmas of educational research and dual epistemology revisited

The truce in the methodology wars rested on this mistaken preference for uniform rational technique in human affairs. This is why it was fragile and ultimately doomed to fail. This preference led to the interrelated assumptions that I have critiqued under the headings mentioned previously, both of which hearken back to the very origins of empiricism: (1) the two dogmas of educational research, which hold that we can distinguish between the cognitive and affective domains, on the one hand, and between facts and values or truth, beauty, and goodness, on the other; and (2) the dual- (or multiple-) epistemology thesis, which states that positivism and constructivism are equally legitimate theories of knowledge.

The first of these refers of course to W. V. O. Quine's influential essay, "Two Dogmas of Empiricism," in which he argued a la Hume that empiricism itself is grounded in two unsubstantiated assumptions. The first holds that statements whose truth-value depends on their meaning, which are often called analytic, can be usefully distinguished from those whose truth-value depends on matters of fact, usually referred to as synthetic. The second maintains that the meaning of statements can be reduced by means of some logical construction to immediate sense experience, which is known as reductionism. There are two ways to sustain the analytic/synthetic distinction. According to the first, we would need to show that statements such as "no bachelor is married" can be transformed into logical truths of the form "no unmarried man is married." This is possible, however, only if "bachelor" is synonymous with "unmarried man," which presupposes that terms such as these can be interchanged without affecting the truth-value of the sentences in which they appear; and this of course is precisely what it means for a statement to be analytic. The second way to sustain this distinction would be to reduce the meaning of all statements to verifiable sense-data, since on this account analytic statements could be seen as extreme cases of meaning that require no verification. The difficulty with this strategy is that empiricists have produced no way of specifying a sense-datum language and showing how to translate the rest of significant discourse, statement by statement, into it. Until they do so, Quine maintains, reductionism must be considered another "metaphysical article of faith."[49]

In educational research these empirical dogmas translated into the positivist belief that truth is a cognitive affair dependent upon scientifically verifiable facts, while beauty and goodness are tied to the emotions expressed in the arts and humanities. Quantitative research was thought to be tough-minded, scientific, and objective, while qualitative methods were tender-minded, humanistic, and subjective. As qualitative inquiry came into its own, its proponents sought legitimacy in accord with cognitive dominance, first by arguing that it has rigorous checks against error analogous to its quantitative counterparts, and subsequently by reference to alternative intersubjective standards such as corroboration, trustworthiness, or authenticity.[50] This strategy, which I called weak empiricism, left the distinctions between cognition and affect and truth, beauty, and goodness intact by means of dual (or multiple) epistemology, which distinguished "between at least two conceptions of knowledge, one that aims to discover and explain relations between dependent and independent variables and another that strives to understand human experiences, norms, and purposes."[51] However, as argued previously, dual epistemology suffers from a self-refuting (or hard) form of relativism that hinders systematic assessment of merit, since each paradigm is thought to have its own assumptions that are protected from critique on the basis of the other. It also discourages mixed methods, since each paradigm is isolated from the other, ontologically, epistemologically, and methodologically. Additionally, it misunderstands Kuhn, who was not a methodological pluralist but held that new paradigms should replace the old ones. Finally, it fails to take on board hard questions about the very possibility of uninterested knowledge, including whether facts can ever be separated from values or causal laws generalized across cultures.[52]

Quine, on the other hand, suggested that the meanings of empirical statements are interconnected with one another in a holistic fashion, which makes talk of the empirical content of single statements misleading, since any statement can be seen to be necessarily true by reconsidering its relation to other statements in a theory in which, at least in principle, everything is open to revision. Ontology is relative, in other words, in the sense that objects of a theory are "cultural posits" decipherable within the context of a theory as a whole or as interpreted or reinterpreted in another theory, not individually as logical representations of sense experience.[53] This is a softer relativism than that embraced by the dual epistemologists since it does not hold that one theory cannot be criticized on the basis of another.[54] It was this sort of relativism that set the stage for Kuhn and Lakatos to argue that research paradigms or programs are what Oakeshott called contingent historical achievements that allow us to "observe" the world around us only at the edges of culture. Although Kuhn and Lakatos may not have been fully aware of it, the upshot of this historical view is to follow Hume in elevating the logical significance of practical or cultural knowledge as the prism through which such "observations" are made, not, as dual epistemologists suggested, to protect one paradigm or program from attack on the basis of another by isolating them from each other. The realm of meaning a la Oakeshott is logically prior to the realm of things and objects; behaviors and events are semantically predicated on performance and occurrences.

Recognizing that cultural meaning is a prerequisite for technical knowledge involves not only blurring the positivist distinction between cognition and affect but also diminishing the difference between science as the arbiter of truth, on the one hand, and the arts and humanities as agents of feeling and value, on the other. The relevant distinction is between neither things and feelings nor facts and values, because Quine's ontological relativism renders them more or less untenable, but rather between two ways of encountering the world outside of consciousness—what Philip Phenix calls "transcendence" and Emmanuel Levinas "the radically other": (1) as a meeting between subjects or (2) as a confrontation between subjects and objects.[55]

In the first instance, as Martin Buber points out, we receive the other into ourselves in a living relationship, allowing it to inform our very perception of the world and the ways we choose to interact within it, the intentions we form, norms we follow, and purposes we pursue.[56] Out of these living relations, we construct, to use John Searle's felicitous phrase, the very "ontological stuff of human civilization,"[57] our grasp of the senses through which we encounter others, the languages we speak, the literatures we study, and the stories we tell our children (which they may later reformulate or reject) about who they are and from whence they have come. The knowledge that we accumulate within these relationships and transmit across the generations is practical not in the procedural sense employed by some pragmatists that only entails solving problems presented in experience, but also in the interpersonal sense that involves relating to the world around us by creating and recreating, interpreting and reinterpreting, together with others with whom we share our lives, ways of what Martin Heidegger called "being-in-the-world."[58] Israel Scheffler called it personal knowledge.

In the second instance, we assert ourselves, imposing interests on others, both material and human, as if they were only objects available for subjugation to our capacity for understanding, manipulation, explanation, prediction, and control. To do so we abstract a technical sort of knowledge— deductive, inductive, and dialectical—from the contingent cultural relationships through which we first meet the world; technical, according to Buber, in the instrumental sense that it can be used to accomplish ends formulated within those very relationships, which privilege the felt needs of others, not a la Dewey of our unencumbered selves. Scheffler called this propositional and procedural knowledge.[59]

Dialogue and the formation of judgment

It is through dialogue of this kind in which we receive a tradition into ourselves, I think, that what Oakeshott called cultural "engagement" transpires. Buber insists that we can relate to objects, events, places, texts, and traditions as subjects by allowing them to inform our very beings just as we can relate to human subjects as if they were objects, using them to achieve some instrumental purpose or other. It is out of this sort of engagement with a variety of traditions that one's capacity to exercise judgment in the process of inquiry emerges. The dialogical process of engaging a tradition of inquiry or research paradigm, then, which begins with understanding and embracing its purposes and intentions before its rules and techniques, is analogous to that of engaging a tradition of social practice such as teaching or learning or schooling in this or another culture by means of such a paradigm. This happens on a number of interconnected levels. On one level, we learn to represent our feelings through a variety of forms that give shape not only to what we express but also to what we can sense and experience. On another level, we learn to interpret these representations in ways that allow us to communicate with others and transmit these representations, where appropriate, across the generations. On a third level, we construct the norms and ideals that govern our social lives. On a fourth level, these norms and ideals in turn become the ethical guideposts for the conduct of inquiry within these social settings.

As we have also seen, Suzanne Langer suggests that moments filled with great emotion, from trepidation to elation, may be best captured in nondiscursive idioms that strive to convey the dynamic shape of feelings in vicarious experiences expressed in such fine arts as sculpture or dance. She contrasts this with discursive expression in which abstract ideas are communicated by means of direct symbols that bear literal or unambiguous relations to the formal conditions they describe. Artistic language such as metaphor can be said to be "alive" on this account, to the extent that it captures the dynamic shape of lived experience, and "dead" when that experience is formalized for the purposes of achieving some instrumental end or objective understanding that lies outside the experience itself. Nondiscursive expression not only gives voice to our feelings in the world, it also forms what we are able to experience and how we are capable of conceiving it, educating our perception by giving shape to our primordial subject–subject engagements. Only later do we abstract the various instrumental techniques of one or another sort of discursive rationality to achieve ends and pursue interests that emerge from this engagement.[60]

As was mentioned in Chapter Three, hermeneutic theorists distinguish between two moments of interpretation. Exegesis involves treating a text or artwork like an object, reading out the meanings that lie within by taking into account the intentions of the author or artist and the linguistic, cultural, or historical contexts in which it was written or created.[61] Eisegesis, on the other hand, involves encountering a text or artwork as if it were another subject, discovering new meanings through the very process of dialogue with it that may not have been intended by the author or artist or previously understood in its linguistic, cultural, or historical context.[62] While the former relies upon discursive reasoning to formalize and justify interpretation, the latter depends upon nondiscursive expression, which gives form to the primordial feelings that emerge from encountering new and innovative ideas and experiences.[63] To offer a formal discursive account of the meanings that lie within a text or work of art, we must first acquire the cultural pre-understanding that emerges from encountering it in dialogue; exegesis presupposes eisegesis; discursive expression presupposes nondiscursive; rational abstraction depends upon artistic engagement. Oakeshott called this cultural pre-understanding "judgment," which is acquired through receiving a tradition of inquiry into oneself by embracing its assumptions and standards of merit. In order to "draw out" the meanings, intentions, correlations, and causes that lie within a culture, we must first participate in it, engaging its modes of understanding, languages and literatures, nuances and narratives, roles and rituals, styles, manners, customs, and intimations of excellence.[64] In the language of anthropology, to analyze a tradition as an outsider, from the etic perspective, we need first to experience it as an insider, from the emit perspective.[65]

Neither positivist social science nor weak empiricist accounts of qualitative inquiry that preserve a rigid distinction between subject and object, knower and known, such as are often found in discussions of phenomenology or ethnography, nor critical social theory that strives to unmask hidden and all too often insurmountable power relations, can claim privilege in the pursuit of truth, the quest for which originates in subject–subject not subject–object relations, in direct encounters with and willingness to receive rather than control the other. And although the feelings that emerge from these encounters are shaped in the nondiscursive processes of artistic form—narratives, symbols, representations, and rituals—the content those feelings convey is fundamentally ethical in character, having to do with how we choose to live together with others. What emerges from subject–subject encounters are not rigid rules or causal laws, but norms of conduct and expression that guide the desires, feelings, and purposes of human subjects in ways that enable them both to engage and understand others as well as to create new meanings to be received and understood by them. Human conduct on this account is both norm-governed and norm-generating, and the norms that emerge from subject–subject encounters are preserved and transmitted across the generations by means of the stories, customs, styles, and nuances of expression that comprise traditions of practice. Understanding these traditions, then, requires first that we grasp the purposes and intentions, the norms that govern conduct and expression, by entering into a dialogue with those who live by them. Only then can we translate the structure of experience from an insider's point of view into the theoretical language of an outsider; or unmask hidden power relations; or measure correlations, causes, and effects, by means of subject–object modes of understanding that offer discursive lenses through which to observe, interpret, and assess human interactions, but which are themselves contingent historical embodiments of culture no less than the traditions they seek to explore.

When it comes to educational research, therefore, what Georg Henrik von Wright once called teleological or purposive explanations are logically prior to causal or scientific explanation.[66] We must first comprehend the reasons why people choose to act or talk in a certain way within the context of the norms, values, or ideals by which he or she lives in order to properly interpret the variables that might influence the choices that they make, which can be understood from a variety of competing theoretical perspectives that draw on distinct modes of disciplinary understanding, including anthropology, sociology, psychology, politics, history, and philosophy. The traditions of educational research include not only the broad methodological categories of quantitative inquiry, qualitative analysis, and critical social theory, therefore, but also the widest possible range of disciplines in the social sciences, the humanities, and the arts, as they are brought to bear on questions relevant to educational policy and practice. Additionally, the ethics of human conduct and expression contained in social and cultural norms provides not only the focus of social and educational inquiry—what we seek to understand and explain—but also the standards according to which we conduct and express that inquiry. We can only grasp another person's purposes and intentions, and hence the variables that might influence them, from within the context of our own.

Viewed in this light, knowledge of human affairs is always the possession of an embodied agent, constrained by language, culture, and history, who grasps, albeit imperfectly, the contours of a world or the meaning of ideas that transcends—exists independently of—his or her limited experience. And this requires—at least as a regulative principle—the existence of a material reality and ethical ideals beyond our own contextualized experience, even if their ultimate shape and content remains shrouded in culture, history, language, and tradition.[67]

Transcendental pragmatism and the practice of inquiry in education

I have called this view transcendental pragmatism. With Oakeshott, James, and Dewey it conceives all inquiry—quantitative, qualitative, and critical—as grounded in historically contingent social and cultural traditions of practices, not universal rational ideals. However, like Oakeshott and James but unlike Dewey, it admits as a Kantian regulative principle—James called it a "working assumption"—the existence of entities, ideas, and ideals that are experienced as "more" or "higher" than human experience, even if we can conceive them only through the prisms of traditions that emerge from the subject–subject encounters in which human cultures originate. The result is what I have called soft, as opposed to hard, relativism, which admits that truth and goodness are tied to cognitive and cultural framework without undermining the possibility of criticizing one tradition on the basis of another.[68]

The positivist seeks to explain events on the basis of causal laws so that they can be predicted and controlled, and the critical social theorist to unmask oppression necessarily hidden in social relations. But we should be wary of these aims, which can be traced to what Oakeshott called the fallacy of rationalism in politics. The fact that another person's behavior can sometimes be predicted does not authorize one to control it, and social relations do not always embody unjust assertions of power. People are subjects, not objects; to understand them we must endeavor to meet them in dialogue; to receive their thoughts, feelings, and desires into ourselves; to allow them, if only for a moment, to use Buber's famous phrase, to fill the firmament; to grasp the norms and ideals, the traditions of practice, through which they have come to comprehend a world that transcends culture through the prism of our own defensible aims and aspirations. Nel Noddings calls this engrossment, or feeling with another, rather than empathy, or putting oneself in her place—it requires a stepping back rather than forward, an act of limitation rather than assertion, of self-control rather than domination over others.[69] Ethics, as Levinas put it, is first philosophy in the study of human subjects, and there is no substitute for this ethical stance if we are to truly understand what it means to educate ourselves and others.[70]

Pedagogy of Difference and the Other Face of Liberalism

The three chapters in Part Three explore the ethical and political consequences of the idea that there are no neutral grounds, rational or otherwise, upon which to base the commonalty of common schooling in liberal democratic societies. There can be no education without faith commitments of some kind or another, so the question becomes what should those commitments be? How can we distinguish between those orientations that promote a modus vivendi for common life across difference in diverse societies and those that do not? What do these distinctions require of the ideologies we teach in schools; of the ways we differentiate between public, particular, and private domains; of our very conceptions of liberal society? How, in other words, can we teach youngsters to celebrate the ways in which they choose to be different while at the same time accepting and respecting the differences of others?

I began to think seriously about these issues after my move to Israel. In the North American context, where Jews live as they have for centuries as a religious and ethnic minority, they tend to regard their identities primarily in religious terms, sometimes reconceived so as to meet the demands of citizenship and minority status in liberal democracies. Only secondarily do North American Jews view themselves as a political or cultural community. In Israel, on the other hand, where Jews constitute a sovereign majority for the first time in two millennia, being Jewish is conceived by most Jewish Israelis first in terms of political community and national culture, and only secondarily as a religion, even among many if not most Orthodox believers. It was only natural that I would focus my attention on religious and spiritual aspects of my identity while living in North America, and that I would shift my focus to its political and national dimensions upon moving to Israel.

I recall, for example, the Jewish pride I would experience in Los Angeles when hosting guests from the wider community at the American Jewish University, where I was Academic Vice President for many years while teaching as an adjunct lecturer at UCLA. When I arrived at the University of Haifa, a Christian Arab graduate student of mine exhibited a similar ethnic and religious pride when he insisted on showing me the Arab Academic College of Education in Haifa, where he earned his first degree. I understood immediately that for him this was the local equivalent of what the American Jewish University had been for me when I lived in Los Angeles and that in his eyes, as well as my own, I was now a professor at Israel's version of UCLA.

But the sovereignty associated with majority status carries with it responsibility, of at least three interrelated kinds. First, I owe it to myself to be able to articulate a reasonable account of the political theory that governs my society. Second, I owe a duty to Jews who continue to live abroad as members of a minority culture in a secular society where the majority of citizens are Christians to defend this grand experiment in Jewish sovereignty against those who would delegitimize it and thereby limit the extent to which Diaspora Jews can or should view this project as part of their own Jewish identities. Third, I have an obligation to ensure that the minorities in the country where I have now become a member of the majority culture are afforded the same if not better rights and privileges than those I enjoyed as a minority citizen in a liberal democracy on the other side of the Atlantic.

During my first year of teaching at the University of Haifa, I came to class one day to find the room half empty. A large group of Arab students who were enrolled in the course were absent. I asked the students in attendance what could have accounted for the large rate of absence. They told me that it was *Eid al-Fitr*, the Feast of Breaking the Fast of the holy Muslim month of Ramadan. I was embarrassed to admit that I had no knowledge of that holiday or its importance to my students and that I found myself behaving as my own university professors had done when they required me to attend class or take exams on Jewish holidays. My first day of graduate school, for example, fell on the lesser-known Jewish holiday of Sukkot, or the Feast of Tabernacles. When I told my professor that I would not be able to attend due to the holiday, he would hear nothing of it. I was required to attend, he said, so that he could "see what I can do." Since travel by car is forbidden to observant Jews on that holiday, I managed to arrange to stay with a colleague who lived walking distance from the campus so that I could at least walk to class and make an appearance. But at the time, I was appalled at the insensitivity of my professor to my religious obligations and dismayed at my powerlessness to do anything about it. Was I to do the same to my own students now that I was in a similar position of authority?

My university in Israel has long since instituted regulations governing the rights of minority students to celebrate their holidays without penalty, and even recognizes three major holidays, one each for Muslims, Christians, and Druze, as days on which the university will not hold class (including *Eid al-Fitr*). But how can I give adequate expression to my own moral sensibilities regarding our obligations to recognize and negotiate difference in diverse liberal societies by justifying regulations of this kind within the framework of a state that purports to be democratic as well as Jewish, both liberal and devoted to the advancement and protection of a particular national culture?

This is the sort of question that came to trouble me as a philosopher of education and that I address in the three chapters that follow. My answers are influenced by the communitarian critique of comprehensive liberalism associated with the likes of Michael Sandel, Michael Walzer, Alasdair MacIntyre, and Charles Taylor, and the diversity liberalism of Isaiah Berlin. In the absence of a neutral "view from nowhere," I argue, the task of liberal democracy is to promote a modus vivendi to negotiate among a rich diversity of incommensurable cultures. To do so, democratic citizens require an education that both initiates them into a heritage of primary identification and exposes them to alternatives from which to develop critical perspective. I call this position the *pedagogy of difference*.

CHAPTER FIVE

Education in Ideology

Introduction

It is commonly accepted that schools inculcate ideologies. State schools initiate students into prevailing political and economic doctrines such as political liberalism, free-market capitalism, or socialism. Faith schools promote the religious beliefs and practices of their sponsoring bodies or denominations. Other affiliation-based schools such as those devoted to particular languages or ethnic identities foster the perspectives of the communities or associations they represent. These ideological orientations appear in different configurations depending on the location of the school and the nature of the commitments in question. Many democracies, including the United Kingdom and Israel, permit state-sponsored faith schools, for example, while the United States does not.

Many people believe that the ideological character of education is unavoidable.[1] All societies inculcate customs and beliefs, they maintain; the question is not whether but what to inculcate.[2] Others find this uncritical acquiescence to ideology profoundly troubling. Students should be taught to evaluate beliefs and practices rationally, they contend, and to embrace only those that can withstand criticism.[3] Uncritical ideological inculcation is indoctrination, not education.[4] Many humanistic and postmodern educators recoil at this elevation of rationality above ideology. Rationalism, they claim, also entails unjustified assumptions; it is no less ideological than the political or religious doctrines fostered in schools.[5] This view is shared by a third group of educators who are as appalled as the rationalists at the imposition of ideas on youngsters in school, but who hold that students should be taught to evaluate doctrines in terms of a logic that serves their own socioeconomic interests, or those of the downtrodden and oppressed, rather than rationalist ideologies of the ruling class or culture.[6] Religious educators are equally troubled by a critical rationality unsympathetic to passionate faith, yet they are no more enamored by the rampant individualism of the humanists, the nihilism of the postmoderns, or the extreme relativism of the critical social theorists.[7]

Can education in particular religious, ethical, or political traditions be distinguished from morally troubling forms of ideological indoctrination without appeal to versions of critical rationalism unsympathetic to those traditions? This question lies at the heart of any inquiry into the sort of curriculum that could initiate students into open society. The stakes in addressing this query are extraordinarily high, since liberal democracies require citizens sufficiently grounded in ethical and political traditions to be capable of exercising self-governance responsibly.[8] If there is no difference between faith, political, or moral *education* and ideological *indoctrination*, it must be admitted that all forms of inculcation are attempts to dominate or even violate the individual; that the difference between initiating people into a way of life and imposing severe physical or psychological pain if they do not is only a matter of degree.[9] Under these circumstances, the very idea of a liberal or democratic education that would promote the rights of people with diverse visions of the good life to live side by side in a common civil society is in serious jeopardy. Yet to maintain such a distinction would appear to require privileging forms of rationality and autonomy that are inconsistent with some religious, political, or moral traditions and that may rely on assumptions that cannot themselves be rationally justified, such as the idea that critical rationality is not just another ideology but the basis for choosing among ideologies.[10]

I maintain that it is possible to educate in ideology without succumbing to indoctrination. Understanding how such an education is possible and the sort of curriculum that flows from it requires delving more deeply into the concepts of ideology, education, and indoctrination. Accordingly, this chapter will be divided into five sections. In the first section, I distinguish between moral (or ethical) and amoral (or nonethical) ideologies.[11] In the second section, I argue that education is first an agent of moral ideology. In the third section, I contend that amoral ideologies incline toward indoctrination. In the fourth section, I respond to some objections to the view that education is an agent of moral ideology from rational, humanistic, radical, and religious perspectives. In the fifth section, I consider the curriculum that flows from the view that education is an agent of ethics. I call it the pedagogy of difference.

Two conceptions of ideology

By the term "ideology," I mean a framework of beliefs and customs that informs or governs some aspect of our individual or collective lives.[12] Matters of value and duty, purpose and meaning, right and wrong, are usually grounded in moral or religious ideologies such as existentialism, humanism, secularism, Protestantism, Catholicism, Judaism, Islam, or Buddhism. Issues concerning power and wealth are often organized around political or economic ideologies such as conservatism, liberalism, socialism, capitalism, or communism. Questions of knowledge and truth are commonly addressed in epistemological and ontological ideologies such as empiricism, positivism, transcendentalism, idealism, realism, rationalism, or pragmatism. Problems relating to expression and beauty are generally framed in terms of aesthetic or artistic ideologies such as classicism, romanticism, expressionism, or symbolism. The term "philosophy"—in the doctrinal sense as in "philosophy of life," rather than the analytic sense concerned with such questions as "What do you mean?" and "How do you know?"—is sometimes used interchangeably with this way of conceiving ideology.

Life is not neatly divided into categories, however, and more often than not ideologies of different types are blurred. Political, religious, moral, epistemological, and aesthetic dispositions are blended to form what have lately been called grand or metanarratives such as modernism, or antinarratives such as postmodernism.[13] These grand narratives have been associated with historical epochs; religious, ethnic, or racial affiliations; linguistic or literary proclivities; local or national identities; gendered perspectives; or sexual orientations. The term "culture" is commonly used to denote these complex networks of cognitive and behavioral dispositions.[14]

All societies may inculcate ideologies in children, but not all ideologies or methods of inculcation are equally suitable to every sort of society. "Closed societies," to use a term coined by Karl Popper, tend to prefer uniform monolithic ideologies transmitted in a manner that prioritizes outcomes over process.[15] The fact that youngsters come to believe and behave in a certain way is more important than how they come to do so. "Open societies," however, require the possibility of multiple competing ideologies that foster self-governance and recognize free choice. Critical rationalism was once thought to be the key to defining both the content and method of instruction to prepare students for citizenship in free societies, because it was thought to provide nonarbitrary, relevant criteria for choosing between competing ideologies that respect the autonomy of individuals. But it turns out that reasons cannot be justified as the nonarbitrary grounds for choosing among ideologies in a way that does not assume what its sets out to prove, since such a justification would itself require a reason. The appeal to reasons appears, therefore, to be as authoritarian as the most uniform ideology found in any closed society. Yet, if there are no criteria for teaching youngsters to choose among competing views, the choices of citizens in open societies will not be free in any meaningful sense of the term, but totally arbitrary according to the whim of the moment. Under such circumstances it is easy for citizens in democracies to make choices that undermine the freedoms they enjoy. Plato called this the "paradox of freedom"—too much freedom yields too little.

To address this dilemma it will be useful to distinguish between two types of ideologies: the moral (or ethical) and the amoral (or nonethical). Terms such as morality and ethics are often used interchangeably in everyday speech as referring to justified or proper conduct. Some philosophers view the former as a narrower and less theoretical category than the latter. Others conceive morality as concerned with norms of correct conduct and ethics as moral philosophy or philosophical thinking about these moral norms. The term "ethics" is also used in a more limited normative sense similar to morality, as in "codes of professional ethics," and the term "metaethics" sometimes overlaps with "ethics" in the broad or theoretical sense as referring to the branch of philosophy concerned with meaning and justification of ethical concepts and principles.[16]

Modern moral philosophy has been greatly concerned with judgments of moral obligation that emphasize such terms as right, wrong, just, unjust, permissible, forbidden, obligatory, and prohibited. These are *deontological* concepts, from the Greek for duty or what one must do. However, an earlier use of the term "ethics" emphasized judgments of moral value concerned with such concepts as good, bad, admirable, deplorable, worthwhile, worthless, virtue, and vice. These are *aretaic* concepts, from the Greek for virtue or excellence.[17]

Socrates asked probably the most fundamental ethical question: How should one live?[18] This prioritizes aretaic over deontological concepts by placing inquiry into the nature of the good life at the center of moral discourse. To understand or do what is right, one must first embrace a larger conception of the good. In fact, we must first consider Socrates's question in order to inquire about the nature of the just society, the proper distribution of wealth, the truths that are worth knowing, and the artistic expression that is meritorious. Sovereignty, as I have quoted Iris Murdoch many times, belongs to the good.[19]

Moral (or ethical) ideologies, then, are comprised of visions of the good that address matters of value and virtue. They reside at the center of the moral life and exercise extraordinary influence over our political, economic, epistemological, ontological, and aesthetic beliefs and practices. They tend to be holistic in that they address significant portions of our lives, but not totalistic in that we may subscribe to a number of conceptions of the good, even those in tension with one another. They are particularistic in that virtues and values are concrete expressions of distinctive cultures, but also pragmatic because they respond to experience and adapt to changes of time and place. They tend to be synthetic in that they are not closed, but open to dialogue and prepared to learn from the ideas and values of competing traditions. Most importantly, they are ethical in that they embrace the conditions of human agency—that people have the freedom of will within reasonable limits to choose their beliefs and behaviors, the moral intelligence to tell the difference between better or worse according to some conception of these notions, and the capacity to err in belief and practice.[20]

Amoral (or nonethical) ideologies, on the other hand, tend to be holistic as well as totalistic—they address the whole of life without allowing for a variety of visions; particularistic but not pragmatic, they are expressed in terms of concrete cultures but unwilling to adapt to changing times and places; non- or antisynthetic, they believe that they contain the whole truth and so have no need to learn from others; and resistant to ethical discourse, they deny the freedom, intelligence, or fallibility of human agents.[21]

This analysis shifts our attention from cognitive to ethical aspects of ideology. John Watt points out that most discussions of ideology in education follow in the footsteps of either Karl Marx or Karl Mannheim.[22] The former understood ideology as the false consciousness that rulers use to dominate. In a classless society grounded in "proper scientific analysis" of political economy, truth, not ideology, would reign. The latter held that all knowledge, save perhaps that of the intellectual elite, is a product of social conditions. Social constructionist and postmodern theorists tend toward even more radical versions of cognitive relativism than that embraced by Mannheim.[23] All of the above, however, understand ideology first in cognitive terms, as ways of conceiving reality, formulating knowledge, or understanding truth.

The present analysis, by contrast, follows the recent neo-Aristotelian revival by suggesting that to be articulate about what we ought to believe we must first get clear about what we mean by such terms as *ought* or *should*, and that this requires a conception of the good.[24] Watt coins the expression "global evaluative orientations" to refer to this ethical aspect of ideology and agrees that it plays a crucial role in the assessment of belief and behavior.[25] He fails to offer moral criteria for assessing evaluative schemes, however, returning instead to the cognitive criterion of "objectivity as comprehensiveness," which involves understanding phenomena from a variety of different viewpoints.[26] This approach risks falling prey to extreme moral relativism by giving equal weight to evaluative orientations regardless of their ethical content. I hold, on the other hand, that we can assess evaluative points of view without succumbing to either radical relativism or absolutist dogmatism by distinguishing the degree to which orientations are suited to ethical discourse and open society on the basis of their commitment to human agency. Open societies tend to rely on moral ideologies infused with concepts of the good, whereas closed societies prefer more uniform, amoral ideologies.

This is a formal and pluralistic account of ethics that outlines the conditions of moral ideologies without totally determining their substance. Freedom, intelligence, and fallibility are by no means morally neutral, but they do allow for a wide degree of pluralism within reasonable limits. Examples of moral ideologies include ethical doctrines such as existentialism, liberalism, utilitarianism, and communitarianism; modern religious orientations such as some, but by no means all, contemporary Christian and Jewish theologies; and premodern religious philosophies that sought to reconcile revelation with reason such as those espoused by Abu Nasr Muhammad Al Farabi, Moses Maimonides, and Thomas Aquinas. Examples of amoral ideologies include extreme left- and right-wing political and religious doctrines such as Bolshevism, fascism, and fundamentalism, and premodern religious orientations such as fatalistic paganism. To distinguish between these two very different sorts of ideologies, I will occasionally use terms such as *vision of the good life* or *conception of the good* to refer to the moral variety, and simply *ideology* to denote the latter.

The divergence between moral and amoral ideologies and its connection to closed and open societies can be sharpened, I think, by reference to a difference between behaviors that conform to laws or rules and activities that follow or are governed by norms.[27] Behaviors in the relevant sense are mechanical acts on the part of a person in which the actor exercises little or no agency. In the most extreme cases governed by natural laws—for instance, when the pulmonary system takes in air, extracts the oxygen, pumps it into the blood stream, and excises carbon dioxide—we perform behaviors without ever thinking a thought, forming an intention or engaging an emotion. This is a necessary form of behavior in Carl Hempel's deductive-nomological sense that, given the covering law and certain preconditions, the results could not be otherwise.[28] That my behavior conforms to the laws of physics or experimental psychology is not a matter of choice and entails no exercise of will.

Rules, in the relevant sense, are akin to natural laws in that they attempt to generate actions without agency, but in this case in situations where the actor could in fact choose to do otherwise. The result is mere (or unintelligent) habit. When it comes to stopping at a red light or driving within the speed limit, for example, we prefer that drivers act out of habit rather than active will. In fact the less they think about it the better, so as to ensure as far as possible the regularity of what might otherwise be erratic and highly dangerous behavior. In these circumstances we often employ behavioral laws, such as various systems of reward and punishment, to induce and condition behavior. I do not generally try to convince a toddler not to put her finger in the electrical socket, or hold the hand of an adult when crossing the street, but instruct her how to behave, rewarding her if she complies and punishing her if she does not. I seek to bypass the will, as it were, and go straight for the behavior.

Activities can be distinguished from behaviors, once again in the revenant sense, in that they entail the exercise of agency—evaluating desires, understanding principles, considering reasons, forming intentions, making and implementing decisions. I choose to take an umbrella in rainy weather, for example, or to worship at a particular time and place and in a certain way. Although there may be natural laws and mechanical rules that apply in such cases, having to do, say, with the way in which rain may affect my health or with regulations to which I have become habituated concerning how, when, or where to pray, there is an additional layer to these behaviors that involves conscious investment of feelings and reasoning. Yet we do not invest ourselves arbitrarily when we act in this way. Our actions follow social or cultural norms informed by reasons, evidence, attitudes, emotions, customs, and values.[29]

Rules tend to be unambiguous and inflexible and are motivated primarily by means of external rewards and punishments. Norms, on the other hand, are more often layered, multifaceted, and open to (even dependent upon) interpretation. They also inform and influence activity intrinsically from within by becoming part and parcel of how we define who we are. This is why we are not always conscious of our implementation of social norms. Our patterns of dress or speech, for example, or the food, music, and art we enjoy, not to mention our engagement with others like or different from ourselves, are all informed by norms that we don't often think about when we employ them.

Thomas Green based the distinction between behaviors and actions on the difference between conforming to a law and obeying a rule or principle of action.

> To learn to obey a rule is not *simply* to acquire a disposition to act in a certain way, but a disposition to act *because* it is the correct way…a rule of action is intended always to discriminate between right and wrong, correct and incorrect performance….Action is never *merely* habitual…action, as opposed to behavior, is always principled, always norm-regarding.[30]

This view appears to conflate what I am calling rules with norms, or more precisely *obeying* a rule with *following* a norm. Principles of action can become routine and rigid and obeying them can readily become a form of unintelligent habit, even if we once adopted them for good reasons.[31] We follow norms, however, as an expression of who we are and an embodiment of how we understand what it means to be a good person. Green's emphasis on principle can also be interpreted as overly cognitive and dichotomous, although this was not necessarily his intention. Norms as I understand them are infused not only with cognitive principles but also with what Charles Taylor calls "imports"—ways "in which something can be relevant or of importance to the desires or purposes or feelings of a subject."[32] And, without underestimating the significance of standards, norms are better thought of as distinguishing degrees of better or worse, rather than dichotomizing right versus wrong or correct versus incorrect.

I refer to this distinction to observe that amoral ideologies preferred by closed societies incline toward rule-conforming behavior, whereas open societies that promote the coexistence of multiple visions of the good require citizens who are capable of self-governance infused by intrinsic and internalized norms. This is why open societies prefer moral ideologies; they require citizens with a refined sense of their capacity for human agency. Taylor reinforces this point when he argues that human agents are distinguished not only by their capacity to evaluate desires quantitatively, on the basis of how much happiness they may enjoy; for example, should I eat lunch, which may preclude swimming, or swim first and eat later—from which I will derive greater overall happiness? Humans also have the capacity to evaluate desires on qualitative grounds. Is it better to exercise courage and loyalty to a friend by saving him in battle, for example, or to save my own life and run? This capacity for qualitative evaluation of desires—Taylor calls it strong evaluation—is closely related to the exercise of responsibility, since we can be held accountable for the moral consequences of our actions because we can evaluate their ethical value. Yet to acquire the norms that enable this sort of evaluation requires initiation into a conception of the good, an ethical vision or moral ideology that offers an account of what it might mean for one sort of desire or action to be better than another. It requires, in other words, an education.[33]

Education and the good life

Philosophers since Plato have held that education in the fullest sense entails the pursuit of worthwhile knowledge or, as Richard Peters put it, that education involves two conditions, one relating to knowledge and the other to desirability.[34] Discussions of education have tended to focus on what students should *know* for some time. Recently, however, greater attention is being paid to what is *worth* knowing.[35] Answering this query requires a conception of what it means for something to be worthwhile. Such a conception is found in responding to Socrates's question of how should one live. This requires a stance concerning what it means to live a good life.[36]

The assumptions of human agency are crucial to any ethical stance. It is pointless for people to consider what sort of life they should live if their beliefs and behaviors are determined by history, society, chemistry, or the gods; if they cannot understand the difference between worthwhile or worthless according to some account of these terms; or if they are destined to be either good or bad by providence or their very nature.[37] To deny agency is to rob life of meaning and purpose; it is to view human existence as amoral, governed by arbitrary and mechanical forces, by fates beyond human comprehension and control, or by nothing at all.[38]

This notion of human agency is also essential to any conception of education. However we conceive the nature of knowledge or whatever we choose to include in the curriculum, we must suppose that the students we are educating and those charged with educating them are free to choose what and whether to learn, capable of understanding basic distinctions relevant to that learning, and equally capable of misunderstanding them. Were this not the case, it would make no sense to speak of education as engagement with worthwhile knowledge, because it would be impossible to make sense of what it could mean for something to be worthwhile. And since conceptions of knowledge and curriculum may vary according to epistemological, political, moral, and other ideological orientations, what conceptions of education must share in common—what makes them conceptions of education rather than of something else, say indoctrination—is a commitment to human agency.

This is not to say that schools are always designed to recognize the freedom, intelligence, and fallibility of teachers and students or that these beliefs are given at birth. In fact, many youngsters are trained in schools or raised in families and cultures that intentionally or inadvertently deny one or more of these assumptions—that conceal from children their potential to become agents of their own attitudes and actions. For these schools, families, or cultures to be engaged in education, however, regardless of ideological orientation, subject matter, or venue, they must seek to instill and strengthen within students the awareness that they are free, intelligent, and fallible human agents, since without awareness of this kind on the part of parents, teachers, and students it is literally impossible to educate.

And this notion of human agency lies at the very heart of moral ideologies grounded in visions of the good life. The conceptual conditions of human agency become part of our lives when they are embodied in concrete relationships, rituals, and virtues—when they are part and parcel of communities committed to visions of the good. Becoming educated, therefore, entails being initiated into a community that embodies the conditions of human agency in concrete social and cultural norms—what Taylor calls "strong values."[39] It requires the inculcation of a moral ideology as a prerequisite for instruction in all other matters. In other words, in educational as in other matters, ethics precedes epistemology, politics, and religion.[40]

The cultivation of our capacity for agency is accomplished through the exploration and acquisition of norms. Green calls this "normation," or the educational formation of conscience—the process through which we embrace those values and virtues that guide us in what Taylor calls "the strong evaluation of desires."[41] Unlike the meaning and application of rules, however, which is uniform and mechanical requiring little understanding, the meanings of norms are layered, nuanced, and complex, allowing many possible paths to implementation. The acquisition of norms is not an unthinking, emotionless, or passive process in which outcomes are predetermined. It is active and engaging, demanding tools for both exegesis—understanding what norms have meant and how they have been applied in the past—and eisegesis—how they may be understood in and the significance they may hold for the present and future. Refining the capacities of human agency, in other words, requires learning to understand, apply, interpret, and create norms within the context of communities or traditions that render them meaningful. It is by means of this process of learning to control the norms that will govern our qualitative evaluation of desires that we acquire the capacity to govern ourselves. Citizenship in open society, in short, calls for membership in distinct norming communities, which requires what I call pedagogy of difference.

Indoctrination and ideology

Philosophers usually conceive indoctrination in terms of the role of appropriate evidence in instruction. An instructor is indoctrinating, in this view, when he or she intends to suppress or avoid appropriate evidence, when instructional methods are employed that ignore or subvert relevant reasoning, or when reasonable argumentation is not or cannot be offered to support the content of instruction.[42] As Green put it, indoctrination entails fostering a nonevidentiary style of belief.[43]

This analysis surely captures something of the epistemological problems with the concept of indoctrination, but not its ethical difficulties. It fails to address the question of why it is morally problematic to suppress evidence or teach something that is not or cannot be grounded in relevant reasoning. Answering this query requires an ethic of belief and behavior—an account of why, under normal circumstances, one should only accept or transmit beliefs and behaviors supported by proper reasoning, and why it would be morally wrong to do otherwise.

One common way of defending an ethic of this kind is by means of a so-called transcendental argument. In this view, the very question why one should only embrace or inculcate beliefs and behaviors supported by relevant argumentation already presupposes that one values reasoning.[44] But this does not seem right. One need not think reasoning desirable to inquire why someone else thinks beliefs or behaviors should be based on them. The question could be posed merely as a matter of curiosity, or in order to understand what makes someone else tick, as an anthropologist might do in studying the strange and unfamiliar customs of a foreign culture.[45]

A more promising account can be found in the conditions of human agency. According to this position, the very ideas of freedom, intelligence, and fallibility, required for meaningful moral judgments, depend upon the possibility of appealing to relevant evidence and reasoning. If my choices are to be other than arbitrary, it must be possible for me to understand within reasonable limits why they may or may not be preferable. This understanding entails the ability to make basic moral distinctions between that which is more or less desirable according to some account of these notions as well as other judgments such as differences between apparent alternatives, including estimations of their possible consequences. To acquire this sort of understanding, and to determine the degree to which it is correct or in error, requires the application of appropriate standards, assessment of relevant reasons, and weighing of pertinent evidence. Evidence-based belief and behavior is desirable, therefore, because without it the very idea of desirability makes no sense.

The moral problem with indoctrination on this account is that it undercuts the conditions of human agency without which moral judgments are meaningless. If education entails nurturing the awareness of the moral potential inherent in each person, indoctrination involves undermining that potential by denying access to the conceptual tools necessary for its realization. Just as education is necessarily an ethical activity, indoctrination is inherently amoral because it undermines the conditions required for ethics and moral discourse to make sense. And this, of course, is why those who indoctrinate will tend to prefer the inculcation of amoral ideologies that are totalistic, that dictate rather than adapt to experience, that are resistant to engagement with alternative or competing orientations, and that deny the conditions of human agency.

As a form of rule-conforming belief and behavior, indoctrination in amoral ideologies is concerned with predetermined outcomes, rather than with understanding, interpretation, and innovation. It seeks conformity of belief and practice by means of pedagogy of uniformity in which the ruling doctrines prevail.

In a well-known analysis, Green argues that training can be understood as the conditioning of habit-conforming behaviors, whereas teaching is a norm-regarding and norm-generating activity (here Green seems to have in mind the broader sense of "norm" rather than the narrower notion of a "rule") because it calls for understanding, interpretation, and creativity. Teaching often requires training, of course. One must learn to read and write in order to interpret or create literature, for example, and to add and subtract to prove mathematical theorems.[46] Indoctrination on this account can be understood as continuing to train in matters that call for teaching, such as the interpretation of poetry, the creation of art, innovation in science, or the worship of God.[47] In a society that prefers the indoctrination of amoral ideology, teaching is rare and it is difficult to imagine how education in the sense considered here could gain a foothold.

Ethics as first philosophy

The distinction between education and indoctrination, I am arguing, is first an ethical one grounded in the difference between moral and amoral ideologies—in the degree to which the conditions of human agency are embraced. There can be education worthy of the name only in moral ideologies, while those that are amoral are best suited to indoctrination. As I have said, when it comes to education, as in other matters, ethics, in the broad formal sense outlined here, is first philosophy.[48] Objections to this view can be formulated from within at least four camps: rationalism, humanism, radicalism, and religion.

Rationalists would argue that the very idea that education is to be distinguished by its commitment to human agency has been advanced here on the basis of reasons. Education, it has been argued, entails engagement with worthwhile knowledge, and for the idea that something is worthwhile to have meaning we must assume that human beings are free, intelligent, and fallible. Reasons, not ethics, come first in educational thought, therefore, because even on this account the deep connection between education and ethics, as well as the distinction between moral and amoral ideologies, must withstand rational scrutiny to be accepted. The distinction between education and indoctrination is primarily epistemological, in this view, and the moral difficulties with the latter stem from undercutting the rational grounds of ethical discourse. Similarly, the preference for moral over amoral ideologies in education stems from the fact that the former tends to be more reasonable than the latter.[49]

This argument reveals the close affinity between the position being advanced here and critical rationalism, so much so in fact that asking whether ethics or epistemology comes first may appear to some as merely academic, with little or no practical consequence. However, the issues at stake here are by no means trivial, since the very possibility of democratic education hinges on successfully maintaining a distinction between education and indoctrination. Unfortunately, the rational view fails because it is incapable of offering a rational response, one that does not presuppose what it sets out to justify, to the question, "Why be rational?"

The ethical view I am advancing abandons the illusion of a rational foundation and posits instead two phases to ideological choices. Our first option is whether we prefer to live in a moral or an amoral world. The very idea that in principle we possess such a choice, of course, presupposes that we have the freedom to make and act on it. In this respect indeterminism or the possibility of choice is basic—some would say ontological—to the position I am advancing. From the assumption that we have freedom of choice within reasonable limits, however, it does not follow that we will always be aware of or exercise it. Yet, to the extent that we prefer a life in which it is possible to differentiate between better and worse according to some account of these notions, a life that can be said in some sense to be good, we must actively embrace and enact the conditions of human agency without which ethical concepts and the very idea of a moral life are meaningless. If this is the life that we choose, we are bound to seek rational justifications for our remaining decisions, since without reasons our preferences become arbitrary and cease to be genuine choices in any meaningful sense.

Humanistic, feminist, and postmodern educators might object that this emphasis on rationality ignores the role of emotion in decision making, and prefers standardization and conformity to individuality and creativity.[50]

However, this orientation does not preclude the possibility that emotions will play an important role in our exercise of free choice. The fostering and maintenance of appropriate feelings is often an important reason why to incline in one direction rather than another. Nor does the view outlined here prefer conformity to creativity. It asserts rather that human agency cannot exist in abstraction. It requires the acquisition of norms situated in ethical communities that can distinguish between novelty and nonsense. There are a variety of such arrangements that embrace human agency, numerous possible moral ideologies from which to choose. Yet the very notion that an idea is novel or a person unique can only be judged from the perspective of a tradition within which an innovation is crafted. Without the ethical substance provided by tradition and collective vision, individualism turns quickly to nihilism and narcissism, and freedom becomes nothing more than the license to do what strikes one's fancy at any given moment. The difference between a life governed by this sort of caprice and one driven by amoral ideology is thin indeed, since both preclude the possibility of self-governance on the basis of critically evaluating alternative courses of action or ways of being.

Many critical social theorists would object to privileging ethics in this way by claiming that ideas such as free will, moral intelligence, and fallibility are themselves value laden, embedded in the ideologies of modernity and democracy, among others, and that freedom is not a privilege enjoyed equally by all.[51] I agree that recognizing human agency is a substantive value choice. Indeed, it is the most basic of such choices, since the possible sense of all other value alternatives turns on the decision whether to acknowledge our potential as moral beings. It does not follow, however, that these values are embedded in the orientations of any particular time, place, or point of view. They are to be found rather in traditions as diverse as the Hebrew Bible, Christian Scriptures, and Aristotelianism in the ancient and medieval worlds, and in a variety of modern moral philosophies from the liberalism of Immanuel Kant and John Rawls to the existentialism of Albert Camus, Jean-Paul Sartre, Martin Buber, and Maurice Merleau-Ponty. Human agency is not the product of a particular culture or religion.[52] Our potential to choose intelligently is part and parcel of the human condition, and awareness of this is a conceptual precondition for all positions that seek to make coherent sense of such notions as duty, virtue, justice, and dignity. Alleviating the servitude and suffering of those denied the privileges of freedom must begin, therefore, with fostering their sense of agency, not, as many critical social theorists assume, in instilling the idea that beliefs and behaviors are determined by ideology, culture, or socioeconomic class.

But is it not coercion to foster values among youngsters not yet developmentally capable of choosing wisely? What is the difference between nurturing this sort of faith commitment, some religious educators ask, and the inculcation of traditional religious beliefs? Does this not prove that at the end of the day education will always amount to indoctrination, and since it has already been admitted that there is no rational foundation to belief, what objection can there be to indoctrinating faith in the God of revelation or intolerance of faiths other than one's own?

This brings us of course to what Peters called the paradox of moral education, the fundamental truth of childrearing every successful parent and teacher realizes sooner or later, that to teach the exercise of free choice requires limiting freedom of choice.[53] From this it does not follow, however, that all instructional intentions are equally desirable, that the inculcation of every faith commitment is morally equivalent to every other, or that all methods of inculcation are to be judged identical. In compelling a youngster to engage in a particular activity, acquire a specific skill, or adopt a certain attitude when they might not otherwise choose to do so, the question is whether the intention is to eventually empower or emasculate the youngster, whether the methods of instruction are designed to enhance or reduce awareness of and ability to exercise age-appropriate self-governance, and whether the faith commitments are understood to be fallible and available to engage competing orientations or dogmatic and closed to such engagement. Many, though by no means all, theistic beliefs are empowering, enhancing, and fallible; most forms of intolerance are emasculating, reductive, and dogmatic.[54]

Ideology and ethics in the curriculum

Ideology plays a role in the curriculum of each of these orientations. The rationalists emphasize critical thinking; the humanists, individual expression; the critical theorists, social criticism; and the religionists, the nurturance of faith. Each orientation has something to recommend it, yet each too often fails to rise above amoral indoctrination to moral education, because it does not sustain or may even supplant human agency. Critical thinking is crucial to any curriculum, but as a means to, not a justification for, the conditions of agency. Individual expression is also important, but creativity can only be judged within the context of a tradition that differentiates it from claptrap. Spotlighting social injustice is certainly worthwhile, but the more critical pedagogy embraces determinism and relativism the greater its tendency to undermine the conditions of moral discourse that render claims of injustice meaningful. And faith in religious and other ideals is vital, but not if it becomes overly dogmatic.

The deep connection between ethics and education discussed here requires what I call pedagogies of *difference*—rather than comprehensiveness or uniformity—that differentiate amoral from moral ideologies, distinguish among distinctive conceptions of the good, and discriminate open from closed orientations to competing ethical visions. Possibilities for critical thinking, individual expression, social criticism, and religious faith all flow from the recognition of difference embedded in such pedagogies.[55]

Pedagogies that distinguish moral from amoral ideologies seek actively to develop human agency. They strive to empower students with an awareness of their freedom to choose and a willingness to exercise that freedom, to enhance their capacity for intelligent choice by sharpening their skill in making relevant moral distinctions and assessing the possible consequences of their choices, and to enable youngsters to recognize and learn from mistakes by engaging a variety of perspectives including those in conflict with their own. This approach is closely allied with education for democratic citizenship, if democracy is conceived as the sort of society that preserves, protects, and defends the moral potential of its citizens—their awareness of and capacity to exercise agency. The values and skills implicit in this approach are shared by diverse communities with competing visions of how to embody them in concrete forms of life. They constitute the foundation of a democratic community of communities or civil society.[56]

However, one cannot engage views different from one's own without understanding one's own orientation, or respect the other without respecting oneself. To acknowledge difference, in other words, one must learn to be different. There can be no common civil society, therefore, without distinct communities that embody the conditions of human agency in concrete visions of the good. Pedagogies of difference entail initiation into such concrete communities. This requires what Miriam Ben Peretz and I call "pedagogy of the sacred,"[57] or what Philip Phenix and Dwayne Heubner referred to as "commitment to transcendence"—higher goods to which one is committed above all others, even if critical reflection could in time yield yet a better way.[58]

Sacred and transcendent ideals, like the conditions of moral discourse and human agency, are to be lived in the here and now, not merely studied in the abstract. For this they must be embodied in traditions of practice or ways of life. Pedagogies of difference call for literacy in such traditions— understanding of their rules and rituals, songs and stories, constitutive texts, and methods of interpretation. Traditions of this kind are not merely stagnant bodies of knowledge and culture to be transmitted, but dynamic and evolving webs of belief and behavior to be transformed; and in the process of transformation they form and reform the teachers and students engaged in the pedagogic process. The citizens that emerge from such an education are not mere reproductions of that which came before, but autonomous selves capable of the responsible and creative decision making that liberal democracy and open society require.

Additionally, learning respect for difference requires exposure to multiple conceptions of the good, not initiation into a single point of view. Initiation into a solitary ethical vision would seem more like training than education in that it would result in an orientation too narrow to allow the sort of critical intelligence required of fallibility. Acknowledging error requires multiple perspectives, since the only way I can identify having gone wrong within a single position is by means of contradiction, whereas engagement with multiple orientations enables assessment of the strengths and weaknesses of each. This is why I have said that moral ideologies are holistic without being totalistic. A purposeful and meaningful life is guided by a variety of visions, provided that tensions between them are not so great as to totally undermine one another.

One can be a Christian teacher who jogs "religiously," a secular lawyer who loves tennis, a dancer from New York devoted to chess, a parent of twins who teaches Hebrew school, and endless other combinations. Some of these identities make greater demands on our self-definition than do others. They reflect longer and richer histories, offer deeper insight into the human condition, or provide a more enduring sense of purpose to life. Sport may play an important part of our lives, but it would be disingenuous to equate the stories of baseball, or rugby, or golf, or tennis with the Christian or Jewish narratives; nevertheless, devotion to sports such as these can have an enduring impact on one's moral life.[59]

Nor is it is enough to be initiated into multiple moral visions inherited from family and community or embraced by proclivity or choice. Pedagogy of difference also requires exposure to attitudes and orientations with which one may not be inclined to agree. Accepting oneself necessitates engaging the other, just as acknowledging the other requires understanding oneself, even or perhaps especially when this is profoundly unsettling. Dialogue and debate among contrasting and conflicting views sharpens understanding of one's own position, fosters learning from other perspectives, and promotes the humble recognition that competing orientations have many advantages of their own.

Conclusion

Education in ideology is possible, therefore, grounded in pedagogies of difference that distinguish moral from amoral ideologies, support commitment to multiple ethical visions, and encourage engagement with others who are different. This orientation requires critical thinking as a means to making and assessing intelligent choices. It makes individuality and creativity possible by promoting contexts in which originality can be distinguished from gibberish. It enables the recognition of injustice by developing the conditions of human agency in which moral judgments make sense. And it fosters nondogmatic faith commitments in higher goods that can be transcended through critical refection. In contrast to the fatalism and pessimism of amoral indoctrination that views life in terms of predetermined necessities, education in ethical vision is optimistic and hopeful that despite current difficulties, with the right choices and the capacity to learn from our mistakes, tomorrow can indeed be better than today.

CHAPTER SIX

Literacy and the Education of Citizens

Introduction

It is commonly accepted that citizens of democratic societies should be literate. To vote, deliberate matters of public concern, or protect one's interests or those of one's family, community, culture, class, race, ethnicity, gender, or sexual orientation requires some ability to decipher language, interpret social cues, understand cultural practices, or grasp—even apply—ethical, political, aesthetic, or other sorts of values. But what does it mean to be literate under circumstances such as these? On John Searle's account, language constitutes the so-called "ontological substance of civilization," the very stuff of which human societies are made.[1] To acquire the ability to use language, in this view, is to learn to express one's purposes or intentions in the context of particular societies, cultures, or traditions. To become literate, then, is to be initiated into a particular community that expresses itself in certain ways and not others; and to inquire about the sort of literacy required of democratic citizens is to ask about the varieties of purposes and intentions with which citizens in democratic societies should be concerned.

Democratic literacy then appears to involve a dilemma. On the one hand, it entails initiation into canons of expression that in the nature of the case will be used by particular communities for the purposes of articulating their customs, beliefs, and practices—in short, their ways of life or concepts of the Good. On the other hand, to limit these canons to a particular group excludes from the language of political power others who are not members of that group. Enfranchising all members of society requires that citizens be provided with skills to articulate their own purposes, intentions, interests, and desires; yet requiring people to adopt a particular way of talking in order to be invited into the corridors of power can deny legitimacy to other modes of expression that may not be favored by purveyors of the current dominant discourse. This is so even if that discourse promotes common canons of communication, since what counts as "common" will itself vary from one community of discourse to another.

This is no abstract problem. Consider Israel, which was conceived as a Jewish and democratic state to provide for the cultural and political aspirations of an ancient people presumably without denying the parallel desires of others. Approximately 80 percent of Israel's citizens are secular and religious Jews, while around 20 percent are Arabs of Muslim, Christian, and Druze dissent, many of whom identify culturally and politically as Palestinians. The language of political discourse into which Jewish Israeli youngsters are initiated in school is grounded in the Modern Hebrew culture created by the founders of Zionism in the first half of the twentieth century. Yet, even though the language of primary education for Palestinian youngsters who are citizens of Israel is Arabic, which is also an official language of the country, Jewish and Zionist history and culture play an important role in the curriculum of Arab Israeli schools and the language in which Palestinian youngsters must matriculate and pursue higher education is Hebrew.[2] It is entirely unclear what ought to count as the sort of literacy necessary for participation in Israeli democracy for these two groups of citizens. On the view that Israel should be a Jewish state, Palestinian Arab language and culture would seem to be excluded from the corridors of power, which could raise questions about Israel's democratic character. However, the claim that democracy requires granting cultural rights to all, which challenges the privilege afforded Hebrew culture, may preclude a nation-state from grounding its political culture in the traditions of a particular people, which as we have seen could in turn undermine the possibility of literacy and hence democracy altogether. Nor is Israel alone in facing this problem; most democratic societies around the world were founded as expressions of particular national cultures, yet face the difficulties of educating significant minority populations whose history, heritage, and language may be different than that of the majority that the state was founded to promote, but who aspire nonetheless to equal rights as citizens.[3]

As we have seen, addressing these sorts of questions requires a philosophical explanation that articulates deeper principles that can mediate between contrasting views or remove the apparent conflict in order to put one's beliefs in alignment.[4] What follows is an attempt to put my own beliefs in alignment by asking how an account of literacy suitable to political education in democratic societies is possible—one that is sufficiently grounded in particular traditions or cultures for the term "literacy" to be meaningful, yet which also takes into account relevant concerns for the enfranchisement of all citizens.

In this chapter I will address this question by assessing the role of literacy in three standard accounts of democratic education—those of republicanism, liberalism, and critical social theory—in light of what John Gray has called the pluralistic face of liberal toleration.[5] Drawing on the political theories of Isaiah Berlin and Michael Oakeshott, I will argue that each of these standard accounts of democratic literacy is problematic: The republican tends to emphasize one particular community to the exclusion of others, while both the liberal and critical promote distinct but equally *universal* ideals at the expense of the *particular* idioms that literacy, and hence democracy, requires.[6] To conclude, I will suggest an alternative grounded in a liberal communitarian view, similar but with some caveats, to what Yael Tamir calls "liberal nationalism." I have referred to the educational consequences of this political theory as the pedagogy of difference.[7]

Rival conceptions of literacy in democratic education

Three traditions of thought dominate the literature of political education in democratic societies, each of which approaches the literacy of citizens differently: republican, liberal, and radical. By political education I mean very broadly here the intentional initiation of members in a society into the concepts, ideals, and practices that are used to govern; and by democracy I mean, again very loosely, a society that, as Abraham Lincoln put it so well, conceives itself as being "of the people, by the people, and for the people," although there is considerable disagreement among the three traditions in question as to who is to be counted as one *of* the people and what it means for government to be *by* and *for* them.

According to the republican tradition, from Aristotle, Marcus Tillius Cicero, and Niccolo Machiavelli to Johann Gottfried Herder and G. W. F. Hegel, and perhaps contemporary communitarians such as Alistair MacIntyre and Michael Sandel, to be a citizen entails membership in a particular group.[8] This might be determined by virtue of lineage or heritage, which is sometimes called ethnic or national republicanism. It may also be a result of having been taught or chosen a particular way of life or concept of the Good, which can be referred to as ethical or ideological republicanism. For government to be by and for the people on this account means that it uses the powers of the state to support and sustain this group or way of life; and to be a literate citizen is to be initiated into the customs, beliefs, and practices of that ethnicity, nationality, culture, or tradition.

When Israeli high school matriculation requires exams in modern Hebrew language and literature or Zionist history for both Jewish and Arab students or when A and O level exams in the United Kingdom demand proficiency in English language and literature or British History from all students regardless of background, and the state allocates funds for teacher preparation, curriculum construction, and classroom instruction in those subjects, or when universities do not hold classes on Jewish holidays in Israel or Christian holidays in France, Germany, or Denmark, or Muslim holidays in Pakistan or Indonesia, these subjects and customs are granted special privilege on republican grounds. To function effectively as a citizen in a national or ideological republic one must speak its language, know something of its history or collective story, and respect its religious and cultural heritage. In Michael Walzer's terms, this is likely to yield a thicker conception of literacy for democratic citizenship, grounded in local culture, language, history, and custom.[9]

According to the liberal account, on the other hand, from Immanuel Kant and John Locke to John Stuart Mill and John Rawls, democratic citizenship is a legal status that requires, among other qualifications, a significant degree of personal autonomy; and for a government to be by and for its citizens entails protecting their fundamental rights to follow a life path of their own choosing, provided, of course, that one's choices do not infringe on the preferences of others.[10] In Eamonn Callan's view, this entails the capacity to assess one's genuine interests realistically according to relevant criteria of rational truthfulness. By interests, in this context, Callan has in mind one's most deeply held convictions and desires, something akin to what Charles Taylor called strong values, not units of utility, benefit, or gain.[11] Additionally, to be an autonomous person in Callan's view, one must possess the independence of mind to pursue these interests even in the face of significant obstacles.[12] Whatever else it may mean, then, to be a literate citizen on this view entails a common conception of critical rationality among groups with alternative visions of the good life upon which individuals can base realistic and independent choices. This view is likely to result in what Walzer calls a thinner account of literacy for democracy, since it will seek a common and neutral discourse in which both to assess personal preferences and deliberate public policies.[13]

In small liberal republics this would constitute a strong basis for common schools in which children of different religions, nationalities, and races, both majorities and minorities, would be educated together. In the Israeli case, for instance, this would suggest that Palestinian and Jewish citizens of Israel be educated together in common schools (they are currently schooled separately) that would teach various aspects of Arab and Hebrew culture to both communities, although perhaps with different emphases for each, but with a common intellectual ethos that emphasized enabling students to cultivate their own interests and arrive at independent choices about fundamental life choices. In large diverse democracies such as the United States, it would mitigate against state-supported separate schools for groups with differing religious or cultural orientations, and for limiting parental rights to religious education. Harry Brighouse, for example, argues against the rights of Amish parents to limit the secondary schooling of their children in order to support their particular faith, on the grounds that it would infringe on the autonomy of their children, and Callan has challenged the rights of parents to bring their children up in a religious tradition altogether.[14]

Finally, according to the main tenets of critical social theory, from Plato to Karl Marx and the Frankfurt school, to the critical pedagogues, postcolonialists, and poststructuralists, all human societies are grounded in fundamental, and possibly insurmountable, conflicts over power.[15] The people, on this account, refers to all members of society, whether or not they are recognized legally as duly constituted citizens, or have more or less power, and for government to be by and for them, it must seek to equalize the distribution of resources among them by taking power from those who have it and allocating it equitably to everyone. At the heart of literacy for democracy according to this position is the recognition of false consciousness or wrongheaded ideology that allows those in power to deny equal distribution of resources to all.

Educational philosopher Ilan Gur-Ze'ev argued, for instance, that Israeli education should abandon the colonial idea that in establishing a state of their own, Jews are coming home, or that they have achieved a utopian or messianic ideal. The Zionists were mistaken.[16] There is no utopia, no home, no ultimate teleological end or messianic time. With George Steiner, Gur-Ze'ev held instead that we all exist in a spiritual Diaspora in which there is no Archimedean point of view from nowhere upon which to base life's meaning and purpose.[17] This is true no less for Jews and Palestinians in the land that one calls Israel and the other Palestine than it is for those who reside abroad. Instead of educating Jewish children in Israel toward a false utopia or Palestinian children in the nostalgic belief that the clock can be turned back to a better time (for them) when there was no Jewish state, both should be engaged in a countereducation that acknowledges the suffering each people has endured, in order to create a new dialogue of coexistence for the future. Following famed critical pedagogue Paulo Freire, this can be accomplished by posing common problems on which teachers and students can collaborate, instead of treating children like banks into which instructors deposit accepted ideologies that reflect current unequal power relations.[18]

Limitations of space do not allow a fully nuanced account that does justice to the rich diversity of opinion within each of these traditions or the deliberations and debates that transpire amongst them. However, I have tried in broad strokes to capture what the various alternatives within each orientation share in common that I take to be problematic. The difficulties I have in mind can be made plain, I think, by reference to what Gray has called the pluralistic face of liberal toleration, though it can be applied to republican and radical political theory as well. "Liberalism has always had two faces," writes Gray:

> From one side, toleration is the pursuit of an ideal form of life. From the other, it is the search for terms of peace among different ways of life. In the former view, liberal institutions are seen as applications of universal

principles. In the latter, they are means to peaceful coexistence. In the first, liberalism is the prescription for a universal regime. In the second, it is a project of coexistence that can be pursued in many regimes.

The philosophies of John Locke and Immanuel Kant exemplify the liberal project of a universal regime, while those of Thomas Hobbes and David Hume express the liberalism of peaceful coexistence. In more recent times, John Rawls and F.A. Hayek have defended the first liberal philosophy, while Isaiah Berlin and Michael Oakeshott are exemplars of the second.[19]

Gray calls the politics exemplified by Kant and Locke universal (some say comprehensive) liberalism and that exemplified by Berlin and Oakeshott a theory of modus vivendi, which Gray writes "is liberal toleration adapted to the historical fact of pluralism." The ethical theory that underpins the search for coexistence among alternative ways of life, therefore, is called "value pluralism." It entails the idea that "there are many conflicting kinds of human flourishing, some of which cannot be compared in value."[20] Simply put, then, my problem with each of these theories of literacy in democratic education is that they do not take sufficient account of the historical fact of pluralism, because they tend to embrace overly rigid approaches to what Berlin dubbed positive liberty and what Oakeshott called rational technique and traditions of practice. Berlin makes the case for pluralism, I think, while Oakeshott shows how respect for difference can be combined with commitment to particular traditions.

Hedgehogs, foxes, and concepts of freedom

Following an obscure fragment from the ancient Greek poet Archilochus, Berlin marked what has become a famous distinction between two sorts of intellectual types—hedgehogs who know one big thing and foxes who know many things.

A great chasm exists between those, on one side, who relate everything to a single central vision, one system less or more coherent or articulate, in terms of which they understand, think and feel—a single, universal, organizing principle in terms of which alone all that they are and say has significance—and, on the other side, those who pursue many ends, often unrelated and even contradictory, connected, if at all, only in some *de facto* way, for some psychological or physiological cause, related by no moral or aesthetic principle. These last lead lives, perform acts, and entertain ideas that are centrifugal rather than centripetal, their thought is scattered or diffused, moving on many levels, seizing upon the essence of a vast variety of experiences and objects for what they are in themselves, without consciously or unconsciously, seeking to fit them into, or exclude them from, any one unchanging, all-embracing, sometimes self-contradictory and incomplete, at times fanatical, unitary inner vision. The first kind of intellectual and artistic personality belongs to the hedgehogs, the second to the foxes; and without insisting on a rigid classification, we may, without too much fear of contradiction, say that, in this sense, Dante belongs to the first category, Shakespeare to the second; Plato, Lucretius, Pascal, Hegel, Dostoevsky, Nietzsche, Ibsen, Proust are, in varying degrees, hedgehogs; Herodotus, Aristotle, Montaigne, Erasmus, Molière, Goethe, Pushkin, Balzac, Joyce are foxes.[21]

Societies conceived by foxes encourage citizens to choose among competing paths to human fulfillment, provided they respect the choices of others, whereas hedgehogs assign privilege to those who follow one particular path. Foxes are drawn to Berlin's negative concept of freedom, the absence of constraints on, or interference with, a person's actions; hedgehogs are attracted to positive liberty, the idea of self-mastery, or self-definition, or control of one's destiny.[22]

Berlin had deep reservations about the latter concept, because of the tendency among those who advance positive accounts of freedom to distinguish between one's actual self that acts in the day-to-day world and some occult entity referred to alternatively as a "true" or "real" or "higher" self, of which a person might not be fully aware. Thus, it is argued that although one's empirical self may indeed feel free, one's true self may actually be enslaved. As Berlin put it so aptly, "once I take this view, I am in a position to ignore the actual wishes of men or societies, to bully, oppress; torture them in the name, and on behalf, of their 'real' selves, in the secure knowledge that whatever is the true goal of man (happiness, performance of duty, wisdom, a just society, self-fulfillment) must be identical with his freedom—the free choice of his 'true', albeit often submerged and inarticulate, self."[23] It is not surprising, then, that Berlin leveled this critique against the potential authoritarianism inherent in the strong Counter-Enlightenment romanticism associated with the likes of Hegel and his right- and left-leaning intellectual descendents, who in many important respects combined the ethical republicanism of Aristotle and Cicero with the dialectical idealism of Plato, to become the progenitors of the more contemporary republican and radical traditions previously mentioned.[24]

Berlin was well aware of the complexities of the many different critical traditions grounded in various forms of dialectical reasoning and conflict analysis, at least as they emerged during his lifetime. He even held that Leo Tolstoy "was by nature a fox, but believed in being a hedgehog,"[25] and he might well have said the same of the likes of Antonio Gramsci, Max Horkheimer, and Theodor Adorno.[26] This said, he had harsher things to say about the intellectual descendents of Plato, Hegel, and Marx than about those of Aristotle, Cicero, and Machiavelli, in part, I think, because he believed that the latter set the stage for the sort of pluralism he embraced in ways that the former did not. We will see subsequently how Oakeshott critiques the lack of pluralism in critical social theory on the basis of a universal application of dialectical logic. Berlin, however, had a slightly different concern in mind—that all too often the ultimate end of conflict analysis is the obliteration of difference altogether. There are, to be sure, social distinctions that ought to be dissolved because they entail an unjust abuse of power, such as those aspects of class, race, gender, ethnicity, religion, sexual orientation, and the like on the basis of which benefits, resources, and opportunities are withheld or verbal, emotional, or physical abuse inflicted. But the exercise of power is not always evil, and its equal distribution not necessarily just. There are many instances where we want and need to rely on the state to use power wisely—in battling corruption, for example, or protecting the weak or the innocent; and some tasks deserve higher reward than others, although well-intentioned people may differ as to what those tasks might be and how large a differential in reward is warranted. Yet, without any "objective" standard of what is to count as just, wise, corrupt, or innocent, we have nothing on which to rely but political tradition in order to distinguish between the just and unjust application of power or distribution of wealth. Berlin was more sympathetic to republicans such as Machiavelli and Herder than to radicals like Marx and Friedrich Engels, therefore, because Berlin believed that, tempered with a strong dose of negative freedom, republicanism might yield a respect for difference that could facilitate ways for deeply distinctive peoples to coexist that are absent from the sort of critical social theories that strive to deconstruct difference altogether.

It may be more surprising, however, to learn that Berlin's reservations concerning the excesses of positive liberty were addressed no less to the monist moral and political theories of Kant and Locke than to the republicans and the radicals. If he viewed Machiavelli and Herder as nascent foxes, he saw these Enlightenment liberals as hedgehogs, headstrong about the capacity of reason to negotiate competing ways of life. Liberalism is normally associated with pluralism, grounded in the right of citizens to choose a concept of the Good over any particular goods they may prefer. This assumes that they can pick freely, based on relevant reasons,[27] and engage in reasonable deliberation to adjudicate disagreements.[28] However, Berlin followed Hegel in holding that our choices are not always as free nor our deliberations as reasonable as they might appear, since the very idea of rational evaluation is historically situated; and though preferring negative freedom, he recognized it too as a historical achievement that tends toward its positive counterpart when transformed into a doctrine that strives for comprehensive influence over the lives of citizens. Thus, he counted as a fairly extreme version of positive liberty the concept of rational autonomy and the pursuit of liberal toleration as a universal ideal found in Kant and Locke.

Berlin parted company with Hegel, however, especially Hegel's left-leaning followers, when they argued that selections can only be genuinely free when power is distributed equally by liberating the weak and oppressed from the ideas and material conditions that render them feeble and subjugated.[29] The ultimate source of human power, Berlin argued, lies not in its uniform distribution, but in the presumption that people can step outside of their current circumstances to choose a new path, despite all of the influences upon them or the forces stacked against them. This is so precisely because our circumstances are not given and even though our choices cannot be based on one view or another of universal reason.[30] His views were thus closer to communitarians such as MacIntyre and Taylor, who held that there is no way to assess rational evaluation other than by appeal to the very rational standards in question, and that without a satisfactory justification of rationality, preferences may be reduced to expressions of mere personal feeling.[31] This confuses freedom with caprice and isolates citizens from one another as they center increasingly on themselves. Meaningful assessment must be based on values that emanate from beyond the self, therefore, linked to historically contingent communities or traditions in which citizens are embedded.[32]

Some liberals, such as Rawls, respond to these objections by pointing out that the weak and oppressed would themselves choose the principle of distributive justice from behind a veil of ignorance and that procedural justice is a neutral mechanism for defending personal choices grounded in affiliation, not a comprehensive doctrine in its own right[33]; and although others take issue with this sort of political minimalism by suggesting that liberal values should influence the private as well as the public domain,[34] most agree that liberal states should protect, not preclude, strong affiliations and situated identities.[35] But these rejoinders fail to address the full weight of Berlin's embrace of the Hegelian assault on Kant and Locke, which questions not only the capacity of reason to adjudicate difference without prejudice, but the very rational grounds of liberalism altogether. Of course, many of the alternatives offered by radical and republican critics of liberalism are not free of difficulties associated with extreme concepts of positive liberty; liberation from false consciousness can lead to new forms of oppression, and traditionalism, if too rigid, may leave little room for those who seek fulfillment outside of prescribed frameworks. This may be why many of them return to some form of liberal justice even after they have criticized it.[36] It appears that with all of its limitations, only some sort of liberal democracy seems to secure the basic rights and liberties, such as free expression, that make criticism possible. But if reason can serve neither as a basis for liberal values nor as a neutral arena for public deliberation, on what grounds can this reengagement with liberalism, however modified, be sustained? This brings us back to Gray's pluralistic liberalism that assumes numerous incompatible forms of human life and pursues a modus vivendi for peaceful coexistence among them.[37]

Callan challenges Berlin's critique of universal (Callan might call it comprehensive) liberalism by questioning whether the distinction between positive and negative liberty can withstand close scrutiny, at least as Berlin has traced it in the history of Western political thought. The difficulty with Berlin's position, writes Callan,

> is that if one looks hard enough at any particular instance of positive or negative liberty, it normally turns out to be describable in terms of the other sort of liberty. One might say that Berlin's putative adherents of positive freedom want the activity of collective self-determination to be free from interference of forces outside the society and disruptive elements within it, while adherents of negative liberty want the individual to be free to determine her life as she pleases within the area of self-regarding conduct. Thus, the dominant interest of Berlin's so-called proponents of positive freedom, given a different but perfectly accurate description of their position, appears to be negative; and the overriding concern of their political adversaries turns out to be with positive freedom, given a similar descriptive change. That is not say that no significant difference exists between the two schools of political thought which Berlin differentiates— there obviously is—but it is a difference to which the ordinary distinction between positive and negative liberty is wholly irrelevant.[38]

But, on Callan's view, what is the difference between the two schools of thought that Berlin delineates? One prioritizes collective goods over individual rights, while the other prefers the right of individuals to choose a concept of the collective Good over any goods they may choose. The former is a common way of conceiving republicanism and the latter a central tenet of universal liberalism. However, this interpretation of Berlin misses the essential point that even the society that promotes individual self-rule, when left untempered by something like Mill's familiar caveat having to do with impinging on the liberties of others, is no less oppressive in its own way than the sorts of extreme right- and left-leaning collectivism to which Callan, along with Berlin, objects. But the desires and aspirations of the others only acquire independent moral standing when we recognize the historical contingency, and hence fundamental diversity, of the very sort of rationality (Callan calls it truthfulness or realism) upon which personal autonomy rests. For if standards to assess ways of life were the same for all, independent of the vicissitudes of history, language, culture, and tradition, then the very idea of self-rule would be meaningless, since universal reason, not personal choice, would in fact govern one's will, the results of which would turn out the same for everyone. Under these conditions, there would be no need in principle for a separate consideration of the other, since everyone's choices would turn out to be the same. In short, it would appear that in this interpretation of Berlin's distinction between positive and negative liberty, Callan, like many universal liberals before him, reveals himself to be a bit of a hedgehog rather than a fox, falling prey to what Oakeshott calls the fallacy of rationalism in politics.

Rationalism in politics and traditions of practice

Oakeshott's critique of rationalism shows that he too was a pluralist, although Gray thought that Oakeshott was overly committed to a single tradition.[39] Oakeshott's mistake, Gray contends, was "to suppose that liberalism must be understood as a system of values, and to seek to replace reference to principle by the guidance of tradition—as if any late modern society...contained only one tradition. If contemporary societies contain several traditions, with many people belonging to more than one, politics cannot be conducted by following any one tradition. It must try to reconcile the intimations of rival traditions."[40] In this assessment, Gray, like many other liberal philosophers, confuses Oakeshott's concern for the political tradition of a single society with the idea that traditions are necessarily closed and rigid, while it is Oakeshott's critique of closed and rigid traditions that in fact points the way to understanding how people who adhere to opposing traditions can coexist and even learn from one another.[41]

As may be recalled from Chapter Four, Oakeshott's position is grounded in a distinction between technical and practical knowledge. The former entails mastery of techniques that can be formulated in propositions—rules, principles, directions, and maxims that can be summarized in books and manuals. The latter exists only in use and is shared or becomes common not by means of formulated doctrines, but through traditions of practice.[42] The problem with rationalism, claims Oakeshott, is that it denies that practical knowledge should be counted as knowledge altogether, since there is no knowledge that is not technical knowledge. For the rationalist, he writes, "the sovereignty of 'reason'...means the sovereignty of technique."[43] The heart of the matter, he continues, "is the pre-occupation of the Rationalist with certainty." The superiority of technical knowledge lay in the appearance that it springs from pure ignorance and ends in complete knowledge.[44] On this account, Thomas Jefferson's declaration, and similar documents of the French Revolution, merely summarized an ideology that Locke had distilled from the English political tradition, on the mistaken assumption that these principles were not the product of civilization, but "discovered in the nature of human reason."[45] However, this passion for logical technique misconceived the proper relation between reason and tradition by confusing genuine knowledge of political affairs with partial truths torn not only from general experience of the world, which is certainly a more reliable guide than the maxims that might be recorded in a book, but also from the traditions of a society, which can take two or three generations to acquire.

The difficulty with universal liberalism, on this view, is that it succumbs to this rationalist infatuation with uniformity and regularity. The consequence for literacy in democratic education is a strong tendency toward what David Tyack called the "one best system," according to which all accounts of how and why children are to be taught to communicate must conform to a universal rational standard.[46] Rawls, for example, calls on citizens in liberal democracies to accept "burdens of judgment" as a common basis for deliberating public goods. Among their other demands, these burdens require that public policies be defended only on grounds accepted by all, without appeal to particular value traditions.[47] A Catholic, in this view, should not make a public case against the legality of abortion on the grounds that human life begins at conception, since this view is limited to particular traditions not held in common by all citizens. However, as Meira Levinson points out, accepting this approach requires embracing an account of how pluralism is to be negotiated in the public domain that itself violates pluralism, since, among other reasons, it requires that our most substantive differences be left at the deliberation-room door.[48] Suggestions that Israel abandon its distinctive Jewish cultural character in order to address injustices done to Palestinians fall prey to this same fallacy of uniform technique. It presupposes a common culture to be transmitted to the young citizens of this state—a culture based on one form or another of universal reason that is not tied to particular language or tradition—when no such culture is possible, since even Enlightenment rationality is embedded in the history of a particular people who lived at a specific time and place.

Critical social theorists also succumb all too frequently to this rationalist fallacy, although they differ with liberals over the technique to which we ought to subscribe. Kant and Locke embraced an empirical-deductive logic with roots going back to Aristotle, whereas Hegel and Marx employed rival versions of dialectical reasoning that began with Plato. "No other technique has so imposed itself upon the world as if it were concrete knowledge," wrote Oakeshott referring to Marx and Engels, and "none has created so vast an intellectual proletariat, with nothing but its technique to lose."[49]

Nowhere is this tendency to reduce complex social relations to abstract and uniform techniques more apparent than in concepts relating to conflict and power associated with critical social theory. Consider the postcolonial claim that Zionism constitutes a form of colonialism, which draws what may be apt parallels between the exercise of Israeli and European power in the Middle East, while denying the deep historic ties of Jews to the land of Israel. To be sure, power relations between Jews and Arabs in Israel and the Middle East have been troubled for centuries, and Zionism most certainly has more than its fair share of abuses to account for, as do all of the other actors in the region; but to reduce these relations to so one-sided a model as colonialism, in which Jews are the intruders and Palestinians the natives, is to misconceive the complexity of the interactions between these peoples in the extreme.[50] It is highly unlikely that a concept of literacy for democratic education based on such an analysis could contribute to a reduction of the many tensions between them, for among many reasons, it would necessitate a call for the nostalgic return to Muslim-dominated Ottoman rule, which predated the arrival of the British in 1917 and the establishment of Israel in 1948—hardly a democratic or pluralistic outcome.

This is not to diminish the attention to power relations brought out by radical social criticism or to suggest that it always or necessarily lacks nuance. Rather, the point is that in a legitimate effort to deconstruct irrelevant differences among people that lead to abuses of authority and inequitable distribution of resources, critical social theories too often delegitimize distinctions in culture and tradition that are essential to the moral bite of their opposition to oppression in the first place, since, as Oakeshott would insist, the ethical evaluation of social conflict is itself historically contingent; or as Michel Foucault has taught us, even dialectical reasoning is a product of power relations and so unavailable as a basis for resisting injustice.

Oakeshott's analysis extends, then, not only to how we understand rational technique but also to the nature of political traditions. Rationalists, he claims, attribute to those traditions "the rigidity and fixity of character" that in fact belongs to the ideological principles born of "arid technique."[51] However, traditions of practice are not limited by one conception or another of rational rules. They are manners of preserving, recalling, and transmitting across the generations knowledge particular peoples have accumulated from the concrete experience of living together as a community.[52] Knowledge of this sort is practical, not technical; it cannot be fully captured by any set of rules, principles, or procedures, or abridged into an abstract political or religious ideology, which although useful can easily distort or mislead; rather it is preserved in the intricacies and details of shared lives, which are communicated in the sundry institutions, rituals, manners, customs, stories, and oddities of which a collective existence is comprised. A tradition of practice, then, is not an inflexible manner of doing things. "It is neither fixed, nor finished; it has no changeless centre to which understanding can anchor itself...no model to be copied or idea to be realized.... Some parts of it may change more slowly than others, but none is immune from change. Everything is temporary."[53] Nevertheless, though dynamic and emergent, traditions are not totally fluid or without identity, since all of their parts do not change at the same time. What accounts for the identity of a tradition is the diffusion of authority between past, present, and future, in which nothing that ever belonged is completely lost. Change within a tradition of practice, then, is normal, though it emerges gradually, not abruptly—by means of undirected evolution, not preplanned revolution.[54]

Unfortunately, the tendency among critics of republicanism is all too often to adopt a dogmatic as opposed to dynamic account of political traditions, closed off from valuable dialogue and debate with alternative views. One example of this is what Sigal Ben-Porath calls the "belligerent concept of citizenship," which emerges when national and personal security are threatened, such as in times of war. It entails a narrowing of three key components of citizenship: (i) civic participation, which is normally voluntary but becomes mandated toward the war effort; (ii) patriotism, which normally reflects pride in democratic ideals but is transformed into unity and solidarity in the face of a common enemy; and (iii) public deliberation, which is normally open and wide-ranging but becomes attenuated when focused on security issues with limited acceptable opinions.[55] These unfortunate tendencies arise under the pressures of war, Ben-Porath argues, because citizenship education is too often viewed as a form of initiation into national identity, which seeks to contain rather than preserve diversity, since it supposes that identification with the nation-state trumps all other identities we may have. Instead, Ben-Porath proposes what she calls expansive education, which conceives citizenship as shared fate, which may entail shared cultural or ethnic identity, but can also be based on other features such as institutional and material linkages.[56]

This alternative seems unobjectionable as far as it goes, but Ben-Porath's complaints about education in national identity appear to be grounded in the very dogmatic conception of tradition that Oakeshott attributes to the rationalists, which too often does not need the threat of war in order to become belligerent. Oakeshott was wrong if he supposed that no traditions of practice function in this way. Some religious and political orientations undoubtedly have a dogmatic tendency to fear the other, and one of the important contributions of critical social theory is to call them to account when they become overly narrow or oppressive. He was correct, however, to point out that many, if not most, traditions of practice are dynamic, not stagnant, and that given the right conditions, they will evolve and adapt to threats of all kinds quite effectively left to their own devices, precisely because they are open to learning from alternative perspectives and from the world in which they are situated. We require, then, not merely an account of citizenship that enables people from diverse backgrounds, such as Jewish and Palestinian Israelis, to view themselves as part of a common enterprise, but also an understanding of the traditions that inform those backgrounds that allows such a dialogue across difference to take place.

Liberal nationalism and the pedagogy of difference

Tamir, a student of Berlin's, outlines a potential basis for such an understanding in her defense of liberal nationalism, in which she uses the term "culture" to refer to something very close to what Oakeshott means by a tradition of practice. With many communitarian critics of comprehensive liberalism, she conceives the citizen and her choices as embedded in shared languages, histories, and customs, not governed solely by disengaged or hypothetical rationality. However, unlike the perfectionism of some communitarians, she adopts an open and reflective rather than a perfectionist account of culture, which assumes that individuals can shape the cultures in which they choose to live, not only base life choices on the cultures they have chosen. Hence, she distinguishes between self-determination and self-rule, the former referring to the right of individuals to public cultural expression and the latter to the right of cultural groups or nations to secure self-determination for their members by means of the state, although state power is not the only way to achieve cultural expression. National privileges are thus intrinsic, not instrumental, values—basic rights owed to every individual, not means to redress collective suffering or promote cultural survival. Concern for the others outside of the immediate circle of national membership is grounded in something akin to what Nel Noddings calls concentric circles of care: "Individuals care most about those in the circle closest to the centre, but are not indifferent to the welfare of those who occupy farther positions."[57]

Finally, in her Preface to the 1995 paperback edition of *Liberal Nationalism*, Tamir distinguishes between national and civic education.

> In a nationally diversified political system, be it a town, a state, a federation, a regional organization, or a global society, it is especially important that all children learn to respect others who have different lifestyles, values, and traditions and view them—qua members of the political system—as equals. Beyond this thin layer each national group should foster among its young knowledge that is relevant to its own particular community, its history, language, and traditions. Separating civic from national education is thus the key for continued peaceful existence of multinational societies…. National groups—minorities and majorities alike—should thus be given the freedom to have their own educational system (whether in the form of separate schools or, preferably…special hours or days) alongside the civic one. Civic education should attempt to create civic friendship among all, but it should attempt to do so not by assimilating all into one culture, but by respecting cultural diversity.[58]

In addition to initiation into their own cultural heritage, "all children should thus acquire some knowledge of the culture, history, and tradition of all national groups that share their political system, and be taught to respect them."[59]

Like Levinson's "weak perfectionism," Tamir's liberal nationalism goes some distance toward managing the tension between the individual rights that democratic citizenship demands and the literacy in particular cultures needed to understand and exercise those rights, or in Berlin's terms, to finding a proper balance between positive and negative liberty.[60] But one wonders whether Tamir, like Levinson, has not leaned too far in the direction of the individual, to the detriment of cultural integrity and continuity, perhaps because Tamir follows the rationalists in misconceiving traditions as rigid and dogmatic. She rejects the idea of cultural "authenticity" being dependent on roles ascribed by some "Council of Elders," since deviating from those roles might be interpreted as "false consciousness" or hiding from one's "true self," both indicators of positive freedom gone awry, and argues instead that "the only authentic and genuine way of life is that freely chosen by each individual for himself."[61] There is, then, "no Archimedean point from which we can evaluate the authenticity of cultures."[62]

> The debate about the nature of authenticity is closely related to the debate about the "thinness" or "thickness" of modern nations. The idea that a nation has undergone a slow and organic process of development is more authentic than one that has developed in a less stable and continuous way, or that a society exhibits a more contiguous set of values and beliefs is therefore more authentic than one that is new, pluralistic, and therefore heterogeneous, should then be viewed with suspicion.
>
> The assumption that individuals can exercise choice regarding both their communal affiliations and their moral identity entails respect for dynamic and pluralistic views of culture. It views with favor the fact that, at any given point in time, different cultural interpretations compete for recognition within each nation. Membership in the cultural community would then be expressed by participating in the debate, rather than by following one specific interpretation.[63]

Thus, Tamir appears to suppose that, with no Archimedean point to evaluate the authenticity of cultures, the only basis on which to make constitutive choices about the person we aspire to be is personal feeling. But it does not follow from the fact that our preferences are historically contingent, determined by neither dogmatic tradition nor universal reason, that the only available option is what Taylor would call weak evaluation, based on mere feeling alone. For constitutive choices to be embedded in culture, as Tamir asserts, requires what Taylor calls strong evaluation, based on norms that emanate from beyond the self.[64] This in turn necessitates a thicker concept of culture or tradition than Tamir appears to allow—one that grows in response to dialogue with opposing views and current events, but that is not within the total control of the individual to shape at the whim of his momentary or personal desires. Traditions that develop organically in response to their environments need not be homogeneous or monolithic. Indeed, the very priority Tamir places on pluralism and heterogeneity is itself the product of such a tradition of practice.

Moreover, without a neutral standpoint, what ought to be the substance of civic as distinguished from national education, in what language should it be taught or on what cultural values can it be based? In the passage cited previously, Tamir appears to endorse state support for education in minority cultures and faiths, which might suggest a multinational approach to civic education. Yet, later on, she equivocates: "Even if social resources are fairly distributed, minority groups will be more limited in their ability to practice their national culture," she writes. "Therefore, due to no fault of society, national minorities may feel culturally deprived and continue to wish that they lived in a community in which they constitute the majority."[65] From this, it might appear that common civic education should be based, as in the United States, on a version of the majority culture that is sufficiently thin so as not to offend minorities. In either case, if this culture is not sufficiently robust to override individual preferences when they run counter to such essential values as respect for difference, it is unlikely that this culture can promote the sort of peaceful coexistence to which Tamir aspires. This necessitates neither a total separation of national from civic education nor a thin culture of mere personal choice. Instead, multinational coexistence requires an education in tradition that is open to dialogue with opposing views within the political system, but that also seeks common ground upon which to build a joint civic education. This may include Ben-Porath's common fate, institutions, and material relations, but it should also involve common historical, religious, and ideological connections. Jewish, Muslim, and Christian religions, for example, all share connections to the narrative of Abraham and Sarah, though the stories they tell about these seminal figures may differ, but all of these stories share connections with modern European Enlightenment culture that gave birth to liberal democracy. Exploring these connections in Jewish and Arab schools in Israel, along with elements of a shared fate, including institutional and material ties, could be the beginning of a common civic curriculum.

Conclusion

For this to be possible, each group requires a robust education in their own tradition, viewed as open and dynamic rather than closed and dogmatic, along with exposure to the traditions of the other. In addition to awareness of the historical contingency of a student's own traditions, cultural initiation also requires a critical aspect that addresses power relations both within that tradition and between it and other traditions. We need, in short, a hermeneutic of dialogue a la Martin Buber and Noddings, not of suspicion a la Freire—one that acknowledges and confirms, rather than accuses, the other. Education in Jewish and Zionist traditions requires a self-examination concerning how Jews have related to one another, for example, across divides of politics, religion, ethnicity, gender, and sexual orientation. But such an education also demands examination of how Jews have exercised power over, in addition to suffering at the hands of, others. Similarly, Arab students of Muslim and Christian origin should be educated in their own customs and beliefs, but also taught to critically examine the cultures and societies from which they have emerged. They should explore historic power relations between Christians and Muslims and, of course, between Christian and Muslim communities and Jews. The civic education that should emerge from this approach cannot be entirely separated from national education; it needs to seek roots within each national culture separately, conceived dialogically and developmentally.

The antidote to rampant rationalism and universal liberalism, as I argue in the coming chapter, is neither a weak personalized culture nor a dogmatic oppressive tradition, but an emergent and dynamic heritage grounded in what Jonathan Sacks calls the "dignity of difference," which admits multiple compelling approximations of the truth and many acceptable visions of how to live.[66] This requires a critical understanding of the tradition into which I was born or with which I choose to affiliate along with an acknowledgment and confirmation of others who are different from me and a willingness to engage them in dialogue. Following Sacks, and in contrast to pedagogies of the oppressed that tend to place responsibility for one's plight on social structures or power relations rather than on oneself, I call this self-critical and dialogical form of education the pedagogy of difference.

CHAPTER SEVEN

What Is Common About Common Schooling?

Introduction

Many liberal political theorists believe that democratic societies require rationally autonomous citizens. A primary aim of schooling in liberal democracies, in this view, is to promote the rational autonomy of students. It follows that liberal societies should sponsor common schools for the children of all citizens and that the curriculum of those schools should emphasize at least those rational traditions that will enhance autonomy and provide future citizens with the critical evaluation skills to make personal life choices and participate in public policy debates. In this view, some sort of rationality constitutes a neutral ground on which to base these choices and debates. However, hard questions have been raised in the philosophical literature concerning this neutral account of rationality. According to one critique, rationality cannot be neutral because it serves the interests of a particular class, culture, race, or gender.[1] Teaching students to evaluate plans and policies on the basis of reason does not enhance their independence, in this view; it enslaves them to power interests that they have not chosen or would not choose, given the opportunity to do so. Another criticism of this position states that rational assessment cannot be justified without appeal to the rational standards in question, which means that those standards must rely on personal or communal preferences that cannot be counted as neutral.[2] A rational approach to the curriculum can prejudice students against certain nonrational life paths, such as those found within particular religious traditions, according to this position, or privilege the knowledge and skills associated with the human and natural sciences over those cultivated within the plastic and performing arts.

Yet, according to most accounts, liberal values and institutions are based on the idea that citizens are free because they have the capacity to evaluate choices rationally and that differences among rival ways of life can be adjudicated by appeal to reason as a neutral court of appeal. To challenge the neutrality of rationality, it would appear, is to call into question the very moral and intellectual sustainability of open, liberal democracy, unless one can appeal to an alternative account of liberalism without neutrality. It is just such an alternative to which John Gray refers when he distinguishes between two faces of liberalism, one in pursuit of regimes that promote an ideal form of life based on universal principles and another seeking a modus vivendi for peaceful coexistence among different ways of living.[3] The belief that liberal democracy depends upon the cultivation of rational autonomy through a common curriculum, I argue in this chapter, is grounded in the liberal doctrine that promotes identification with an ideal form of life based on universal principles. After discussing some of the main difficulties with this view, I will outline an approach to schooling in open, liberal democracies based on the pursuit of coexistence among different ways of living. This alternative challenges the tendency in large diverse democracies (such as the United States and the United Kingdom) to prefer so-called common to particularistic or affiliated education, thereby placing many types of secular and faith schools on a more equal footing and providing moral justification for education in the national cultures of small liberal republics (such as Denmark, Israel, and Lithuania) that maintain special relationships to particular groups while acknowledging the rights of all citizens.

Rational autonomy is associated with schooling for both personal and public reasons. The first sort of reason has to do with the role of rational evaluation in making choices that will lead to a fulfilling life; the second with the function of autonomy in the justification and operation of the liberal state. On the first line of reasoning, common schools should promote rational autonomy because it has a greater capacity than heteronomy to enable students to flourish; in the second account, schools should do so because the legitimization and functioning of the liberal democratic state requires rationally autonomous citizens. Accordingly, this chapter will be divided into four sections. The first section will consider personal arguments for autonomy as a basis for common schooling. The second section will discuss the role of autonomy in the justification of the liberal state. The third section will situate these arguments in what Gray has called universal liberalism and sketch an alternative account of liberalism grounded in what has come to be called value pluralism. The final section will argue that a genuine commitment to liberal pluralism requires an education rooted in dynamic traditions—not neutral rationality or prevailing dogmas—that engage opposing perspectives, reinterpret current practice, and acknowledge that all people are inherently equal and worthy of respect. In the previous two chapters, I have called this sort of education the pedagogy of difference.[4]

Autonomy and human flourishing

Harry Brighouse argues that, on the personal level, education should aim at enabling people to lead flourishing lives, which are characterized by at least two criteria. First, flourishing lives are worth living, which means that they contain a selection of "objective goods."[5] Second, for a person *to flourish* within such a life, they have to identify with it, to live it "from the inside," as it were.[6] What counts as an objective good is not a straightforward affair, but it is not very controversial that some practices and ideals are better for us than others and that different people may be fulfilled by quite diverse combinations of goods. Nor is it a particularly contentious matter that for a life to be fulfilling, one must identify with it. Brighouse uses the term "autonomy"—"the opportunity to make and act on well-informed and well thought out judgments"[7]—to denote how one comes to live inside a way of life and concludes not only that (1) "the basic methods of rational evaluation are reliable aids to uncovering how to live well" but also that (2) "they are the only aids that can be identified and taught."[8]

He offers the following reasons to support these conclusions:

Rational reflection can help us to detect inconsistencies and fallacious argumentation, and to uncover misuse of evidence. It helps us to see whether a choice coheres with our given judgments, including our judgments about what kind of person we ought to be. It also helps us to evaluate the ways we are attached to other people, and to carry out our altruistic obligations and goals more effectively.... It is important to notice that rational reflection can, and often does, lead us to affirm our existing traits, values, commitments, and attachments.[9]

This account is problematic for several reasons.[10]

First, rationality cannot itself withstand the test of rational evaluation without presupposing the very rational standards one would be evaluating.[11] Consider a person who has had no exposure to rational discourse, such as Jean-Jacques Rousseau's Emile, who was raised in the wild.[12] How could one go about demonstrating to him that the canons of rational assessment are indeed valid, other than by means of the very logical laws one has set out to defend? But to assume that those laws are valid is to presuppose the very point one has set out to demonstrate, which is to succumb to a form of circular reasoning that those very laws reject. Immanuel Kant tried to ground the a priori principles of reason in the very makeup of human consciousness,[13] and so as a liberal follower of Kant, Brighouse might respond that, in a sense, Emile already understands these principles. An education in rational evaluation, in this view, is intended to draw out of him logical capacities that are already implicit within, not to demonstrate their truth or validity. However, few today believe in such universal cognitive structures; and it was his suspicion of such a belief that very likely led Rousseau to suggest that introducing Emile to the civilized discourse governed by rational evaluation is closer to coercion than persuasion.[14]

My second concern has been brought home by critical social theorists in education—Marxists, neo-Marxists, and poststructuralists—who argue that any standards one might employ to formulate judgments about the sort of person I should be will be tied to economic, ideological, or cultural interests; and any attempt to liberate those judgments from such interests on rational grounds of one kind or another will itself entail the exercise of power. So while the appeal to rational evaluation may be intended to free youngsters from the undue power that their parents exercise over their lives, in order to enable them to make their own autonomous choices, it may in fact merely subjugate them to other economic, ideological, or cultural interests that may or may not be consistent with what is best for them.[15]

Third, as I will argue at greater length in what follows, it is entirely unclear how we could go about determining what is best for a person other than within the context of a tradition concerning what ought to count as better or worse. And although there are many rational traditions that address this concern in productive and interesting ways, not all ethical traditions will necessarily withstand the test of reason, including, as I have indicated, perhaps even those very rational traditions themselves.[16] This is not to say, of course, that the radical perspectives mentioned fair any better in this paradoxical terrain, for on their own account they too must be tied to economic, ideological, cultural, or other interests, the liberation from which will only land them in some new set of power relations. Richard Peters was right when he noted that in order to foster moral independence we have no choice but to restrict it, and once having done so it is notoriously difficult to sort out how we can free a child from the grip of those initial acts of coercion.[17]

My fourth difficulty with Brighouse's account of the role of autonomy in education has to do with what might get left out as a candidate for the sort of life consistent with human flourishing. I have in mind those religious traditions that call upon the faithful to believe in God and obey divine commandments, even when there is no apparent rational justification for doing so. There are, of course, reasons why a person might choose such a path other than on the basis of valid proofs for the existence of God or logical explanations of particular religious practices, such as the promise of eternity inherent in Pascal's wager or of a meaningful life in William James's will to believe.[18] Nor is a religious way of life for everyone; indeed, for divergent thinkers in some traditions or for women in others or when imposed through force or violence, such a life can be downright oppressive. But it cannot be denied that many people have come to lead very wholesome and worthwhile religious lives on nonrational grounds, such as naïve religious faith, the homes in which they were raised, or an epiphany that led to conversion. It is hard to imagine that the standards of rational evaluation would not discourage youngsters from choosing such a nonrational path, which would deny them opportunities for existential purpose that have sustained people for centuries through the joys and trials of life. Of course, this difficulty may not be a consequence of all accounts of rational autonomy, and we will consider in what follows at least two views that attempt to address the issue, but it does seem to be a problem for Brighouse's position.

My fifth problem with rational assessment as the best way to get inside a way of life is that it requires us to do just the opposite. To compare and contrast rival orientations we need to view them from without, as a journalist or sociologist or historian might describe them, not from within, as an insider might experience them. Indeed, the whole point of such an exercise is to gather and assess evidence objectively, without regard to the sorts of subjective attachments that characterize the life of an insider. Yet, it is the value of just such a particular set of attachments that we are expected to judge when we rationally assess the alternatives; and to make such a judgment would appear to require the very sort of immersion into one way of life at the expense of others that Brighouse is at pains to critique as ruinous to autonomy. One is at a loss to understand how decisions of this sort can properly be called rational when the most pertinent evidence required to make them is summarily ruled out of court.

Consider the case that Brighouse discusses of "people who experience their sexuality as fixed and inadaptable."

> A homosexual who experiences his homosexuality as unchangeable simply cannot live, from the inside, a way of life in which those who refrain from heterosexual marriage and childrearing are social outsiders. Trapped in such a way of life, he will be alienated from it. It may be a very good way of life, but it is not one that *he* can endorse from the inside, and is therefore not one that *he* can live well.[19]

But if he is old enough to experience his sexuality as inadaptable, he is already inside a life with real subjective attachments and experiences, some of which may have taught him that his sexuality is either fixed or flexible and others that it is either forbidden or permitted. The problem for him is not to choose impartially among an array of alternatives, but to determine—at least in part on the basis of his own subjective experience— whether he wants to remain in his current life or to opt for another, either by seeking to change the tradition that informs it or by abandoning that tradition altogether. Doing so, however, may put him at odds with a family or community or God that he holds most dear. I can hardly imagine a more deeply emotional choice. Reason may be helpful in sorting out some of the issues in this case (which is, in fact, one of the roles attributed to it by Brighouse in the passage quoted here), but it is highly unlikely that rational evaluation can on its own carry the burden of such a weighty decision.

Autonomy and the liberal state

Meira Levinson grapples with a number of these issues in her "weak perfectionist" account of rational autonomy as a source of legitimacy for the liberal state.[20] Before outlining her own approach, she identifies some of the main difficulties within prevailing comprehensive and political liberal theories by distinguishing between three commitments of liberalism: (A) an acceptance of deep irremediable pluralism in modern society; (B) a concern for public legitimization of the state based on a principle of justice; and (C) a belief that this legitimization project yields substantive liberal freedoms and institutions. Uniting all three commitments in one coherent theory of liberalism is difficult. Joseph Raz, for example, rejects legitimization as unattainable in light of the fact of pluralism and so argues for the value of autonomy—the capacity to form, revise, and rationally pursue a worthwhile human life—in a way that bridges directly from pluralism to substantive liberal institutions.[21] John Stuart Mill, on the other hand, sacrifices (or misconstrues) the depth of modern pluralism in favor of linking legitimization directly with substantive liberal institutions via an argument for the value of autonomy (or "individuality").[22] What links Raz and Mill, writes Levinson, "is a belief in the value of autonomy for both itself and as a means of justifying substantive liberal freedoms."[23] This strand of political thought, she explains, has come to be called "comprehensive" or "perfectionist" liberalism, since it promotes rationality as a substantive liberal value to guide personal value choices, in addition to its neutral role in adjudicating between rival ways of life. As such, this account of liberalism is subject to at least the first four objections raised here in connection with Brighouse's view of autonomy, which is also a case of comprehensive liberalism: the absence of a noncircular justification of rationality, the possible connection between rationality and nonrational power interests, the role of context in determining sources of value, and the tendency within rationalism to delegitimize nonrational sources of value such as naive religious faith.[24]

In contrast to comprehensive liberalism, John Rawls contends that all three of the commitments Levinson highlighted can be coherently unified in a more limited "political" liberal theory.[25] He avoids autonomy as a substantive value in favor of the two moral powers of human beings: (1) the capacity for a sense of justice and (2) the capacity for a conception of the good. In the first instance, Rawls reinterprets pluralism through what he calls the "burdens of judgment," the acceptance of which is one element of the sense of justice required for citizens to reach agreement on the legitimate principles that should govern the state. Reasonable people differ over what is most important in life for at least six reasons: (i) conflicting evidence, (ii) disagreement over the relative weight of evidence, (iii) the indeterminacy of "hard cases," (iv) the influence of past on present experience, (v) the incommensurability of values, and (vi) the circumscription of value within any particular society.[26] To accept these so-called burdens of judgment as sources of reasonable disagreement, Rawls contends, is to accept a particular account of pluralism, not only to acknowledge it as a fact. This leads citizens to seek principles of justice compatible with every reasonable person's conception of the good, rather than to convince others to adopt a view of the state grounded in a particular way of life. To accept the burdens of judgment, in other words, is "to accept their consequences for the use of public reason in directing the legitimate exercise of political power."[27] The difficulty with this position, Levinson argues, is that by requiring citizens to alter their understanding of pluralism, as opposed to asking them merely to accept its existence, Rawls violates the boundaries of pluralism itself; and in so far as accepting this account requires people to realize that theirs is not the only reasonable way to live, it demands that, at least in their capacity as citizens, they exercise a rudimentary level of autonomy. This would appear to leave Rawls in much the same position as Raz and Mill vis-à-vis the neutrality of rational autonomy.[28]

If Rawls intended his account of the first moral power to tie pluralism to the legitimization project via the burdens of judgment, he sought to link legitimization to substantive liberal institutions by means of the second moral power, "the capacity to form, to revise, and rationally to pursue…a conception of what we regard for us as a worthwhile human life."[29] Since the liberty to pursue a vision of the good is a primary freedom protected by liberal states, and one's present way of life may require occasional if not regular revision, participants in the legitimization process must assume that citizens can not only form but also revise their life paths. From this Rawls derives other substantive liberties, such as freedom of conscience, which is required to allow one to recognize and acknowledge mistakes, and freedom of association with like-minded citizens, which is needed for there to be meaningful freedom of conscience. But the capacity to form, revise, and pursue a vision of the good, Levinson points out, is just what we mean by rational autonomy. Rawls's justification of substantive liberal institutions, therefore, does not escape reliance on autonomy as a positive, and hence nonneutral, value any better than his reading of pluralism via the prism of the burdens of judgment.[30]

To address these difficulties, Levinson offers an account of liberalism that embraces a view "which values individual autonomy, but does not discriminate against those who do not exercise autonomy in their own lives,"[31] provided they see themselves as what Rawls called "self-authenticating sources of valid claims"[32] and as what Stanley Benn dubs "autarchic persons" who intentionally affect change in the world, take responsibility for their actions, and are able to have a conception of the good.[33] Levinson contends that this requires more than a thin or formal account of autonomy, such as that advanced by Gerald Dworkin. In his view, autonomous individuals are those who evaluate and revise first-order desires, which are of the form "I want X," by means of second-order desires, which take the form "I want to want X," in order to ensure that the desires they act upon are those with which they identify or "adopt as their own." Dworkin argues that formalism—the fact that an account does not distinguish between autonomous and heteronymous people based on the content of their desires—is an advantage because it allows that heteronymous lifestyles (such as those that follow divine commandments) can be freely chosen and so these lifestyles should be protected by liberal institutions.[34] Levinson, on the other hand, thinks that it is strange to subsume heteronymous values under the rubric of autonomy, since it allows people to enslave themselves and continue to be regarded as autonomous, among other reasons. Consequently, she opts for a more substantive account of the concept.

According to Levinson, an autonomous person must be situated in a coherent cultural orientation, possess a well-developed personality (emotionally, intellectually, spiritually, aesthetically, and morally), and embrace a plurality of constitutive desires and values. Cultural coherence enables an individual to identify with a source of value other than mere personal preference upon which to base second-order evaluations of first-order desires; possessing a well-developed personality allows a person to base autonomous choices on complex interactions among a wide variety of personal abilities and commitments; and embracing a plurality of constitutive desires and values drawn from distinct, even rival, sources provides a vantage point from which to critically assess one set of desires and actions on the basis of another. Levinson's efforts to acknowledge the roles of culture, nonrational dimensions of personality, and human agency in making substantive life decisions is most welcome, but she may not have gone far enough. The difficulty with her account is that it falls prey to a version of the fifth objection raised here in connection with Brighouse's view of autonomy: It requires a person to stand inside and outside of a way of life at the same time. On one hand, the autonomous person is to be situated inside a coherent cultural orientation, and, on the other, she is to embrace a plurality of values, including some that conflict with the culture in which she is situated. This is thought to allow critical assessment of all or part of that cultural orientation, from the outside, but seems more likely to leave a child confused. Additionally, as I have argued, it is not at all clear how an outside perspective enables one to understand what it means to experience a particular culture as an insider, which would appear to be the crucial sort of evidence required in order to decide whether this is the sort of life one wants to lead. It is the subjective experience of a tradition from the inside that is most important in deciding whether to adopt it, and exposure to a different life path as an outsider that offers the opportunity to consider whether to take a closer look, from the inside.[35]

The other face of liberalism

Brighouse's flourishing and Levinson's weak perfectionism both falter, because each of them conceives liberalism as a universal form of life, however limited, based on rational autonomy.[36] As noted in the previous chapter, Gray calls this universal liberalism.[37] In terms made popular by Isaiah Berlin, which are also mentioned in that chapter, universal liberals such as Brighouse and Levinson tend to become hedgehogs who know one big thing—rational autonomy—instead of foxes who knows many things— rival traditions.[38] Despite their avowed commitment to pluralism, they interpret liberalism along the lines of Berlin's positive concept of freedom— the idea of self-mastery, or self-determination, or control of one's destiny— rather than in reference to negative liberty—the absence of constraints on, or interference with, a person's desires and actions. And as is well-known, the difficulty with an overenthusiasm for positive freedom is the tendency of those who endorse it to impose a way of life on people who might choose otherwise, because it is thought to be in their best interest.[39] Put simply, by imposing rational neutrality (even in a weak form) on Levinson's second and third liberal commitments, public legitimization and substantive freedoms and institutions, universal liberalism runs afoul of Levinson's first liberal commitment, the irremediable fact of pluralism.[40] The alternative sort of liberalism exemplified by Berlin is a theory of modus vivendi, which has no truck with ideal regimes, but seeks terms on which different ways of life can live together. Modus vivendi, writes Gray, "is liberal toleration adapted to the historical fact of pluralism." The ethical theory associated with this historical turn in liberal thought has been called value pluralism— the idea that "there are many conflicting kinds of human flourishing, some of which cannot be compared in value."[41] This is a much more tentative and cacophonous liberalism than that associated with the foundational aspirations of rationalism.[42]

As was noted previously, Michael Oakeshott took the underlying problem of universal liberalism to be its embrace of rational rules, procedures, and techniques as the exclusive basis of political knowledge, when to be meaningful all such technical knowledge must be interpreted in the context of a political tradition grounded in practice.[43] Gray believed Oakeshott to be wrong in replacing principle with tradition as a basis for liberalism, which as I responded earlier confuses concern for the political tradition of a single society with the idea that traditions are necessarily closed and rigid.[44] The fact that Oakeshott considered liberalism to be a particular political tradition in no way infringes on his commitment to diversity, which is evident in his view that education entails the cultivation of personal identity through engagement with the many modes of understanding that comprise cultures.[45] Indeed, toleration of the very range of orientations inherent in Gray's pursuit of coexistence is possible only within the context of a political tradition of the sort Oakeshott endorses.[46]

The point to be emphasized here is that it is difficult to comprehend what value pluralism could possibly mean without appeal to some conception of tradition. Even if we assume that there are many rival traditions and that people might adhere to more than one of them, meaningful as opposed to merely personal choices must be grounded in strong values that are embedded in one or more of those traditions. To say that the renewal of liberalism entails a modus vivendi for coexistence among rival forms of life, a supposition that is itself situated in a particular historical perspective, presumes that people adhere to one or more of the rivals. But to assume that democratic societies are or ought to be indifferent with regard to the orientations citizens may consider is to entertain the very mistaken view from nowhere upon which universal liberalism rests.[47] In the absence of rational neutrality, the liberal challenge is to discern how prevailing traditions can serve as a source of, rather than a hindrance to, moral independence and to ensure that relevant rights and liberties are not denied to citizens affiliated with minority cultures or those of the weak or powerless. The question is not whether pluralistic liberalism entails initiation into traditions, but rather what sort of traditions do societies that embrace value pluralism require.[48]

Liberal societies that seek peaceful coexistence among rival ways of life should initiate students of both majority and minority cultures into "dynamic" versions of the traditions to which they are heir. In addition to celebrating their own legacies, dynamic traditions are willing to engage opposing perspectives and reinterpret current practice. They are also committed to the idea that all people, regardless of background or affiliation, have the capacity for free agency and so are inherently equal and worthy of respect.[49] What binds the majority of citizens together in most societies is not the presumption of a neutral public square, but a shared way of life. In small liberal republics such as Denmark, Israel, and Lithuania, for example, it is extraordinarily difficult for public functionaries, from schoolteachers to heads of state, to hide behind an illusion of neutrality; they are friends of your brother, or related to your sister-in-law, or neighbors down the block, or, sometimes, enemies across the fence. The issue, however, is one of principle, not merely size—large democracies also depend upon face-to-face associations.[50] Most people who acquire a commitment to the rule of law or a constitution or a system of checks and balances do so because of stories they tell about themselves and their families, about their history or destiny or mission, in their own language and through the media of their own culture.[51] There is more than one way to live such a life— to recount such narratives or speak such languages or participate in such cultures or understand such histories or conceive such destinies or grasp such missions; and there will likely be citizens whose heritages, languages, and origins are different from those of the majority. To the extent that we deny citizens opportunities to participate in the process of interpretation, or restrict engagement with alternative or rival traditions, we render communal customs increasingly mechanical and limit their potential to bind people together through shared moral meanings and practices; and to the extent that we deny minority cultures, or those of the underprivileged or the oppressed, access to public expression and resources, we limit the likelihood that citizens so affiliated will choose to identify with the liberal state. Additionally, education in liberal societies should cultivate within students a proclivity for dialogue among conflicting orientations. To say that discussions within and among traditions lay beyond rational neutrality does not mean that they are devoid of intelligent discourse or critical assessment, but that such discourse and assessment may not always be readily accessible to all. Public deliberation will consequently demand communication among diverse, even incommensurable, goods without recourse to a common rationality that can serve as a neutral meeting ground.

Moral agency and liberal democratic education

The antidote to rampant rationalism and universal liberalism, then, is neither extreme separatism nor total anarchy, but recognition of what Jonathan Sacks calls the "dignity of difference," which admits multiple compelling approximations of the truth and many acceptable visions of how to live.[52] One can acquire the capacity to make independent choices, given that we can never stand outside of the lives we lead, by learning to be different and to respect the difference of others. This requires coming to understand myself, both past and present, and being prepared to assume responsibility for my future. It also requires coming to understand others who are different from me, both past and present, and recognizing that it is they, not I, who should assume responsibility for their future. Following Sacks, and in contrast to pedagogies of the oppressed that tend to place responsibility for one's plight on social structures or power relations rather than on oneself,[53] I call this the pedagogy of difference.[54]

The understanding that I have in mind here is not derived from the sort of evidence-based propositional or rule-based procedural knowledge discussed by Israel Scheffler, although theoretical evidence and practical procedures are by no means irrelevant to it.[55] Martin Buber would have referred to these as examples of objective knowledge, because they are intended to serve the instrumental objectives of subject–object or I–It relationships. The understanding that the pedagogy of difference requires, however, is closer to what Buber called subjective knowledge, which is acquired through personal encounters among human subjects—husbands and wives, parents and children, teachers and students, friends and lovers—and between those subjects and the data and ideals that inform and give direction to their lives.[56]

In this sort of encounter, one stands inside a way of life and receives it into oneself, rather than standing outside of it in order to compare it with others. Under these conditions, the distinction between autonomy and heteronomy is a bit misleading, since the boundaries between inside and outside the self are blurred. A way of life that on one account might have been perceived as external becomes the very content through which one achieves self-definition. The result is strong subjectivism, which supplies the values for what Charles Taylor calls strong evaluation of second-order desires that govern decisions constituent of who I chose to be—should I tell the truth to help a friend even when it may bring me harm, or embrace my homosexuality even though my religious tradition teaches that I should not?[57] On the other hand, without a foundation for the neutrality of reason, the objective comparisons of one way of life to another from the outside inherent in Brighouse's critical assessment or Levinson's plurality of desires and values too often end up in a weak form of subjective evaluation based on a person's momentary feelings—today I will try this way of life, tomorrow another.

To make life choices intelligently, then, I need to stand firmly within a way of life that offers me guidance in doing so. Hence, when parents believe that their way of life is best for human flourishing given the alternatives, they have a solemn duty as loving guardians and teachers, not a right or a privilege, to pass it on as a legacy that will ultimately enable their children to make intelligent and independent decisions as adults.[58] But what if this way of life seeks to dominate a child's independent judgment so completely that she will make only the narrow choices it prescribes or in a way that precludes consideration of all other options? Brighouse asks us to consider such a case when he refers to the Amish, a quasi-separate religious community in the Midwestern United States that challenged the law requiring youngsters to attend school until the age of sixteen and won a reduction to the age of fourteen. In the famous United States Supreme Court case of *Yoder v. Wisconsin*, the litigants argued that the requirement "violated their right to freedom of conscience, because during the early teen years, children are especially vulnerable to secular influences, so subjecting children of that age to formal education jeopardizes their belief in God and, ultimately, their opportunity for salvation."[59] Brighouse worries that this decision unduly allows parents to restrict opportunities for their children to make well-informed life choices on their own and that "autonomy is important enough to justify a requirement that all children be subject to an education designed to facilitate it."[60] But this would enable the state or some other agent to impose a comprehensive liberal view of the world on all children, even when their parents do not agree, which, as we have seen, cannot be sustained on rational grounds and so is no less an act of coercion than that of the parents themselves.

The pedagogy of difference offers an alternative way of accounting for cases of this kind grounded in the recognition that education in identity is intended to initiate people into a life worth living. For such a life to be good in any normative sense of the term, we must suppose not that those who would live it are rationally autonomous beings, but rather that they are independent moral agents, free within limits to choose between several life paths and capable of distinguishing between them.[61] People who have the capacity to understand and interpret desires, beliefs, and behaviors are at liberty to choose among them, and because of this liberty can be held accountable for the consequences of their choices.[62] If the Amish and communities like them want their children to assume eventual responsibility for their way of life, it is imperative that as they mature these children be encouraged to embrace this way of life, within limits, of their own free will. It is precisely for that reason that once they have reached maturity, the Amish send their young adults away for a time, to allow them to return to the community—or not—freely. Thus, the pedagogy of difference requires not only a deep immersion in the stories and practices of the tradition into which one is being initiated, but also opportunities to learn of other traditions and to experience them as well, though as something of an outsider, both to appreciate those who are different from me and to consider whether or not to join them. To understand myself, I must encounter the other; but to genuinely encounter the other, I must also understand myself. I can only freely choose a way of life, either the one offered by my parents or some other, if I have a thorough and loving grounding in one way of life, as well as an exposure to some of the alternatives. Exposure to traditions other than my own accomplishes a version of the critical assessment to which both Brighouse and Levinson aspire, but grounded in an initiation into the strong values of a particular tradition that does not require the embrace of two or more opposing perspectives at the same time and does not presume rationality as a neutral "view from nowhere" from which to assess alternative lifestyles.

Of course, some families, schools, communities, or societies are less cognizant than others of the need to prepare students to make life choices by fostering awareness of free agency. To the extent that these institutions suppress or deny human agency, they limit the capacity of their members for responsible moral decision making. Since *moral* discourse presupposes agents who can opt in or out of a way of life as they are given to understand it, suppression of agency leads to *amoral* communities that are closed to outside alternatives and that favor indoctrination into a mechanical rule-bound existence over education in a freely chosen ethical or religious identity.[63] However, for the state to intervene in such an instance and to impose a comprehensive liberal or rational view on a closed community for the sake of a child would undermine the very freedom of choice upon which human agency relies, and so would serve only to jeopardize the moral legitimacy of the state itself. This would do nothing to liberate the child from the coercion of such a community, which can only be accomplished through an exercise of her own free will.

Clearly, if a child is physically or emotionally mistreated in some way, the state has an obligation to protect her whether or not she is living in a closed or open community, although it may sometimes be difficult to reach agreement concerning what it means to be mistreated. The same would hold for any community that would seek to impose itself on another, or on the public at large, for example, through force and violence such as attacks on abortion clinics or other acts of terror. Additionally, although I agree with Brighouse that the state may have an interest in providing funds to religious schools open to alternative points of view,[64] my own view is much more positive about the contribution of dynamic faith traditions to liberal democracy, but more negative concerning the call of closed communities on the public purse, since it is unlikely that the alumni of their schools will possess the moral independence required for democratic decision making and responsibility. However, other than in such obvious or extreme cases, it is an entirely contestable matter whether a child would be better off living in one sort of community or another, since there is no way to conceive what might be better or worse for the child other than in the context of the religious or secular ethical traditions that govern our collective lives.

Conclusion

In contrast to the universal view of liberalism advanced by Brighouse and Levinson, the ethical and political philosophy most compatible with the pedagogic and educational views expressed here involves a tradition-oriented or communitarian reading of value pluralism. I have called it communitarian liberalism (or liberal communitarianism).[65] Since a neutral form of rational autonomy is indefensible, moral agency must be founded on the genuine relationships of students to families, communities, and traditions (including, of course, rational traditions), provided students are prepared to consider opposing views, revise current practice, and acknowledge the rights of all. Education in religious faiths or initiation into particular cultures is not antithetical to liberalism; nor should it merely be tolerated in a democracy, as implied by Brighouse and Levinson, as a lesser alternative to mainstream rationalism. Rather, education in dynamic traditions has a profound contribution to make to the preparation of democratic citizens who can assess the choices and assume the responsibilities required of self-governance, since there are no grounds upon which to base these decisions and responsibilities outside of the traditions of conscience that foster human agency. There are many good reasons other than the pursuit of an illusive rational autonomy why liberal societies might choose to support schools that offer a broad secular education to their children. However, schools affiliated with particular traditions, communities, or cultures are likely to do as well, if not better, than so-called common schools at initiating students into the dynamic traditions that liberal democracies require.

PART FOUR

Intelligent Spirituality in the Curriculum

Part Four collects three essays that consider what it would mean to design a curriculum concerned with the sort of pedagogy described in Part Three of this volume. How, I ask, should particular commitments to moral and religious traditions be included in the curriculum, while at the same time promoting an understanding and genuine concern for fellow citizens who are different culturally, racially, religiously, linguistically, or by virtue of gender or sexual orientation? What is the proper relation between the prevailing secular orientation and particular moral and religious traditions, between openness to a variety of alternatives and devotion to the faith of one's ancestors?

Like most of the other essays in this volume, these were written after *Reclaiming Goodness*, influenced by the relational ethics of my teacher Nel Noddings, along with those of Martin Buber and, more recently, Emmanuel Levinas. Among my most important experiences in graduate school was teaching Buber's *I and Thou* in Nel's graduate seminar on philosophy of education, where she worked out some of the ideas that were later associated with what became known as the "ethic of care." However, these chapters are distinguished even more emphatically by the fact that they were penned under the influence of my engagement with the life and thought of Terence McLaughlin, which began shortly after my move to Haifa in 1999. It culminated in an invitation for a 2003 study leave in Cambridge as a Visiting Fellow at St. Edmund's College, where Terry was a long-standing Fellow, and the Faculty of Divinity's Center for Advanced Religious and

Theological Studies. Like he did for many others with whom he came into contact, Terry had a profound impact on me, both personally and professionally, and his untimely passing in March 2006 dealt a severe blow to the international philosophy of education community. In 2000, we were brought together by the editors of the *Blackwell Guide to Philosophy of Education* to write a joint essay on religion and spirituality in education, and learned through the process of writing that essay that, though he was a devout Catholic and I a serious Jew, we shared similar views on the nature of religious faith and its relation to democratic values. Terry called this position "openness with roots" and argued that it is entirely consistent with the sort of autonomy required of democratic citizens. He called this approach to moral independence "autonomy via faith."

To distinguish this account of moral independence from the sort of rational autonomy often associated with comprehensive liberalism, I have tended to follow Charles Taylor in referring to my own understanding of this sort of independence as "human agency." The sort of tradition that seeks to engage a view of transcendence consistent with this sort of agency, I dub "intelligent spirituality." Together these terms point to the sort of hermeneutic we need to embrace in interpreting both liberalism and faith traditions—if we are to find the Aristotelian golden mean in which the two find common cause.

The first two chapters in this part explore the relation between this account of agency and spirituality to leading theories of curriculum and moral education. The third chapter is a revised edition of a paper first published in a Terrence McLaughlin tribute volume entitled *Faith in Education*, which is an expanded version of my Terrence McLaughlin Memorial Lecture given at the Institute of Education, University of London, in June 2007. It takes up McLaughlin's side of a debate with Stanford University's Eamonn Callan over the liberal rights of parents to educate their children in religion. I include it here in revised form because it constitutes a seminal point in the philosophical project recorded in this volume. Although written initially as a defense of what I take to be McLaughlin's view on religious initiation in liberal democracy, it has also come to serve as a summary of my own views on the subject to date.

CHAPTER EIGHT

Human Agency and the Curriculum

Introduction

Philosophers have long held that education in the fullest sense entails initiation into communities in pursuit of worthwhile knowledge.[1] As I argued in Chapter Five, addressing the question of what is *worth* knowing requires a conception of what it means for something to be worthwhile,[2] regardless of how one conceives the nature of knowledge; and this entails a stance concerning what it means to live a good life.[3] Yet recent curriculum thought has tended to deny or undermine one or another aspect of the key assumption upon which a meaningful account of desirability depends—that people are the agents of their own beliefs, desires, and actions. This renders a significant encounter between the curriculum and substantive ethics highly problematic.[4]

In this chapter, I examine how four seminal curriculum theories relate to human agency: those of Ralph Tyler, Joseph Schwab, Elliot Eisner, and the critical pedagogues. Although they do not exhaust the rich variety of alternatives within the curriculum field, these theories provide a glimpse of how curriculum studies writ large have grappled with Socrates's question. They have exerted considerable influence on major traditions of curriculum thought, are illustrative of the prevailing assumptions among a number of leading orientations, and address a breadth of behavioral, cognitive, emotional, and political aspects of human experience with which the curriculum ought to be concerned.[5] Before turning to these curriculum orientations, however, I should say more about the connection between ethics, human agency, and the curriculum.

Ethics and human agency

Crucial to any ethical stance, I have been arguing, is the assumption that human beings possess agency. This means that they have the freedom, within reasonable limits, to choose their beliefs, desires, and actions; the intelligence to distinguish between better and worse according to some conception of these notions; and the capacity to make mistakes in what they believe, feel, and do.[6] I have called these the conditions of moral or ethical discourse: freedom, moral intelligence, and fallibility.[7] It is pointless for people to consider what sort of life they should live if their beliefs and behaviors are determined by history or society or chemistry or the gods, if they cannot understand the difference between worthwhile or worthless according to some account of these terms, or if they are destined to be either good or bad by providence or their very nature.[8]

These conditions can be clarified by reference to three concepts that emerge in Charles Taylor's conception of human agency: self-determination, self-expression, and strong evaluation. Free will is related to self-determination. Taylor follows Immanuel Kant in believing that personal autonomy is a "transcendental condition" of ethics, an assumption we must make for any conception of normative discourse to make sense. Ethics is concerned with persuading a person to discipline her will to act or arrange her life in a certain way. If it is not, in fact, within a person's sphere of influence to direct her will, if she is not in this sense autonomous, then it is futile to endeavor to persuade her to desire this rather than that or to behave in this way rather than that, since she is not the agent in charge of her desires or behavior.

Moral intelligence is connected to what Taylor calls self-expression. He follows G. W. F. Hegel in recognizing that for a person to be able to exercise autonomy, she must be able to ground her choices in some sort of reasoning or understanding; otherwise her choices would not actually be hers, but rather a product of caprice.[9] This requires "horizons of significance" or "transcendental ideals" embedded in moral traditions sufficiently "thick" to sustain meaningful moral choice—not mere reflections of arbitrary taste, personal whim, or momentary feeling—to which competing conceptions of the good give expression, even if we cannot agree on their content.[10]

For self-expression to be meaningful, moreover, we must suppose that people have the capacity to engage in a particular kind of self-evaluation. This is connected to what I have called fallibility, or the capacity to err. Unlike animals that possess only first-order desires concerning such needs as food, procreation, and survival, humans also possess second-order desires— desires about desires—in which they evaluate their primary preferences.[11]

It is useful to distinguish between two sorts of second-order desires. I can choose, in the first instance, between, say, two flavors of ice cream. Taylor calls this "weak evaluation," because the decisive factor in choosing one flavor over another is how I feel at the moment. Today I feel like choosing vanilla, but tomorrow I might prefer chocolate. I can also choose, however, between risking my life to save a friend in battle or running away to save myself. The crucial factor in this instance is not how I feel at a given moment, but how I assess the worth of a particular feeling. I might consider the desire to save a friend courageous or generous, for example, and the motivation to run cowardly or selfish. Or, I might think it foolish to risk my life for another, and eminently sensible to look out for myself first. It is this sort of assessment, which Taylor calls "strong evaluation," that we must express in making autonomous ethical decisions, if they are to be meaningful in other than a weak sense. Humans require strong values upon which to base ethical judgments, but they do not always live up to those values. However, they are capable of recognizing when they do not do so, through a process of self-examination that includes strong evaluation of their own desires and behaviors.[12]

Whatever else it presupposes, then, to the extent that it is concerned with worthwhile knowledge, curriculum thought must assume that teachers and students possess agency, that they are capable of self-determination, self-expression, and strong evaluation. In what follows, I argue that Tyler runs afoul of self-determination, Schwab of self-expression, Eisner of strong evaluation, and critical pedagogy of all three.[13] This has led me to the conclusion that the role of ethics in curriculum discourse needs to be reconsidered. In the final section of this chapter, I make some preliminary suggestions as to what this might entail.

The Tyler rationale

Tyler is often associated with the technological movement in curriculum thought.[14] He responded to the so-called "scientific curriculum making" of Franklin Bobbitt and W. W. Charters, according to which the curriculum should prepare students for adult life.[15] The tasks to be mastered to that end are to be determined by means of a statistical survey of daily adult behaviors.[16] Unfortunately, this assumes that current adult behaviors are those that ought to be taught to children, which, as Boyd Bode pointed out, is not always the case.[17] Additionally, it assumes that we can conclude from the way things are how they ought to be, and as David Hume long ago pointed out, this is logically problematic.[18] This problem is commonly associated with what G. E. Moore called the "naturalistic fallacy,"[19] although Moore's formulation differed in significant ways from Hume's.[20]

Tyler addressed this, among other concerns, by suggesting that three sources be consulted to determine curriculum objectives: the learners themselves, the social environment, and the subject matter. By comparing an assessment of what students know in a given field to what the society and subject matter require them to learn, we can establish the proper objectives in each discipline. Since there are likely to be many more objectives than can be attained, the results of this process should be sifted through two screens—the philosophy of the school and the psychology of learning. The first establishes the normative priorities of the school and the latter the appropriate developmental stages at which each priority should be addressed.

To establish the objectives of a language or mathematics curriculum, for instance, we should first assess what the students already know and compare this to what the social environment and subject matter require. French or American schools will demand different levels of language proficiency at home than they do abroad, and a math program in a science magnet school will have different expectations than that of an arts-centered school. Whatever the environment, the subject matter will require much more than can be accomplished in any given academic year. So the school philosophy should be consulted to establish priorities, and educational psychology should be consulted to determine developmental appropriateness. The school philosophy can help to allocate resources such as instructional time, money for textbooks, language labs, and other instructional aids. Educational psychology will assist in deciding what students of a given age can be expected to achieve.

Once the objectives have been determined, Tyler then asked the curriculum planner to consider the experiences that might ensure that they are achieved, the ways in which those experiences should be organized, and how they ought to be evaluated. Tyler was among the first curriculum theorists to conceive the curriculum process in terms of student learning and social conditions, rather than subject matter alone. He held that objectives should be stated in terms of measurable student outcomes, that a variety of experiences in addition to frontal instruction can assist students in achieving those objectives, that student interest is an important guide in choosing among the available experiential alternatives, that experiences should be organized to emphasize conception connection among disciplines, and that the curriculum planning process is not complete until student achievement has been achieved. Despite these contributions, however, he did not succeed in overcoming the normative difficulties that plagued his predecessors.

In a well-known critique, curriculum historian Herbert Kliebard pointed out that to assess students' knowledge or the demands of any given subject matter, we must first know what subjects are to be taught.[21] However, this is the whole point of curriculum development—to determine what those subjects ought to be. In other words, according to Kliebard's critique, to determine what subjects should be taught we must already know what they are. The sources of objectives may help to refine the desired behaviors the curriculum should seek to attain, but at the end of the day the real work of curriculum development comes down to the normative philosophy of the school, which is predetermined by the adult society. Yet, Tyler offers no guidance as to how to evaluate competing claims among normative philosophies of education. Like his predecessors Bobbitt and Charters, he uncritically assumes that the way things are is the way they ought to be.

But Tyler's difficulties with the normative side of the curriculum run deeper than this. Kliebard also questioned the morality of manipulating educational environments to achieve predetermined behavioral objectives.[22] Does not the very idea of stating curriculum aims in terms of predetermined measurable objectives presume that the outcomes of learning can be controlled by the educational experiences in which the learner is required to participate? Where is the will, or desire, or interest of students in this scheme? To be sure, Tyler calls upon the curriculum planner to measure the interests of students in assessing the needs of the learners, and even asks that student interest be taken into account when planners select educational experiences for learners. Yet in the final analysis, the interests of society— expressed in the philosophical screen and translated into experiences designed to ensure outcomes—will always trump student desires. It would appear that interest is to be consulted, in Tyler's curriculum, primarily for the purpose of packaging predetermined social objectives to make them appealing to students, rather than to actively engage their genuine aspirations and concerns.

Tyler might respond, of course, that aspirations are socially determined, and that one purpose of the curriculum is to shape student desires according to social needs, or at least to provide a basis upon which autonomous decisions might later be founded. Communities of all sorts—political, cultural, religious, linguistic, or ethnic—have legitimate interests in inculcating their particular concerns in their children.[23] But this response misses the key point: Kliebard questioned not only the inadequacy of Tyler's approach to competing social needs and rival educational philosophies but also the morality of his assumption that learning should be defined primarily in terms of experiences designed to produce predetermined outcomes. Tyler did not consider whether students might at any time embrace those outcomes, either when they are asked to achieve them, or later on when, according to some views, people are better prepared by virtue of accumulated learning or maturity to make such assessments. Nor did he suggest that the task of the curriculum is to form student desires by persuading them to appreciate or encouraging them to choose certain ends over others. Rather, the only way for students to embrace desired outcomes, according to the Tyler rationale, would be through experiences that are prearranged to produce those outcomes, whether or not a student might at some point be so convinced or inclined. Yet, the very idea that social or any other sort of interests are *morally* legitimate only makes sense when we recognize that people, including students, are agents endowed with the capacity for self-determination. We flatten the ethical significance of social or other concerns, therefore, to the extent that we ignore, suppress, or subvert this essential human capacity.

A second defense of Tyler's position might claim that this critique conflates two different sorts of actions or policies: (i) those that undermine the autonomous actions of particular people under certain circumstances, thus impeding their capacity for moral judgment, and (ii) those that implicitly deny a presupposition of moral agency, such as autonomy, even though the people subject to those policies might nevertheless remain moral agents. Kliebard's position pertains to the first sort of actions or policies, it might be argued, whereas the thesis of this chapter, that contemporary curriculum theory is conceptually ill-equipped to assess the worth of the learning that it prescribes, relates to the second. However, this distinction does not appear to withstand criticism. A curriculum theory prescribes policies concerning what to teach children in school and how to teach it to them. To say that an approach to curriculum implicitly denies this or that supposition of agency (or anything else for that matter) can mean nothing other than that it directs school personnel to relate to students in particular ways. To conceive of curriculum in ways that undermine the autonomy of this or that student, therefore, is just what it means to deny, implicitly or otherwise, that self-determination is a condition of moral agency necessary to make sense of judgments about the value of the learning a curriculum prescribes.

By attempting to sideline the will of students, Tyler undermines a key assumption of human agency necessary for normative discourse to have meaning. There is a deep tension within a curriculum that offers an account of what is most worth knowing, which is what the Tyler rationale proposed to do, but that flattens the self-determination of students; for the very idea of something being worthwhile requires the assumption that, within reasonable limits, students are agents of their own desires, beliefs, and actions.

Schwab and the structure of the disciplines

An especially influential approach to the academic curriculum during the past half-century was launched in the 1960s as "the structure of the disciplines" movement. Schwab, Tyler's colleague at the University of Chicago, was a towering figure in this tradition.

Schwab and his structuralist colleagues responded to the rapid growth of knowledge by arguing that the curriculum could no longer provide students with a comprehensive knowledge of any given subject matter, since scientific discovery is moving so rapidly that what is believed to be true today may turn out to be false tomorrow. Instead of focusing solely on the substance of a discipline, its basic concepts and findings, the curriculum should also teach the syntax of a discipline, its methods of discovery and justification. Such an inquiry-based curriculum would teach students not only the matter of a discipline, as Richard Peters called it,[24] but, more importantly, its epistemological form—the tools of investigation and critical assessment used by scholars to discover new knowledge.[25] For this reason, the structuralist approach to curriculum has sometimes been associated with what came to be known as the "discovery method."[26]

How are we to devise such a curriculum? Schwab had a unique and ingenious answer. Following Aristotle's distinction between theoretical knowledge (*Sophia*) and practical wisdom (*Phronesis*), he held that curriculum is a practical, not a theoretical, discipline.[27] Its aim is not to discover laws of nature, society, behavior, or education, but to translate those discoveries into practical strategies for teaching the structure of disciplines. The products of curriculum development are alternative lesson plans that anticipate instructional challenges in teaching a particular subject matter, not experiences designed to meet objectives measurable by the tools of social or behavioral science.

Arriving at such plans is a complex process, because the disciplines to be taught and the research that provides guidance for how to teach them are not static doctrines to be memorized and applied, but dynamic disciplines rich with scholarly discussion and debate. The challenge is to create an ongoing conversation between those working to discover new disciplinary and pedagogic knowledge and those endeavoring to teach students in school. This process, which Schwab called "curriculum deliberation," engages representatives of the essential ingredients of curriculum in dynamic discussions about how best to translate theory into practice. He called these ingredients "commonplaces"—teaching, students, subject matter, and milieu. Since there is no one right way to teach a discipline, the creation of practical pedagogic wisdom requires the "arts of eclectic," an integrated application of the most compelling and relevant theories from both the subject matter itself and the study of how best to teach it.[28] Lee Shulman was later to call this sort of practical wisdom "pedagogic-content knowledge," the unique understanding that is accumulated in the teaching of an academic discipline.[29]

Unlike Tyler and the curriculum technologists, Schwab and his structuralist colleagues were not ambivalent about normative discourse in curriculum thought. But they were ambiguous. A normative educational philosophy is implied in the communal requirements of what Schwab called milieu. However, Schwab is unclear about whether normative philosophy should provide the conceptual and ethical frame that guides curriculum deliberation. If so, how is it to be determined, given Schwab's complex, plural, and evolving conception of theory? If normative visions of education are to be considered as but one of a number of types of theories to be taken into account during the process of deliberation, how can it be said that the curriculum subscribes to a normative vision?

This ambiguity is related to an epistemological problem with curriculum structuralism that raises questions about the second condition of human agency—moral intelligence and self-expression. In arguing that scientific theories are more tentative and partial than was previously supposed, Schwab became an early critic of naïve empiricism and a pioneer of postpositivism in educational research.[30] Since the findings of inquiry are underdetermined by data, theoretical expectations and conceptual frameworks play a significant role in the formulation of explanations. These frameworks are organized into disciplines or forms of knowledge each with its own assumptions, concepts, and methods of inquiry. This leads to a strong form of cognitive relativism, which holds that truth is a function of conceptual framework.

Although it does not follow logically from his epistemological position, Schwab appears to treat moral traditions like structures of knowledge. Since all moral positions are underdetermined by reasoning, and no argument exists that can sustain the superiority of one over another, normative positions must be evaluated within the context of the conceptual frameworks within which they are formulated, and a variety of competing (even contradictory) positions should be considered in making curriculum decisions. Ironically, and I believe unintentionally, this sort of relativism, both cognitive and moral, undermines the very critical spirit that the structuralists such as Schwab sought to promote, because it implies that it is senseless or unreasonable to criticize one framework on the basis of the assumptions of another. According to this view, the only sort of criticism permitted must come from within a conceptual scheme, and if a particular tradition or discipline cares little for logical consistency, even internal criticism may be ruled out.[31]

Schwab admitted that "the charge of relativism can be fairly laid against" his viewpoint.[32] Yet he embraced this sort of relativism in response to the dogmatism of scientific positivism, which held that truth and goodness could be only defined in terms of a very narrow empiricism. His intention was to create an eclectic basis for educational practice in which a rich variety of normative as well as empirical traditions, from Plato and Aristotle to Sigmund Freud and B. F. Skinner, could play equally challenging roles in making curriculum decisions. As he put the point, "if scientific knowledge can be sought in many ways, it is not because science is a game, a systematic delusion, or the pursuit of metaphors of mnemonics. Rather ... it is because nature is so rich in matters to be learned and scientists so apt in finding ways to learn them."[33]

In throwing out arbitrary and overly simplistic empirical standards, however, Schwab may have gone too far, by blurring important epistemological distinctions between truth and falsehood. And in adopting a parallel stance toward moral traditions, Schwab may have embraced an overly eclectic attitude toward normative visions of education that weakens our capacity to identify value differences between better and worse. This threatens the possibility of moral intelligence and self-expression. If every moral tradition is as good as every other, it becomes impossible in principle to distinguish between good and bad or right and wrong according to any theory. Of course, one might respond a la Alasdair MacIntyre that certain goods are internal to discipline-based practices and that the comparative worth of various moral ideals and traditions can only be judged from the perspective of the various moral ideals and traditions available to us.[34] However, MacIntyre assumes with Aristotle that rival moral traditions struggle to grasp a common *telos*, or ultimate good, unarticulated in Schwab's writings, even if they may never reach agreement as to its most adequate formulation. For self-expression to be morally meaningful, it must reflect more than mere personal or conceptual or collective preference. This is not to say that there is only one moral tradition that can provide a normative frame for curriculum deliberations, but rather that any putative conception of the good must appeal to horizons of significance that transcend the indeterminate circumstance in which we find ourselves, even if we may not be able to agree as to their nature or content.[35]

Eisner's aesthetic humanism

If Tyler's technological curriculum focuses on producing desired behaviors and Schwab's academic structuralism on cognitive processes, the humanistic curriculum turns our attention to emotional dimensions of education. One important theorist in this tradition is Eisner, who is known for his systematic exploration of art as a root metaphor for the processes of teaching and educating.[36]

To conceive education as an art requires an aesthetic theory. For this, Eisner turned to Suzanne Langer's analysis of art as the symbolic expression of feeling. As seen previously, Langer grounded art in two important distinctions: between discursive and nondiscursive expression, and between logical and dynamic form.[37] Discursive expression is abstract, conceptual, and theoretical. We use it to communicate about our world in daily and academic life, from shopping lists and travel directions to scholarly discoveries and scientific theories. Nondiscursive expression, on the other hand, is concrete, particular, and experiential. We use it to communicate about dimensions of experience where words and concepts fail us—for instance, in expressing intense emotions such as love or anger. This sort of expression often relies on religious rituals, artistic symbols, or metaphoric language to create immediate, virtual, or vicarious experience.

Logical form, according to Langer, is rigorous, structured, and fixed. It is concerned with the precise measurements and conceptual contours of reality. For instance, two lampshades that share precisely the same profile but for size can be said to have the same logical form. Dynamic form, on the other hand, speaks to the shape of experiences that are fleeting and in flux. The description of an automobile accident by a police officer, for example, will strive to express the logical form of the events in discursive language: when the accident happened, the direction of each car before they collided, where they ended up immediately afterwards, and so on. But the stories told by the drivers to their families and friends will be filled with emotion. They will seek to capture the emotional shape of the accident through expressive language that involves the listener in a vicarious experience of it.

The academic curriculum prefers discursive expression of logical form. It aims to convey concepts, methods of inquiry, and truths in the precise theoretical language associated with scholarship. The fine arts, on the other hand, aim to capture the dynamic form of human feeling in nondiscursive expression such as symbols and metaphors.[38] To take seriously the image of teaching and education as fine arts, then, we must understand how they use nondiscursive expression to capture and communicate the shape of human feeling. Eisner offers such an understanding by rethinking curriculum content and evaluation, rather than in a new approach to its design and construction.

Eisner conceives curriculum subject matter in terms of what he calls "forms of representation." In contrast to the structure of a discipline that emphasizes its mode of inquiry, the notion of a form of representation stresses a mode of expression. "People don't paint what they see," Eisner is fond of musing "they see what they can paint." The shape of consciousness is determined by the ways we represent experience, not by how we study it. Art and science are both forms in which we represent what we experience. Excluding forms of representation such as the fine arts from the curriculum, as so often occurs in state schools, denies students the opportunity to appreciate the sort of experience that the arts capture, indeed to enjoy those experiences altogether. In terms of the Hegelian formulation borrowed from Charles Taylor as previously discussed, limiting the forms of representation in the curriculum restricts the capacity of students to acquire new and unimagined traditions and media within which to exercise self-expression. The optimum curriculum will expose students to as many forms of representation as time and other resources permit.[39]

If the curriculum initiates students into a collection of artistic forms, the evaluation of curriculum entails appreciating and critiquing the ways in which those forms have been represented. To view teaching and education as fine arts requires that assessment be conceived as artistic connoisseurship and criticism. Connoisseurship refers to the refined taste for a particular art form—taste that is acquired through extensive personal experience as either a creator or student of that art. It involves the capacity for judging quality, for assessing the artistic merit of a particular work of art. Educational connoisseurship, then, is a form of understanding what goes on in classrooms based on personal experience. Educational criticism, on the other hand, is a form of representing that knowledge. It involves commenting on pedagogic activities in rich, metaphoric terms in order to transform how we perceive and do our educational work.[40]

This conception of curriculum and evaluation expands our thinking about the tasks of education by placing the affective domain and subjective experience at its core. It recognizes that the curriculum needs to influence feeling and creative self-expression as well as thinking, to foster love of learning, mold commitment and dedication, and shape the student's deepest appreciation of what it means to be devoted to people and ideals. Following Plato, Schwab called this the education of "eros."[41] It is not enough to teach about friendship and fellowship, we must engage students with comrades; it is not enough to discuss love of community, or tradition, or beauty, or God, we must involve students in symbolic activities that facilitate these sorts of emotions; and it is not enough to deliberate about those who are different, we must engage students actively and creatively with the Other.

Nevertheless, although Eisner is acutely sensitive to the impact of what we choose not to teach, he offers little guidance concerning how to make those choices.[42] If every form of representation is as suitable for inclusion in the curriculum as any other, how are we to distinguish between those that are more or less worthwhile? Under these circumstances, it is difficult to assess whether or to what degree particular curriculum alternatives are more or less desirable. This undermines the third assumption of moral agency mentioned here, fallibility, or the possibility of being wrong.[43] The very self-expression Eisner seeks to promote would appear to require what Taylor calls strong values that enable the assessment of the quality of an experience.[44] Yet, Eisner shies away from such strong evaluation when he fails to offer an account of how to distinguish the relative worth of forms of representation that compete for time and resources in the curriculum. In short, Eisner's aesthetic approach to self-expression appears to rely on too "weak" or "thin" or "merely" personal an account of the values needed to make curriculum decisions and assess classroom experience.[45]

This point is driven home, it seems to me, by Eisner's tendency to posit a personal conception of connoisseurship as the primary source for assessing the merit of educational experiences. This weakens the meaning of the term "merit." It is not enough for educational criticism to reeducate our perception of educational events according to the connoisseurship of an experienced educator alone. For this sort of personal assessment to be meaningful, it must carry weight because the connoisseur has acquired an appreciation for a standard of excellence; and for such standards to have meaning, they must appeal to strong values that transcend self and society.[46] Yet it is the very possibility of this kind of strong evaluation that Eisner appears to avoid in stressing the role of personal understanding in the assessment of school programs.

One might respond, of course, that standards of merit are implicit within the forms of representation themselves. If the connoisseur is to base her assessment of an educational program on a merely personal interpretation of these contextualized standards, however, the attendant conception of merit remains weak, since assessment will be grounded primarily on individual taste. We might suppose, on the other hand, that standards of excellence are agreed upon by recognized practitioners of various activities or discourses. Unfortunately, this could too easily lead to a self-refuting form of relativism that assumes, for example, that programs can only be assessed according to standards internal to a particular viewpoint or tradition. But this would imply that one would have to accept the presuppositions of a particular form of representation in order to criticize it. Moreover, if a tradition rejects the very idea of a standard of merit, it would be difficult to sort out what educational criticism or assessment in this context could possibly mean. To engage in what Taylor calls strong evaluation requires that connoisseurs assess the quality of, not merely express, their own personal or collective preferences, and for this to be possible, the standards of merit that they employ need to emanate from beyond the narrow confines of self or community or form of expression. However, Eisner's tendency to situate the source of aesthetic authority within either individual connoisseurs or communities of practitioners appears to preclude such a transcendent point of view.

Critical pedagogy and the radical curriculum

Eisner wrote of the three curricula that all schools teach: the explicit curriculum that is announced in brochures, course syllabi, and textbooks; the implicit curriculum, which is embedded in classroom norms and student–teacher relations; and the null curriculum, which refers to what we do not teach.[47] Practitioners and policy makers often ignore the latter two curricula. For critical social theorists such as Michael Apple, however, the implicit and null curricula are not merely ignored; they are hidden by those in power. Grounded in critical social theory (Marxism, neo-Marxism, postmodernism), this approach to curriculum seeks to expose unspoken assumptions of schooling in order to reveal how education is used by dominant classes and cultures to reproduce the power relations embedded in the status quo.[48]

Critical social theorists hold that beneath the surface of social life lies conflict between the powerful and the powerless.[49] Those who have power based on wealth, lineage, or majority rule use culture to impose on others an ideology that sustains their power. This ideology or discourse—expressed in language, media, religion, knowledge, morality, and education—obscures the fact of oppression from those who are enslaved, to the degree that some even prefer subjugation to liberation. Marx called this "false consciousness."[50] Marxist and neo-Marxist theorists are considered modernists. They believe that false consciousness can be overcome for a liberated consciousness based on total equality of material and cultural resources. Postmodern theorists, on the other hand, are more pessimistic. In their view, power is inherent in all human activity. We can only become conscious of domination, not overcome it.[51] Both believe that epistemological ideas such as truth and knowledge and moral ideas such as right and wrong have no "objective" basis outside of the power interests they serve. However, to the former, all beliefs and behaviors are ideological save those dedicated to liberating the oppressed, whereas, to the latter, beliefs and behaviors are comprised of dominating discourses from which there can be no liberation.[52] The task of critical pedagogy, an educational orientation influenced by critical social theory, is to expose the hidden tools of domination utilized by those in power so that students can embrace more authentic ideologies and discourses that reflect their own cultural, social, and political interests.[53]

Critical social analysis assumes that all education is either ideological or an expression of hegemonic discourse. The question is not whether but which ideology to inculcate, or, alternatively, not whether but which discourse to expose.[54] It might appear that this is entirely consistent with my call for a return to substantive ethics in curriculum thought,[55] but this is not so, because radical curriculum theory uses such terms as ideology and discourse in what I have called an amoral (or nonethical) rather than a moral (or ethical) sense. Recall that moral ideologies and discourses embrace the conditions of human agency. They are not moral in the sense that they embrace a particular substantive ethic, although the conditions of moral agency are by no means value-free, but in that they accept the transcendental conditions that make it possible to have meaningful ethical discourse. Amoral ideologies and discourses, on the other hand, deny these conditions. They assume that beliefs and behaviors are not chosen, but determined by family, or socioeconomic class, or culture.[56]

By advocating that children ought to be liberated from or made conscious of hegemonic culture in order to serve ideological interests or new discourses they may not necessarily embrace, radical curriculum theory employs such terms as ideology and discourse in an amoral sense; and since all truths and values are relative to class, culture, race, or gender, save those for the modernists that reflect the necessity of liberating the oppressed, there is no way to assess whether the interests of a particular child, however they might be interpreted, are in fact being served by this new ideology of liberation or exposed hegemonic discourse.[57] This undermines all three assumptions of human agency. The child does not make choices that give expression to her own strong values, either now or upon reaching maturity. Values are not chosen at all, but determined by ideology, culture, class, or dominant discourse. It is assumed, therefore, that she will express the values of her culture or social class and embrace liberation as defined by others, whether or not she would choose such a form of liberty for herself. Positions of this kind do not engage substantive ethics; they render such an engagement deeply problematic.[58]

Consider one representative illustration. At the end of *Education and Power*, Apple writes with critical appreciation of political economists and cultural reproduction theorists in education:

> Thus, a particular kind of discipline has been required here, one that is critical of overly reductionist and economist categories that have proven in the long run to be damaging to the Marxist tradition, and

one which—at the same time—interrogates the school with an interest in uncovering the roots of domination and exploitation that undoubtedly exist. This...involves criticizing a tradition and using it at the same time.... While it is important to realize that schools do reproduce gender relations and the social relations of reproduction, "behind their backs," they also reproduce historically specific forms of resistance."[59]

Based on this, I have suggested strategies and action on a variety of fronts: within schools and universities involving curriculum, democratizing technical knowledge, using and politicizing the lived culture of students and teachers, etc.; and outside the school involving both educational practices in progressive labor unions, political and feminist groups, and so on, and in political action to build a mass socialist and democratic movement in the United States.[60]

The ideological agenda of this perspective is clear; and my point is not that this agenda makes no contribution to curriculum thought and practice. Rather it overreaches because of an ambivalence concerning free choice. Apple suggests strategies to uncover the roots of "exploitation" and "domination" as critical pedagogy sees it, presumably to liberate students so that they can make choices based on the radical insights they have gained. But what of a young woman who finds fulfillment in a particular religious orientation that Apple might consider oppressive of women, or a young man who would prefer to remain loyal to his family or community, even though this may require submitting to the authority of parents or tradition? Surely these young people should be offered opportunities to move on if they so choose. By exposing hidden structures and forces that would deny or subvert such opportunities, critical thought in education makes a significant contribution. But with equal surety, these youngsters should be allowed to decline opportunities to look elsewhere without disrespect if this is their preference, and here it seems to me is where the trouble begins.[61]

Radical curriculum theory too often appears to embrace what Isaiah Berlin called liberty in the "positive sense," which addresses the question, "What, or who, is the source of control or interference that can determine someone to do, or be, this rather than that?"[62] Berlin argues that what gives plausibility to this sort of reasoning is that

we recognize that it is possible, and at times justifiable, to coerce men in the name of some goal (let us say justice or public health) which they would, if they were sufficiently enlightened, themselves pursue, but do not, because they are blind or ignorant or corrupt. This renders it easy for me to conceive of myself as coercing others for their sake, in their, not my, interest. I am then claiming that I know what they truly need better than they know themselves.[63]

The tendency to decide what is best for someone, whether or not he or she would agree, is often more subtle in the views expressed by Apple and his colleagues than in the left- and right-leaning orthodoxies to which Berlin was referring when he wrote these words; indeed Apple himself as cited here criticizes some of these very orthodoxies. Nevertheless, these tendencies can be found, for example, in the ways radicals sometimes use the term "progressive" to suggest that those who do not embrace their views are "backward" or "regressive"; or the designation "democratic" to hint that those who do not endorse Apple's mass socialist movement are less democratic or undemocratic; or the expression "resistance" to intimate that those in favor of reproducing some of the social relations opposed by radicals are sympathetic to oppression.[64] The problem, of course, is not in the use of these terms per se—other movements have described themselves as "progressive," or "democratic," or dedicated to "resistance," but rather in the exclusiveness (almost intolerance) with which these terms are too often appropriated, in ways that cast aspersions on the views or actions of those who might use them differently, or who are not comfortable with the style of argumentation associated with critical social theory, or who believe that their interests lie elsewhere—implying that those uses or discomforts or interests are morally suspect or expressions of a false or inauthentic self, because they do not sense the need to "resist" "domination" or "exploitation," as conceived in critical, or poststructural, or postcolonial, or some other critical social theory.[65]

My point is not that radical curriculum theory is illiberal because it fails to embrace autonomy, but rather that in diminishing the significance of human agency, it tends to undermine the *moral* bite of the claim that one group or another has suffered oppression, because it undercuts the conditions necessary for ethical concepts to be meaningful altogether.[66] Instead, its antidote—"liberation" or "critical consciousness"—runs the risk of replacing one form of subjugation with another.[67] In an amoral universe, power—not ethics—is the primary court of appeals; and force of one kind or another too often appears to be the only recourse to resolve differences or redress perceived injustice.[68]

Human agency in the curriculum

To speak of ethics in the curriculum does not require an alternative account of instructional content, design, or evaluation, which might well be derived from an eclectic application of these and other curriculum orientations, taking into account some of the difficulties I have mentioned. Rather, to engage ethics in the curriculum requires a conception of what it means for an educational program to be better or worse, and this can be articulated only within the context of a conception of the good. Although there is no single ethical vision that all curricula are bound to promote, they must embrace the formal criteria without which the very idea of an ethical stance is meaningless in other than a weak sense—that people have the capacity for agency. However, this capacity is not an innate ability that will develop on its own. Indeed, the awareness and facility for agency can be just as easily ignored or suppressed as fostered, so it is a fundamental task of every curriculum to promote an awareness of the capacity for agency among those it proposes to influence. Let us conclude then by considering how each of the conditions of agency—free will or self-determination, moral intelligence or self-expression, and fallibility or self-evaluation—might be incorporated into the curriculum.

Free will or self-determination

To foster free will and self-determination, the primary concern of any curriculum must be the ultimate independence of children, their ability upon reaching maturity to understand within reasonable limits the options they face and the consequences of choosing one direction over another, and their ability to make intelligent choices based on this understanding. Whatever value educators may attribute to this or that subject matter or pedagogy, cultivating the moral potential of the child as a human agent is always of greater importance, since without an awareness of our capacity for agency, the very idea of something being important makes no sense.[69] We teach subject matter not to liberate students from forms of oppression that they may or may not agree to perceive as such, but to give them greater cognitive and affective control over their own lives.[70] This sort of education is associated with what Berlin called liberty in the "negative sense," which is concerned with the question, "What is the area within which the subject—a person or group of persons—is or should be left to do or be what he is able to do or be, without interference by other persons?"[71]

   To live meaningfully in and contribute productively to a society conceived in such a conception of liberty requires the ability to assess not only the strength of an argument, but also the quality (according to some conception) of a piece of art or literature, the significance of a historical or a sociological development, or the contribution of a scientific or technological innovation as well as the capacity to understand or reproduce them.[72] Education for self-determination implies fostering a critical stance toward subject matter, not only in the sense of the ability to employ and assess reasons,[73] but also—and perhaps more importantly—in terms of the capacity to appraise quality or significance, to evaluate not only the amount of happiness one may achieve by making one choice rather than another, or the strength of the reasoning that favors that choice, but also the relative worth of the satisfaction that may be realized from making it.

Moral intelligence or self-expression

Qualitative judgments of this kind, however, only make sense within the context of ethical orientations that enable one to say that this is more important than that. And to make such judgments possible, a tradition must meet at least two conditions. First, to serve as a basis for a person's self-determined choices—what Taylor calls a "source of the self"—a moral tradition must be an expression of one's identity, integral to how one conceives who one aspires to be.[74] Second, to achieve this level of ownership and investment, a tradition needs to be sufficiently robust and emotionally compelling to inspire affiliation and identification.

As to the first condition Martin Buber's distinction between objective and subjective learning can help to clarify what it means for a tradition to become part of one's identity. Buber, it should be recalled, distinguished between two moments in relationships. One can relate to another as a subject to an object—what Buber called I–It relations—in which the subject uses the object to achieve some instrumental end; or one can also relate to another as a subject to another subject—what he called I–Thou relations—in which, at least for a few precious moments, to use Buber's beautiful language, "the other fills the firmament." There is a receiving of the other into oneself, a mystical union of sorts in which it becomes difficult to distinguish between one's own feelings and those of the other. The other, in this sense, becomes part of me, and I become part of the other.[75]

Buber applied this analysis to relations between students and subject matter. One can relate to learning as a subject to an object, in which case the knowledge acquired is employed to achieve some instrumental end, such as professional development, technological innovation, or even the advancement of knowledge. This attitude clearly plays an important role in the curriculum and is indicative of much, if not most, of the learning that takes place in schools. However, one can also relate to subject matter as one subject to another, in which case the knowledge acquired becomes part of my very being, integrated into my conception of who I choose to become.[76] For an ethical orientation to be a sufficiently integral expression of oneself to serve as a source for self-determined choice it must be transformed from this sort of objective into subjective learning.[77] From this it does not follow that ethical sources are merely "subjective" in the weak sense that they reflect one's personal taste or feelings at a particular moment. They are subjective rather in a strong sense in that they connect one's inner life with horizons of significance that transcend the self, so that the demands of community or tradition or nature or God become part and parcel of who one chooses to be.

As to the second condition—a sufficiently robust and emotionally compelling tradition—Michael Walzer's distinction between "thick" and "thin" moral theories can be useful in clarifying the sort of traditions that are the most likely candidates for promoting this sort of self-expression. We can distinguish, Walzer argues, between two different interrelated kinds of moral argument, "a way of talking among ourselves, here at home, about the thickness of our own history and culture … and a way of talking to people abroad, across different cultures, about a thinner life we have in common…. There are the makings of a thin and universalistic morality inside every thick and particular morality."[78] The conditions of human agency adumbrated here are clearly part of that thin universalistic ethic that many cultures and moral traditions share in common. And a curriculum concerned with engaging worthwhile knowledge will of necessity initiate students into some notion of common humanity or civil society, since, as I have been arguing, to count as ethical orientations, competing conceptions of the good must embrace and promote at least the assumptions of human freedom, intelligence, and fallibility.[79]

However, for this thin universalistic ethic to be sufficiently meaningful to serve as a source for self-determined choices, it must be embodied in the practices of a local community that displays the features of what Walzer calls moral maximalism: "It will be idiomatic in its language, particularist in its cultural references, and circumstantial in two senses of that word: historically dependent and factually detailed. Its principals and procedures will have been worked out over a long period of time through complex social interactions."[80] This is so for at least two reasons. First, this is how social and other goods present themselves in our lives. "The process as a whole," Walzer continues, "is surely misrepresented when it is described … as if it had been guided by a single, comprehensive, and universal principle. All such principles are abstractions and simplifications that, when analyzed, reveal their idiomatic, particularist, and circumstantial character."[81] Second, in order to undergo the transformation from objective to subjective learning, an ethic needs to be sufficiently emotionally compelling to engage a student's moral imagination. One is moved to live in this way for love of country, or culture, or family, or tradition, or reason, or God, or something else that has the capacity to ignite a commitment sufficiently passionate to serve as the guidepost of one's life. Robust and detailed cultural narratives, symbols, and artifacts that reflect the complexities and perplexities of real life are better able to inspire this level of commitment than high-level abstractions.[82]

Fallibility or self-evaluation

To assume that students are fallible and to promote strong evaluation means, among other things, that the moral understanding necessary to acquire or construct worthwhile knowledge is not innate but learned, that it is not in a person's very nature to grasp the wisdom of an ethical tradition or to behave well or poorly. Students might just as readily misunderstand as understand that tradition, or choose poorly as wisely. Whether or not they do so is a contingent matter, which implies that if they, in fact, comprehend the tradition's conception of what counts as worthwhile, or learn to desire or appreciate something of particular value, or choose to follow a virtuous course of action, they are to be credited with a meritorious intellectual, emotional, or practical accomplishment. And if they fail to achieve this understanding or appreciation, or to exercise this choice, they are in some measure responsible for the failure.

This is not to say that there are no factors beyond the student's control. All students are disadvantaged in some way or another, and some are obviously more advantaged than others—economically, intellectually, emotionally, artistically, and physically. Surely curriculum theory and educational policy should consider whether, when, and how to address these imbalances.[83] However, in so far as we are unwilling to hold students accountable for any portion of their learning, or to see them as responsible in some way when they miss the mark, they will face grave difficulty in acquiring or constructing or doing whatever a tradition deems appropriate with the knowledge that it considers to be worthwhile. An equally, if not more, important curricular and educational task, therefore, is to cultivate within students this sense of responsibility and accountability. This requires that students be encouraged to experience the exhilaration of genuine accomplishment when they succeed and to examine their own beliefs, desires, and actions when they have not achieved all that they had hoped. What might I have done differently? Where have I missed the mark? The strong evaluation required of future life choices begins with an assessment of the quality of personal investment a student has made in the learning process.[84]

Although this may sometimes mean that students will need to face uncomfortable aspects of their own personalities, and this can result in fear or stress, the upside is that they will come to recognize that they have the capacity to change course, to make a difference. What they do, feel, and think does in fact matter; and their inherent worth is to be discovered not in the feeling that they will get it right no matter what, but rather in the realization that they matter even when they get it wrong, indeed because they have the capacity to get it wrong, since were this not the case, it would literally make no sense to speak of anything mattering at all. Students can thus learn to accept themselves as imperfect but nonetheless worthwhile beings, even as they strive to improve where they can. The recognition that I am inherently worthwhile even though I make mistakes, coupled with the awareness that I have the capacity to contribute to a better tomorrow for myself and others, is a source of profound joy.[85]

Conclusion

A meaningful account of curriculum must begin with what can count as desirable, with what it means for knowledge on any account to be considered worthwhile, with the conditions of human agency. Attempts to conceive the curriculum in terms of establishing, realizing, and evaluating behavioral objectives, or the structure of disciplines or knowledge or rationality, or forms of aesthetic representation and evaluation, or the liberation of the oppressed have tended to undermine one or more of these conditions. To engage worthwhile knowledge requires that the curriculum not only presuppose these conditions as human capabilities but also actively promote them. This requires that students learn to make independent choices grounded in assessments not only of the reasoning entailed but also of the relative worth of various human activities and that these choices express their personal identification with thick ethical traditions within which strong evaluation makes sense. It also requires students to recognize that in the context of those traditions, they have the capacity to err in what they think, feel, and do, but that they can also change course and make a difference. This is a source of fear and trepidation, but also of great joy. Cultivating this sort of existential joy is, to my mind, the highest aspiration of any curriculum.

CHAPTER NINE

Moral Education and Liberal Democracy

Introduction

In *Reclaiming Goodness* I argued that the recent spiritual awakening can be understood as a response to a political success and moral failing of modernity. The political success entails the creation of modern liberal democracies that enable people of conflicting conceptions of the good to live in a common civil society. A consequence of the openness such a society requires, however, is sustained difficulty in cultivating particular visions of the good. Here is where the moral failure can be found. Over the recent past, parents and teachers have too often become inarticulate and insecure about what to say to children concerning how best to live their lives and the children of these confusing and uncertain times have begun to search elsewhere for responses to perennial existential questions.[1]

This argument grounds the spiritual quest in the search for a moral life, in the classical sense, of a life worth living. One sensible answer to this quest is what I call intelligent spirituality, which entails cultivating an authentic or excellent version of one's self in a learning community with a vision of a higher good.[2] In this chapter, I argue that liberal democratic societies require citizens with "thick" authentic identities characterized by particular as well as civic virtues cultivated in separate as well as common communities committed to visions of a higher good. Education in intelligent spirituality, in other words, is a liberal democratic imperative.

The account of moral education developed here prefers a liberal communitarian version of character education to a number of other influential approaches, such as cognitive moral developmental, the ethic of care, critical pedagogy, and more conservative interpretations of character education.[3] Without discounting the importance of the commons, it also places an educational burden on particular communities for cultivating the authentic self that democracy requires. Additionally, it shifts the responsibility for moral and citizenship education from schools alone to communities in which schools play a partial, if significant, role. Finally, it blurs differences between social science and the humanities in examining good practice in moral education and proposes renewed respect for the humanistic disciplines—literature, the arts, history, philosophy, and theology—to examine ethical heritage as a resource for pedagogy and educational policy as well as for subject matter content.[4]

The chapter is divided into five sections. In the first section, I examine the case for robust authenticity and "thick" identity in liberal democracy. In the second section, I examine four influential approaches to moral education: cognitive moral development, the ethic of care, critical pedagogy, and character education, in order to show that the latter has the best chance of educating democratic citizens with "thick" identities. In the third section, I examine several objections to character education and respond with a more refined, liberal communitarian account. In the fourth section, I review the conception of goodness as intelligent spirituality that this alternative requires. In the final section, I explore the sources of practical wisdom needed to implement this sort of moral education.

Thick identity and liberal democracy

We saw in Chapter Five that the terms *morality* and *ethics* are often used interchangeably in everyday speech as referring to justified or proper conduct, philosophers often viewing the former as a narrower and less theoretical category than the latter.[5] Over the past quarter-century, however, communitarian philosophers have recaptured an earlier, perhaps more original, use of the term "ethics" as having to do with what Bernard Williams called Socrates's question, how should one live?[6] They point out that since Immanuel Kant moral philosophy has been more concerned with judgments of moral obligation than judgments of moral value. Theories concerned with the former (which emphasize such terms as right, wrong, just, unjust, permissible, forbidden, obligatory, and prohibited) are often called deontological, from the Greek for duty or what one must do, while those focused on the latter (which examine such concepts as good, bad, admirable, deplorable, worthwhile, worthless, virtue, and vice) are called aretaic, from the Greek for virtue or excellence. Socrates's question is aretaic because it inquires about the nature of a good or worthwhile life.[7]

In addition to Kant, utilitarianism has also been influential in modern moral philosophy. Both defend the sort of liberal democracy mentioned at the outset that enables people with conflicting answers to Socrates's question to live together in a common civil society. In a broad sense, both utilitarian and Kantian ethics can be understood as aretaic theories, since utilitarianism is concerned with maximizing *goods* and Kantians view justice, fairness, and reasonableness as *virtues*. Using the term in this way blurs the distinction between judgments of moral obligation and judgments of moral value, however, since both utilitarians and Kantians have been especially concerned with the justification of moral obligation by grounding it in either the categorical imperative or the principle of utility. Jan Steutel and David Carr suggest, therefore, that we distinguish between virtues ethics in a broad sense that includes the utilitarian and Kantian accounts and in a narrower sense that excludes them.[8]

For example, both utilitarian and Kantian ethics prefer that individuals be allowed to choose their way of life, although they offer different accounts of what this implies. On the other hand, several, though by no means all, virtues ethics view their way of life imposed as obligatory due to external authorities such as families, communities, churches, and states. As John Stuart Mill put it, "the only freedom which deserves the name is that of pursuing our own good in our own way, so long as we do not attempt to deprive others of theirs or impede their effort to obtain it."[9]

Unfortunately, the utilitarian defense of this liberal principle is caught on the horns of a dilemma. The only criterion upon which to make moral judgments, in this view, is an aggregate of goods—the greatest good for the greatest number. What counts as a good to be included in this calculation, however, can only be determined according to individual preferences. Yet, if each person is to judge what is good for himself or herself according to his or her own unabated preference, on what grounds can we prefer such values as tolerance or freedom or fairness, or indeed the utility principle itself, to goods that emanate from less tolerant or liberal orientations, such as the preference of an unborn fetus's life to the choices of its mother, the importance of students praying to a particular God in common schools whether or not they or their parents believe in that God, or even the supremacy of one group over another? "The relativist defense of liberalism," as Michael Sandel wrote, "is no defense at all."[10]

On the other hand, if we take that aggregate seriously, what would prevent a public consensus or large majority from imposing its will on a small minority? "If enough cheering Romans pack the Coliseum to watch the lion devour the Christian," continues Sandel, "the collective pleasure of the Roman's will surely outweigh the pain of the Christian, intense though it may be."[11] From a Kantian perspective, "A wholly instrumental defense of freedom and rights not only leaves rights vulnerable, but fails to respect the inherent dignity of persons. The utilitarian calculus treats people as means to the happiness of others, not as ends in themselves worthy of respect."[12]

The Kantian solution to this dilemma is to draw a distinction between the Right and the Good, "between a framework of basic rights and liberties, and the conceptions of the good that people may choose to pursue within that framework."

For Kantian liberals, then, the right is prior to the good, and in two senses. First, individual rights cannot be sacrificed for the sake of the general good, and second, the principles of justice that specify these rights cannot be premised on any particular vision of the good. What justifies the rights is...that they comprise a fair framework within which individuals and groups can choose their own values and ends, consistent with a similar liberty for others.[13]

John Rawls became the leading contemporary defender of this view of Kantian liberalism due to the extraordinary influence of his theory of justice as fairness,[14] and the communitarians became its primary critics.

Recalling the arguments of Hegel against Kant, the communitarian critics of modern liberalism question the claim of the priority of the right over the good, and the picture of the freely-choosing individual it embodies. Following Aristotle, they argue that we cannot justify political arrangements without reference to common purposes and ends, and that we cannot conceive our personhood without reference to our role as citizens, and as participants in a common life.[15]

Liberal democracy requires a citizen tied to others, in this view, by common purposes and ends shared in a common life. But how can persons of this kind define and acquire for themselves identities connected to others in the cultural context of modernity—or late-modernity—in which disconnected individualism is so rampant? To this Charles Taylor responds that the modern pursuit of individuality itself constitutes an ideal with which individualists, indeed all moderns, already identify. Following Lionel Trilling,[16] he calls it authenticity—the idea of being true to one's self. "There is a certain way of being that is *my* way. I am called to live my life in this way and not in imitation of anyone else's."[17] But, he suggests, I can define a standpoint of this kind for myself that is not trivial, "only against a backdrop of things that matter...only if I exist in a world in which history, or the duties of citizenship, or the call of God, or something else of this order...matters crucially."[18] Authenticity, Taylor continues, "is not an enemy of demands that emanate from beyond the self; it presupposes such demands."[19]

To define an identity sufficiently robust for democratic citizenship, one that enfranchises me to choose my own way of life, requires that I already find myself within such a way of life. Even the decision to leave a community presupposes involvement in the very communal identity I choose to reject. There can be no choice, no self-governance without a context from within which to choose.[20] Justice and fairness also require embodiment in a tradition. To preserve the Right, one must also embrace the Good.

The return of character education

The growth of the field of moral education over the past half-century can be understood in light of these developments in the field of ethics and moral philosophy. Lawrence Kohlberg rejected what he called somewhat flippantly the old "bag of virtues" approach to moral education in favor of a middle ground between values clarification, which he thought to be too relativistic and subjective, and Emile Durkheim's socialization orientation, which he saw as too routinized and indoctrinary.[21] Kohlberg's critique of values clarification and socialization can be understood as a rejection of the two horns of the utilitarian dilemma. In this view, values clarification presupposes the subjectivist assumption that youngsters already possess values in need of clarification, and that the standard for assessing the worth of those values lies within them. Socialization, on the other hand, represents the social consensus (the Romans) that imposes itself on small minorities (the Christians) whether they like it or not, and on everyone else intersubjectively.

According to one influential reading, Kohlberg's initial solution was strictly deontological, to conceive moral education as promoting the development of moral thinking, defined in terms of Kant's rational structure of consciousness.[22] The highest form of moral reasoning is associated with the categorical imperative—treat others as ends not means—and the liberal principle—all deserve freedom of choice provided another's freedom is not infringed. The stages of moral growth were conceived in terms of Jean Piaget's theory of cognitive development, which attempted to chart the developmental patterns of these structures.[23] The research paradigm was heavily quantitative. It measured the growth of moral thinking by placing responses of students to irresolvable moral dilemmas on a six-staged developmental scale.

Communitarians, however, are not the only critics of Kantian liberalism. Prior to the liberal–communitarian debates, at least two other critiques of Kant emerged that share aretiac tendencies with the communitarians. Frankfurt school neo-Marxists elaborated upon collectivist themes in G. W. F. Hegel and followed Plato in arguing that a liberal framework of rights masks oppression and dominance by those in power. Existentialists such as Martin Buber developed subjectivist themes in Hegel by claiming that the Kantian critique of utilitarianism did not go far enough; it continued to view people as objects isolated from rather than as subjects in relation to one another.

The two most powerful critiques of the cognitive developmental tradition in moral education came from intellectual descendents of these traditions of thought. Jurgen Habermas of the Frankfurt school argued that Kohlberg's research program was more hermeneutic than quantitative, which was one of the reasons why it was so difficult to articulate an unambiguous methodology for coding responses to moral dilemmas according to stages of moral development. There can be no moral thinking other than in the context of a community of discourse, argued Habermas, so what Kohlberg's research has actually shown is not the psychological structure of individual moral growth, but rather the tendency of rational communities to gradually reject the hegemonic dominance of others.[24]

Carol Gilligan and Nel Noddings were influenced by Buber in arguing that moral rules and principles are not reliable guides to moral behavior.[25] They argued that moral growth is more affective than cognitive—better conceived as grounded in feelings of care than in justifiable moral rules and principles. Rules are grounded in object–object or instrumental relationships. Buber called them I–It relations. Caring, on the other hand, requires the meeting of two subjects in a moment when the other "fills the firmament," to cite Noddings's reference to Buber.[26] He called those moments of meeting I–Thou relations. One result of this critique is a moral subject who no longer stands alone, but who is situated in relation to others. Both feminists turned to interpretive traditions of research to make their case, Gilligan to qualitative social research and Noddings to philosophical phenomenology.

Kohlberg's reaction to this criticism toward the end of his career was to contextualize the Kantian subject as Habermas and the care ethicists recommended by situating students in just communities. Only in communal contexts, he now argued, can real, as opposed to hypothetical, moral dilemmas arise that will precipitate moral growth. He also recognized that there may be a stage of moral development beyond the categorical imperative that grounds moral behavior and attitudes in transcendent higher goods. In moral education the Good was beginning to emerge once again from the shadow of the Right.

This reflects a return of the very aretiac "bag of virtues" Kohlberg had rejected, albeit in an updated, more sophisticated rendition, in the form of a communitarian account of moral education that has become known as character education. Though character education is a complex movement with a variety of strands, some of which will be differentiated and critiqued in what follows, in general it entails the cultivation of enduring traits or virtues through guidance and experiences that involve imitation, habituation, insight, sympathy, sensitivity, and sensibility.[27]

Character education reconsidered

But why return to virtues and character? Why not simply embrace the Frankfurt and feminist alternatives to the cognitive developmental approach? One answer is that goodness is a wide enough category to embrace both critical pedagogy and the ethic of care in a pluralist account of possible conceptions of the good. However, this is no more satisfying than referring to Kant and Mill as virtues ethicists; it blurs important distinctions and disagreements between what might be perceived as left- (neo-Marxists and existentialist) and right- (conservative communitarian) leaning interpretations of Hegel.

In her book, *Educating Moral People: A Caring Alternative to Character Education*, Noddings acknowledges that caring is a virtue of sorts and that her account of moral education shares much with the communitarians.[28] However, she worries about the tendency of character educators to impose a conception of the good on youngsters without adequately taking into account their feelings and interests. She also challenges the grounding of ethics in community and tradition, which is not enjoyed by all, does not always conjure positive connotations, and, like rules, is no guarantee of moral outcomes. One-on-one relationships, rather than community or tradition, are a more reliable ground for ethics and moral education.

Similarly, proponents of critical pedagogy argue that the imposition of a conception of the good on youngsters is always an act of hegemony and domination, if not also an act of violence, against the subject upon which it is being imposed. The moral life cannot possibly be cultivated through such dominance or violence to the self, they argue. Genuine moral education requires that youngsters be prepared to resist this sort of oppression by means of countereducation.[29]

These arguments highlight some of the differences between the character, caring, and radical conceptions of moral education. Yet they do not adequately address the problem that motivated the communitarians to reassert a preference for the Good over the Right, which is this: How can we conceive of a self that is sufficiently robust to sustain the burdens of liberty and democracy without smothering that person with so many externally imposed virtues that he or she loses the ability to act or think independently? To use Michael Walzer's felicitous terminology, the sort of character education the feminists and the radicals critique assumes a self that is too "thick" to meet this challenge, while the alternatives they propose are too "thin."[30]

To clarify this point, it will be useful to note two approaches to character education identified by Terence McLaughlin and J. Mark Halstead. "Nonexpansive" conceptions of character education involve "a deliberate effort by schools, families, and communities to help young people understand, care about, and act upon core ethical values," in which the rationale is "significantly limited," the qualities of character or virtues are viewed as "fundamental or basic," and the pedagogy prefers "direct teaching" and "practice of these traits" to "the development of moral reasoning."[31] "Expansive" conceptions of character education, on the other hand, ease these restrictions.[32] They offer "sophisticated and nuanced" accounts of liberal democracy as part of their rationale for character education, promote emergent as well as fundamental or basic qualities of character and virtues, such as the requirements for democratic citizenship, and emphasize a role for reasoning in the cultivation of these attributes.[33]

The feminist and radical objections noted here conflate these two sorts of character education by assuming that the nonexpansive account applies to the whole character education movement. They are right to point out that nonexpansive character education may lead to undesirable moral consequences, especially in the context of a democratic society. The Good is not merely preferred on this view; it dominates the Right by imposing too much on the individual and limiting opportunities for reflection and choice. Neither the radical nor the relational alternatives are preferable, however, since the radical self is "thinner" than its Kantian counterpart and the relational self, though "thicker," is not "thick" enough.

The difficulty with the radical self can be seen by returning to the radical contention that all normative education constitutes a form of dominance or violence. If every moral idea or piece of culture offered to the child violates his or her individuality, and we are to arm him or her with the ammunition to counter the violence of moral education in order to make way for a personally constructed self, what precisely is the ethical identity of the youngster to be constructed of? Not only is the heritage of family, community, or tradition unavailable to the child on this account, for the very teaching of such a heritage is an act of domination or violence, even the rules and rights of the Kantian liberal framework that protect the right to choose one's own vision of the good are precluded.

It is more difficult to see the problem with relational ethics, since Buber followed Hegel in contextualizing the Kantian self by relating it to others and care ethicists followed Buber in doing the same to Kohlberg's adaptation of Kant. The difficulty with this view is that we cannot understand what it might mean to relate to or care for someone unless the concepts are situated in a way of life that attributes meaning to these activities. An act might be interpreted as relating or caring in one context and as something very different in another. Meeting and caring cannot be grounded in one-to-one relationships alone; they require context in which the concept has meaning. Just as we cannot conceive our personhood as citizens outside of a common life, we cannot conceive ourselves as relational or caring persons except in a community or tradition of discourse. Buberian meeting and the ethic of care offer steps in the direction of such a conception, since two people meeting one another in relation constitute a nascent community. However, for this sort of meeting to sustain liberal democracy, it requires greater historical and social depth than Buber and Noddings appear to allow.[34]

One could, of course, respond that the likes of Buber and Noddings have articulated traditions that give meaning to concepts such as relation and care—Buber's in his interpretation of Hassidism and Noddings's in giving voice to the traditions of the Mother. If so, then they too intuit the need to ground relation and care in wider contexts. The dangers of character education that concern Noddings lie not in a moral education rooted in community and tradition per se, but rather in the conceptions of goodness that particular communities and traditions embrace.

Character education and intelligent spirituality

Expansive character education does not require a particular conception of goodness, but a framework that picks out those putative ethical visions that fill the moral void of modernity without doing damage to the demands of democracy. If neo-Kantian liberalism constitutes a framework of rights necessary for liberal democracy, liberal communitarianism proposes a complementary framework of goods that can live within the limits of democracy. The criteria for the sort of good that meets both the political demands of liberalism and the moral demands of communitarianism, however, are just those that correspond to the very meaning of the concept of goodness itself.

To the degree that putative ethical visions stray toward the vacuousness of the left-leaning or the nonexpansiveness of the right-leaning Hegelians, they undermine the very core of what it means to have a conception of the good life. And this core lies at the very heart of democracy because the crucial virtues of democracy are built into the very concept of value itself. To deny them is not to embrace some alternative vision of the good; it is to deny the very possibility of goodness altogether. In an important sense, then, nonexpansive character education is not actually moral education at all, but closer to political or religious indoctrination.[35]

I argued in *Reclaiming Goodness*, and reiterated in Chapter Five of this book, that a vision of the good life is ethical, holistic, pragmatic, and synthetic.[36] The first and last of these criteria attend to demands of liberalism, while the middle two address the quest for meaning and purpose.

First, "good" is used here in the ethical sense of the term. In general we use terms like good and bad in the ethical sense to describe persons or groups of persons, including their acts, traits, emotions, dispositions, intentions, motives, and the like. We use evaluative terms in a nonethical sense to describe objects, processes, or states of affairs to which we might ascribe excellence that is not connected to persons, such as beautiful art, good food, or fine wine. The main difference between these two ascriptions of value has to do with human agency.[37] Unlike objects, people can take responsibility for what they do because they are the agents of their actions; they are, within limits, both free to choose and capable of understanding the moral meaning of their choices. As a result people are also capable of being wrong, both in what they believe and in how they decide to act.[38] The moral sense of the good is incompatible, therefore, with fatalism or strong determinism, "the view that what we do is wholly controlled by something independent of our choices and desires," but consistent with weaker forms of determinism in which external causes influence but do not control our choices.[39]

There can be no moral or ethical discourse if we deny these three conditions, since it makes no sense to speak of moral obligations or traits unless there are moral agents who can act upon or possess them. To the extent that a putative vision denies one or more of these conditions, it limits the extent to which it constitutes an ethical vision and hence its capacity to fill the moral vacuum liberalism requires. As was emphasized in the previous chapter, I refer to them, therefore, as the conditions of moral agency and ethical discourse: freedom, intelligence, and fallibility.[40]

It is worth emphasizing that these are not merely liberal or modern values smuggled in, as it were, to adjudicate among putative ethical visions. They are found in traditions as diverse as the Hebrew and Christian Bibles, medieval Aristotelianism, and modern existentialism, all of which understood that if people cannot influence their actions and understand the difference between better and worse according to some account of these terms, or if it is in their very nature to do or be either good or bad, then it simply makes no sense to assess their character or behaviors in moral terms. Human agency, it seems, is built into the very concept of goodness.

This capacity to influence, within reasonable limits, one's own destiny in such a way that is neither a function of previous causes nor a matter of chance, but of choice, intent, and purpose, lies at the very heart of the democratic ethos. It is because human beings are agents capable of governing their own actions that they are also capable and worthy of governing their collective lives. Democracy is a form of government over a society of moral agents, and the first task of liberalism is to protect the capacity of democratic citizens to exercise their agency. The first task of moral education is likewise the cultivation of moral agency, which links it inextricably with the cultivation of the capacity for democratic citizenship.[41]

Second, goodness is also holistic in that it offers a vision of a whole life. Socrates's question, Williams points out, "is not immediate; it is not about what I should do now, or next. The Greeks themselves were much impressed by the idea that such a question must, consequently, be about a whole life and that a good way of living has to issue in what, at its end, would be seen to have been a good life."[42]

It does not follow, however, that such a life must be totalistic. One can embrace a variety of ethical visions grounded in religious, national, professional, artistic, recreational, and many other sorts of values. Each can make demands on one's whole life, from dusk to dark, birth or adulthood to death. Yet they are often integrated with one another as well. Communities of primary identity provide the ideals and role models within which we define ourselves.[43] Some are "thicker" than others, however, because they make greater demands on our self-definition, reflect longer and richer histories, offer deeper insight into the human condition, or provide a more enduring sense of purpose to life.[44]

One can celebrate many, but not all, ethical visions. Some traditions contradict one another, or preclude accepting the values or ideals of one community while remaining a member of another. The mainstream Jewish view, for example, is that the messiah has yet to arrive, which precludes the possibility of a person being simultaneously Jewish and Christian by accepting Jesus as the messiah. Since the values and interests of communities can conflict, we are wise to also live in a community of communities that protects both our right and the right of others to pursue our own primary goods. This is the liberal democratic community. Passion for communities of primary identity needs to be tempered with commitment to the wider public life and loyalty to the state that embodies this public life needs to be balanced with concern for particular identities.[45] Total identification with the state, even a liberal democratic one, runs the risk of right-leaning Hegelian nonexpansiveness no less than total identification with a religious or ethnic group.

Schools cannot bear the entire burden of moral and citizenship education in liberal societies, therefore; they require collaboration with families and communities or, when these are absent, surrogates to serve in their stead. The sort of communities required for this education combine the characteristics of what Ferdinand Tonnies referred to as "*Gemeinschaft*" and "*Gesellschaft*" and what Durkheim called mechanical and organic community.[46] *Gemeinschaft* communities are family or tribal organizations in which traditions, roles, and rules are clear. They are mechanical in the sense that they are close, closed groups that are given, usually by birth, rather than chosen. *Gesellschaft* communities are modern, open, and organic in that people choose to join for social, economic, ideological, or other reasons. The former are often associated with obligations, a sense of belonging, nostalgia or romanticism, collective memory, narrative, and relationships; the latter with autonomy, choice, reason, historical criticism, rational discourse, and rules. Expansive character education is cultivated through a delicate (and often uneasy) balancing of these tendencies. This entails an attempt to overcome the false dichotomy between romanticism and rationality, feelings and reasons, emotion and intelligence, in order to offer an account of the moral life that is both emotionally and intellectually satisfying.[47]

Liberal societies nevertheless do require both common and separate schools in some form or another. The common vision of democratic community and particular visions of separate communities should be reflected in both institutions, although with different degrees of emphasis and ends in view. Common schools should actively encourage and sustain students' distinctiveness without aiming to initiate them into particular communities. Separate schools, whether full-time or supplemental, should initiate into particularity identity, but not without proper attention to the commons as well. In both cases, the juxtaposition of particular with common identities, and of differing versions of particularity with one another, necessitates a synthetic hermeneutic, which is discussed in what follows. The question of where parents choose to educate their children depends, among many other considerations, on the balance of parental commitment to the various communities into which they would like to see their children initiated.[48]

Third, goodness is pragmatic, not only because it is allied in important respects with William James and John Dewey[49] but also in the sense that virtues are expressed in terms of concrete practical examples; be like this person, follow that role model; embrace such virtues as: *integrity*, a passionate willingness to enact an ethical vision wholeheartedly; *humility*, an awareness that one could be wrong despite a heartfelt commitment to a particular way of life; *literacy*, an understanding of the doctrines, narratives, symbols, rituals, methods of interpretation, and forms of criticism of the communities to which one belongs; and *fulfillment*, the joy of recognizing that I can make a difference in my own life and in the lives of others.[50]

The logic of virtues is not that of deontological judgment that applies general rules to particular behaviors. It is rather one of aretaic judgments, in which excellence is a transcendent quality discovered and illustrated through complex concrete cases. This is why narratives, symbols, and rituals play an important part in communicating goodness across the generations. It does not follow, of course, that we can say nothing abstract or general about virtues. When we do, however, we are putting in discursive terms what we have experienced in concrete cases, rather than determining what to do in a particular case on the basis of a rule.[51]

Finally, goodness is synthetic. The recognition of my own fallibility and that of my own community's or tradition's vision of the good means that I am able and I should be willing to learn from other conflicting visions, provided, of course, that they too accept the conditions of moral agency and ethical discourse. Additionally, since living in a community with a conception of the good also requires the liberal democratic community of communities, goodness as a synthetic concept implies that there is a constant reading and rereading of tradition both as an insider and as an outsider.[52] This calls for an ongoing hermeneutic process that Simon Rawidowicz called "interpretatio"—the negotiation between exegesis (reading out) and eisegesis (reading in), explication and appropriation, meaning and significance, history and memory, to balance the demands of loyalty and belonging, on the one hand, with openness and receptivity to alternative perspectives, on the other.[53]

Some have found answers to this quest for a vision of the good life within themselves, others in a sense of solidarity and belonging, and others still in the renewal of ritual and relation to God. I refer to these as subjective, collective, and objective orientations to spirituality.[54] Each has much to recommend it, provided it is not taken to undesirable extremes. To avoid the extreme subjectivism possible in searching to define one's self, the radical relativism that could flow from the idealizing of a particular group, and the dogmatism often associated with religious ritual and worship of God, I introduce the idea of transcendence developed by Philip Phenix and Dwayne Huebner.[55] According to this view, even though there could always be another time, a different place, or a better way, for our ethical visions to make sense we must suppose, if only as a regulative principle, that they refer to a reality that lies beyond our experience of time, space, and value. Robert Adams put it as follows in referring to finite and infinite goods: "many finite, one infinite."[56] I refer to this as a higher, rather than highest, good, since we can always improve upon our most recent representation of it.[57]

Intelligent spirituality refers to those visions of the good life that integrate subjective, collective, and objective orientations to goodness while avoiding the dangerous extremes of each by embracing the conditions of ethical discourse, on the one hand, and the regulative principle of transcendence, on the other. This is the sort of spirituality that responds to the moral failure that spawned the current quest, without undermining the political success that makes it possible.[58]

This does not mean that to be ethical or moral one must believe in God. But it does imply that one must believe that something is of value beyond one's self and one's community. Thomas Green makes this point in discussing the importance of the sacred in moral education. "To think of the absence of the sacred," writes Green, "that is, its total absence, is to conceive a condition in which nothing excites horror. And in such a world, moral education cannot gain a foothold."[59] This sense of the sacred need not be religiously "tethered," to use an expression McLaughlin and I developed elsewhere,[60] but it must transcend personal and communal meaning to recognize the possibility of a reality beyond our experience of space, time, and value to which our various visions of the good allude. Another aim of moral education, then, is the cultivation of an awareness of transcendence.

Moral education in this view is about the acquisition of a spiritual or ethical identity grounded in particular and common communities that are bounded by ethical discourse, on the one hand, and transcendence, on the other. This sort of identity is defined in terms of the ideals with which one identifies, not as psychological or sociological processes.[61] It is not built into the structure of consciousness or given at birth either full-blown or in a nascent form that will unfold naturally. I am hesitant, therefore, to speak of "spiritual development." What is "given" or "built in" is a potential, the possibility of gradually realizing that I can actually take hold of my own destiny and significantly influence the course of my life and the lives of others. This potential must be nurtured, cultivated, and exercised. It is something like a muscle, or our capacity for language, or what Elliot Eisner calls a form of representation.[62]

However, the result of not educating the capacity for moral agency is the impoverishment of will, not merely of mind, as Eisner would have it. To the extent that awareness of moral agency is ignored or suppressed, a person's moral horizons become increasingly limited; and to the extent that it is engaged, the opportunities for meaning and purpose are enhanced. It is an illusion, therefore, that nonexpansive communities, fundamentalist religion, or total identification with the state increases moral clarity and purpose. In a very deep sense, these orientations undermine the very possibility of living a worthwhile life altogether. I prefer, therefore, to speak of spiritual or ethical identity as cultivated or educated rather than developed or transmitted. This entails initiation into learning communities through the study, practice, and celebration of their visions of a higher good.

The practice of moral and spiritual education[63]

The very nature of goodness, then, lends itself to a view of liberal communitarian democratic education that is expansive. But how is it possible to initiate into communities with intelligent conceptions of goodness in ways that do not undermine their expansiveness? Even McLaughlin and Halstead question whether civic democratic virtues embraced by Amy Gutmann and Eamonn Callan, such as justice, reasonableness, and deliberativeness, can be cultivated, especially in the early years, without relying on them at least to some degree. If they are assumed, however, then nonexpansive and expansive approaches to character education may not be as clearly distinguishable from one another as was supposed, since the very civic virtues upon which democratic citizenship rests are imposed in a nondemocratic and unreasonable fashion.

This is, of course, the paradox of moral education to which Richard Peters referred long ago.[64] Addressing it will normally require the exercise of a certain amount of external authority and rote learning, which often makes it difficult to distinguish between initiation into more and less democratically orientated traditions, especially at the early stages. The crucial question is whether this authority and habituation is intended to enhance or suppress the moral agency of the learner, and this can often be detected even when the students are young. How, for example, does the educator relate to questions, or disagreements, or independent initiative on the part of the student? Education for moral agency will seek to validate inquisitiveness and independence even as it seeks to initiate the student into communities in which queries and autonomy are meaningful.

There are no rules for negotiating this delicate balance. It calls for what Aristotle called *Phronesis*, or practical wisdom. In contrast to *Sophia*, which is concerned with theoretical description of physical and metaphysical reality, *Phronesis* entails understanding what one ought to do and how one ought to live.[65] What are the sources of such wisdom?

As was noted in the previous chapter, Joseph Schwab worked out an especially compelling account of practical wisdom in education. For Schwab the outcome of educational thought could never be usefully conceived in the theoretical terms of the positivistic natural sciences. Human behavior is simply too complex, intentional, and unpredictable to be described by covering laws alone. In four well-known essays on "the practical," he argued that education is not so much a way of thinking as a way of doing, a synoptic activity infused with conflicting needs, information, values, and ideals that can be enriched and improved in light of often contradictory but illuminating theoretical constructs from a variety of disciplines. Instead of picturing education as the application to pedagogy of psychological and sociological laws, Schwab suggested a process of curriculum deliberation in which developmental psychologists, learning theorists, sociologists of contemporary society, and subject-matter experts would debate alternative conceptions of what and how to teach. This paved the way for integrating quantitative social science into a more interpretive, Aristotelian form of educational thought, concerned with exploring transcendent norms illustrated in concrete cases in order to illumine practice.[66]

Some of the central features of Schwab's account can be summarized as follows: (1) Content and pedagogy are not as readily distinguishable from one another as has often been thought in educational research and curriculum thought. (2) Schools are intimately tied to the communities they serve. (3) We need to consult the content about how to teach, not only abstract rules of pedagogy—Lee Shulman later called this pedagogic content knowledge.[67] (4) Life in classrooms, as Philip Jackson called it, is a complex enterprise, the study of which calls for engagement with this complexity, recognizing that any description or abstraction of it will necessarily be partial, incomplete, underdetermined by data, and fallible.[68] (5) Teaching is a fundamentally moral activity and schools are infused with a moral life—again following Jackson's terminology—that lives and breathes in a rich cultural and communal context.[69] (6) One important role for curriculum specialists—Eisner calls them educational connoisseurs—is to create integrated interpretations of this complexity to illumine perception and improve practice.[70]

These observations suggest a research program in moral education that blurs some of the distinctions between the social sciences and the humanities, and that lends renewed respect to the roles of literature, the arts, history, philosophy, and theology in examining pedagogy and policy, as well as curriculum content. The study of intelligent spirituality as a practice, in other words, stands at the crossroads of humanistic and qualitative social inquiry in education.[71] Let us briefly consider the logic, data, outcomes, and methodology of such a research program.

The logic of virtue, as mentioned here, is one of discovering transcendent qualities in concrete cases, not applying abstract rules to particular behaviors. Virtues can be elusive and nuanced and are best understood in relation to the character of a whole person. They are best captured in what Suzanne Langer called nondiscursive communication, such as symbols, rituals, and stories, that gives expression to the dynamic form of concrete wholes, much as a dry river bed encapsulates the water's ebb and flow at a particular point in time.[72] The nuances and complexities of the virtue of integrity, for example, can be explored in studying the biblical character of Noah, who is said to have been "a righteous and integral person in his generation."[73] A host of questions follow. Given what he did, why would the text describe him as righteous or integral or wholehearted? Why in his generation? Does this mean that his character illustrates the virtue of integrity for a particular time rather than for all time? Is it possible to describe such a virtue for all time? And so on. Or we could look to a description of contemporary teachers, such as Ms. Payton, Mr. Peter, Mr. James, and Ms. Smith, depicted so beautifully by David Hansen in *The Call of Teaching*.[74]

The data to be examined in studying the cultivation of character, therefore, need not be restricted to contemporary educational practice, which has been the focus of modern educational research in one form or another since its inception. We can also learn from literary figures, artistic expression, historical cases, philosophical inquiry, and theological interpretation, indeed from all of the forms in which ethical heritage has been represented across the generations—including, of course, contemporary educational policy and pedagogy. It seems fairly obvious from Schwab's account that the humanistic disciplines should play important roles as sources of subject matter in moral education. It is less apparent, however, that literary and historical traditions represent a repository of ancient and medieval wisdom concerning pedagogy and policy in moral education that is an untapped resource of contemporary educational scholarship. Nicholas Burbules and McLaughlin, for example, examined the pedagogy of Jesus as a model for contemporary ethical instruction, while Shmuel Glick and I have explored questions raised for the teaching of texts by the developmental curriculum of the Talmudic rabbis, and Yusef Waghid has studied the implications of texts from the Koran for democratic education.[75]

All of these authors were writing for general audiences that are not necessarily Christian, Jewish, or Muslim. The assumption is that there are norms, maxims, and parables embedded in ancient literary, artistic, historical, philosophical, and theological sources that can transcend time and space to speak to moral educators in a host of contexts today. This is not a parochial nonexpansive research program, in which we examine our own traditions in order to reproduce them across the generations. It is rather an expansive program addressed at a wide audience that encourages contemporary as well as ancient traditions to speak to one another across the boundaries of time, place, and contemporary life. It is certainly appropriate for the curriculum and pedagogy of particular faith schools. The more interesting challenge is to make this sort of research relevant for the practice of moral education in the commons as well.

Moreover, the practices and narratives of ethical heritage are found not only in schools, or stories about teachers, or histories of education. They are found in the communities and contexts in which those schools, teachers, and educations have lived. Lawrence Cremin made this point beautifully in his "ecological" description of the interdependence of family, school, and church in nineteenth-century small-town America.[76] Studying the

Phronesis of moral and spiritual education requires that we cast a wide net, both vertically through time and horizontally across contemporary life, to explore the contexts, both actual and virtual, in which persons of exemplary character have lived good lives and, through their example, taught others to do the same.

This broad conception of *Phronesis* might be thought of as an adaptation of Shulman's notion of the wisdom of teacher practice to the education of intelligent spirituality. Shulman argued that we can discover principles, parables, maxims, and norms of good teaching by holistic examination of good teachers at work.[77] I am arguing that we can enhance our grasp of the wisdom it takes to cultivate intelligent spiritual identity by studying communities and traditions, both contemporary and historical, which have successfully transmitted conceptions of the good across the generations.[78] The outcomes of these studies might be conceived as grounded theories of ethics in education that describe transcendent norms of education in intelligent spirituality grounded in the doctrines, narratives, parables, symbols, rituals, and conceptions of interpretation and criticism of particular traditions and communities.[79]

The methodologies for such investigations are fully described in many volumes devoted to qualitative social inquiry, literary and art criticism, historiography, and philosophical and theological methodology. I want to add one point to these discussions. If the study of moral education entails documenting and interpreting traditions of practical wisdom, its aim must be not only explication for its own sake but also reeducation, renewal, regeneration, and reconceptualization of current practice. This requires exegesis of tradition, in which we attempt to uncover its plain meaning and significance to those who lived or wrote it. It also involves the appropriation of traditions in which we translate them from one context and adapt them to another. This process of adaptation is sometimes called eisegesis. Rather than remaining with the exegete, loyal solely to the meaning of tradition for the context in which it was created, the eisegete is loyal to a tradition as it evolves through time and is imbued with a desire to enable that tradition to speak to contemporary circumstances as well.[80]

When the twelfth-century biblical scholar Rabbi Shlomo ben Yitzhak wrote that a biblical verse calls for interpretation or when his grandson, Rabbi Shmuel ben Meir, wrote that commentary should reveal the plain meaning of texts updated each day, both tried to capture the delicate balance between exegesis and eisegesis.[81] Following William Frankena's parody of Kant on the interdependence of the Good and the Right, we might say that exegesis without eisegesis is dead, but eisegesis without exegesis is wild.[82] In qualitative educational research, a similar balance is required in the tension between participation and observation, between experiencing a culture "subjectively" as an insider, and then describing it "objectively" so that it can be made understandable and relevant to an outsider. Eisner refers to the task of reeducating our perception, and thereby updating pedagogical traditions, as educational criticism, a form of educational inquiry analogous to assessment in literature and the arts.[83]

Intelligent spirituality offers an alternative account of moral education, therefore, that avoids both dogmatism and relativism and that reflects the communitarian defense of democracy. Like James, more enamored of tradition than Dewey, but sharing some of his suspicions of it, this position could be fairly characterized as a "liberal communitarian" approach to moral education.

CHAPTER TEN

Religious Initiation in Liberal Democracy

Introduction

This chapter reconsiders a well-known debate between Terence McLaughlin and Eamonn Callan over parental rights and religious upbringing. Although the debate centered on a disagreement about the meaning of moral autonomy and religious understanding, I argue that a deeper difference is at stake concerning the very character of liberal society. McLaughlin's position appears to reflect an interpretation of the sort of value pluralism associated with Isaiah Berlin and Michael Oakeshott that John Gray called the other face of liberalism.[1] Callan is a well-known proponent of comprehensive—Gray called it universal—liberalism associated with Immanuel Kant and John Locke and with several influential interpretations of John Rawls.[2] McLaughlin apparently favored a richly pluralistic society populated by citizens whose moral independence is embedded in thick cultures that may be tied to intelligent religious communities infused with subject–subject understanding expressed as "beliefs in" dynamic faith traditions. Callan, on the other hand, supports a more uniform society peopled by rationally autonomous citizens who prefer "sophisticated" to "simple" religion—one reasonable, the other dogmatic—based on subject–object understanding stated as logically or empirically assessed "beliefs that" something is the case.

This chapter is divided into five sections. In the first section, I summarize the debate between McLaughlin and Callan over parental rights and religious upbringing, including Callan's latest challenge to McLaughlin's claim that religious initiation yields a unique, autonomy-enhancing understanding of faith.[3] Such an understanding, asserts Callan, satisfies neither believers nor unbelievers. I disagree, arguing that despite his elaborate account of appreciative understanding from an insider's perspective, Callan's brand of liberalism is far too intolerant of "belief in" dynamic faiths, which it reduces to logically or empirically assessable "beliefs that" something is the case. In the second section, I explore the distinction between "belief that" and "belief in," and in the third and fourth sections, I show how the "unbeliever's objection" misunderstands the former and the "believer's objection" misconceives the latter. In the final section, I return to the underlying debate over the nature of liberal society, which lies at the heart of the intellectual journey depicted in this book.

Two concepts of autonomy

McLaughlin's initial essay addressed the claim that parents in a liberal society have no right to raise their children in a particular faith since religious upbringing entails indoctrination and undermines moral autonomy.[4] Following Bruce Ackerman, McLaughlin argued that parents are justified in fostering a stable and coherent "primary culture," which may be infused with religion, since children are not born fully fledged participants in the liberal form of life and their subsequent development into autonomous adults depends on it.[5] Indoctrination can be avoided by exposing children to influences other than the religion in which they are raised and accepting that they may eventually choose a path different from that of their parents. "The essential freedom of the act of faith must be preserved," he wrote. "Religious liberal parents may well hope that their child's eventual autonomy will be exercised in favor of faith; but in the logic of their own religious—as well as liberal—position, this must remain a hope rather than a requirement." McLaughlin called this "autonomy via faith."[6]

Callan responded by suggesting that parents may have a *weak* right to *expose* children to religion as part of a primary culture, provided the youngsters are encouraged to remain agnostic until mature enough to decide for themselves, but not a *strong* right to *instill* faith, regardless of whether or not it is abandoned later.[7] All indoctrination entails the inculcation of beliefs without due regard for relevant evidence, he argued. Weak indoctrination infringes sufficiently on self-determination to be "evil" even if it does not produce unshakable belief.[8] Callan would have us believe that there is something like an inverse relation between the extent to which a child is raised inside of a religious tradition and the amount of rational autonomy that will thereby be fostered. Reason, not religion, should guide life choices, according to Callan, including those about whether or not to be religious, and too vigorous an imposition of religious faith at a young age hampers the development of the relevant rational faculties. We might dub this position "autonomy via reason."

In his rejoinder, McLaughlin challenged the relevance to autonomy of the distinction between weak and strong religious upbringing, claiming that "Callan too quickly dismisses the significance of being on the inside of religion for the capacity to understand and evaluate it, and he is over-confident about the value and significance for understanding of the sort of *explanations* which parents are invited to give children."[9] The thrust of this rejoinder can be summarized as follows:

(1) Religious initiation yields understanding unavailable by other means that enhances the autonomy of children to make informed choices about leading a religious life.

(2) Religious initiation is therefore justifiable since enhanced autonomy based on informed choice is in the interest of children.

(3) Hence, parents have a strong right to initiate their children into religion.

Callan calls statement 1 the "initiation thesis," which is the premise for statements 2 and 3. He now concedes that parents may have a strong right to initiate their children into religion (statement 3), not because religious upbringing is in their best interest (statement 2), but because the state should intervene in the parental upbringing of children only in cases of extreme harm.

> The best thing to do for our children and what we have the right to do are not the same thing…. A good argument for moral limits on parental rights would have to show that the behavior to which parents have no right infringes on the basic interests of the child to such a degree that interference on the part of others might be justified to prevent that behavior.[10]

He also concedes that religious upbringing could be in the interest of children (statement 2), *if* religious initiation indeed yields a unique understanding that enhances religious choices (statement 1). The point of this thesis "was to justify religious upbringing in the sense that it could be shown to be in the interests of children in devout families who receive it."[11] However, he challenges the idea that religious initiation yields an understanding of religion that is unproblematic (statement 1).

Following Jonathan Kvanvig, Callan suggests that religious upbringing is surely intended to yield an appreciative understanding of religion from an insider's perspective, subject, of course, to critical judgment, rather than knowledge of its main concepts and their relations to one another.[12] But, he claims, this satisfies no one. From the believer's point of view, religious initiation so conceived transforms religion into a way to acquire an appreciative understanding of religion, whereas to the faithful, religion is the end not the means. From the unbeliever's vantage point, even if religious initiation leads to an understanding of religion otherwise unavailable, this comes at the price of inculcating possible falsehoods in ways that might be harmful to children.

> On the one hand, the justification (of religious initiation) fails for the religious believer because it inverts the proper relation between understanding and faith; on the other hand, it fails because though religious upbringing enhances growth of understanding in some respects, it thwarts its development in other respects that cannot be reasonably dismissed as unimportant.[13]

According to this logic, even if statement 3 is true, it does not follow from statement 2, and even if statement 2 follows from statement 1, the initial premise is objectionable to both believers and unbelievers. McLaughlin's rejoinder does not demonstrate, therefore, that children are better off having received a religious upbringing than they would be if exposed to matters of faith when old enough to decide for themselves. Hence, Callan asks rhetorically, "Why bring the kids into this?"

Callan acknowledges that he and McLaughlin "wandered together into a thicket of densely entangled questions," the complexity of which "outstripped" their understanding;[14] so in contrast to his previous "brazen confidence," he tempered his current remarks.[15] "It would be painful to learn," he laments, "that I am no wiser now than I was in our original dispute that I had merely traded old mistakes for new ones, though I cannot think of anyone I would have preferred to learn from than McLaughlin."[16] No one, least of all me, can replace Terry McLaughlin, and to the best that I can tell, Callan appears not to have made any new mistakes in his current contribution. Rather, despite increased wisdom in many other matters, he may have repeated a few of the old ones. McLaughlin would have maintained, I think, that both of Callan's objections to the initiation thesis falter, one because he failed to comprehend the consequences of "believing in" a personal God or faith tradition for religious understanding, the other because he presupposed that key articles of faith can be reduced to logically or empirically assessable "beliefs that" something is the case. Both errors stem from the faulty assumption that one or another account of critical rationality can serve as a neutral criterion, rather than nonneutral cultural inheritances, against which all perspectives, including religion, must be adjudicated.

Two types of faith

Martin Buber distinguished between two types of faith: *belief that* such and such is the case and *belief in* someone or something.[17] The former is a cognitive state concerning a proposition or set of propositions one affirms to be true; the latter depicts a relationship of trust and loyalty between persons or between people and significant events, symbols, places, and stories.[18] The one is captured well in the Greek *pistis*, especially as used by Paul in conceiving the Church as a transnational group of individuals who affirm a set of beliefs about Christ. The other is expressed in the Hebrew *emunah*, which in its biblical use refers to a people's trust in the God whose teaching constitutes the center of their collective life. This harsh dichotomy does not appear to get the story quite right, however, since these two senses of belief appear to be interconnected. We believe that many things are true about people in whom we trust, for example, and it makes little sense to be loyal to someone without affirming her existence. Additionally, Jesus was himself a rabbinic Jew who was as likely to speak of *emunah* as *pistis*, and the encounter of the sages with Greek thought eventually introduced into Judaism, at least in some circles, the idea that membership requires belief that certain dogmas are true.[19] Buber's distinction is better understood as depicting two aspects of faith rather than a sharp difference between Christianity and Judaism. One aspect stresses ways of talking across cultures about a thin life we might share in common, grounded in rational, subject–object knowledge; the other emphasizes thicker local practices grounded in interpersonal subject–subject experiences that are linguistically idiomatic, culturally particular, and historically situated.[20] Priority placed on one or the other has a profound impact on how religion is conceived.

Consider the distinction once made by the well-known medieval rabbi and poet Yehuda Halevy between the God of the Philosophers and the God of Abraham.[21] The former is the metaphysical deity discovered through the power of reason—the transcendent good of Plato and prime mover of Aristotle, who is the beginning and end of the universe but incapable of caring about the suffering of individual people. The latter is the personal God of revelation who enters history and engages human beings, who cares deeply about people living in concrete communities, and who reaches out to liberate them from bondage, redeem them from sin, and teach them a path to righteousness. Halevy wrote to prioritize the God of Abraham over the God of the Philosophers, to defend the advantages of tradition by exposing the limitations of reason. But the distinction between a thin universal dimension of religion conveyed in abstract doctrines and thick particular traditions expressed in local customs relates to nontheistic faiths, such as Buddhism, as well.

From Philo Judaeus of Alexandria in the first century until Baruch (Benedict) Spinoza in the seventeenth, Muslim, Jewish, and Christian philosophers such as Mohammed Al Farabi, Moses Maimonides, and Thomas Aquinas prioritized *pistis*, belief that the philosopher's God exists, over *emunah*, faith in the God of revelation; revelation was to be justified on rational grounds, not the other way around.[22] This led to a different dichotomy in which religious beliefs that squared with Aristotle were considered more sophisticated and less dogmatic than those that did not. When Aristotle's metaphysics crumbled under the weight of Cartesian skepticism, many intellectuals assumed that the more "naïve" aspects of religion grounded in mere local custom and "irrational superstition" would follow suit, to be replaced by more rigorous beliefs based on the sort of empirical inquiry established by Francis Bacon.[23] However, when David Hume employed the same Cartesian skepticism a century later to show that Bacon's method produced results that were merely contingent, not necessary, Kant awoke from his dogmatic slumber to argue that empiricism only makes sense when coupled with the assumption that causation is built into the rational structure of consciousness, not things-in-themselves.[24] This entailed a new philosophical idea of God as the beginning and end of reason, not the universe, and a new universal religion, within the limits of reason alone.[25] Many responded to Enlightenment intolerance for tradition by imitating the inflexibility of the empirical reasoning that had come to dominate the discourse in which they now felt compelled to defend their faith, but which had not previously characterized religion.[26] This widened the gap between sophisticated and naïve religion. Many devotees of Enlightenment considered traditionalism obscurantist and dogmatic while more than a few traditionalists referred to Enlightenment rationalism as self-obsessed and morally vacuous.

Halevy, on the other hand, never conceded the priority of reason over revelation and so would not accept the dichotomy between sophisticated and simple faith. Tradition is often a more reliable source of truth than reason, he argued. Intelligent religion is grounded in historically situated beliefs and practices handed down from parents to children and teachers to students, which may not necessarily echo the latest conclusions of human inquiry. This is not to say that reason is to be rejected altogether; for example, it is useful in explaining particular faiths across cultures. Rather, it ought to be contextualized and its limitations acknowledged. In contrast to the speculative character of Aristotelian metaphysics, Halevy based his preference for tradition on the accuracy with which rabbinic scholars preserved what he took to be eyewitness testimony to the divine–human encounter across the generations. Were he alive today, Halevy could not deny the extraordinary advances of empirical science; but he could point with some satisfaction to the enhanced logical status granted to tradition, albeit of a more scientific nature, in explaining this success by such postpositivist historians and philosophers of science as Thomas Kuhn and Imre Lakatos.[27]

Rationalism tends toward universal political theories in which power is allocated to those who have achieved self-control by freeing themselves from error. Callan's autonomy via reason is but one example. Traditionalism of the sort described here inclines toward political pluralism in which power is vested in those who resist the impulse to impose themselves on others, which is an alternative sense of self-control born of relations to individuals, community, history, or God, similar to McLaughlin's autonomy via faith. Berlin called one positive, the other negative liberty.[28] The former can be seen in social democratic and comprehensive liberal doctrines associated with Jean-Jacques Rousseau, Karl Marx, and their intellectual heirs, on the one hand,[29] and with Kant, Locke, and their descendants, on the other, especially Rawls;[30] the latter finds its modern expression in what Gray called the other face of liberalism, associated with the likes of Johann Herder, Thomas Hobbes, Edmund Burke, and more recently, Oakeshott. [31]

"Belief that" and the unbeliever's objection

Callan distinguishes between relational knowledge and appreciative understanding and admits that one important requirement of the latter is the capacity to appreciate religion from an insider's perspective.[32] But he conceives religion as something like an object that is to be understood by an appreciating subject.

> Appreciative understanding of Catholicism requires that one take up the perspective of a practicing Catholic, at least by imagining oneself into that perspective.... One must be able to consider how the world looks to someone, for example, who believes that bread becomes the body of Christ in the Mass. And how the world looks at such moments is only intelligible by virtue of a distinct range of emotional susceptibilities, such as reverence in response to the putative presence of God.[33]

> Callan does maintain that appreciative understanding is "objectual" rather than "propositional," the one being followed by a direct object such as the presidency, or the president, or the English language, and the other involving understanding that such and such is the case.[34] However, his critical criterion of appreciative understanding appears to render this distinction irrelevant, since it reduces key articles of faith to beliefs evaluated according to rational criteria, where truth is conceived as correspondence between an understanding subject and the object to be understood. The degree to which one understands a religious doctrine "cannot be sundered from questions of whether one is right or wrong about the truth of whatever propositions" comprise it. "The best appreciative understanding requires wise, sometimes harshly critical, judgment regarding its object, as well as appropriate perspective taking."[35]

The problem with religious upbringing for the unbeliever, according to Callan, concerns instances when the critical requirement might be violated, not merely because these beliefs could be false, but also because they constitute part of a "normative identity that the child is expected to embrace, and as such, they are apt to be peculiarly resistant to rational revision once they are embraced."[36] The difficulty with this objection is not in the reduction of "belief in" to "beliefs that" something is the case. As I have said, believing in someone makes no sense without believing that she exists. The question rather is whether it is possible to test beliefs of this kind against the standards of "harshly critical" judgment or to "rationally revise" them without reference to a tradition—whether there is a neutral "view from nowhere" that is not itself embedded in some web of commitments against which to assess these beliefs.

Willard Van Orman Quine thought not. As discussed concerning the dogmas of educational research in Part Two of this volume, he pointed out that philosophers from Gottfried Wilhelm von Leibniz to Kant distinguished between two such critical criteria: those that depend on the logical relation between concepts, such as Anselm's argument that divine existence can be derived from the idea that "God is that than which a greater cannot be conceived," and those that refer to the empirical world, such as the belief that God entered history to redeem the Hebrews from slavery. Each is related to one of Quine's two well-known dogmas of empiricism: (1) that statements whose truth-value depends on their meaning can be usefully distinguished from those whose truth-value depends on matters of fact and (2) that the meaning of statements can be reduced by means of some logical construction to immediate sense experience. As we have seen, both turn out to be indefensible.[37]

Quine proposed instead that meanings are interconnected with one another in holistic webs of beliefs, which makes talk of the empirical content of single statements misleading, since any statement can be seen as necessarily true by reconsidering its relation to other statements in a theory in which, at least in principle, everything is open to revision. Ontology is relative, in other words, in the sense that objects of a theory are "cultural posits" decipherable within the context of a theory as a whole or as interpreted or reinterpreted in another theory, not individually as logical representations of sense experience.[38] This is a soft relativism that admits the logically benign and somewhat obvious claim that truth (and by extension goodness) is relative to conceptual framework, not the hard and incoherent variety that rejects the possibility of criticizing one framework on the basis of another.[39] All forms of relativism, Callan's protestations to the contrary notwithstanding, are not bad philosophy.[40]

Quine's ontological relativism set the stage for the likes of Kuhn and Lakatos to argue that scientific paradigms and research programs contain core beliefs that are tested against experience only at the edges;[41] for Michel Foucault and Oakeshott to maintain, each in his own way, that even when we revoke a theory in the human as well as the natural sciences, we do not escape the grip of framework;[42] and for Alasdair MacIntyre to apply these insights to religious traditions.[43] Except in the rare circumstance when it is transformed by revolutionary experiences—a new revelation or a miraculous event or some mystical practices—criticism of a faith tradition normally entails engagement with internal standards, such as rabbinic or canon law, which themselves can be subject to considerable debate within a community. It may also involve external sources—history, archeology, evolutionary biology, philosophical theology, critical social theory, other religious traditions, or secular perspectives—which may stimulate reconsideration or even rejection of important beliefs and practices, but hold no prima facie privilege over the tradition itself.[44] For example, many religious Zionists see the establishment of the State of Israel as foreshadowing redemption, which has inspired debates over liturgies celebrating Israel's independence; and Anglicans are engaging both internal and external sources of criticism when they consider the role of homosexuality in their Church.

The extent which Callan reduces religious "belief in" to logical or empirical "belief that" can be seen in his distinction between "the faith of the simple" and the faith of "substantially educated and autonomous adults."[45] He illustrates this distinction by reference to Elizabeth Anscombe's lovely essay "On Transubstantiation." Simple faith can be seen in the case of a three-year-old child Anscombe once saw who prostrated himself before his mother when she returned from taking communion. "Is he in you?" the child asked, to which his mother responded affirmatively.[46] The child bowed reverently. According to the Catholic doctrine of transubstantiation, the wafer and wine become the body and blood of Christ—the host—when consecrated by the priest during the Eucharist, which celebrates the last supper of Jesus. Receiving the host from the priest and ingesting it after it is consecrated constitutes participation in Holy Communion. This sort of belief is best imparted first through participation in religious ritual, Anscombe suggests, in which awe and wonder can be nurtured in the youngster through whispering exhortations, drawing reverential attention, and encouraging imitation and engagement.[47] Direct classroom instruction about the beliefs embedded in such ritual and how they relate to one another should come later. Sophisticated belief can be found in a theologian Anscombe once knew who, along with the Vatican Council, wanted to "alter or water down" faith. He deplored the prostration of the child before his mother's belly as silly, perhaps even idolatrous. Anscombe guessed that the theologian was losing faith, which (sadly in her view) turned out to be the case.[48]

In contrast to Anscombe, Callan appears to prefer sophisticated to simple piety, a distinction that she, like Halevy, rejected out of hand.[49] This can be discerned from the discussion of a similar distinction between "simple" and "sophisticated" integrity in his book on political education, *Creating Citizens*; one entails wholehearted fidelity to roles and beliefs harmonized to minimize friction and untainted by hypocrisy or evasion, while the other combines "vigorous faith" with the "possibility of reasoned vindication."[50] The former may include cases of "crazy dogmatism" or "forms of fundamentalism which deny that faith must be freely given,"[51] whereas the latter requires both keeping religion out of the public domain, which only entertains public reason untainted by particular perspectives, and tolerating opposing views including unbelief, if not also entertaining the possibility that they may indeed be true. Accepting these conditions, which according to Rawls are among the burdens of judgment expected of all liberal citizens, is a high-wire act.[52] To stay on the wire, respect for fellow citizens "must be regarded not only as an authentic virtue; it must be prized as the paramount virtue." To relax in our respect is to open the door to contempt toward those who reasonably disagree with us. If this approach is compatible with fundamentalism, it will have to be a very different kind from those that are currently familiar, and the inculcation intended to sustain it "would have to depart drastically from the insular dogmatic education that characterizes garden-variety fundamentalism."[53] To be both a person of faith and a liberal citizen, in other words, one must "stay on the wire" by abandoning simple for sophisticated integrity.

This preference for sophistication is grounded in yet another form of integrity that Callan dubs "reflection," which entails "standing for one's own best judgment about how to live," rather than an inner consistency or integration of the self.[54] He cites the richly variegated life of the Yiddish novelist Isaac Bashevis Singer. In contrast to Jacob of Josefov, protagonist of his novel *The Slave*, who held fast to his simple faith despite hardship and religious doubts, Singer succumbed to uncertainty and abandoned the devout faith of his youth when exposed to secular literature and modern science.[55] In his autobiographical *Love and Exile*, Singer depicts himself as "a philanderer with ascetic leanings … whose restless imagination seems the only fixed point of his identity."[56] Although able to sympathetically portray the virtues of Jacob of Josefov, he could also "celebrate the implacable skepticism and contempt for tradition of a man who is Jacob's spiritual opposite."[57] Such a person, to be sure, must impose some order on his life.

> Yet if one lives in consciousness of the variety of good lives, it is natural to want to encompass many values in one's life, and so instead of the tight cohesion of a life of simple integrity one ends up with a pattern rather more messy and unsteady, but perhaps richly fulfilling for all that.[58]

Paradoxically, those open to the diversity of goods will also be conscious of the losses their openness exacts.

> But on reflection one may decide that the gains offset the loss or that what is lost is not a real option anyhow. Giving up on the good life as a linear quest may occasion a painful feeling of disorientation. But it may also yield a powerful sense of liberation.[59]

This then is Callan's default position, the "other" against which religious initiation is to be judged when it is expected to yield understanding unavailable by "other" means, the "open" field of play in which the "vigorous faith" of the sophisticated believer must be "vindicated" and the simple faith of the child "rationally revised." This is Rawls's public sphere, infused with public reason, maintained by the burdens of judgment, untainted by any parochial perspective.

But this picture of rational reflection as completely open to multiple conceptions of the good is indefensible unless one accepts the sort of reductionism that Quine has challenged or the neutrality of the very rational reflection in question, which results in a circular argument unacceptable on rational grounds.[60] Oakeshott would see in this preference for reasoned reflection an instance of the fallacy of rationalism in politics, the false idea that human affairs can be adequately captured by means of abstract and rigid concepts and techniques such as those taught in empirical science and by both universal liberals and critical social theorists.[61] All of these are but convenient techniques for summarizing more complex manners, customs, symbols, and stories by means of which people live with others. The summaries he called technical and the lived complexities practical knowledge. One can be formulated in propositions, rules, principles, directions, and maxims; the other exists only in the human relations in which communal life is conducted and is shared by means of practical traditions, not theoretical doctrines. Oakeshott traced the source of this fallacy to a preoccupation with certainty by the likes of Rene Descartes and Bacon, but it in fact goes back to Plato's, and to some degree Aristotle's, preference for theory over practice and the idea that power should be vested in those whose belief—*pistis*—is free from error. The Hebrew Bible offered an alternative account, however, grounded in a covenant of faith— *emunah*—between free people and a moral God preserved in traditions comprised of sacred narratives and revered customs and ceremonies.

Callan claims that for a believer to accept the burdens of judgment entails "variation on the conflict between Athens and Jerusalem that was powerfully evident near the very beginnings of their tradition and has shaped its development ever since."[62] Athenian philosophy represents the antecedents of liberal toleration based on universal rationality, in this analogy, while the revealed religion of Jerusalem signifies the inflexible dogma or unsubstantiated local custom that is to be tolerated, but only under the condition that it is transformed from simple to sophisticated, by means of reconciliation with reason. But Plato's, and to a lesser extent Aristotle's, rationalism was anything but tolerant of difference; and this so-called reconciliation is more like a subjugation of revelation by reason than an acknowledgment of each based on mutual recognition. For all of his talk of tolerance, Callan's liberalism appears to follow in these Athenian footsteps. He shows little patience for biblical *emunah* or one or another traditional account of the human encounter with transcendence, casting these as "simple," and taints them with the brush of "crazy dogmatism" or "garden variety fundamentalism." To the extent that this sort of liberalism is prepared to entertain religious initiation at all, it appears to prioritize inflexible *pistis*, such as the rationally vindicated belief that the philosopher's god exists, over *emunah*, faith in a living God or dynamic tradition.

Ironically, the simplicity and rigidity that Callan and other like-minded rationalists attribute to religious tradition in fact belongs more properly to the rational principles born of "arid technique," which entered into religion in response to rationalism.[63] As noted previously, a tradition of practice is not an inflexible manner of doing things. "It is neither fixed, nor finished; it has no changeless centre to which understanding can anchor itself."[64] It is normal for traditions of practice to change, which emerges gradually in part through contact with other viewpoints. The relevant educational issue concerns a faith's willingness to permit learning from alternative perspectives, not the rational sophistication of its beliefs.[65]

The "unbeliever's objection" fails, then, since it misconstrues religion by reducing key articles of faith to a series of beliefs that something is the case assessed according to untenable logical or empirical criteria. This results in a false dichotomy between simple and sophisticated religion that privileges an incoherent account of reflection as a default position against which life paths are to be adjudicated and falls prey to the false idea that human affairs, including religion, can be adequately captured in abstract rational techniques torn from practical experience preserved in dynamic cultural inheritances.

"Belief in" and the believer's objection

The believer's objection also fails, because the primary sort of understanding that is achieved through initiation into religion is characterized not by the appreciation of an object such as a work of art or some putative theological truth—God's existence or transubstantiation—but by entering into relation with another subject in an intimate I–Thou moment in which, to use Buber's words, the other fills the firmament.[66] To the believer, the presence of God is all too real, not "putative" or "imagined," experienced in a "'meeting" between subjects that Buber called "dialogue." The result is not any sort of "objectual" understanding at all, but a form of insight into oneself and others that is achieved by a letting go, at least in part, in order to receive another subject. Parker Palmer called this self-knowledge as one might be perceived by another, by God or Jesus or Allah or Buddha or a beloved friend.[67] It is a form of what Israel Scheffler called personal, as opposed to propositional or procedural, knowledge that entails a meeting of two subjects, not the confrontation of a subject with an object to be understood—the presidency or the English language—or the acting of a subject upon the objective world—electing a candidate or speaking English.[68] In these instances, claims Buber, one engages the world to achieve an instrumental purpose, to grasp a concept or master a practice. However, in a subject–subject encounter, we set aside interest in order to receive the other with no end in view other than the meeting itself. Thus Buber even allows that we can encounter a prized location or event or work of art or sacred text in this way, provided we receive each for its own sake, not for some instrumental purpose, in which case one's self-perception can be transformed no less than in meeting other humans or God, since we can come to view ourselves in a new light.[69]

Many mystical traditions depict insight of this kind metaphorically by reference to intimate relations between two people: knowledge in the biblical sense, as when "Now the man knew his wife Eve."[70] The insight that is achieved "resides" in neither subject alone but in the encounter between them—a new intersubjective entity into which, at least for a moment, one loses oneself in the other. According to Thomas Merton, it is by means of such insight that we learn to let go of the egotism and self-centeredness inherent in what he calls our "false" selves, which drives us to impose our individual ambitions or aspirations—our will—on others, in order to discover a more genuine or authentic version of ourselves in which the needs and feelings of others take precedence over our own.[71] From a less theological point of view, Nel Noddings describes this process in terms of one-caring who receives the feelings of one-cared-for, which confirms in each an elevated sense of self.[72]

Moral independence, in this view, is to be found in the contraction, not the assertion of self; in receiving, not interfering, with others; in what Noddings calls "engrossment."[73] This may be why Berlin preferred negative to positive liberty, because it entails an acknowledgment of the independence of the other rather than an assertion or imposition of self. Although religion is not the only path to this sort of insight, nor is it central to every faith tradition, the capacity to engage another in this way is among the most important disciplines that the rituals of worship make possible; it is what a devout Christian can experience when she ingests bread and wine as embodiments of Jesus, what an observant Jew might feel upon bending the knee before the Holy One in silent devotion, what a religious Muslim could undergo in prostrating himself before Allah, and what may transpire for a Buddhist when she loses herself in meditation. In this experience, one meets the divine or transcendent in an interpersonal encounter, mediated by the customs and ceremonies of a tradition that shapes perceptions based on centuries of human encounter with what Rudolph Otto called the "Holy," Paul Tillich the "Ultimate," and Philip Phenix "Transcendence." And when we confront this "True Reality," to use Mircia Eliade's term, in whatever tradition we may find it, we learn among other lessons that although we may possess some truths, we do not in and of ourselves embody the Absolute Truth; although we may all be the children of God, none of us *is* God; although every human being may contain a glimpse of the Divine, we are not ourselves divine; although each of us is holy, we do not possess Ultimate Holiness, either as individuals or collectives.[74] Self-determination begins, on this account, by acknowledging the other, not centering on the self.

Yet, although we are not God, we are or can be like God—by recognizing that engrossment entails learning to control ourselves, not dominate others. At the end of the day, both partners in dialogue remain responsible for themselves, however transformed by the encounter they may be. Consider again the Eucharist, which commemorates the last supper of Jesus. This was a Passover Seder, which retells the story of Israelite liberation from an Egyptian Pharaoh who believed himself divine and so entitled to enslave others. "Let My people go," demanded Moses in God's name, "so that they may celebrate a festival for Me in the wilderness."[75] To celebrate this God is to be liberated from the enslavement of the Egyptian and every other Pharaoh by accepting a revelation that calls us to receive others and to respect their independence. When the Israelites rejected this message by worshipping a golden calf, the very symbol of Pharaoh's power, the text ritualized the liberation from bondage by requiring the sacrifice of a calf in the worship of God.[76] This sacrifice was institutionalized in the Jerusalem cult for close to a thousand years. When the Temple was destroyed by the Romans in the first century, it was replaced in Christian worship by accepting the sacrifice of Jesus and in Jewish worship by penitential prayers. The spiritual challenge embodied in devotion of this kind involves learning the self-control to respect others by receiving rather than imposing oneself upon them.[77]

It may well have been into just this sort of encounter that Anscombe wished to see her young friend initiated, the appropriate response to which is what Abraham Joshua Heschel called awe and wonder.[78] Perhaps this is why the youngster was seen as getting it right while the theologian began to get it wrong, since the former bowed reverently while the latter sought to objectify and rationalize that which eludes objectivity and reason. Buber points out how the insight of an I–Thou moment can be lost when we attempt to view it from an objective standpoint—for example, when dialogue between subjects is used for some purpose other than the meeting itself. As discussed previously, Suzanne Langer suggests that moments filled with great emotion of this kind, from trepidation to elation, may be best captured in nondiscursive idioms that strive to convey the dynamic shape of feelings in vicarious experiences expressed in such fine arts as sculpture or dance.[79]

Religious customs and ceremonies can be understood in this way as enabling the worshipper to vicariously experience the dynamic feelings of those whose direct encounters with the Divine have been authenticated by tradition and captured in symbols and rituals. Consider the Jewish liturgical formula known as the *kedusha*, or sanctification of the Deity. At the climax of the worship service, when supplicants experience themselves as standing directly before God, they repeat the words that, according to the book of *Isaiah*, the angels recite in the Divine presence: "Holy, Holy, Holy is the Lord of Hosts, His presence fills the Earth"[80] and then the words that according to the book of *Ezekiel*, the angels respond to one another: "Blessed be the Presence of the Lord in His place."[81] Worshippers stand before God, in this tradition, and grasp the meaning of holiness in their lives, by reenacting these prophetic experiences in Isaiah's and Ezekiel's own words. The problem with Anscombe's theologian, on this view, is not that he acknowledged the role of metaphor in worship, but that for him the lived religion that the metaphor was to have facilitated was in the process of dying, and with it the metaphor itself, not the least because he confused rational theological understanding with an act of faith. As Oakeshott observed, rationalism often shares with dogmatism a literalism that is uncharacteristic of a dynamic tradition.[82]

The insight born of lived religious experience knows no age, though it can mature and in many traditions involves skill that requires practice, like playing a musical instrument or speaking a language. These are preserved in the narratives, symbols, and customs that comprise what Oakeshott called a tradition of practice. The earlier one begins, the more accomplished one can become; and the skill with which one is able to express oneself shapes what one is capable of feeling, not only what one is able to express.[83] The capacity to experience faith is learned, then, through the artistry of worship—what Heschel called *prayers of empathy* that teach us to feel the Divine presence, in contrast to *prayers (or acts) of expression*, in which we give voice to what we already feel.[84] When Anscombe's young friend learned to take communion, he was learning a prayer of empathy; when he bowed spontaneously before his mother, he engaged in an act of expression. I know many adults who feel uncomfortable in the synagogue, and so avoid, even denigrate, Jewish worship, because they never learned the requisite skills at a sufficient level of proficiency to participate competently. Of course this reaction could also be a consequence of being wrongly taught in dogmatic or abusive ways or simply because it does not inspire the relevant feelings of reverence, in which case one should be free to seek a life path elsewhere. However, the answer to Callan's question about bringing the kids into such a tradition is clear: Doing otherwise substantially diminishes their capacity to intelligently choose such a life for themselves.

On this account, the believer's objection is no objection at all, since to acquire insight of this kind is just what it means to embrace faith in another subject, divine or otherwise. In this sense faith in the other is not merely a belief that some metaphysical object exists, but rather trust in the reciprocity that any genuine relationship entails. The default position for the believer—Heschel called it an ontological presupposition—is the reality of a dialogue seeking God, not neutral reflection; and the insight that engaging this God involves is not a means to some other end, it is the end.[85] This is the very heart of what the Hebrew Bible means by *emunah*, which conceives the mutual obligations that emerge from the Divine–human encounter in covenantal terms, though other traditions may conceive them differently. This sort of faith is neither simple nor sophisticated but intelligent—intellectually, emotionally, and morally—well informed by an ever-emerging tradition of practice that preserves the insights of previous generations while adapting to changing times and circumstances, and afraid of neither doubt nor criticism, but aware that living in relation involves acknowledging our mistakes—including God's—and then accepting one another despite them.[86] In the dynamics of such dialogue, the dichotomy between heteronomy and autonomy is blurred, since the so-called external demands of the other—lover, one-cared-for, nature, history, community, sacred text, God—are embedded along with my own concerns in the relationship that we now share, and the reasons why one might assent to those demands are to be found in the reciprocity that such a relationship entails. This is why recitation of the commandment "You shall love the Lord your God with all your heart, with all your soul, and with all your might"[87] is preceded in Jewish liturgy with the words, "You have loved us with abundant love, O Lord our God…enlighten our eyes to understand your Torah and dedicate our hearts to observe your commandments,"[88] indicating that in choosing a religious life, one is responding to the Divine love embodied in the gift of revelation.

The other face of liberalism revisited

Rational reflection cannot be presupposed as a default position with respect to competing traditions that espouse conceptions of the good. As Callan himself suggests, its values are part and parcel of one such tradition that entails the embrace of particular liberal virtues and beliefs.[89] "Future citizens must be taught to think in particular ways about doctrines that properly lie outside the scope of public reason," he contends. "The moral authority of the family and the various associations in which the child grows up must be questioned to the extent that the society contains reasonable alternatives to whatever that authority prescribes."[90] To propose this particular tradition as a universal ideal, to use Gray's formulation, against which other ways of life are to be judged, entails not pluralism but yet another case of the sort of positive liberty about which Berlin expressed deep reservations:

> Once I take this view, I am in a position to ignore the actual wishes of men or societies, to bully, oppress; torture them in the name, and on behalf, of their 'real' selves, in the secure knowledge that whatever is the true goal of man (happiness, performance of duty, wisdom, a just society, self-fulfillment) must be identical with his freedom–the free choice of his 'true', albeit often submerged and inarticulate, self.[91]

Nor can the best interests of children, or what might be considered harm, be determined in any meaningful way other than within the context of rival traditions of political, religious, cultural, or educational practice. As McLaughlin pointed out:

The indeterminacy of the child's interest provides a starting point not only for arguments emphasizing parents' 'non-paternalistic' rights over their children but also for arguments claiming that, in the midst of perplexity, parents are in the best position to perceive and determine any paternalistic intervention that may be justified on behalf of the child.[92]

Neither the cause of pluralism (or ecumenism) nor the best interests of children are served by such a false sense of unrestricted openness.

This is to say nothing against reflective integrity as a way of life other than that it has no privileged standing as a criterion against which to judge other life paths. In a liberal society it must compete with all the rest on a playing field in which numerous incommensurable traditions, cultures, and religions vie for the allegiance of citizens who are free to combine them in whatever ways and at whatever levels of commitment they see fit, without any preconceived rules of engagement. Callan, following Rawls, holds that the task of liberal theory should be to rise above a mere modus vivendi that keeps peace among the competitors, to achieve a consensus concerning how the competition is to be conducted, governed by public reason, the burdens of judgment, and other liberal values and doctrines. Yet, without the possibility of rational neutrality or privilege in some form, a modus vivendi for peaceful coexistence may be the best that liberal democracy can achieve; in which case, there can be no warrant whatsoever to holding initiation into religion hostage to a view of reflection that is unsustainable as a universal ideal. I have tried to show, on the other hand, that some religious orientations entail an alternative account of openness, understood as receptivity to difference grounded in respect for cultural inheritance—for example, the biblical notion of interpersonal trust as the basis of a covenant among free people who control the impulse to impose themselves on others.[93] This constitutes the grounds of a more pluralistic liberalism.

It is, alas, now impossible to ascertain whether the sort of religion I have described is what McLaughlin had in mind in coining the expression *autonomy via faith* or whether he would have embraced my strong endorsement of Berlin's brand of value pluralism. The foregoing undoubtedly reflects more my view than his; but it was a profound commitment to both intelligent faith and the deep pluralism required for it to prosper that we held in common, I believe, and it was this capacity to embrace the other by recognizing the divine spark in each person that inspired me to call him my friend. It is certainly not the only interpretation of autonomy that meets the demands of democratic citizenship, but neither can it be so easily dismissed as Callan suggests. Noddings put it well when she commented that intelligent believers and unbelievers may have more in common with one another than with unintelligent believers and unbelievers; and it is surely intelligence born of reasonable, reflective, religious, or other traditions that lies at the heart of the moral independence that democratic citizenship requires.[94]

PART FIVE

Epilogue

I conclude with two chapters that respond to criticisms that have been raised about the views expressed here, especially concerning religious initiation in liberal democracies and the ties between spirituality and both ethics and critical thinking. Chapter Eleven is the only chapter in this volume that was not published previously. It arose out of a private conversation I had with Eamonn Callan at the book launching for *Faith in Education: A Tribute to Terence McLaughlin* in 2009. My paper on religious initiation for that volume (which is reprinted in slightly revised form in Chapter Ten in this volume) was based on a 1984–1985 debate between Callan and McLaughlin in the *Journal of Philosophy of Education*. Callan pointed out that subsequent to 1985, McLaughlin had published a good deal on the subject of religious upbringing in liberal democracy, and Callan intimated that this work might cast McLaughlin's views in a different light than the interpretation I offered in my 2009 paper. I took the conversation as an opportunity to situate my depiction of "autonomy via faith" in McLaughlin's later work and to respond to important questions raised by Michael Hand at the end of the McLaughlin tribute. Of particular interest in this chapter is my discussion of McLaughlin's critique of Israel Scheffler on education in Judaism. Scheffler's philosophy of Jewish education was influenced by Mordecai Kaplan, a leading American Jewish theologian who sought to reconcile John Dewey's naturalism with both the national and religious aspects of Jewish civilization. McLaughlin was critical of a natural theology that eschews a transcendental God, at least in part because it tends to subjugate substantive faith traditions to the confines of an especially secular brand of liberalism, a view that I share.

Chapter Twelve builds on this discomfort with Dewey's religious naturalism by responding to another sort of criticism that is often raised about the views developed here, well articulated in Kevin Gary's generous review of *Reclaiming Goodness*. He asks, first, whether I have conflated spirituality with morality; and second, whether I have underestimated the tensions between spirituality and critical thinking. I rejoin in the first instance that Gary has not adequately distinguished between the deontological morality associated with the sort of comprehensive liberalism discussed in Chapter Eleven and the more ancient tradition of aretaic ethics consistent with the liberal account of communitarianism defended in Chapter Nine and Isaiah Berlin's pluralistic account of liberalism outlined in Chapter Six. The spiritual quest of recent years is a response to the failure of the deontological ethics of comprehensive liberalism to offer meaning, which is found in comprehensive visions of the good. Hence, this use of the term "morality" should undoubtedly be distinguished from contemporary references to spirituality. But not "ethics" in the aretaic sense of the term, the revival of which I argue goes hand in hand with the current spiritual awakening. In the second instance I suggest that Gary has not adequately distinguished between Aristotle's notions of *Sophia* and *Phronesis*, or theoretical reason and practical wisdom. The sort of critical thinking associated with the theoretical reason of liberal rationalism may indeed be in tension with the current spiritual quest, but not the normative judgments of merit and quality that are the hallmark of practical wisdom. It is within this practical ethical discourse that the spiritual quest properly resides, a discourse more open than that of Dewey or other comprehensive liberals to the sort of religious transcendentalism embraced by William James.

For liberals like me who have devoted substantial portions of our lives to the religious upbringing of children and to educating them in cultural and national affiliations, the issues that this debate brings to the fore are not merely academic. Among the kids Callan asks about in posing the question, "Why bring the kids into this?" are my own children and students. I recall sitting in synagogue one Shabbat morning as I pondered Callan's thoughtful challenge to McLaughlin, asking myself whether I had been engaged in religious indoctrination for these many years. Had I acted in a manner that was morally damaging to my nearest and dearest? I was on sabbatical in Berkeley at the time, and the synagogue in which I was sitting was the very one in which I had been raised. This rekindled that feeling of my youth when the liberalism I encountered appeared to be less accepting of difference than it promised. So I have a deeply personal stake in getting this account of the relations between liberalism, religion, and education right.

My defense of McLaughlin on religious initiation in liberal society, on the one hand, and of the transcendental possibilities of neo-Aristotelianism, on the other, offers an account of inquiry in liberal democratic education that is accepting of robust affiliation with particular cultural traditions. McLaughlin's concept of "openness with roots" corresponds in many respects to what I have called pedagogy of difference. Both require intense exposure to robust spiritual perspectives, whether or not they are tethered to particular faith traditions, alongside openness to others who are different—both human and, where relevant, divine; and both are grounded in the neo-Aristotelian revival associated with liberal communitarianism and diversity liberalism defended in the final chapter. In this view, education in intelligent spirituality properly conceived can play an important role in the preparation of citizens for open, pluralistic, liberal democratic societies.

CHAPTER ELEVEN

To the Truth, Roughly Speaking

Introduction

In Chapter Ten, I took up the late Terry McLaughlin's side in a well-known dispute with Eamonn Callan over the liberal right of parents to educate their children in religion. I argued that McLaughlin favored the sort of robust pluralism according to which the personal autonomy of liberal citizens may be embedded in thick cultures infused with "belief in" dynamic faith traditions, whereas Callan supports a more uniform liberal society peopled by rationally autonomous citizens whose religious and other commitments are based on logically or empirically justified "beliefs that" something is the case.[1] McLaughlin's view is in keeping with the sort of covenantal theology found in the Hebrew Scriptures, I suggested, and most probably in the sacred texts of other faiths as well, which is often misunderstood by those who ground their liberalism in a narrow account of rationality.

Two concerns have been raised regarding this view. First, even if McLaughlin embraced a covenantal account of faith, this is irrelevant to Callan's objections concerning the liberal right of parents to instill that faith in children.[2] Second, by focusing on McLaughlin's 1984 essay and 1985 rejoinder to Callan and not McLaughlin's subsequent essays on religious and liberal education, I may not have fully appreciated the subtleties of McLaughlin's liberalism.[3] "It is alas now impossible to ascertain," I concluded, "whether the sort of religion I have described is what McLaughlin had in mind ... or whether he would have embraced my strong endorsement of ... value-pluralism."[4]

Although space limitations did not permit consideration of McLaughlin's later work in the tribute volume, his latter views are indeed accessible and worthy of examination. In this chapter I respond to these concerns by situating my defense of McLaughlin in his subsequent work in order to clarify some important nuances in McLaughlin's and ultimately my own account of knowledge, liberalism, and liberal education.

This chapter is divided into five sections. In the first section, I summarize the initial debate between McLaughlin and Callan, including Callan's most recent rejoinder in the tribute volume and my defense of McLaughlin from the previous chapter in this volume. In the second section, I respond to Michael Hand's defense of Callan, in which he argues that the distinction between "belief in" and "belief that" is irrelevant to Callan's objections. This leads to a more detailed discussion in the three final sections concerning the difference between religious understanding from the outside and from the inside, on the one hand, and between appreciative understanding and openness with roots, on the other.

Many of us who knew and loved Terry remember the toast with which he would often begin a meal. "To the truth," he would state, firmly lifting a glass, and then with a wry smile and twinkle in his eye, he would add: "roughly speaking." Although he apparently believed in absolute truth (including in the existence of a personal God), as Karl Popper famously put it, he did not believe that anyone has it in her pocket.[5] It is this fine-tuned view of transcendence that guided McLaughlin's account of faith in liberal education, I will argue, as it does my own.

McLaughlin on religious initiation

McLaughlin argued that parents are justified in fostering a stable and coherent primary culture in their children, which may include religion, provided they are exposed to alternative views and free to choose a different life path than that of their parents upon reaching adulthood. Among other reasons, their development into autonomous adults depends upon it. He called this position "autonomy via faith."[6] Callan responded that parents may have a *weak* right to *expose* their children to religion but not a *strong* right to *instill* faith, since reason, not religion or culture, should be the basis of life choices, and religious upbringing hampers rational development. I called this position "autonomy via reason."[7] McLaughlin rejoined that "Callan too quickly dismisses the significance of being on the inside of religion for the capacity to evaluate it." Religious initiation yields understanding unavailable by other means that enhances the capacity of children to make informed choices about religious life.[8] In the tribute volume, Callan retorted by claiming that McLaughlin's rejoinder, which he dubbed the "initiation thesis," satisfies neither the believer nor the unbeliever:

> On the one hand, the justification of religious initiation fails for the religious believer because it inverts the proper relation between understanding and faith; on the other hand, it fails for the unbeliever because though religious upbringing might enhance the growth of understanding in some respects, it thwarts its development in other respects that cannot be reasonably dismissed as unimportant.[9]

In defense of McLaughlin, I held that the believer's objection fails because it supposes that one can distinguish the sort of understanding that is achieved in the midst of belief or faith *in* someone or something and an act of faith itself, such that one could be said to lead to the other (understanding to faith or faith to understanding). But precisely the opposite is the case when faith is understood as a covenantal concept. To acquire a deeper understanding of oneself in relation to another—a lover or friend or one-cared-for or tradition or God—is just what it means to have faith in the other. To dissect the relationship by means of the sort of analysis or justification to which the objection refers is to commit a version of what Michael Oakeshott called the fallacy of "rationalism in politics"—the false idea that human affairs can be adequately captured by means of abstract and rigid techniques rather than concrete and dynamic "traditions of practice," preserved, for example, in the artistry of worship, among other rituals, customs, and ceremonies.[10] Autonomy via faith, on this account, entails the discipline or control of self required to receive or become engrossed in another person or tradition.

The unbeliever's objection also fails, I contended, because it reduces beliefs *in* someone to beliefs *that* something is the case, adjudicated according to neutral logical or empirical criteria. This falls prey to one or both of Willard Van Orman Quine's famed "dogmas of empiricism" that analytic can be distinguished from synthetic statements, or logical from empirical truths, and that the meaning of all statements can be reduced to sense data.[11] Quine proposed instead that meanings are interconnected with one another in holistic webs of belief such that the "objects" of a theory are but "cultural posits," decipherable only within the context of the theory as a whole or from the perspective of another theory.[12] That autonomy can only properly be understood in relation to one's capacity to logically or empirically assess the truth-value of statements is indefensible, therefore, since this very idea is itself the product of a tradition of thought that is not fully sustainable by a priori reason. It does not follow that autonomy via reason is to be rejected, however, or that it cannot or should not be combined in some way with autonomy via faith (McLaughlin was clearly in favor of such a combination), only that it is one of several rival accounts that must compete for the loyalty of adherents in a liberal society, each with their own strengths and weaknesses. Isaiah Berlin called this stance value pluralism.[13]

Two types of faith revisited

In his concluding remarks to the McLaughlin tribute, Hand responded to my defense of McLaughlin by asserting that even if I am right about Callan's misreading of religious understanding, this misses the point of the believer's objection.[14]

For the believer, what justifies the enterprise of religious upbringing is "the possibility of faith and salvation," not "whatever understanding the possibility happens to presuppose." Religious understanding does not enter into the believer's justification, so disagreements about its nature are by the by.[15]

But covenantal faith is not a product of or a pathway to religious understanding. It just *is* such an understanding, achieved in contraction rather than assertion of self, to receive or accept the demands of others. "I live to serve," Terry was want to say. Faith of the sort he advocated is lived in service to others. This requires a form of self-control or self-discipline into which children can be initiated without fear of indoctrination, provided they are exposed to alternatives and free to choose other paths as they mature. Self-assertion, though not problematic in the nature of the case, can lead to a centering on the self in which people see themselves as gods, entitled to impose on others. "Every human being has the right to seek religious truth and adhere to it freely," McLaughlin wrote.

No one is to be forced to act against his or her conscience.... To proclaim or to offer faith is not to engage in the "moral violence" of imposition. In the covenantal tradition, we are not ourselves divine, but strive to imitate the Divine by our willingness to place others—God, community, tradition, family, friends and loved ones—before ourselves.[16]

Salvation is earned, on this account, through a life of service. One learns to live such a life by following the example of those who do so—through the wisdom of practice, not rational justification—what Aristotle called *Phronesis*, not *Sophia*.

In *Phronesis*, practical knowledge of the good is related to intelligent and personally engaged sensitivity to situations, individuals (including oneself) and a tradition of belief and life, in making inherently supple and non-formulable practical judgments about what constitutes an appropriate expression of the good in a given circumstance.[17]

If grasping the meaning of "belief in" is "by the by" according to Hand, understanding how "beliefs that" are themselves embedded in traditions is equally beside the point.

The unbeliever's objection … certainly assumes that the ability to subject one's beliefs to rational criticism is valuable…. It is only criticism from a putatively tradition transcending point of view to which Alexander objects, he is quite at ease with rational criticism of one tradition from the perspective of another. Fairly obviously, though, religious indoctrination is as inimical to the kind of criticism Alexander favors as to the kind he rejects. The unbeliever's objection about beliefs imparted to children by "characteristically admired and loved adults"…is that subjecting them to any form of criticism, tradition-transcending or tradition-embedded is extraordinarily difficult. Asserting that one form of criticism is in any case ruled out by other considerations scarcely addresses that worry.[18]

However, if the idea of a tradition-transcendent view from nowhere is ruled out of court, then the only sort of criticism possible—rational or otherwise—must be tradition embedded, either from within a tradition or from the perspective of another. Callan is quite right to worry about the sort of religious initiation that precludes criticism of this kind, but this is not the approach to religious upbringing that McLaughlin advocated. He agreed with Callan that an initiation into faith that is totally closed to alternatives—religious and nonreligious options—would be tantamount to untenable indoctrination and sought to preclude just such an approach through the complement to autonomy via faith, "openness with roots." According to this idea, education in religion, or what McLaughlin called (in work we completed together) religiously tethered spirituality, must entail exposure to alternative perspectives in addition to a primary culture, so as to ensure that the child will be free to choose a life path without coercion.[19]

> On the side of "openness," liberal democratic societies should be committed, within familiar limits, to a robust pluralism that accommodates a diversity of religious and spiritual belief, commitment, and activity and ensures the development for individuals of the tools of self-definition.… On the side of "rootedness," however, liberal democratic societies also have an interest in the flourishing, again within familiar limits, of forms of religious and spiritual belief, commitment, and activity that constitute not only important contexts for the formation of persons and of democratic character, but also resources for the shaping of lives.[20]

Callan is also right to be concerned about the difficulty of fostering such a critical stance, but this concern applies to all traditions, including rational ones. It does not undermine the idea that a youngster will be in a better position to decide whether or not to choose a religious life having lived one, under the relevant conditions of openness. The dispute between McLaughlin and Callan, then, concerns whether *some* account of religious initiation is justifiable, not whether *all* of them are; and the unbeliever's objection only gains a foothold as a complaint against McLaughlin if one privileges the unbeliever's perspective as neutral vis-à-vis that of the believer, because it is based on rational reflection; and this, as I have demonstrated, is an untenable position. The existence of a plurality of rival and incommensurable cultures and traditions competing for our devotion is inescapable. A critical attitude can only be acquired under these circumstances by combining initiation into the internal standards of one tradition with exposure to alternative perspectives—education in religion and spirituality from the "outside" as well as the "inside." The former views issues of meaning, truth, and value "primarily as matters for exploration, discussion, and critical assessment," in which no one tradition is given normative preference. The latter refers to forms of education that are "appropriate for those within a particular religious or spiritual tradition, or those being initiated into such a tradition."[21]

Two type of religious understanding

We can distinguish, then, between two sorts of understanding in the religious domain, understanding about religion "from the outside" and religious understanding per se "from the inside." In the one, as I have argued, a subject acquires knowledge or appreciation of an object, whereas in the other a subject receives or accepts another subject into himself or herself; one is associated with "belief that," the other with "belief in." Although I surmised this distinction from his early dispute with Callan and our later work together, McLaughlin discussed its consequences for education in religion and spirituality in a number of subsequent important essays. For example, in his analysis of education, spirituality, and the common school, he argued that the former is most appropriate for nonconfessional situations such as common schools in pluralistic, liberal democratic societies in which no one religious or spiritual tradition is given normative preference.[22] On the other hand, in his defense of separate schools for religious and other communities and in his account of the distinctiveness of the Catholic school, he held that the latter is more suitable to religious upbringing in the home or to initiation into particular traditions in faith schools, though not without concomitant exposure to the former to some degree as well.[23] His discussion of Ludwig Wittgenstein on religion and education, however, illuminates a more nuanced account of this distinction that addresses not only the limitations of the believer's and unbeliever's objections, but also the contribution of Callan's analysis to religious education.[24]

McLaughlin pointed out that among the many contemporary philosophers and educationalists who espouse what he called the "Liberal Rational" (LR) approach to education in religion and spirituality, some acknowledge a difference between understanding from the outside and the inside, whereas others do not.[25] Callan does. However, following Wittgenstein on education and religion, McLaughlin further argued that many LR advocates who acknowledge that religion should be understood from the inside fail to fully comprehend its meaning and complexity. Callan falls into this camp as well. According to the first account of LR:

> Education in religion, at least in the common schools of a pluralistic liberal democracy, should aim not at fostering religious belief and practice

in students but at their achievement of understanding in this domain....
The forms of commitment it seeks to bring about are those of the
educated, rather than the religious, person.... Students should be made
aware that the domain of religion, though worthy of engaged attention,
involves uncertainty and controversy and the question of religious faith
and practice is therefore a matter for personal reflective evaluation,
decision, and response.[26]

This formulation of LR, although supported by familiar arguments and
addressed to the common schools of pluralistic, liberal democracies, "also
calls into question the character and legitimacy of education in religion in
religious schools." A second formulation of LR, which is more sympathetic
to religion, would stress that

the view is not expressing hostility to religious faith as such, but seeking
to achieve for individuals an appropriate degree of objectivity of
judgment and self-determination.... Nor need the complexity involved
in achieving understanding in the religious domain be overlooked or
oversimplified. The significance of the "internal" perspective ... is typically
acknowledged.... Since this general view rules out the formation and
maintenance of faith, attempts are made to satisfy the requirements of this
"internal" perspective through such strategies as sympathetic imaginative
participation.[27]

Callan's account of appreciative understanding in the religious domain
would appear to place him in this second LR camp. In contrast to Jonathan
Kvanvig's relational understanding, which requires "an internal grasping of
appreciation of how various elements in a body of information are related
to each other," appreciative understanding "entails grasping the meaning
of something in a way that registers its true value, and to that extent, being
able to respond with the emotions that benefit its true value."[28] This entails
not only the sort of critical assessment that I have discussed at length, but
also a perspectival requirement.

Appreciative understanding of Catholicism requires that one take up the
perspective of a practicing Catholic, at least by imagining oneself into
that perspective provisionally...Any religion must be understood from
the inside if it is to be understood (in the appreciative sense) at all.[29]

But, McLaughlin asked: "Can the demands of the 'internal' perspective
be adequately satisfied by strategies such as 'sympathetic imaginative
participation?'"[30] From Wittgenstein's point of view, at least as McLaughlin
read it, the answer is clearly no. Religious experience is more particular
than general, according to McLaughlin on Wittgenstein. Hence, religious
understanding, from the inside, is achieved primarily by living a religious

life. Presenting religion as uncertain or controversial, even sympathetically or appreciatively, misrepresents important elements of such a life.[31] It does not follow that in order to engender any understanding in the religious domain whatsoever, the democratic common school should teach youngsters to confess one religious faith or another; those schools celebrate diversity, not a particular religious way of life.[32] They should promote religious understanding from the outside, not the inside, to which Callan's account of appreciative understanding offers a welcome contribution. Properly taught sympathetic appreciation could help "elucidate" a particular life of faith, to use D. Z. Phillips's terminology.[33] Although McLaughlin emphasized that several problems facing "elucidation" remain unexplored, such as the difficulty of bringing about an "intellectually and spiritually sophisticated" understanding of the nature and force of orthodoxy and orthopraxis, it might assist nonreligious students in understanding some very general characteristics of religious life and aid children of one faith in appreciating key aspects of another.[34]

To those who would seriously consider embracing a particular faith tradition, however, and to families and educational institutions outside the common sector that aim to initiate students into such a tradition, appreciative understanding is no substitute for what Phillips called "advocacy," which leads to the acceptance of a particular way of life. However, McLaughlin was also quick to point out that from a Wittgensteinian perspective, religious advocacy (or initiation) does not preclude allowing, even teaching, students to question key articles of faith. Forms of religious life have their own criteria of assessment, and the initiation process, if it is to involve education not indoctrination, should prepare students to apply these criteria to important religious doctrines and practices. Additionally, Wittgenstein would not preclude criticizing one faith tradition from the perspective of another, including the assessment of particular theological positions by reference to appropriate external rational criteria, provided that appropriate steps are taken to ensure proper understanding of the relevant standards and concepts of opposing traditions and that one is not granted privilege over the other. Here again, Callan's appreciative understanding could be most helpful, as a way of understanding another faith tradition from the outside.[35]

Appreciative understanding versus openness with roots

McLaughlin illustrated the complexities of this more nuanced difference, between *appreciative understanding* of religion from the outside and *openness with roots* grounded in religious understanding from the inside, in a comparison of Richard Peters and Israel Scheffler on religion and education.[36] McLaughlin noted that Peters saw himself as "something of an outsider to religious faith and experience."[37] Peters offered a sympathetic appreciation of religious life based on his own membership in the Society of Friends (Quakers), albeit as one who, on his own account, "is on the fringe of that society."[38] Yet he also noted that the Quaker allergy to dogma and authority, and its emphasis on "individual spiritual insight," makes it a form of religion that is "not alien to the person who believes in the use of reason."[39] Religion, on Peters's account, "is grounded in an experience that is accessible in principle to any reflective person: awe," which is an emotion "of overwhelming significance" inextricably "shot through with contingency."[40] The appropriate response to such feelings, which result from confronting the contingency of creation and appreciating the limits of reason, is to express and endorse them in symbolic forms of worship— prostration, praying, singing, and public rituals. Religious experience of this kind enhances morality, rather than superseding it, by emphasizing particular values, such as respect for persons, which "passes into reverence and love" when "viewed in the broader context of human life on earth."[41] According to McLaughlin, and he emphasized that Peters might well have agreed, although this account offers "a foundation for the religious sense and for religious attitudes and reactions," it is "unduly thin." It provides no detailed treatment of how these foundations could be related to "more developed religious beliefs, rituals, and practices of the sort found in a thicker religious tradition such as Judaism."[42] Peters did not explore the educational implications of this view of religion for education in religion and spirituality in the common or separate schools of pluralistic, liberal democracies, McLaughlin points out, but he could well insist that at least in the common schools of those societies pupils should be given opportunities to reflect on these issues without being expected to share Peters's perspective on them.[43]

By way of comparison, McLaughlin considers the life and work of Scheffler.[44] Unlike Peters's marginal religious affiliation, Scheffler was raised in an Orthodox Jewish family, educated in Jewish faith schools up to and including his ordination as a rabbi by the Jewish Theological Seminary of America, and was traditionally observant throughout his life. He was also a leading philosopher who, in light of the relationship between democracy and reason, held that common education in a liberal society should "liberate the mind, strengthen its critical powers, inform it with knowledge and the capacity for independent inquiry, engage its human sympathies, and illuminate its moral and practical choices."[45] Scheffler would appear then to be the ideal candidate to illustrate McLaughlin's concept of "openness with roots." Indeed, Scheffler even referred to himself as an "intellectual bilingualist" committed at once "to the universalistic character of philosophy, with its emphasis on skepticism, rationality, objectivity and the like, on the one hand, and to religious belief and practice, on the other."[46] Yet, on closer inspection, Scheffler's profile may be more closely aligned with the sophisticated, as opposed to the simple, believer to which Callan referred and to which I responded in our respective contributions to the McLaughlin tribute. Whereas simple is transformed into sophisticated religion through a subjugation of faith by reason in which religious understanding from the inside is overtaken by that from the outside, the covenantal faith inherent in McLaughlin's "openness with roots" entails a dialogue between the two that results in what I call intelligent spirituality. As I argued previously, such a faith is "informed by an ever-emerging tradition of practice that preserves insights from previous generations while adapting to changing times and circumstances" that is "afraid of neither doubt nor criticism."[47]

McLaughlin was especially concerned with the "historical and naturalistic approach" to Judaism and Jewish education that Scheffler learned from his teacher at the Seminary, the great Reconstructionist rabbi and theologian, Mordecai Kaplan.[48] This orientation

> "eschews apologetics and builds on the firmest views available in general scholarship, rational philosophy, and scientific research." Thus, "our independent conceptions of truth, logic, and evidence" take precedence over the inherited text and religious practice as they stand, and require that their epistemic and moral authority be reassessed and reinterpreted.[49]

Setting aside whether rabbinic tradition is amenable to so extensive a reinterpretation, there appears to be considerable tension between Scheffler's preference for truth, logic, and evidence, on the one hand, and his concern for inherited tradition, on the other. In his approach to general education, which is based on the former, Scheffler holds that we must "surrender the idea of shaping or molding the mind of the pupil."[50] Yet in his account of Jewish education, which appeals in some sense to the latter, he aims to nourish, support, and perhaps even mold the child in membership of a distinctive cultural community. Scheffler seems to view the texts, doctrines, and rituals of Judaism, to the extent that they refer to, or imply, transcendent or metaphysically significant realities and claims, as literally false, positing instead that when properly translated, they provide a concrete commentary on life not available in the abstract observations of science. The particular contribution of the Jewish tradition lies instead in the "reflexive symbolic impact" of ritual that assists participants in relating "to higher values and more exalted purposes."[51] The uniqueness of this contribution remains entirely unclear, however, if, in order to remain valuable, the ideals of Jewish tradition must be translated into the naturalistic truths that Scheffler espouses in his approach to general education. Under these circumstances, asked McLaughlin, how can one justify "molding" the child in the spirit of Judaism when, properly translated, its values are just those of the liberal democracy that calls us to surrender such an approach? And why is the survival of this culture to be considered valuable when its distinctive beliefs, values, and practices appear to be either false or expressed with equal or better clarity in those of contemporary society? McLaughlin wondered, therefore, whether the privileging of rational over traditional concepts and practices in this reinterpretive project, which may look more like the thin view offered by Peters than the more robust vision one might have expected, is capable of preserving significant Jewish continuity.[52]

The contours of McLaughlin that are alternative to sophisticated religion, "openness with roots," can be seen in his commentary on Scheffler's account of the educative role of ritual in Jewish education. When engaging ritual, Scheffler insists on "a critical search for clarity" based on philosophical reflection in which pupils are called to ask themselves the question that Kaplan famously asked his students at the Seminary where Scheffler was ordained: "Do you truly believe what you are saying?"[53] This is the beginning of Scheffler's, and Kaplan's, reinterpretive project. Following John Dewey, Kaplan called it Reconstructionism. McLaughlin insisted, however, that getting this project of reconstruction off the ground requires a judicious mixture of "acceptance" (belief in), on the one hand, with the "critical search for clarity" (belief that), on the other.[54]

> "Acceptance," in the sense of a willingness of pupils to participate in ritual and to let it "speak" to them through its various modes without an undue concern about clarity of meaning, seems necessary if ritual is to have any authority, force, and stability, and if it is to exercise its distinctive educative effect.... Ritual elements may symbolize many things, and through many processes and modes, often simultaneously.... It is this feature of ritual which renders it open to the sort of reinterpretation attempted by Scheffler.... However, despite its interpretive flexibility, ritual requires an attitude of "acceptance" if it is to yield its multiple meanings and not to disintegrate, suffer abandonment or be replaced by new capriciously invented rituals lacking the same depth and range of symbolic significance.[55]

McLaughlin went so far as to suggest that there are times when "acceptance" (belief in) should take precedence over "critical engagement" (belief that).

> The educative value of rituals consists in part in their stability and "givenness" and these may be undermined by too great a preoccupation with critical clarity of meaning, where every ritual engagement becomes the occasion of a seminar.[56]

Reinterpretation of the sort Scheffler advocates invites pupils to consider their own independent beliefs in ways that "may draw attention away from the rituals themselves." This runs the risk, McLaughlin continued, of "underplaying the authoritativeness of the ritual, and the seriousness and tenacity of engagement with the tradition." Some students may ask, for example, why, once the reinterpreted insights have been gained in the shape of some "general exemplars, their ritualized embodiment continues to have any value and force."[57] Scheffler might respond to these concerns by suggesting that the right balance between "acceptance" and "critical clarity" requires a form of Jewish practical wisdom that yields a plurality of ideological approaches to Jewish life. Although McLaughlin otherwise takes a positive view of *phronesis*, in this instance in which the very stability of the tradition may well be undermined, he asked whether

> these elements of plurality and commonality can be coherently held together in an established way of life in light of a re-interpretive approach to the religious elements of the tradition of the sort which Scheffler outlines…. Education, and indeed life itself, cannot take place in a vacuum. They require tradition and substance, and traditions cannot be easily invented or reinvented from scratch.[58]

The intelligent faith born of "openness with roots" requires practical wisdom of a more grounded nature, according to McLaughlin, that exercises "balanced judgment" between a tradition of practice that is sufficiently "established" to engage alternative traditions and those alternatives themselves. In this sort of encounter the two traditions meet on a level playing field in which one does not dominate the other.[59]

Hard versus soft value pluralism

A balanced approach of this kind requires a sophisticated and subtle account of the liberal tradition. I argued that McLaughlin was a value pluralist in the spirit of Berlin and Oakeshott, in which the dynamic traditions and intelligent religion inherent in "autonomy via faith" and "openness with roots" are viewed as allies, even resources, certainly not threats, to the sort of liberalism McLaughlin embraced. In contrast, Callan is among those friendly critics of Rawls's political liberalism who point out that despite his best intentions, Rawls did not escape a more comprehensive or ethical form of liberalism. Without the possibility of rational neutrality in some form, I held, a modus vivendi for peaceful coexistence among rival incommensurable inheritances "may be the best that liberal democracy can achieve."[60] In his later work, especially his well-known distinctions between maximal and minimal citizenship and citizenship education and the burdens and dilemmas of common schooling, McLaughlin articulated some of the complexities of such a modus vivendi. His account of these complexities allows yet another distinction to be drawn between a hard form of value pluralism, associated, for example with the likes of William Galston,[61] of whom McLaughlin was somewhat critical, and his own softer, more nuanced approach to the topic, which is sympathetic to John Tomasi's liberalism without justice, which in turn echoes Berlin's value pluralism.

It is useful to begin by distinguishing between two sorts of conceptions of the good—one that advances the beliefs, practices, and interests of a particular culture that may live in proximity to other cultures and another that seeks common ground across different cultures.[62] Each of these can be conceived on a continuum between thicker and thinner conceptions, where the degree of thickness or thinness can be assessed according to the extent to which a version of the good seeks to impose itself as a form of what Berlin called positive liberty on all aspects of life and so is closed off to dialogue with alternative points of view, as opposed to negative liberty, which refrains from imposition on others.[63] A very thick particular conception of the good would look like an extreme form of ethnic or civic republicanism or religious fundamentalism, whereas a very thick version of the common good across difference, for example one that imposed liberal toleration as a universal ideal, would be tantamount to an extreme form of comprehensive liberalism. As conceptions of the commons thicken, they tolerate increasingly thinner particular ways of life. Conversely, as particular conceptions of the good become thicker, they tolerate thinner approaches to the common good across difference. Comprehensive liberal states that have a relatively thick conception of the commons, for example, often require particular identities to diminish the extent to which they rely on deeply held beliefs for public purposes. Thus Rawls's conception of public reason permits justification of public policies based only on burdens of judgment shared by all, which precludes particular constituencies from defending their positions based on certain cherished convictions. On this account, a devout Catholic would not be allowed to oppose public support for abortion or same-sex marriage on religious grounds. Conversely, thick republican states will tend to marginalize public expression of customs, languages, or commitments that diverge from the prevailing ethnic, civic, or religious ethos. Even though Hispanics represent a large minority in California, for example, English, not Spanish, remains the primary if not exclusive language of public discourse.[64]

McLaughlin's distinction between minimal and maximal citizenship, conceived again as a continuum not a dichotomy, concerns the identities, loyalties, political involvements, and social prerequisites of effective citizens in relation to the common conception of the good across difference in open, pluralistic, liberal democracies.[65] On the minimal side of the continuum, the identity conferred on the individual through citizenship is merely formal or juridical, loyalties and responsibilities are viewed primarily as local or parochial, involvements are seen as serving interests that are individual or sectoral, and prerequisites for membership are essentially legal or official. According to the maximal view, on the other hand, "the citizen must have a consciousness of him or herself as a member of a living community with a shared democratic culture involving obligations and responsibilities as well as rights."[66] The more a conception of citizenship leans toward the minimal end of this continuum, the thinner its conception of the common good, and the greater its capacity to embrace a dogmatic view of particular traditions or cultures that are so excessively thick as to be virtually closed to alternative perspectives. Conversely, the more an interpretation of citizenship leans toward the maximal end of the continuum, the thicker its concept of the common good, and the greater its need to understand tradition as dynamic by embracing somewhat thinner accounts of culture that appreciate the benefits of engaging opposing viewpoints. In principle, McLaughlin pointed out, the liberal commons should be "free of significantly controversial assumptions and judgments," and hence sufficiently thin to allow, even encourage, "the freedom of citizens to pursue their diverse private conceptions of the good within a framework of justice."[67] It should not, however, be so thin as to permit all forms of dogmatism or intolerance.

McLaughlin's distinction between light and heavy burdens, conceived again as a continuum, not a dichotomy, also relates to the "unifying, common, or public" aspects of schooling in pluralistic, liberal democracies.[68] Toward the light end of this continuum are to be found burdens of unifying aspects of schooling that invoke relatively uncontroversial values reflected in a wide consensus that bridges social divides, while on the heavy end are burdens of greater complexity and sophistication that require more sustained argument and deeper understanding (such as the educational role and limitations of personal autonomy or the proper balance between unity and diversity in democratic societies), which in the nature of the case will be more controversial. According to McLaughlin, the burdens that can be identified concerning unifying aspects of democratic schooling generate a range of corresponding dilemmas regarding the "diversifying, non-common, or non public" dimensions of education in pluralistic, liberal societies. These are dilemmas, not problems or difficulties, since they are often intractable and must be navigated, not resolved, to achieve the trust and support of diverse communities. McLaughlin articulated criteria for justifying both common and separate schools based on balancing fairly heavy burdens with their corresponding dilemmas.[69]

Value pluralists share with other liberals a concern to protect the rights of democratic citizens to choose their own life path, whether this entails following the comprehensive good into which they are born, some other way of life, or no systematic orientation whatsoever. They also agree with other liberals that this will require a common life across difference, of greater or lesser thickness, that establishes shared values and procedures that enable people of deep difference to live together in peace. As we have seen, John Gray follows Thomas Hobbes in calling these shared values and procedures a modus vivendi.[70] However, value pluralists differ from comprehensive or universal liberals over both the extent of this common life and how it is to be achieved. On the one hand, comprehensive or universal liberals tend to embrace a fairly thick conception of the common good that is achieved according to some rational foundation—often an actual, implied, or hypothetical contract agreed upon by rationally autonomous individuals stripped of their particularity. Some also call this approach ethical liberalism, since liberal toleration is embraced as a universal ideal. Value pluralists, on the other hand, hold that whether the commons is thinner or thicker, it must be negotiated on the basis of dialogue among deeply different cultures and communities. Hard value pluralists view the modus vivendi, or vision of the common good, across difference, as relatively thin, and consequently conceive democratic citizenship as relatively minimal. They tend to prefer pluralism to other social values, for example, by protecting forms of dogmatic tradition that may be intolerant of difference to some degree. Softer approaches to value pluralism balance pluralism with other commitments required for peaceful coexistence. They embrace a somewhat thicker view of the commons, therefore, and more maximal concepts of democratic citizenship.

Although his penchant for complexity often makes it difficult to pin McLaughlin down on these matters, it would not be too far off to say that he was a soft value pluralist.

> Both minimalist and maximalist interpretations of "education for citizenship" are controversial. Minimalist interpretations … are open to accusations of uncritical socialization, not least into the unexamined political values which they often embody. On the other hand, maximalist interpretations … are in danger of presupposing a substantive set of "public virtues" which may exceed principled consensus that exists or can be achieved.[71]

He was critical of Galston's conception of civic education, therefore, as relying upon an unduly thin view of the commons. Galston embraced too minimalist an approach to democratic citizenship, argued McLaughlin, settling for conspicuously light common burdens that posit aspects of nationality and culture as given and so beyond critical examination.[72] Although McLaughlin could be viewed as a kind of "diversity liberal" in that he defended particular virtues, especially those based on faith, from the tyranny of a narrow account of reason, he eschewed as false Gaston's dichotomy between diversity and autonomy, in which it is suggested that it is sufficient for citizens in diverse democracies to be merely autarchic rather than autonomous. The rational deliberation and self-determination of the autarchic person does not call into question fundamental matters of belief or conviction, such as prevailing social or political structures.[73] Although McLaughlin favored autonomy via faith, which prefers other- to self-centered ethics, he neither insulated faith from critique nor opposed autonomy via reason. On the contrary, he advocated a dialogue between the two, provided it was based on the proper degree of mutual understanding in which one did not dominate the other. Above all, McLaughlin viewed the free choice of citizens as paramount, especially in matters of faith.

On the other hand, although he shared much with Callan's comprehensive liberalism, including the desire to balance unity with diversity and promote civic respect for difference, McLaughlin was also concerned about the tendency of comprehensive liberals to inadvertently prefer unity over diversity.[74] Views of this kind may devolve into a universal ethical stance, "through the back door," he suggested, by basing common values on an unexamined presumption of shared rationality rather than on dialogue and debate.[75] The burdens of a common life across difference embraced by this comprehensive approach to liberalism are indeed heavier than those inherent in Galston's view, since they require a significant degree of critical engagement, especially concerning private goods such as those of faith traditions. But they may not be heavy enough. Public virtues are not always subjected to the same degree of scrutiny as private virtues. Nor is sufficient attention paid to the ways in which private virtues, especially those grounded in faith, are sometimes excluded from public discourse.[76]

Although his interpretation of liberalism was in many respects closer to that of Callan than Galston, neither, in McLaughlin's view, took sufficient account of the dilemmas that are attendant to their respective perspectives. Common schools, argued McLaughlin, should be based

> on a rationale which goes beyond the minimalistic yet which does not stipulate unequivocal value influence based on an ethical or comprehensive liberalism.... Students in such schools must achieve a grasp of the salience of public values for political purposes, but also come to appreciate the limitations of these values with respect to overall moral evaluation and life considered more broadly.[77]

Such an awareness requires that students learn a kind of "moral bilingualism," which involves accepting the potentially transformative implications of public virtues in a liberal society, while at the same time acknowledging that "the common school must not underplay the role which reasonable moral views in the non-public domain play in overall moral evaluation and in human life more generally."[78] For example, the commons ought to promote a fine-grained understanding of respect. Civic respect is not the only form of respect, and "the common school should not convey the impression that giving 'respect' requires the necessary approval of the choices which people make within the limits of their rights."[79] Thus, Catholic students whose faith tradition does not sanction homosexuality should learn civic respect for gays, lesbians, bisexuals, and transgender people, on the one hand, but without undermining respect for their nonpublic religious inheritance, on the other. Instead of Galston's hard diversity liberalism and

Callan's comprehensive liberalism, McLaughlin appeared to prefer a softer value pluralism that is sympathetic to Tomasi's liberalism without a neutral concept of justice.[80] Tomasi places even heavier burdens on the commons by requiring a more balanced approach to public and private goods, in which each is subjected to equal scrutiny and considered in relation to the other.[81] This sort of liberalism is in keeping with Berlin's preference for negative over positive liberty, which holds that even liberal toleration is a product of what Oakeshott called historically contingent traditions of practice.

I am grateful to Michael Hand and Eamonn Callan for helpful comments that led to clarification of important nuances in McLaughlin's position as well as my own. However, neither Hand's critique nor McLaughlin's later writings lend credence to the claim that properly understood belief in someone or something—religious understanding from the inside—is irrelevant to Callan's objections or that my focus on the text of McLaughlin's debate with Callan in the 1980s rather than his later writings led to a misconstrual of McLaughlin on either religious initiation or liberalism. On the contrary, McLaughlin's rejoinder stands that "Callan too quickly dismisses the significance of being on the inside of religion for the capacity to evaluate it," as does my assessment that the sort of intelligent religion McLaughlin had in mind is in keeping with a form of value pluralism in which faith, when tied to a relevant account of openness, is seen as an ally, even a resource, but certainly not a threat, to open, pluralistic, liberal democracies.

CHAPTER TWELVE

Spirituality, Morality, and Criticism in Education

Introduction

In his thoughtful review of *Reclaiming Goodness*, Kevin Gary captured many of the most important themes that I addressed in that book while raising two apprehensions about intelligent spirituality.[1] His first concern relates to what he takes to be my failure to adequately distinguish between spirituality and morality; his second deals with the role of criticism in spirituality and spiritual education. In this chapter I will consider each of these apprehensions in turn.

Spirituality and morality

Gary summarizes my view as follows: "Essentially the current spiritual failure ... consists of the inability of modern thought to offer a compelling ethical vision. As a consequence, there is an absence of holistic ideals to live by. This accounts for the self-centered fragmentation of modern life, which has in turn led ... to a gross instrumentalism that lacks higher purpose."[2] So far so good.

Into this vacuum, he suggests, I offer spirituality as the remedy. On my account, Gary contends, "spirituality neatly responds to the malaise of modern life by offering meaningful substantive visions of goodness that contemporary, secular moral frameworks lack. Spirituality is expansively defined as living by and acquiring visions of goodness." This, he opines, is where my analysis is most helpful: "It provides a framework for situating many voices within spirituality thus enabling meaningful dialogue and exchange across traditions."[3] It is at this point that Gary begins to lose the thread of my argument.

What does the concept of spirituality mean?

It is not *I* who offers spirituality as a remedy for the malaise of modern life, but the many people who have begun to search for spirituality in the recent decades. I ask why it is that so many have joined this quest and what it would mean to them for it to be successful; and I conclude that they are searching because *modernity*, or more precisely modern liberal moral theory, has failed to offer meaning and purpose to their lives—not secularism, *modernity*. Indeed, I take great pains to avoid false dichotomies between secularism and religion or, as Terence McLaughlin and I put it in another context, between tethered and untethered concepts of spirituality;[4] and I point out that modern religious institutions such as liberal churches and synagogues have been accused of being no less empty of meaning and purpose than so-called secular institutions such as state schools in many liberal societies. Nor, I contend repeatedly, does religion have a monopoly on spirituality. On the contrary, many concepts of spirituality are more inclusive than religion, allowing believers and nonbelievers to engage in a common discourse about the meanings and purposes of their lives.

This is why my account of spirituality is expansive—because these are the meanings attributed to the term by those who use it in the current context, not because I have chosen (arbitrarily) to define spirituality in this way. If this entails a "risk of conflating spirituality with morality," as Gary contends, it is not I (or at least not I alone) who has taken this risk, but the variety of theologians, educators, and public figures who have made such wide use of the term. The question to be asked of my analysis, then, is whether it fairly accounts for the many complexities that arise from such a broad use of the concept. That Gary finds this analysis helpful suggests that his response to this question might well be affirmative.

The same can be said concerning his query about the necessity of the spiritual turn. It is not I who has called for a spiritual awakening, but the many seekers who have begun to explore spirituality. Nowhere do I say that spirituality is the only or a necessary response to the moral crisis of modernity. Such a claim entails a coercive ethos that requires a spiritual response of everyone who wishes to address the weaknesses of Enlightenment morality. But this is the opposite of my position, which is avowedly noncoercive and places a premium on freedom and fallibility. Yet many people apparently feel a need to respond to this crisis in ways that involve spirituality, as they conceive it. The task of *Reclaiming Goodness* was to understand what they mean by the term, to examine why they feel this need, and to explore some of the connections and tensions between the spiritual quest and such concepts as education and democracy.

Should spirituality be distinguished from ethics?

But is this risk of conflating spirituality with morality as troubling as Gary portrays it? I think not; and understanding why not will help, I believe, to illumine the nature of this spiritual yearning. To this end, it is useful to recall the well-known distinction, discussed in Chapter Nine of this volume, between deontological and aretaic forms of normative discourse. The former is often associated with modern moral philosophy since Immanuel Kant. It attempts to understand norms in terms of duty. The latter recalls an ancient concern for excellence or virtue by engaging Socrates's famous question: How should one live? By addressing this query, we conceive of what it might mean to live a good life, from which may follow a variety of beliefs, behaviors, and desires. The term "morality," in the narrow sense of justified obligation, is often associated with the modern deontological tradition of normative thought. The term "ethics," on the other hand, is very often linked to an earlier aretaic tradition that examines the nature of the good life, though it is also sometimes associated with deontology, as in such expressions as "metaethics," which deals with principles for justifying moral obligations, or "professional ethics," which relates to codes of practice.[5]

The point of my analysis was to show that the current wide use of this term "spirituality" is very often motivated by a concern to live a good life that ancient and medieval philosophers associated with ethics, in the aretaic sense of the term. Yet, when Gary accuses me of conflating spirituality with morality, it is unclear to which of these orientations he is referring. His formulation of the problem in terms of spirituality versus morality suggests that he has in mind something like modern moral thought, with its deontological emphasis. He asks, for example, whether a person can articulate a holistic vision of the good that transcends the self without resorting to the language or resources of spirituality. This returns us to the dichotomy between secularism and religion, which presupposes that concepts sometimes associated with God and religion, such as spirituality, are unnecessary unless proven otherwise. This distinction is grounded in Enlightenment thinking that sought a public domain of civil discourse based on the sort of universal rationality used to justify Kantian deontology.

The impression that Gary's desire to distinguish spirituality from morality rests on the assumptions of modern moral philosophy is reinforced by his reference to William James's polemic against the secular moralist, who lacks the will to enact normative convictions.[6] On Gary's reading, James thinks that religious experience, which Gary appears to identify with spirituality, can step in where the secular weakness of will leaves off; although it is entirely unclear from Gary's brief account of it what sort of spirituality this would entail or why it would motivate the secularist to enact his or her moral convictions. His complaint that intelligent spirituality "does not go far enough in addressing the interior failings that can paradoxically impede or catalyze spiritual growth"[7] suggests a version of what I have called subjective spirituality that locates the source of worthwhile living within the self. If this is correct, however, I have difficulty understanding Gary's objection. I have discussed the dynamics of inner life at length, as part of a search for the discovery of a desirable version of oneself within the context of a community possessing a higher good. I have also commented extensively on the significance of human frailty and fallibility in this search. The crucial point, however, is that rigorous distinctions between secular and religious, inner and outer, or spirituality and morality, have no place in the aretaic tradition, in which the language of meaning and purpose so common to today's spiritual seekers plays a central role.

Yet, Gary also recognizes that the deontological justifications of Enlightenment morality "proved flimsy and gave way to a base emotivism that has deprived contemporary society of a normative vision of goodness."[8] And his prime example of the nonspiritual secularist is a "contemporary Aristotelian." This might suggest that his complaint about lack of boundaries between spirituality and morality in my analysis is concerned with the linkage of spirituality to ethics in the aretaic sense. But if this is the case, I again do not know what to make of his complaint. The whole point of ethics in this sense is to conceive how best to live; and there are a variety of traditions, religious and secular, theistic and nontheistic, tethered and untethered, within which people envisage such a life. The contemporary spiritual quest, in all of its forms and expressions, I argue, entails a reemergence of concern for what it might mean to live well or wisely that had been ignored or even suppressed by the modern, deontological tradition of moral thought. To insist that this spiritual discourse be rigorously distinguished from morality is to ask that we return to the very forms of moral reflection that proved to be problematic and that led to spiritual crisis in the first place.

Spirituality and criticism

This aretaic orientation can also help to clarify my position concerning the role of criticism in intelligent spirituality. In this connection Gary agrees that "critical thinking is certainly indispensable for appraising spiritual education and spiritual traditions…. However, it can also be an impediment to spiritual awareness and practice."[9] To drive this point home, he draws our attention to neo-Thomist philosopher Josef Pieper's approbation of Thomas Aquinas's distinction between *ratio* and *intellectus*. The former, Pieper argues, refers to the mind's capacity for discursive or critical thinking, while the latter relates to the mind's capacity for awe and beholding.[10] Gary illustrates this distinction by reference to Abraham Joshua Heschel's notions of awe and wonder.[11] "It is not my contention," Gary continues, "to re-create the dichotomy between spirituality and rationality that Alexander is at pains to overcome, but rather to draw attention to this distinction that has implications in how spiritual education is enacted." "Alexander's happy marriage between spirituality and critical thinking," he concludes, "is somewhat specious."[12]

The problem with this complaint is not that Gary has inappropriately situated my analysis in Enlightenment thought, as he may have done in reference to the connection between spirituality and morality, as previously stated, since the allusion to Thomas Aquinas quite properly places the discussion in the sort of Aristotelian—or more precisely neo-Aristotelian—discourse where it belongs. Rather, the difficulty here can only be identified by understanding where within Aristotle's analysis of rationality and ethics contemporary discussions of spirituality ought to be situated, how the current neo-Aristotelian revival differs from its premodern Aristotelian ancestors, and what counts as criticism in this neo-Aristotelian context.

What sort of activity is spirituality?

Recall that Aristotle distinguished between the practical wisdom suitable for understanding how personal and political affairs ought to be conducted and theories about how the world works. As discussed previously in this volume on numerous occasions, he called the former *Phronesis*. It consists of ethical and civic virtues required for living a good life and creating a just society. Though alluding to higher ideals, virtues are always expressed in terms of local cultures and customs. He dubbed the latter *Sophia*. It attempts to grasp physical and metaphysical reality by means of two sorts of reasoning: *techne*, which reveals what he called the efficient or mechanical causes of events, and *episteme*, which focuses on teleological or final causes. Efficient causes precede events, "pushing" them into being, as it were, by disrupting or intervening in a state of affairs in a random or chance manner. Teleological causes, on the other hand, "pull" an event toward a natural or intrinsic state, one that is part of the very design of things. Since events cannot be explained without reference to a larger order in which they are set, the whole possesses a greater degree of reality than the parts. Teleological explanations are more fundamental than mechanical explanations, in Aristotle's view, because they tie physical to metaphysical reality.[13]

Aquinas's *ratio*, in these terms, constitutes the process of teleological reasoning, *episteme*, by means of which we come to conceive the ultimate cause of all existence, namely God. *Intellectus* is what we do once we have realized the magnificence of such an ultimate reality and its significance for the very purpose of existence itself. For Aquinas, in other words, rational contemplation is the end of the sort of thinking associated with *Sophia*, not nonrational experience as Gary suggests. To be sure, teleological reasoning, *episteme*, is different in several respects from the kind of rationality some philosophers of education associate with critical thinking. The former is concerned with ultimate purposes whereas the latter, under the influence of empiricism, often emphasizes what Aristotle called efficient causes or *techne*. Gary's complaint does not quite hit the mark, therefore, since in the scholastic tradition, contemplation of the Divine is quite a bit more rational than his account of *intellectus* would appear to allow.[14] However, he may be correct that an undue emphasis on technical forms of reasoning, especially in their modern skeptical formulations, could have an adverse effect on spiritual pursuits.

But difficulties with Gary's concern about connecting spirituality to criticism run deeper than this. Indeed, it strikes at the heart of my view of what the current spiritual awakening is all about. To see why, let us turn for a moment to the Jewish case that Gary introduced into the discussion by reference to Heschel. Actually, the Jewish counterpart to the sort of Catholic scholasticism represented by Aquinas was not Heschel, a twentieth-century rabbi and theologian, but the twelfth-century rabbi and philosopher Moses Maimonides, who argued that the rational contemplation of God is the ultimate end of human existence.[15] Heschel, on the other hand, was heir to a great Hassidic dynasty and sought ways to translate basic concepts of Jewish mysticism into a contemporary idiom. According to this mystical tradition, we meet God in the context of direct religious experience, not through rational contemplation, for which he used the terms awe and wonder. And this experience is achieved by means of religious practices that, in the Jewish tradition, are delineated in terms of Divine commandments.[16]

For the likes of Heschel, then, the basic category of spiritual experience is *Phronesis*, not *Sophia*. On this account, faith—a religious or tethered approach to spirituality—is not a product of theoretical reasoning that yields belief *that* such and such is the case. Rather, it is embedded in particular communities and embodied by the traditions of thought and practice within which those communities celebrate their highest ideals. It involves, in other words, belief *in* a particular way of life. It is just such a practical orientation to spirituality that I proposed in *Reclaiming Goodness*, and that I defended on behalf of McLaughlin in Chapters Ten and Eleven here. The sort of intelligence that ought to be embedded in the spiritual quest, I contend, is connected to concrete practices rather than abstract beliefs. To clarify what kind of thinking this sort of spiritual practice entails, I need to say more about how the current neo-Aristotelian revival understands practical reasoning.

How does neo-Aristotelianism differ from Aristotelianism?

Following Martin Buber's distinction between "belief that" and "belief in," Menachem Kellner points out that until Maimonides, classical rabbinic Judaism was characterized by the sort of practical wisdom illustrated here by Heschel's theology, in which abstract or theoretical beliefs about such matters as how the world came into being or who created it were embedded in traditions of practice.[17] The same might be said of other faith traditions as well. Along with Al Farabi and Aquinas, Maimonides followed a neo-Platonic interpretation of Aristotle, in placing *Sophia*, and in particular *episteme*, or abstract teleological reasoning, at the center of the spiritual life. One can only be saved or liberated, in this view, by accepting an account of ultimate truth consistent with how each of these philosophers interpreted his own religious tradition. As mentioned previously, Isaiah Berlin referred to this as a positive concept of liberty, the intolerance of which has wreaked havoc throughout history on people whose faith differed from those in power, such as reformers, dissidents, and unbelievers.[18]

Modern philosophers successfully challenged this point of view by undermining scholastic arguments for the existence of God. But they did not abandon the Aristotelian preference for theoretical styles of reasoning. Kant, for example, grounded his view of the moral and religious life in an account of practical reason that was situated in the same cognitive structure as pure reason. The result was a highly formalized, almost mathematical, morality according to which all normative obligations would be derived from a single axiom—the imperative to treat other humans as ends not means—and a uniform Idea of God or Numenon—the actual world as it ought to be—in which pure and practical reason meet.[19] Michael Walzer called this sort of abstract universalism a thin moral tradition,[20] and it is precisely this sort of thinking that led critics such as Alasdair MacIntyre, along with many spiritual seekers, back to Aristotle's aretaic orientation, which promotes thicker, contextualized, concrete ways of living.[21]

However, this return to Aristotle's notion of practical wisdom does not entail a revival of the absolutist metaphysics characteristic of his medieval disciples. Rather, it involves a more dynamic transcendentalism associated with the likes of James.[22] According to this more dynamic view, to avoid the quagmires of self-defeating relativism potentially inherent in modern openness to alternative perspectives, we must assume as a regulative principle some transcendental ideal, or *telos*, toward which competing ethical visions aspire, even though we may not be able to agree on its content. In fact, it is part of the very meaning of the concept of goodness in the ethical sense that each of these alternatives might turn out to be false. Were this not the case, we would be compelled by logic or nature, rather than choice, to embrace one point of view, which, as I have argued at great length, undermines the possibility of discourse being ethical in any meaningful sense of the term. This allows for a pluralistic account of the liberal democratic tradition in which competing conceptions of the good are able to live side by side, while at the same time encouraging the embrace of substantive conceptions of the good. The sort of reasoning that this involves is indeed teleological, but situated in practical rather than theoretical considerations, where the purposes with which we are concerned are chosen by human agents rather than determined by logic or nature or history or God. On what bases do we make these choices?

What sort of thinking does spirituality entail?

To avoid undermining democratic pluralism, I argued that spiritual responses to the ethical failings of modernity need to be intelligent, in addition to embracing freedom and fallibility. That is, they must assume that people have the capacity to assess the relative merits of different actions, beliefs, or desire according to some conception of what it means for activities, beliefs, and desires to be meritorious. Were it not for our capacity to make normative distinctions such as these, our choices would be arbitrary rather than free and we would be unable to discern the degree to which the paths we have chosen are better or worse, given some conception of what it means for a path to be worthwhile.

To clarify the sort of thinking these sorts of choices entail, it is useful to make reference once again to Charles Taylor's notion of strong evaluation. Recall that Taylor accepts Harry Frankfurt's distinction between first-order desires, such as the need to be satiated or the inclination to avoid danger, and second-order desires, which are desires about desires. Humans share the capacity to have first-order desires with other animals, but only we are able to formulate desires by means of which we can evaluate other desires.[23] Taylor observed, however, that there are in fact two sorts of second-order desires. We can assess the worth of a desire on the basis of momentary feelings or in relation to the amount of pleasure we might enjoy. Today I like vanilla ice cream, but tomorrow I may prefer chocolate, or if I swim before I eat lunch then I can enjoy my exercise without risking a cramp in the water. Taylor calls these weak evaluations, since nothing of significance turns on the calculation I may make at any given time. However, life also presents us with harder choices. Should I save my friend in battle, or run to save myself? This sort of decision entails a choice about the very sort of person I want to be, which requires a qualitatively different sort of judgment. To be meaningful in other than a weak sense, Taylor argues, evaluations of this kind require strong values concerning what counts as a worthwhile life grounded in community or tradition or God—or something other than the self alone.[24]

The spiritual quest is about coming to identify with strong values such as these, embedded in communities of ethical practice that draw on religious, cultural, aesthetic, intellectual, linguistic, and other sorts of traditions; and it is in this sense that intelligent spirituality entails a capacity for criticism. There is nothing spurious at all, therefore, about the so-called marriage of spirituality with critical thinking in this qualitative—practical and teleological but not technical—sense of the term. On the contrary, without the ability to evaluate whether life choices are worthwhile, it would be impossible to make sense of what it could mean to live a purposeful life. As I have argued, this is the whole point of a spiritual quest. Good qualitative judgments, however, do not come easily. We must learn to make them, preferably from those who have acquired wisdom by practicing a particular spiritual tradition. This is why the concepts of education and spirituality are so closely intertwined.

NOTES

Introduction

1   W. James, *Pragmatism and Other Writings* (New York, NY: Penguin Classics, 2000), 7–24.
2   D. Tyack, *The One Best System: A History of American Urban Education* (Cambridge, MA: Harvard University Press, 2007).
3   H. A. Alexander, *Reclaiming Goodness: Education and the Spiritual Quest* (Notre Dame, IN: University of Notre Dame Press, 2001).
4   P. H. Phenix, "Transcendence and the Curriculum," *Teachers College Record* 73, no. 2 (1971): 271–83.
5   Alexander, *Reclaiming Goodness*.
6   H. A. Alexander, "Education in Ideology," *The Journal of Moral Education* 34, no. 1 (2005): 1–18 (revised here as Chapter Five); H. A. Alexander, "Human Agency and the Curriculum," *Theory and Research in Education* 3, no. 3 (2005): 343–69 (revised here as Chapter Eight).
7   H. A. Alexander, "Moral Education and Liberal Democracy: Spirituality, Community, and Character in an Open Society," *Educational Theory* 53, no. 4 (2004): 367–87 (revised here as Chapter Nine).
8   H. A. Alexander, "Literacy and Citizenship: Tradition, Reason, and Critique in Democratic Education," in *Philosophy of Education in the Era of Globalization*, eds Y. Raley and G. Preyer, 30–50 (New York, NY: Routledge, 2010) (revised here as Chapter Six).
9   H. A. Alexander, "A View from Somewhere: Explaining the Paradigms of Educational Research," *Journal of Philosophy of Education* 40, no. 2 (2006): 205–22 (revised here as Chapter Two).
10 For example, J. Royce, *The Basic Writings of Josiah Royce*, Vol. 1 and Vol. 2, ed. J. J. McDermott (New York, NY: Fordham University Press, 2005).
11 M. Oakeshott, *Rationalism in Politics and Other Essays* (London: Methuen, 1962).
12 James, *Pragmatism*, 10–11.
13 R. Rorty, *The Consequences of Pragmatism* (Minneapolis: University of Minnesota Press, 1982), xii–xlvii.
14 James, *Pragmatism*; J. Habermas, *Knowledge and Human Interests* (Boston, MA: Beacon, 1972); T. Nagel, *The View from Nowhere* (Oxford: Oxford University Press, 1986).
15 R. J. Nash, *Faith, Hype, and Clarity: Teaching about Religion in American Schools and Colleges* (New York, NY: Teachers College Press, 1999), 19–20.
16 D. E. Purpel, *The Moral and Spiritual Crisis in Education* (Granby, MA: Bergin and Garvey, 1988).
17 R. Nozick, *Philosophical Explanations* (Cambridge, MA: Harvard University Press, 1981), 8.

18 James, *Pragmatism*, 28.
19 James, *Pragmatism*, 29.
20 James, *Pragmatism*, 11.
21 James, *Pragmatism*, 14.
22 James, *Pragmatism*, 29–30.
23 J. Dewey, *Democracy and Education* (New York, NY: Macmillan, 1916).
24 Rorty, *Consequences of Pragmatism*.
25 James, *Pragmatism*, 38–40 (italics in the original).
26 I. Berlin, *Four Essays on Liberty* (Oxford: Oxford University Press, 1969).
27 A. MacIntyre, *After Virtue: A Study in Moral Theory* (Notre Dame, IN: University of Notre Dame Press, 1984); A. MacIntyre, *Whose Justice, Which Rationality?* (Notre Dame, IN: University of Notre Dame Press), 1989.
28 K. Lewin, *Field Theory in Social Science* (New York, NY: Harper and Row, 1951).
29 T. Parsons, *The Social System* (Glencoe, IL: The Free Press, 1951); C. W. Mills, *The Sociological Imagination* (Oxford: Oxford University Press, 2000).
30 R. S. Peters, *Ethics and Education* (London: George, Allen, and Unwin, 1966).
31 R. K. Merton, *Social Theory and Social Structure* (New York, NY: Free Press, 1968).
32 J. Schwab, *Science, Curriculum, and Liberal Education* (Chicago: University of Chicago Press, 1982).
33 H. A. Alexander and A. Bursztein, "The Concept of Translation in the Philosophy of Education," [in Hebrew], in *Studies in Jewish Education* 11, eds J. Cohen, E. Holtzer and A. Isaaacs, 337–54 (Jerusalem: The Magnes Press of the Hebrew University of Jerusalem, 2007); H. A. Alexander and A. Bursztein, "Normative Deliberation in Education," [in Hebrew], in *Educational Eclectics: Essays in Memory of Shlomo (Seymour) Fox*, eds S. Wygoda and I. Sorek, 149–69 (Jerusalem: Mandel Foundation and Keter Publisher, 2009).
34 Aristotle, *Metaphysics*, trans. D. Bostock (Oxford: Clarendon Press, 1994).
35 Oakeshott, *Rationalism in Politics*.
36 Plato, *The Republic*, trans. R. Waterfield (Oxford: Oxford University Press, 2008).
37 Y. Halevy, *Kuzari: An Argument for the Faith of Israel* (New York, NY: Schocken Books, 1964).
38 D. Reisman, "Al-Farabi and the Philosophical Curriculum," in *The Cambridge Companion to Arabic Philosophy*, eds P. Adamson and R. Taylor, 52–71 (Cambridge: Cambridge University Press, 2005); M. Maimonides, *Guide to the Perplexed*, trans. M. Friedlander (New York, NY: Dover, 1956); T. Aquinas, *On the Truth of the Catholic Faith*, trans. A. Regis (New York, NY: Doubleday, 1955).
39 D. Hume, *An Enquiry Concerning Human Understanding* (Oxford: Oxford University Press, 2007).
40 I. Kant, *Prolegomena to Any Future Metaphysics*, trans. G. Hatfield (Cambridge: Cambridge University Press, 2004).
41 I. Kant, *Religion Within the Limits of Reason Alone* (New York, NY: Harper Torchbooks, 1960).
42 G. W. F. Hegel, *Philosophy of Right* (Oxford: Oxford University Press, 1967).
43 W. V. O. Quine and J. S. Ullian, *The Web of Belief*, 2nd ed. (New York, NY: Random House, 1978).
44 W. V. O. Quine, *Ontological Relativity and Other Essays* (New York, NY: Columbia University Press, 1969); Oakeshott, *Rationalism in Politics*.

45 M. Buber, *I and Thou* (New York, NY: Touchstone, 1996); E. Levinas, *Humanism of the Other*, trans. N. Poller (Urbana-Champaign, IL: University of Illinois Press, 2005); Oakeshott, *Rationalism in Politics*; J. Sacks, *The Dignity of Difference*, rev. ed. (London: Continuum, 2003).

46 H. A. Alexander, "Schools without Faith," *Religious Education* 76, no. 3 (1981): 307–21 (revised here as Chapter One).

47 See Chapter Five.

48 H. A. Alexander, "Aesthetic Inquiry in Education: Community, Transcendence, and the Meaning of Pedagogy," *Journal of Aesthetic Education* 37, no. 2 (2003): 1–18 (revised here as Chapter Three).

49 Oakeshott, *Rationalism in Politics*; M. Oakeshott, *On Human Conduct* (Oxford: Clarendon Press, 1975).

50 H. A. Alexander, "Traditions of Inquiry in Education: Engaging the Paradigms of Educational Research," in *A Companion to Research in Education*, eds A. D. Reid, E. P. Hart, and M. A. Peters, 13–25 (Dordrecht: Springer, 2014).

51 Berlin, *Four Essays on Liberty*; Oakeshott, *Rationalism in Politics*; M. Sandel, *Liberalism and the Limits of Justice* (Cambridge: Cambridge University Press, 1998), C. Taylor, *The Ethics of Authenticity* (Cambridge, MA: Harvard University Press, 1991); M. Walzer, *Thick and Thin, Moral Argument at Home and Abroad* (Notre Dame, IN: University of Notre Dame Press, 1985).

52 W. A. Galston, *Liberal Pluralism: The Implications of Value Pluralism for Political Theory and Practice* (Cambridge: Cambridge University Press, 2002).

53 J. Gray, *Two Faces of Liberalism* (London: New Press, 2002); R. Rorty, *Contingency, Irony, and Solidarity* (Cambridge: Cambridge University Press, 1989), 44–69.

54 See Chapter Five.

55 See Chapter Six.

56 H. A. Alexander, "What Is Common about Common Schooling: Rational Autonomy and Moral Agency in Liberal Democratic Education," *Journal of Philosophy of Education* 41, no. 4 (2007): 609–24 (revised here as Chapter Seven).

57 See Chapter Eight.

58 See Chapter Nine.

59 T. H. McLaughlin, "Parental Rights and the Religious Upbringing of Children," *Journal of Philosophy of Education* 18, no. 1 (1984): 75–83; T. H. McLaughlin, "Religion, Upbringing and Liberal Values: A Rejoinder to Eamonn Callan," *Journal of Philosophy of Education* 19, no. 1 (1985): 119–27; E. Callan, "McLaughlin on Parental Rights," *Journal of Philosophy of Education* 19, no. 1 (1985): 111–18; E. Callan, "Why Bring the Kids into This? McLaughlin and Anscombe on Religious Understanding," in *Faith in Education: A Tribute to Terence McLaughlin*, ed. G. Haydon, 9–26 (London: Institute of Education, University of London, 2009).

60 H. A. Alexander, "Autonomy, Faith, and Reason: McLaughlin and Callan on Religious Initiation," in *Faith in Education: A Tribute to Terence McLaughlin*, ed. G. Haydon, 27–45 (London: Institute of Education, University of London, 2009) (revised here as Chapter Ten).

61 T. H. McLaughlin, "Citizenship, Diversity, and Education: A Philosophical Perspective," *Journal of Moral Education* 21, no. 3 (1992): 235–50.

62 W. Galston, "Civic Education in the Liberal State," in *Liberalism and the Moral Life*, ed. N. L. Rosenblum, 89–101 (Cambridge, MA: Harvard University Press, 1989); W. A. Galston, *Liberal Purposes: Goods, Virtues, and Diversity in the Liberal State* (Cambridge: Cambridge University Press, 1991).

CHAPTER ONE

1   M. Eliade, *The Sacred and the Profane* (New York, NY: Harcourt, Brace, and Javanovich, 1987).
2   W. James, *The Will to Believe and Other Essays* (New York, NY: Dover, 1956), 1–31.
3   Parsons, *Social System*, 12, 36–37.
4   K. W. Bolle, *The Freedom of Man in Myth* (Nashville, TN: Vanderbilt University Press, 1968); M. Eliade, *Myth and Reality* (New York, NY: Harper and Row, 1963), 1–38.
5   M. Eliade, *Myths, Dreams, and Realities* (New York, NY: Harper and Row, 1957); F. Musgrave, *Ecstasy and Holiness* (Bloomington: Indiana University Press, 1974).
6   M. Walzer, *Exodus and Revolution* (New York, NY: Basic Books, 1986).
7   Hume, *Enquiry Concerning Human Understanding*.
8   R. Rubenstein, *The Religious Imagination* (New York, NY: Bobbs and Merrill, 1968).
9   Alexander, *Reclaiming Goodness*; H. A. Alexander and T. H. McLaughlin, "Education in Religion and Spirituality," in *The Blackwell Guide to Philosophy of Education*, eds N. Blake, P. Smeyers, R. Smith, and P. Standish, 356–73 (Oxford: Blackwell Publishing, 2003).
10 D. Huebner, *The Lure of the Transcendent*, ed. V. Hillis (New York, NY: Routledge, 1999).
11 A. de Tocqueville, *Democracy in America*, trans. G. Lawrence, ed. J. P. Mayer (New York, NY: Harper and Row, 1996), vol. II, part II, chap. 12, 534–35.
12 W. James, *The Varieties of Religious Experience* (New York, NY: Signet Classics, 1958), 383–85.
13 Bolle, *Freedom of Man*.
14 James, *Varieties of Religious Experience*, 54.
15 L. S. Vygotsky, *Mind in Society* (Cambridge, MA: Harvard University Press, 1978); M. Ramirez and A. Castaneda, *Cultural Democracy, Bicognitive Development and Education* (New York, NY: Academic Press, 1974).
16 F. Tonnies, *Community and Society*, trans. C. P. Loomis (New York, NY: Harper and Row, 1957); E. Durkheim, *The Division of Labor in Society*, trans. W. D. Hall (New York, NY: Macmillan, 1984).
17 V. Frankl, *The Doctor and the Soul* (New York, NY: Random House, 1973).
18 James, *Will to Believe*, 76, 120.
19 E. W. Eisner, "The Impoverished Mind," *Educational Leadership* 35, no. 8 (May 1978): 615–23. Eisner coined the term "null curriculum," as opposed to "explicit" and "implicit" curricula, to refer to the consequences of excluding a major form of human representation such as the fine arts from the school. See: E. W. Eisner, "The Three Curricula that All Schools Teach," in *The Educational Imagination: On the Design and Evaluation of School Programs*, 1st ed., 97–107 (New York, NY: Macmillan, 1979).

20 S. N. Eisenstadt, *From Generation to Generation* (Glencoe, IL: The Free Press, 1956), 148–49.

21 Eisenstadt, *From Generation to Generation*, 174.

22 F. Musgrave, *Youth and the Social Order* (Bloomington: Indiana University Press, 1964).

23 J. S. Coleman, *The Adolescent Society* (Glencoe, IL: The Free Press, 1962), 2.

24 R. E. Callahan, *Education and the Cult of Efficiency* (Chicago, IL: University of Chicago Press, 1962).

25 Callahan, *Education and the Cult of Efficiency*, 23.

26 H. M. Levin, *Workplace Democracy and Educational Planning* (Paris: Institute of International Education, UNESCO, 1978).

27 F. Bobbitt, *How to Make a Curriculum* (New York, NY: Houghton Mifflin, 1924).

28 R. Gange, "Educational Technology as Technique," *Educational Technology* 8 (November 1968): 5–18.

29 T. Rozak, *The Making of a Counter Culture* (Garden City, NY: Doubleday, 1968), 16.

30 R. Descartes, *Discourse on Method and Related Writings*, trans. D. M. Clark (London: Penguin Books, 1999), 16.

31 J. Locke, *An Essay Concerning Human Understanding* (New York, NY: Oxford University Press, 1979), book II, chap. 1, par. 2.

32 W. James, *The Meaning of Truth* (New York, NY: Longman, Green, 1909), v–viii.

33 A. Tarski, "The Semantic Conception of Truth," *Philosophy and Phenomenological Research* 4, no. 3 (1944): 341–76.

34 M. Weber, "Science as a Vocation," in *From Max Weber*, eds H. H. Gerth and C. W. Mills, 129–58 (New York, NY: Oxford University Press, 1946), 146.

35 Callan, "Why Bring the Kids into This?"

36 G. Spindler, *Education and the Cultural Process* (New York, NY: Holt, Rinehart, and Winston, 1974), 279.

37 L. Raths, M. Harmin, and S. Simon, *Values and Teaching* (Columbus, OH: Merrill, 1966), 19; L. Kohlberg, "Moral Education in the Schools: A Developmental Approach," *School Review* 74, no. 1 (1966): 1–30.

38 See Chapter Nine.

39 P. W. Jackson, *Life in Classrooms* (New York, NY: Holt, Rinehart, and Winston, 1968).

40 Jackson, *Life in Classrooms*, 48.

41 Jackson, *Life in Classrooms*, 54.

42 G. Rosenfeld, *Shut Those Thick Lips: A Study of School Failure* (New York, NY: Holt, Rinehart, and Winston, 1971), 37.

43 K. Kenniston, *The Uncommitted: Alienated Youth in American Society*, 1st ed. (New York, NY: Harcourt, Brace, and World, 1965), 168.

44 P. McLaren, *Life in Schools: An Introduction to Critical Pedagogy in the Foundations of Education*, 2nd ed. (White Plains, NY: Longman, 1994), 5.

45 McLaren, *Life in Schools*, 9.

46 McLaren, *Life in Schools*, 18.

47 R. Larkin, *Suburban Youth in Cultural Crisis* (New York, NY: Oxford University Press, 1979), 210, quoted in McLaren, *Life in Schools*, 18.

48 McLaren, *Life in Schools*, 18.

49 H. Brighouse, *On Education* (New York, NY: Routledge, 2005), 14–15.

50 E. W. Eisner, "Educational Connoisseurship and Educational Criticism: Their Forms and Uses in Educational Evaluation," *Journal of Aesthetic Education* 10, no. 3/4 (1976): 135–50.
51 Eliade, *The Sacred and the Profane*, 211.
52 Alexander, *Reclaiming Goodness*, 7.
53 T. Kuhn, *The Structure of Scientific Revolutions* (Chicago, IL: University of Chicago Press, 1962).
54 For example, A. Comte, *Introduction to Positive Philosophy* (London: Hackett, 1988).
55 B. V. Hill, "Do Religious Studies Belong in the Public School?" *Religious Education* 75, no. 6 (1980): 659–66.
56 James, *Will to Believe*, 24.

CHAPTER TWO

1 The term "positivism" is usually used in a sweeping sense among educational researchers to refer to the epistemological orientation most commonly associated with empirical research in the natural or exact sciences. This view affirms with scientific positivists that empirical truth is to be discovered by means of controlled experiments alone, and with the logical positivists that the aim of the experimentation is to verify causal laws for purposes of explanation, prediction, and control. Qualitative researchers differ as to whether they follow the Anglo-American distinction between the sciences and humanities and so cede the term "scientific" to the exact sciences, or the German distinction between *Naturwissenschaften* and *Geisteswissenschaften*, and so refer to qualitative research as scientific only in a different sense.
2 Nozick, *Philosophical Explanations*, 8.
3 E. Guba, "The Alternative Paradigm Dialogue," in *The Paradigm Dialogue*, ed. E. Guba, 17–27 (Newbury Park, CA: Sage, 1990); E. Guba and Y. Lincoln, *Fourth Generation Evaluation* (Newbury Park, CA: Sage, 1989); E. Guba and Y. Lincoln, *Naturalistic Inquiry* (Beverly Hills, CA: Sage, 1985).
4 G. H. von Wright, *Explanation and Understanding* (Ithaca, NY: Cornell University Press, 1981); C. P. Snow, *The Two Cultures* (Cambridge: Cambridge University Press, 1990); L. J. Cronbach, "Beyond the Two Disciplines of Scientific Psychology," *American Psychologist* 30 (1975): 116–26.
5 Kuhn, *The Structure of Scientific Revolutions*.
6 M. Q. Patton, *Qualitative Evaluation and Research Methods* (Newbury Park, CA: Sage, 1990); M. Q. Patton, *Qualitative Evaluation Methods* (Thousand Oaks, CA: Sage, 1980).
7 H. A. Alexander, "Cognitive Relativism in Evaluation," *Evaluation Review* 10, no. 3 (1986): 259–80.
8 G. Biesta and N. C. Burbules, *Pragmatism and Educational Research* (Lanham, MD: Rowman and Littlefield, 2003); R. B. Johnson and A. J. Onwuegbuzie, "Mixed Method Research: A Research Paradigm Whose Time Has Come," *Educational Researcher* 33, no. 7 (2005): 14–26.
9 Nagel, *View from Nowhere*.
10 This chapter can be viewed as an attempt to articulate a version of pragmatism that embraces a less radical form of relativism than that of Richard Rorty

a la Richard Bernstein. See Rorty, *Consequences of Pragmatism*, and
R. J. Bernstein, *Beyond Objectivism and Relativism: Science, Hermeneutics,
and Praxis* (Philadelphia: University of Pennsylvania Press, 1983), 197–206.

11   Guba, "Alternative Paradigm Dialogue"; Guba and Lincoln, *Naturalistic
Inquiry*; Guba and Lincoln, *Fourth Generation Evaluation*; Patton, *Qualitative
Evaluation Methods*; Patton, *Qualitative Evaluation and Research Methods*;
R. E. Stake, *The Art of Case Study Research* (Thousand Oaks, CA: Sage,
1995); E. W. Eisner, *The Enlightened Eye: Qualitative Inquiry and the
Enhancement of Educational Practice*, 2nd ed. (Upper Saddle River, NJ:
Prentice-Hall, 1998).

12   H. Giroux, *Border Crossings: Cultural Work and the Politics of Education*
(New York, NY: Routledge, 2005); S. Aronowitz and H. Giroux, *Postmodern
Education: Politics, Culture and Criticism* (Minneapolis: University of
Minnesota Press, 1993); McLaren, *Life in Schools*; M. W. Apple, *Ideology
and Curriculum* (New York, NY: Routledge, 1979); M. W. Apple, *Education
and Power* (New York, NY: Routledge, 1985); T. Popkewitz, *Paradigm and
Ideology in Educational Research: The Social Functions of the Intellectual*
(London: Falmer, 1984).

13   D. T. Campbell and J. Stanley, *Experimental and Quasi-Experimental Design
for Research* (Chicago, IL: Rand McNally, 1963); W. R. Shaddish, T. D. Cook,
and D. T Campbell, *Experimental and Quasi-Experimental Designs for
Generalized Causal Inference* (Boston, MA: Houghton Mifflin, 2002).

14   D. C. Phillips, "A Guide for the Perplexed: Scientific Educational Research,
Methodolatry, and the Gold versus Platinum Standards," in *A Companion to
Research in Education*, eds A. D. Reid, E. P. Hart, and M. A. Peters, 129–40
(Dordrecht: Springer, 2014).

15   M. J. Feuer, L. Towne, and R. J. Shavelson, "Scientific Culture and Educational
Research," *Educational Researcher* 31, no. 8 (2002): 4–14.

16   F. Erickson and K. Gutierrez, "Culture, Rigor, and Science in Educational
Research," *Educational Researcher* 31, no. 8 (2002): 21–25; E. St. Peter,
"'Science' Rejects Postmodernism," *Educational Researcher* 31, no. 8
(2002): 25–28; M. Eisenhart, "Hammers and Saws for the Improvement of
Educational Research," *Educational Theory* 55, no. 3 (2005): 245–61.

17   K. R. Howe, "The Question of Educational Science: Experimentism vs.
Experimentalism," *Educational Theory* 55, no. 3 (2005): 307–21.

18   P. A. Moss, "Understanding the Other/Understanding Ourselves: Toward
a Constructive Dialogue about 'Principles' in Educational Research,"
Educational Theory 55, no. 3 (2005): 268–83; see von Wright, *Explanation
and Understanding*.

19   T. A. Schwandt, "A Diagnostic Reading of Scientifically-Based Educational
Research," *Educational Theory* 55, no. 3 (2005): 285–305; Howe, "Question
of Educational Science"; Phillips, "Guide for the Perplexed."

20   Johnson and Onwuegbuzie, "Mixed Method Research," 16; Ken Howe makes
a similar argument against what he calls the "incompatibility thesis." However,
not all dual-epistemology advocates hold quantitative and qualitative
inquiry to be incompatible. Indeed, some hold that qualitative inquiry
in some sense complements the quantitative. Both versions of the thesis,
however, are flawed for the reasons mentioned, see K. R. Howe, "Against
the Quantitative-Qualitative Incompatibility Thesis, or, Dogmas Die Hard,"

Educational Researcher 17 (1988): 10–16 and K. R. Howe, "Getting Over the Quantitative-Qualitative Debate," *American Journal of Education* 100 (1992): 236–56.

21 S. D. Sieber, "The Integration of Fieldwork and Survey Methods," *American Journal of Sociology* 73 (1973): 1335–59; A. Tashakkori and C. Teddloe, *Mixed Methodology: Combining Qualitative and Quantitative Approaches* (Thousand Oaks, CA: Sage, 1998); J. W. Creswell, *Research Design: Qualitative, Quantitative, and Mixed Approaches* (Thousand Oaks, CA: Sage, 2003).

22 Johnson and Onwuegbuzie, "Mixed Method Research," 17. This is part of a wider tendency in the natural and human sciences toward what Clifford Geertz has called "blurred genres," see C. Geertz, *Local Knowledge: Further Essays in Interpretative Anthropology* (New York, NY: Basic Books, 1983), 19–35.

23 Kuhn, *Structure of Scientific Revolutions.* Jerome Bruner appears to make a similar point when he distinguishes between paradigmatic and narrative forms of inquiry, a distinction that parallels the German differentiation between *Naturwissenschaften* and *Geisteswissenschaften*, as opposed to the Anglo-American natural science, social science, and the humanities. Ironically, most commentators on Kuhn, both pro and con, interpret *The Structure of Scientific Revolutions* as a relativistic tract, which undermines the very foundational account of empirical science that constructivists who propose to complement rather than challenge positivism appear to protect. Yet, the human sciences turn out to be paradigmatic in a much deeper sense than Kuhn allowed for the natural sciences, in that they entail the documentation and creation of examples and illustrations of transcendental ideals to which all academic inquiry alludes in one form or another, even though they may lie beyond our direct grasp; see I. Lakatos and A. Musgrave, eds, *Criticism and the Growth of Knowledge* (Cambridge: Cambridge University Press, 1970) and J. S. Bruner, *Actual Minds, Possible Worlds* (Cambridge, MA: Harvard University Press, 1986).

24 Campbell and Stanley, *Experimental and Quasi-Experimental Design*; C. G. Hempel, *The Philosophy of Natural Science* (Englewood Cliffs, NJ: Prentice-Hall, 1966); E. Nagel, *The Structure of Science: Problems in the Logic of Scientific Explanation* (London: Routledge and Kegan Paul, 1961).

25 E. W. Eisner, *The Educational Imagination: On the Design and Evaluation of School Programs*, 3rd ed. (Saddle River, NJ: Prentice-Hall, 1994), 236–42; Eisner, *Enlightened Eye*; Guba and Lincoln, *Naturalistic Inquiry*.

26 Guba and Lincoln, *Fourth Generation Evaluation*; L. Richardson, "Writing: A Method of Inquiry," in *Handbook of Qualitative Research*, eds N. K. Denzin and Y. S. Lincoln, 923–48 (Thousand Oaks, CA: Sage, 1994).

27 A. J. Onwuegbuzie, "Positivists, Post-Positivists, Post-Structuralists, and Post-Moderns: Why Can't We All Get Along: Towards a Framework for Unifying Research Paradigms," *Education* 122, no. 3 (2002): 518–30.

28 M. Chatterji, "Evidence on 'What Works': An Argument for Extended-Term Mixed-Method (ETMM) Evaluation Designs," *Educational Researcher* 34, no. 5 (2005): 25–31; G. K. Chesterton, *Orthodoxy* (New York, NY: Dodd, Mead, & Co., 1952), 14.

29 Hume, *Enquiry Concerning Human Understanding.*

30 Kant, *Prolegomena*; Kant, *Critique of Pure Reason* (New York, NY: Macmillan, 1970).

31   G. W. F. Hegel, *Reason in History*, trans. R. S. Hartman (Minneapolis, MN: Bobbs-Merrill, 1953); G. W. F. Hegel, *The Phenomenology of Spirit*, trans. A.V. Miller (Oxford: Clarendon Press, 1978).

32   Isaiah Berlin traces the origin of this tradition to Vico and Herder, see I. Berlin, *The Proper Study of Mankind*, eds H. Hardy and R. Hausheer (London: Random House, 1998), 243–435.

33   Comte, *Introduction to Positive Philosophy*.

34   Hume, *Enquiry Concerning Human Understanding*.

35   M. H. Lesnoff, *The Structure of Social Science* (London: Allen and Unwin, 1974).

36   K. R. Popper, *The Logic of Scientific Discovery* (London: Routledge, 1992); K. R. Popper, *Objective Knowledge* (Oxford: Clarendon Press, 1972).

37   D. C. Phillips and N. C. Burbules, *Postpositivism and Educational Research* (Lanham, MD: Roman and Littlefield, 2000).

38   I. Lakatos, *The Methodology of Scientific Research Programs* (Cambridge: Cambridge University Press, 1978).

39   E. Husserl, *The Crisis of the European Science and Transcendental Phenomenology*, trans. D. Carr (Evanston, IL: Northwestern University Press, 1970).

40   R. Descartes, *Discourse on Method*; R. Descartes, *Meditations on First Philosophy*, trans. J. Cottingham (Cambridge: Cambridge University Press, 1996).

41   E. Husserl, *Cartesian Meditation: An Introduction to Phenomenology*, trans. D. Cairns (The Hague: M. Nijhoff, 1960); E. Husserl, *Ideas: A General Introduction to Pure Phenomenology*, trans. W. R. Boyce Gribson (London: Allen and Unwin, 1967).

42   F. Nietzsche, *The Birth of Tragedy, The Gay Science, Thus Spoke Zarathustra, and On the Genealogy of Morals*, ed. D. B. Allison (Lanham, MD: Rowman and Littlefield, 2001).

43   A. Schutz, *Life Forms and Meaning Structure*, trans. H. R. Wagner (London: Routledge and Kegan Paul, 1982); A. Schutz and T. Luckmann, *The Structures of the Life World*, trans. R. M. Zaner and J. Tristram Engelhardt (Evanston, IL: Northwestern University Press, 1983).

44   Aristotle, *Metaphysics*; N. H. Smith, *Charles Taylor: Meaning, Morals, and Modernity* (Cambridge: Polity, 2002), 35–41.

45   M. Heidegger, *Being and Time*, trans. J. Stambaugh (New York, NY: SUNY Press, 1996).

46   J. Dewey, *How We Think* (Boston, MA: Heath, 1910); J. Dewey, *Logic: A Theory of Inquiry* (New York, NY: Henry Holt, 1938).

47   See Biesta and Burbules, *Pragmatism and Educational Research*; S. J. Maxcy, "Pragmatic Threads in Mixed Methods Research in the Social Sciences: The Search for Multiple Modes of Inquiry and the End of Philosophical Formalism," in *Handbook of Mixed Methods in Social and Behavioral Research*, eds A. Tashakkori and C. Teddlie, 51–90 (Thousand Oaks, CA: Sage, 2003).

48   C. Taylor, *The Explanation of Behavior* (London: Routledge and Kegan Paul, 1964); Smith, *Charles Taylor*, 33–57. Taylor directed this critique at the human sciences alone; but if natural science is itself a cultural phenomenon, then it too must be understood as bound up with human

purpose and meaning. C. Geertz, "The Strange Estrangement: Taylor and the Natural Sciences," in *Philosophy in an Age of Pluralism*, ed. J. Tulley, 83–95 (Cambridge: Cambridge University Press, 1994).

49 James, *Meaning of Truth*, 29. In this connection, Mill was not far off the mark in referring to social and human studies as moral sciences, even if his account of the nature of those studies may have been overly enamored with positivist conceptions of the physical sciences. J. S. Mill, "The Logic of the Moral Sciences", in *Collected Works of John Stuart Mill*, Vol. 8, ed. J. M. Robson (Toronto: University of Toronto Press, London: Routledge and Kegan Paul, 1977), 832–952; also I. Murdoch, *The Sovereignty of Good* (London: Routledge and Kegan Paul, 1970).

50 Phenix, "Transcendence and the Curriculum"; Alexander, *Reclaiming Goodness*; also Alexander, "Education in Ideology," where I argue that dogmatic ideals are essentially amoral or nonethical in the sense that they flatten possibilities for the exercise of human agency (see Chapter Five).

51 H. G. Gadamer, *Truth and Method* (New York, NY: Crossroad, 1989); Moss, "Understanding the Other"; David Bridges has called this process "fiction written under oath," which entails, as I understand it, a commitment to express to the best of one's ability ideals that transcend human existence or experience, D. Bridges, *Fiction Written under Oath: Essays in Philosophy and Educational Research* (The Hague: Springer, 2005).

52 Plato, *Phaedrus*, trans. R. Waterfield (Oxford: Oxford University Press, 2002); also P. Bourdieu, *The Logic of Practice*, trans. R. Nice (Cambridge: Polity Press, 1990).

53 Plato, *Republic*.

54 See Chapter Nine.

55 On the idea of dynamic form, see S. Langer, *Problems of Art* (New York, NY: Scribners, 1954); also see Chapter Three.

56 Thus, among today's most compelling reconstructions of scientific explanation after Hume is Peter Lipton's notion of "inference to the best possible explanation." P. Lipton, *Inference to the Best Explanation* (London: Routledge, 1991).

57 W. Feinberg, *Understanding Education: Toward a Reconstruction of Educational Inquiry* (Cambridge: Cambridge University Press, 1983).

CHAPTER THREE

1 Alexander, "Cognitive Relativism in Evaluation"; Eisner, *Educational Imagination*, 3rd ed.; Eisner, *Enlightened Eye*; Richardson, "Writing: A Method of Inquiry"; J. L. Kimcheloe and P. McLaren, "Rethinking Critical Theory and Qualitative Research," in *Handbook of Qualitative Research*, eds N. K. Denzin and Y. S. Lincoln, 138–57 (Thousand Oaks, CA: Sage, 1994).

2 Kuhn, *Structure of Scientific Revolutions*.

3 C. Norris, *Against Relativism: Philosophy of Science, Deconstruction, and Critical Theory* (Oxford: Blackwell, 1997).

4 P. Wexler, *Holy Sparks: Social Theory, Education, and Religion* (New York, NY: Macmillan, 1997), 139–51; P. Palmer, *To Know as We Are Known:*

Education as Spiritual Journey (San Francisco, CA: Harper and Row, 1983); Huebner, *Lure of the Transcendent*, 353.

5   E. W. Eisner, *The Art of Educational Evaluation: A Personal View* (London: Falmer, 1988), 189–200; I. Scheffler, *In Praise of the Cognitive Emotions and Other Essays* (New York, NY: Routledge, 1991), 3–17.

6   Callahan, *Education and the Cult of Efficiency*.

7   R. Rist, "On the Relation among Educational Research Paradigms," *Anthropology and Education Quarterly* 8, no. 2 (1977): 37–57; M. Q. Patton, *Utilization Focused Evaluation* (Thousand Oaks, CA: Sage, 1978).

8   E. R. House, *The Logic of Evaluative Argument* (Los Angeles, CA: UCLA Center for the Study of Evaluation, 1977); E. Guba, *Toward a Methodology of Naturalistic Inquiry in Education* (Los Angeles, CA: UCLA Center for the Study of Evaluation, 1978).

9   A. Peshkin, "The Researcher and Subjective Reflections of Ethnography of Schooling," in *Doing Ethnography of Schooling: Educational Ethnography in Action*, ed. G. Spindler, 48–67 (New York, NY: Holt, Reinhart, and Winston, 1982).

10 Patton, *Qualitative Evaluation Methods*, 17–21; Guba and Lincoln, *Naturalistic Inquiry*, 14–69.

11 P. Berger and T. Luckmann, *The Social Construction of Reality* (New York, NY: Penguin, 1969).

12 Of course, qualitative research is only naturalistic in part. Participant observation and interviews are both intrusive procedures; see H. A. Alexander, "Is Phenomenology the Basis of Qualitative Inquiry?," in *Proceedings of the Philosophy of Education Society 1987*, ed. B. Arnstein, 379–89 (Champaign, IL: The Philosophy of Education Society, 1988).

13 E. G. Guba and Y. S. Lincoln, *Effective Evaluation* (San Francisco, CA: Jossey-Bass, 1981), 58–127.

14 von Wright, *Explanation and Understanding*; C. Weiss, *Evaluation Research* (Englewood Cliffs, NJ: Prentice Hall, 1972).

15 C. Geertz, *The Interpretation of Cultures* (New York, NY: Basic Books, 1973), 3–32.

16 N. Denzin, *The Research Act*, 3rd ed. (Englewood Cliffs, NJ: Prentice Hall, 1989); Guba and Lincoln, *Effective Evaluation*, 102–107; Guba and Lincoln, *Naturalistic Inquiry*, 305–307.

17 B. G. Glazer and A. Strauss, *The Discovery of Grounded Theory* (Chicago, IL: Aldine, 1974).

18 Husserl, *Ideas*; A. Schutz, *On Phenomenology and Human Relations* (Chicago, IL: University of Chicago Press, 1970).

19 J. Spradley, *The Ethnographic Interview* (New York, NY: Holt, Reinhart, and Winston, 1979); J. Spradley, *Participant Observation* (New York, NY: Holt, Reinhart, and Winston, 1980); A. Strauss, ed., *George Herbert Mead on Social Psychology* (Chicago, IL: University of Chicago Press, 1977); G. Ryle, *The Concept of Mind* (New York, NY: Harper and Row, 1949); P. Winch, *The Idea of Social Science and Its Relation to Philosophy* (London: Routledge and Kegan Paul, 1958).

20 E. W. Eisner, "Aesthetic Modes of Knowing," *Learning and Teaching the Ways of Knowing, NSSE Yearbook* 48, no. 2 (1985): 23–36; J. Dewey, *Art as Experience* (New York, NY: Perigee Books, 1980); Langer, *Problems of*

Art; N. Goodman, *Languages of Art* (Indianapolis, IN: Bobbs-Merrill, 1968);
N. Goodman, *Ways of Worldmaking* (Hassocks: Harvest Press, 1978).

21   H. A. Alexander, "Empathy and Evaluation: Understanding the Private
Meanings of Behavior," *Studies in Philosophy of Education* 22, no. 4 (1991):
123–34.

22   J. F. Lyotard, *The Postmodern Condition: A Report on Knowledge*
(Minneapolis: University of Minnesota Press, 1979).

23   Richardson, "Writing: A Method of Inquiry," 518.

24   H. Siegel, *Relativism Refuted* (The Hague: Reidel, 1987).

25   Scheffler, *In Praise of the Cognitive Emotions*, 15.

26   N. Goodman, "Art as Inquiry," in *Aesthetics Today*, eds M. Philipson and
P. Gudel, 301–21 (New York, NY: Meridian, 1990).

27   Scheffler, *In Praise of the Cognitive Emotions*, 9; Goodman, *Languages of Art*,
251.

28   Goodman, "Art as Inquiry," 315.

29   Langer, *Problems of Art*, 21–22.

30   Eisner, "Aesthetic Modes of Knowing"; Huebner, *Lure of the Transcendent*,
29–30.

31   Palmer, *To Know as We Are Known*, xv.

32   Phenix, "Transcendence and the Curriculum"; Heubner, *Lure of the
Transcendent*, 358–69; Buber, *I and Thou*.

33   E. W. Eisner, *Cognition and Curriculum Reconsidered* (New York, NY:
Teachers College Press, 1994).

34   P. J. Pelto and G. H. Pelto, *Anthropological Research: The Structure of Inquiry*
(Cambridge: Cambridge University Press, 1978), 62–66.

35   E. D. Hirsch, *Validity in Interpretation* (New Haven, CT: Yale University Press,
1971).

36   Gadamer, *Truth and Method*.

37   Eisner, *Art of Educational Evaluation*, 105; J. Dewey, *Art as Experience*.
Eisegesis does not replace exegesis. Rather, creative interpretation must be
rooted in contextual meaning.

38   I. Kant, *The Critique of Judgment* (Oxford: Oxford University Press, 1988),
212–13.

39   P. K. Feyerabend, *Science in a Free Society* (London: Verso, 1982).

40   J. Keats, "Ode on a Grecian Urn," in *The Complete Poems*, ed. J. Barbard, 344
(New York, NY: Viking Press, 1977).

41   Murdoch, *Sovereignty of Good*, 77–104.

42   I called these ethical or moral versus nonethical or amoral ideologies. See
Chapter Five.

43   K. Marx and F. Engels, *The German Ideology* (New York, NY: Prometheus,
1998); Apple, *Ideology and Curriculum*.

44   Kincheloe and McLaren, "Rethinking Critical Theory."

45   McLaren, *Life in Schools*, 166–91.

46   Alexander, *Reclaiming Goodness*, 37–50.

47   Murdoch, *Sovereignty of Good*, 85.

48   Alexander, *Reclaiming Goodness*; see Chapter Nine.

49   J. J. C. Smart, *Ethics, Persuasion, and Truth* (London: Routledge and Kegan
Paul, 1984), 84.

50   MacIntyre, *After Virtue*.

51 H. A. Alexander, "Elliot Eisner's Aesthetic Theory of Evaluation," *Educational Theory* 36, no. 3 (1986): 259–70; S. Blackburn, *Essays in Quasi-Realism* (Oxford: Oxford University Press, 1993).

52 Norris, *Against Relativism*, x.

53 R. G. Collingwood, *The Principles of Art* (Oxford: Clarendon, 1964).

54 Phenix, "Transcendence and the Curriculum"; Huebner, *Lure of the Transcendent*, 360.

55 P. Tillich, *The Dynamics of Faith* (New York, NY: HarperCollins, 1986).

56 Alexander, *Reclaiming Goodness*, 145–51.

57 Murdoch, *Sovereignty of Good*, 17.

58 E. Cassirer, "The Educational Value of Art," in *Symbol, Myth, and Culture*, ed. D. P. Verne, 196–215 (New Haven, CT: Yale University Press, 1979).

59 Kant, *Critique of Pure Reason*, 532–49.

60 Alexander, *Reclaiming Goodness*, 161; Levinas, *Humanism of the Other*. See Chapter Ten.

61 C. Taylor, "Interpretation and the Sciences of Man," in *Philosophy and the Human Sciences* (Cambridge: Cambridge University Press, 1985), 15–57.

62 T. F. Green, "Teaching, Acting, and Behaving," *Harvard Educational Review* 34, no. 4 (1964): 507–24; T. F. Green, *The Activities of Teaching* (New York, NY: McGraw-Hill, 1971).

63 R. S. Peters, "Education as Initiation," in *Philosophical Analysis and Education*, ed. R. D. Archambault, 87–112 (London: Routledge and Kegan Paul, 1972); P. H. Hirst, *Knowledge and the Curriculum* (London: Routledge and Kegan Paul, 1974); M. Oakeshott, "Religion and the Moral Life," in *Religion, Politics, and the Moral Life*, ed. T. Fuller, 39–45 (New Haven, CT: Yale University Press, 1993); T. F. Green, *Voices: The Educational Formation of Conscience* (Notre Dame, IN: University of Notre Dame Press, 1999); P. H. Phenix, *Realms of Meaning* (New York, NY: McGraw-Hill, 1964); Eisner, *Cognition and Curriculum Reconsidered*; Palmer, *To Know as We Are Known*, 21; Alexander, *Reclaiming Goodness*, 183–201.

64 Green, *Activities of Teaching*; P. W. Jackson, *The Practice of Teaching* (New York, NY: Teachers College Press, 1986), 115–45.

65 Huebner, *Lure of the Transcendent*, 360.

66 Aristotle, in *Poetics*, ed. T. J. Saunders, trans. T. A. Sinclair (London: Penguin Classics, 1981), chaps. 1–3; Huebner, *Lure of the Transcendent*, 60.

67 Alexander, *Reclaiming Goodness*, xii.

68 Huebner, *Lure of the Transcendent*, 23–35.

69 Eisner, *Cognition and Curriculum Reconsidered*.

70 J. Schwab, "The Practical: Arts of Eclectic," in *Science, Curriculum, and Liberal Education*, eds I. Westbury and N. Wilkof, 322–64 (Chicago, IL: University of Chicago Press, 1978); L. S. Shulman, "Those Who Understand: Knowledge Growth in Teaching," *Educational Researcher* 15, no. 2 (Feb. 1986): 4–14.

71 Schwab, "The Practical: Arts of Eclectic."

72 Eisner, *Educational Imagination*, 3rd ed., 212–344; Eisner, *Enlightened Eye*, 63–168.

73 Eisner, *Enlightened Eye*, 89–105.

74 S. L. Lightfoot, *The Good High School* (New York, NY: Basic Books, 1983), 16.

75 Langer, *Problems of Art*, 1–12, 44–58.

76 Eisner, *Educational Imagination*, 3rd ed., 237–42; Eisner, *Enlightened Eye*, 107–20.

77 Guba and Lincoln, *Naturalistic Inquiry*, 289–331.

78 T. A. Schwandt, "Constructivist, Interpretivist Approaches to Human Inquiry," in *Handbook of Qualitative Research*, eds N. Denzin and Y. S. Lincoln, 118–37 (Thousand Oaks, CA: Sage, 1994).

79 Y. S. Lincoln and E. G. Guba, "But Is It Rigorous? Trustworthiness and Authenticity in Naturalistic Evaluation," in *Naturalistic Evaluation*, ed. D. D. Williams, 73–84 (San Francisco, CA: Jossey-Bass, 1986), 83.

80 Guba and Lincoln, *Fourth Generation Evaluation*.

81 Richardson, "Writing: A Method of Inquiry," 517.

82 Eisner, *Educational Imagination*, 3rd ed., 229–30.

83 Eisner, *Educational Imagination*, 231–32.

84 Palmer, *To Know as We are Known*, 13.

85 Murdoch, *Sovereignty of Good*, 90.

86 Murdoch, *Sovereignty of Good*, 87–88.

CHAPTER FOUR

1   Callahan, *Education and the Cult of Efficiency*; Tyack, *One Best System*; H. Kliebard, *The Struggle for the American Curriculum, 1893–1958*, 3rd ed. (New York, NY: Routledge, 2004).

2   Comte, *Introduction to Positive Philosophy*.

3   K. Egan, *Getting It Wrong from the Beginning: Our Progressivist Inheritance from Herbert Spencer, John Dewey, and John Piaget* (New Haven, CT: Yale University Press, 2004).

4   D. J. Clandinin and F. M. Connelly, *Narrative Inquiry: Experience and Story in Qualitative Research* (San Francisco, CA: Jossey-Bass, 2000); Eisner, *Enlightened Eye*; Rist, "Relation among Educational Research Paradigms"; Stake, *Art of Case Study Research*.

5   Kincheloe and McLaren, "Rethinking Critical Theory."

6   Guba, *Toward a Methodology*; Guba, "Alternative Paradigm Dialogue"; Guba and Lincoln, *Naturalistic Inquiry*; Patton, *Qualitative Evaluation Methods*; Patton, *Qualitative Evaluation and Research Methods*.

7   P. Freire, *Pedagogy of the Oppressed* (New York, NY: Continuum, 2000); McLaren, *Life in Schools*; Popkewitz, *Paradigm and Ideology*.

8   Alexander, "View from Somewhere," 209 (see Chapter Two).

9   The National Research Council of the American Academy of Science offered a broader account of "rigorous science" that recognized the academic respectability of a variety of methodologies in educational research that included such qualitative disciplines as educational anthropology, but a number of critics point out that this view does not veer very far from the narrow empiricist path (see Feuer, Towne, and Shavelson, "Scientific Culture"; Eisenhart, "Hammers and Saws"; Erickson and Gutierrez, "Culture, Rigor, and Science"; Moss, "Understanding the Other"; St. Peter, "'Science' Rejects Postmodernism"; and Chapter Two.

10 Alexander, "View from Somewhere," 208–12 (see Chapter Two).

11 Alexander, "View from Somewhere."

12 See Chapter Three.

13 M. Oakeshott, *The Voice of Liberal Learning* (New Haven, CT: Yale University Press, 1989); Oakeshott, *On Human Conduct*; Oakeshott, *Rationalism in Politics*.

14 Oakeshott, *Voice of Liberal Learning*, 64.

15 Oakeshott, *Rationalism in Politics*, 10–11.

16 Oakeshott, *On Human Conduct*, 40–41. Oakeshott was not especially rigorous about the way he used such terms as "behavior," "conduct," "skills," or "abilities." He sometimes referred to a tradition of practice, for example, as a tradition of behavior, when by the idea of practice he clearly had in mind meaningful conduct, not merely observable or unintelligent actions. Similarly, he describes skills as abilities of lesser complexity, and often uses the term "complex abilities" to denote more sophisticated capacities. To simplify, I use the term "behavior" to denote activities that are less, and "conduct" endeavors that are more, meaningful or intelligent. Similarly, I use "skills" to denote less, and "abilities" more, complex capacities (see H. A. Alexander, "Engaging Tradition: Michael Oakeshott on Liberal Learning," in *Learning to Live with the Future*, eds A. Stables and S. Gough, 113–27 (New York, NY: Routledge, 2008).

17 Hempel, *Philosophy of Natural Science*; Nagel, *Structure of Science*.

18 Campbell and Stanley, *Experimental and Quasi-Experimental Design*; Shaddish, Cook, and Campbell, *Experimental and Quasi-Experimental Design*.

19 R. Bogdan and S. K. Bilken, *Qualitative Research for Education*, 5th ed. (Boston, MA: Allyn and Bacon, 2006).

20 Alexander, "Aesthetic Inquiry in Education," 2–6 (see Chapter Three).

21 For example, Bourdieu, *Logic of Practice*; Freire, *Pedagogy of the Oppressed*; G. Lucas, *Critical Anthropology* (New York, NY: New School for Social Research, 1972). Marx and Engels were among our most incorrigible political rationalists in Oakeshott's view. In reference to dialectical materialism, he wrote that "no other technique has so imposed itself upon the world as if it were concrete knowledge; none has created so vast an intellectual proletariat, with nothing but its technique to lose." Oakeshott, *Rationalism in Politics*, 26.

22 Marx and Engels, *German Ideology*; M. Horkheimer and T. Adorno, *Dialectic of Enlightenment* (Palo Alto, CA: Stanford University Press, 2007); M. Foucault, *The Order of Things: An Archeology of the Human Sciences* (New York, NY: Routledge, 2001); M. Foucault, *The Archeology of Knowledge and Discourse on Language* (London: Pantheon, 1982).

23 L. Althusser, *Writings on Psychoanalysis* (New York, NY: Columbia University Press, 1999), 7–32.

24 P. Ricoeur, *Freud and Philosophy*, trans. D. Savage (New Haven, CT: Yale University Press, 1970); P. Ricoeur, *The Conflict of Interpretations*, trans. D. Ihde (Evanston, IL: Northwestern University Press, 1974); P. Ricoeur, *Hermeneutics and the Human Sciences*, trans. J. B. Thompson (Cambridge: Cambridge University Press, 1981).

25 L. Harvey, *Critical Social Research* (New York, NY: Routledge, 1990).

26 Oakeshott, *Rationalism in Politics*, 9.

27 Oakeshott, *On Human Conduct*, 54.

28 Oakeshott, *On Human Conduct*, 61.
29 Oakeshott, *Rationalism in Politics*, 129.
30 Oakeshott, *Voice of Liberal Learning*, 69.
31 Oakeshott, *Rationalism in Politics*, 11–12.
32 Oakeshott, *Rationalism in Politics*, 31.
33 Oakeshott, *Rationalism in Politics*, 32.
34 Oakeshott, *Rationalism in Politics*, 33.
35 F. Bacon, in *The New Organon*, eds L. Jardine and M. Silverthorne (Cambridge: Cambridge University Press, 2002); Descartes, *Discourse on Method*; Oakeshott, *Rationalism in Politics*, 15.
36 Plato, *Phaedrus*; Plato, *Republic*.
37 Aristotle, *Metaphysics*; Smith, *Charles Taylor*, 35–41; Taylor, *Explanation of Behavior*; Taylor, *Philosophy and the Human Sciences*, 15–57.
38 Hume, *Enquiry Concerning Human Understanding*.
39 Kant, *Prolegomena*; Kant, *Critique of Pure Reason*.
40 Popper, *Logic of Scientific Discovery*; Popper, *Objective Knowledge*.
41 Lakatos, *Methodology of Scientific Research Programs*.
42 Hegel, *Reason in History*.
43 Marx and Engels, *German Ideology*.
44 Foucault, *Order of Things*; Foucault, *Archeology of Knowledge*.
45 Husserl, *Ideas*; Husserl, *Cartesian Meditation*.
46 Alexander, "View from Somewhere," 212 (see Chapter Two); Alexander, "Is Phenomenology the Basis."
47 James, *Pragmatism*; Dewey, *Logic*.
48 W. James, *A Pluralistic Universe* (Lincoln, NE: University of Nebraska Press, 1996); Alexander, "Engaging Tradition."
49 W. V. O. Quine, "Two Dogmas of Empiricism," in *From a Logical Point of View* (Cambridge, MA: Harvard University Press, 1999), 20–47.
50 Alexander, "Aesthetic Inquiry in Education," 2–6 (see Chapter Three).
51 Alexander, "View from Somewhere," 206 (see Chapter Two).
52 Alexander, "View from Somewhere," 209.
53 Quine, *Ontological Relativity*, 26–69.
54 H. A. Alexander, "Liberal Education and Open Society: Absolutism and Relativism in Curriculum Theory," *Curriculum Inquiry* 19, no. 1 (1989): 11–32; Alexander, "Cognitive Relativism in Evaluation."
55 Phenix, "Transcendence and the Curriculum"; Levinas, *Humanism of the Other*.
56 Buber, *I and Thou*.
57 J. Searle, *The Construction of Social Reality* (New York, NY: The Free Press, 1995), 1–30.
58 Heidegger, *Being and Time*.
59 I. Scheffler, *Conditions of Knowledge* (Chicago, IL: University of Chicago Press, 1983).
60 Langer, *Problems of Art*.
61 Hirsch, *Validity in Interpretation*.
62 Gadamer, *Truth and Method*.
63 Alexander, "Aesthetic Inquiry in Education," 5 (see Chapter Three).
64 Oakeshott, *On Human Conduct*, 54.
65 H. R. Bernard, *Research Methods in Anthropology* (Lanham, MA: Rowman and Littlefield, 1995).

66   von Wright, *Explanation and Understanding*.
67   Alexander, "View from Somewhere," 214 (see Chapter Two).
68   Alexander, "View from Somewhere," 212–15.
69   N. Noddings, *Caring: A Feminine Approach to Ethics and Moral Education* (Berkeley: University of California Press, 1984), 30.
70   Levinas, *Humanism of the Other*.

CHAPTER FIVE

1   W. F. O'Neil, *Educational Ideologies: Contemporary Expressions of Educational Philosophy* (Santa Monica, CA: Goodyear Publishing, 1981).
2   G. S. Counts, *Dare the Schools Build a New Social Order* (Chicago, IL: University of Chicago Press, 1981).
3   H. Siegel, *Educating Reason* (New York, NY: Routledge, 1988).
4   I. A. Snook, *Indoctrination and Education* (London: Routledge and Kegan Paul, 1972).
5   Aronowitz and Giroux, *Postmodern Education*.
6   Apple, *Ideology and Curriculum*.
7   Purpel, *Moral and Spiritual Crisis*; M. Rosenak, *Commandments and Concerns: Jewish Religious Education in a Secular Age* (Philadelphia, PA: Jewish Publication Society, 1987).
8   Oakeshott, "Political Education," in *Rationalism in Politics*, 111–36.
9   I. Gur-Ze'ev, *Destroying the Other's Collective Memory* (New York, NY: Peter Lang, 2003), 1–24.
10   Alexander, *Reclaiming Goodness*, 156–62.
11   I use the term "amoral" rather than "immoral" here, since without a conception of agency, it is impossible to make sense of normative statements altogether—to distinguish between that which is to be positively valued or counted as moral and that which is not.
12   This is a generous account of ideology that entails the possibility that ideologies can be assessed both positively and negatively. They can be better and worse, true and false, and falsifiable as well as nonfalsifiable. In contrast, Karl Popper uses the term "ideology" as something like an antonym of theory. On his account, only theories can be proven false, while ideologies cannot be. This is closer to what I have called amoral (or nonethical) ideologies. I might have referred to the moral (or ethical) ideologies as open, since on the account presented here, they are open to engagement with other moral (or ethical) ideologies. I chose not to do so, however, to avoid the confusion that might arise from Popper's negative accounting of ideologies, on the one hand, and my contention that moral (or ethical) ideologies can be found in what he called open societies, on the other; cf. J. Lorrain, *The Concept of Ideology* (London: Hutchinson, 1979).
13   Lyotard, *Postmodern Condition*.
14   Geertz, *Interpretation of Cultures*.
15   K. R. Popper, *The Open Society and Its Enemies* (London: Routledge and Kegan Paul, 1963).
16   W. K. Frankena, *Ethics*, 2nd ed. (Englewood Cliffs, NJ: Prentice-Hall, 1973), 4–9.

17 Frankena, *Ethics*, 9–10. Some philosophers have found it useful to make a rather rigid distinction between the terms *morals* and *ethics*, reserving the former for the concern in modern philosophy since Kant with deontological questions and the latter for the premodern and post-MacIntyre, neo-Aristotelian interest in virtues and values. Since I hold that the aretaic focus on conceptions of the good is logically prior to and wider than matters of duty, it could readily be argued that the two sorts of ideologies I have distinguished should be called ethical and nonethical rather than moral and amoral. While I agree with this point in principle, and explicitly endorse it in Chapter Twelve, in everyday speech, especially among educators, the terms ethics and morality are used more or less interchangeably, and attempts to insist upon more restrictive uses of the terms lead more often to confusion than to increased clarity. For example, although character education fits squarely into the Aristotelian concern for virtues and should hence be referred to as education in ethics, it is regularly designated as moral education, in part perhaps to contrast it with other more Kantian approaches such as those of cognitive developmentalists influenced by Kohlberg. In this chapter, therefore, I follow the tendency among educators to use the terms interchangeably.

18 B. Williams, *Ethics and the Limits of Philosophy* (Cambridge, MA: Harvard University Press, 1985).

19 Murdoch, *Sovereignty of Good*.

20 Alexander, *Reclaiming Goodness*, 140–50; see Chapter Nine.

21 The term "amoral" is used by some philosophers to designate activities for which moral or ethical assessment is irrelevant, such as tennis or cooking. I use the term in a different sense, which suggests that when the conditions of human agency are denied, moral assessments are meaningless, even concerning matters where they would otherwise be relevant, such as the oppression of the poor or unequal or unfair distribution of economic and other resources in society. In all events, I am not inclined to separate categories such as sports or food so readily from value concerns (consider, for example, questions of sportsmanship or vegetarianism).

22 J. Watt, *Ideology, Objectivity, and Education* (New York, NY: Teachers College Press, 1994), 1–26; Marx and Engels, *German Ideology*; K. Mannheim, *Ideology and Utopia* (London: Routledge and Kegan Paul, 1936).

23 Berger and Luckmann, *Social Construction of Reality*; Lyotard, *Postmodern Condition*.

24 MacIntyre, *After Virtue*; MacIntyre, *Whose Justice, Which Rationality?*

25 Watt, *Ideology, Objectivity, and Education*, 82–83.

26 Watt, *Ideology, Objectivity, and Education*, 125–28.

27 My analysis here follows Green, "Teaching, Acting, and Behaving," although it is strikingly similar to Oakeshott on the difference between human behavior and human conduct. See Chapter Four.

28 Hempel, *Philosophy of Natural Science*.

29 To the extent that these entail some sort of intentional inquiry, John Dewey might have called these intelligent, as opposed to unintelligent, habits. See J. Garrison, "John Dewey's Theory of Practical Reason," *Educational Philosophy and Theory* 31, no. 3 (1999): 291–312.

30 Green, "Teaching, Acting, and Behaving," 509–16.

31   N. Noddings, *Educating for Intelligent Belief and Unbelief* (New York, NY: Teachers College Press, 1993); Noddings, *Caring*.

32   C. Taylor, *Human Agency and Language* (Cambridge: Cambridge University Press, 1985), 48.

33   Taylor, *Human Agency and Language*, 15–44.

34   R. S. Peters, *The Concept of Education* (London: Routledge and Kegan Paul, 1967).

35   C. Higgins, "Teaching and the Good Life," *Educational Theory* 53, no. 2 (2003): 131–54.

36   J. White, *Education and the Good Life: Autonomy, Altruism, and the National Curriculum* (New York, NY: Teachers College Press, 1991).

37   These three conditions are interrelated. The most basic is indeterminism, or the idea that within reasonable limits we are in fact the agents of our actions and beliefs. However, without some understanding of the moral and practical significance of our options, it is difficult to imagine how our choices could be other than arbitrary. Some conception of moral understanding is required. Similarly, if we choose as we do only because it is in our very nature to do so, then we could not exercise choice in any meaningful sense. To be the agents of our actions, therefore, requires not only that we possess some sort of moral understanding but also that we can get it wrong, because we are fallible. Here again my use of the term "fallible" is broader than Popper's. It includes the possibility of moral as well as cognitive mistakes. This latter condition is especially important—and controversial—in discussing matters of religious doctrine and faith.

38   Alexander, *Reclaiming Goodness*, 44–48.

39   C. Taylor, *Sources of the Self: The Making of Modern Identity* (Cambridge, MA: Harvard University Press, 1989), 16–32.

40   Levinas, *Humanism of the Other*.

41   Green, *Voices*; Taylor, *Human Agency and Language*, 15–44.

42   Snook, *Indoctrination and Education*.

43   Green, *Activities of Teaching*, 29–33.

44   H. Siegel, "Can Rationality Be Redeemed?" in *Philosophy of Education Yearbook 1996*, ed. F. Margonis, 74–76 (Champaign, IL: Philosophy of Education Society, 1997).

45   H. A. Alexander, "Rationality and Redemption: Ideology, Indoctrination, and Learning Communities," in *Philosophy of Education Yearbook 1996*, ed. F. Margonis, 65–73 (Champaign, IL: The Philosophy of Education Society, 1996); Alexander, *Reclaiming Goodness*, 156–62.

46   Green, "Teaching, Acting, and Behaving"; Green, *Activities of Teaching*.

47   Alexander, *Reclaiming Goodness*, 143–44.

48   Levinas, *Humanism of the Other*.

49   Siegel, *Educating Reason*.

50   Noddings, *Caring*; Aronowitz and Giroux, *Postmodern Education*.

51   Apple, *Ideology and Curriculum*.

52   Some Eastern religions, such as certain interpretations of Buddhism, teach transcendence of self. Many of these hold, with a number of Western mystical traditions, that abandoning a false sense of self yields a truer, more authentic person who is in greater control of her being, since she has come to understand the nature of existence more deeply. This way of thinking is

quite in keeping with the conception of agency required for ethical discourse and moral ideologies. Other orientations preach a wholesale abandonment of self, losing it within God or the cosmos altogether. These orientations tend to abandon the sort of human agency discussed here, and to that extent may be at odds with the conceptions of freedom and responsibility consistent with open society and democratic citizenship.

53 R. S. Peters, *Psychology and Ethical Development* (London: George Allen and Unwin, 1974).

54 Tillich, *Dynamics of Faith*.

55 The pedagogy advanced here might be viewed as an educational extension of arguments advanced by Jonathan Sacks in his *Dignity of Difference*.

56 Alexander, *Reclaiming* Goodness, 198–203; Galston, "Civic Education"; Galston, *Liberal Purposes*; Galston, *Liberal Pluralism*.

57 H. A. Alexander and M. Ben Peretz, "Toward a Pedagogy of the Sacred: Transcendence, Ethics, and the Curriculum," in *Spiritual Education, Cultural, Religious, and Social Differences: New Perspectives for the 21st Century*, eds J. Erricker, C. Ota and C. Erricker, 34–47 (Brighton: Sussex Academic Press, 2001).

58 Phenix, "Transcendence and the Curriculum"; Huebner, *Lure of the Transcendent*; Alexander, *Reclaiming Goodness*, 145–47.

59 Consider, for example, the ways in which athletics entail discipline, strategic thinking, and a commitment to fairness, and how team sports promote the values of teamwork and cooperation in addition to competitiveness. See Chapter Nine.

CHAPTER SIX

1 Searle, *Construction of Social Reality*.

2 This is so at least at the level of research universities. There are a few undergraduate colleges in Israel that teach in Arabic.

3 Y. Tamir, *Liberal Nationalism* (Princeton, NJ: Princeton University Press, 1995), 124–30.

4 Nozick, *Philosophical Explanations*, 8.

5 Gray, *Two Faces of Liberalism*.

6 Oakeshott, *Rationalism in Politics*; Berlin, *Four Essays on Liberty*.

7 Tamir, *Liberal Nationalism*; also see Chapters Five, Seven, and Nine.

8 Aristotle, *Politics* (London: Penguin Classics, 1981); M. T. Cicero, *The Republic and the Laws*, trans. N. Rudd (Oxford: Oxford University Press, 2009); N. Machiavelli, *The Prince* (New York, NY: Bantam, 1984); I. Berlin, *Three Critics of Enlightenment: Vico, Hamann, and Herder* (Princeton, NJ: Princeton University Press, 2001), 168–242; Hegel, *Philosophy of Right*; MacIntyre, *After Virtue*; MacIntyre, *Whose Justice, Which Rationality?*; Sandel, *Liberalism and the Limits of Justice*.

9 Walzer, *Thick and Thin*; The first published version of this chapter (Alexander, "Literacy and Citizenship") made the common mistake of associating Terence McLaughlin's well-known distinction between maximal and minimal citizenship education with Michael Walzer's equally well-known distinction

between thick and thin moral traditions. However, McLaughlin's distinction considers the extent to which an education prepares youngsters to embrace values that allow for a common civic life across difference, not the particular moral traditions with which they may be encouraged to identify. See McLaughlin, "Citizenship, Diversity, and Education" and Chapter Eleven.

10 I. Kant, *Groundwork for the Metaphysics of Morals*, trans. A. Zweig (Oxford: Oxford University Press, 2002); I. Kant, *Critique of Practical Reason*, trans. M. Gregor (Cambridge: Cambridge University Press, 1997); J. Locke, *Two Treaties of Government* (Cambridge: Cambridge University Press, 1988); J. S. Mill, *On Liberty*, in *Collected Works of John Stuart Mill*, Vol. 18, ed. J. M. Robson (Toronto: University of Toronto Press, London: Routledge and Kegan Paul, 1977); J. Rawls, *A Theory of Justice* (Cambridge, MA: Harvard University Press, 1971); J. Rawls, *Political Liberalism* (New York, NY: Columbia University Press, 1993).

11 Taylor, "What is Human Agency?" in *Human Agency and Language*, 15–44.

12 E. Callan, *Autonomy and Schooling* (Kingston and Montreal: McGill-Queen's University Press, 1988), 25–55.

13 Walzer, *Thick and Thin*. In McLaughlin's view, education in what Walzer refers to as thin moral traditions that reach across difference can be situated on a spectrum between maximal and minimal education in citizenship, to the extent that they encourage values associated with peaceful coexistence and democratic governance; see McLaughlin, "Citizenship, Diversity, and Education," and Chapter Eleven.

14 Brighouse, *On Education*, 13–14; Callan, "McLaughlin on Parental Rights."

15 Plato, *Republic*; K. Marx, *Critique of Hegel's Philosophy of Right* (Cambridge: Cambridge University Press, 1970); Horkheimer and Adorno, *Dialectic of Enlightenment*; Freire, *Pedagogy of the Oppressed*; E. Said, *Orientalism* (New York, NY: Vintage Books, 1979); Foucault, *Order of Things*.

16 I. Gur-Ze'ev, *Beyond the Modern-Postmodern Struggle in Education* (Rotterdam, The Netherlands: Sense, 2008).

17 G. Steiner, *After Babel: Aspects of Language and Translation* (Oxford: Oxford University Press, 1998).

18 Freire, *Pedagogy of the Oppressed*; P. Freire, *Education for Critical Consciousness* (London: Continuum, 2005).

19 Gray, *Two Faces of Liberalism*, 2.

20 Gray, *Two Faces of Liberalism*, 6.

21 I. Berlin, *The Hedgehog and the Fox: An Essay on Tolstoy's View of History* (New York, NY: Simon and Schuster, 1953), 3.

22 Berlin, *Four Essays on Liberty*.

23 Berlin, *Four Essays on Liberty*, 133.

24 I. Berlin, *Against the Current: Essays in the History of Ideas* (Princeton, NJ: Princeton University Press, 1997), 1–24.

25 Berlin, *The Hedgehog and the Fox*, 5.

26 A. Gramsci, *Selections from the Prison Notebooks* (New York, NY: International Publishers, 2008); Horkheimer and Adorno, *Dialectic of Enlightenment*.

27 J. Raz, *The Morality of Freedom* (Oxford: Clarendon Press, 1986); Brighouse, *On Education*.

28 A. Gutmann and D. Thompson, *Democracy and Disagreement* (Cambridge, MA: Harvard University Press, 1998); J. Raz, *Engaging Reason: On the Theory of Value and Action* (Oxford: Oxford University Press, 2002); Rawls, *Political Liberalism*.

29 I. M. Young, *Inclusion and Democracy* (Oxford: Oxford University Press, 2002); Freire, *Pedagogy of the Oppressed*; McLaren, *Life in Schools*.

30 J. Gray, *Isaiah Berlin* (Princeton, NJ: Princeton University Press, 1996).

31 MacIntyre, *After Virtue*; Taylor, *Sources of the Self*; Taylor, "What is Human Agency?" in *Human Agency and Language*, 15–44.

32 Sandel, *Liberalism and the Limits of Justice*; Taylor, *Ethics of Authenticity*.

33 J. Rawls, *Justice as Fairness: A Restatement* (Cambridge, MA: Harvard University Press, 2001); Rawls, *Theory of Justice*; Rawls, *Political Liberalism*.

34 E. Callan, *Creating Citizens: Political Education and Liberal Democracy* (Oxford: Clarendon Press, 2004); A. Gutmann, *Democratic Education* (Princeton, NJ: Princeton University Press, 1987); J. Tomasi, *Liberalism beyond Justice: Citizens, Society, and the Boundaries of Political Theory* (Princeton, NJ: Princeton University Press, 2001).

35 W. Feinberg, *Common Schools/Uncommon Identities: National Unity and Cultural Difference* (New Haven: Yale University Press, 2000); W. Feinberg, *For Goodness Sake: Religious Schools and Education for Democratic Citizenry* (New York, NY: Routledge, 2006).

36 S. Macedo, *Liberal Virtues: Citizenship, Virtue, and Community in Liberal Constitutionalism* (Oxford: Oxford University Press, 1990).

37 Gray, *Two Faces of Liberalism*.

38 Callan, *Autonomy and Schooling*, 10.

39 Oakeshott, *Rationalism in Politics*.

40 Gray, *Two Faces of Liberalism*, 32–33.

41 Alexander, "Engaging Tradition."

42 Oakeshott, *Rationalism in Politics*, 10–11.

43 Oakeshott, *Rationalism in Politics*, 11.

44 Oakeshott, *Rationalism in Politics*, 12.

45 Oakeshott, *Rationalism in Politics*, 28.

46 Tyack, *One Best System*.

47 Rawls, *Political Liberalism*.

48 M. Levinson, *The Demands of Liberal Education* (Oxford: Oxford University Press, 1999).

49 Oakeshott, *Rationalism in Politics*, 26.

50 The very name Palestine, for what Jews have historically called Israel, was chosen by the Romans after their conquest in the first century—ostensibly to indicate that the land belonged not to the Jews but the Philistines, a people who resided in the southwest coastal region of that land around 800 years earlier. Muslim Arabs arrived in the seventh century and until very recently did not use the designation Palestine for the land. It was reintroduced by the British when they acquired a mandate to rule from the League of Nations in 1917, probably to identify their own empire with that of the Romans. Although people certainly have the right to choose the names by which they prefer to be called, one can only wonder whether the choice of such a name as the national designation for Arab residents of that land after the establishment of the State of Israel in 1948 did not entail an allusion to its anti-Jewish

origins. Relations between Jews and Arabs in the region, as I said, are not easily summarized in a single technique of conflict analysis or dialectical reasoning.

51 Oakeshott, *Rationalism in Politics*, 31.
52 Oakeshott, *Rationalism in Politics*, 123.
53 Oakeshott, *Rationalism in Politics*, 128.
54 Oakeshott, *Rationalism in Politics*, 126.
55 S. R. Ben-Porath, *Citizenship Under Fire: Democratic Education in Times of Conflict* (Princeton, NJ: Princeton University Press, 2006), 11–14.
56 S. R. Ben-Porath, *Citizenship under Fire*, 23–27.
57 Tamir, *Liberal Nationalism*, 109.
58 Tamir, *Liberal Nationalism*, xxix.
59 Tamir, *Liberal Nationalism*.
60 Levinson, *Demands of Liberal Education*.
61 Tamir, *Liberal Nationalism*, 51.
62 Tamir, *Liberal Nationalism*, 52.
63 Tamir, *Liberal Nationalism*, 51.
64 Taylor, *Ethics of Authenticity*; Taylor, "What is Human Agency?" in *Human Agency and Language*, 15–44.
65 Tamir, *Liberal Nationalism*, 56.
66 Sacks, *Dignity of Difference*.

CHAPTER SEVEN

1 Freire, *Pedagogy of the Oppressed*; McLaren, *Life in Schools*; Apple, *Ideology and Curriculum*; Apple, *Education and Power*.
2 MacIntyre, *After Virtue*; MacIntyre, *Whose Justice, Which Rationality?*
3 Gray, *Two Faces of Liberalism*.
4 H. A. Alexander, "Educating Identity: Toward a Pedagogy of Difference," in *Religious Education as Encounter: A Tribute to John Hull*, ed. S. Miedema, 45–52 (Münster: Waxmann, 2009).
5 Brighouse, *On Education*, 15.
6 Brighouse, *On Education*, 15–16.
7 Brighouse, *On Education*, 14.
8 Brighouse, *On Education*, 19.
9 Brighouse, *On Education*, 20.
10 Alexander, "Educating Identity."
11 Alexander, *Reclaiming Goodness*, 156–62.
12 J-J Rousseau, *Emile, or Treatise on Education* (Amherst, NY: Prometheus Books, 2003).
13 Kant, *Prolegomena*; Kant, *Critique of Pure Reason*.
14 cf. MacIntyre, *After Virtue*; MacIntyre, *Whose Justice, Which Rationality?*
15 For example, McLaren, *Life in Schools*; Apple, *Ideology and Curriculum*; Aronowitz and Giroux, *Postmodern Education*.
16 Walzer, *Thick and Thin*; Oakeshott, *Rationalism in Politics*; see Chapter Eight.
17 Peters, *Psychology and Ethical Development*.
18 B. Pascal, *Pensees* (London: Penguin, 2000); James, *Will to Believe*.

19 Brighouse, *On Education*, 17 (emphasis in original).
20 Levinson, *Demands of Liberal Education*.
21 Raz, *Morality of Freedom*.
22 Mill, *On Liberty*.
23 Levinson, *Demands of Liberal Education*, 15.
24 Gray points out that Raz is a value pluralist (Gray, *Two Faces of Liberalism*, 96–99) and that Mill's writings exhibit a tension between universalism and pluralism (Gray, *Two Faces of Liberalism*, 29–31). Yet both argue that liberal values should play a role in the lives of private citizens beyond that of negotiating between competing perspectives. Hence they can be counted for the present purposes as comprehensive liberals (Galston, *Liberal Pluralism*, 8–9).
25 Rawls, *Political Liberalism*.
26 Rawls, *Political Liberalism*, 54–58.
27 Rawls, *Theory of Justice*, 86.
28 Levinson, *Demands of Liberal Education*, 17.
29 Rawls, *Political Liberalism*, 302.
30 S. Macedo, *Diversity and Distrust: Civic Education in a Multicultural Democracy* (Cambridge, MA: Harvard University Press, 2000); Callan, *Creating Citizens*; Tomasi, *Liberalism beyond Justice*.
31 Levinson, *Demands of Liberal Education*, 21–22.
32 Rawls, *Political Liberalism*, 32.
33 S. Benn, *A Theory of Freedom* (Cambridge: Cambridge University Press, 1988); Levinson, *Demands of Liberal Education*, 22–24.
34 G. Dworkin, *The Theory and Practice of Autonomy* (Cambridge: Cambridge University Press, 1988).
35 On the idea of education in a tradition "from the inside" and "from the outside," see Alexander and McLaughlin, "Education in Religion and Spirituality," 363–73; and Chapter Eleven.
36 Levinson (*The Demands of Liberal Education*, 6) states explicitly that she identifies with the liberal tradition that was transformed during the past thirty years by John Rawls, rather than that of Thomas Hobbes, though she may disagree with Gray as to whether Hayek and Raz are universal liberals or value pluralists.
37 Gray, *Two Faces of Liberalism*.
38 Berlin, *The Hedgehog and the Fox*.
39 Berlin, *Four Essays on Liberty*.
40 Levinson (*The Demands of Liberal Education*, 63) writes that "the ideal liberal school establishes a plural community whose structure and content are dictated by the overriding goal to foster the development of children's autonomy—a community instantiated by the norms of critical inquiry, toleration, and reflectiveness." This is a pluralism that excludes traditions that do not embrace rationality as a standard for critical assessment or autonomy as a value. If Levinson's ideal liberal schools receive preferential treatment by the state, it is difficult to understand how this does not "discriminate against those who do not exercise autonomy in their own lives" (Levinson, *The Demands of Liberal Education*, 22). To be fair, Levinson did state that it is hard to hold the three liberal commitments together in a single coherent account of liberalism; but surely she did not mean by this that we are to sacrifice pluralism on the alter of rationalism.

41 Gray, *Two Faces of Liberalism*, 6.
42 For a critique of Gray's account of value pluralism, see K. A. Appiah, *The Ethics of Identity* (Princeton, NJ: Princeton University Press, 2005), 36–42.
43 Oakeshott, *Rationalism in Politics*, 1–36.
44 Oakeshott, *Rationalism in Politics*, 31; Gray, *Two Faces of Liberalism*, 32–33; see Chapter Six.
45 Oakeshott, *Rationalism in Politics*, 135; Oakeshott, *Voice of Liberal Learning*.
46 Alexander, "Engaging Tradition."
47 Nagel, *View From Nowhere*.
48 This, of course, is the question Rawls was trying to address in his notion of "reasonable comprehensive doctrines." The problem with this view, I am arguing, is that the burdens of judgment upon which it relies result in too restrictive an account of the doctrines permitted in liberal societies and hence too truncated an account of pluralism; see Rawls, *Political Liberalism*, 58–66, and Tomasi, *Liberalism beyond Justice*.
49 The Hebrew Bible has been read in this way by a number of political traditions, sometimes in dialogue with philosophers from Aristotle to Dewey, although it has also been interpreted contrary to this spirit as well; see R. N. Bellah et al., *Habits of the Heart: Individualism and Commitment in American Life* (Berkeley: University of California Press, 1986); Walzer, *Exodus and Revolution*; Sacks, *Dignity of Difference*; and Chapter Ten.
50 Bellah et al., *Habits of the Heart*; Tocqueville, *Democracy in America*.
51 The narrative might include neutrality as an aspiration or ideal, but not based on Kant's a priori reason or Rawls's burdens of judgment, see R. Covers, "Nomos and Narrative," *Harvard Law Review* 97, no. 4 (1983): 1–68.
52 Sacks, *Dignity of Difference*.
53 Freire, *Pedagogy of the Oppressed*.
54 Alexander, "Educating Identity"; Terence McLaughlin referred to a similar perspective in his expression "autonomy via faith," although without making the distinction between liberalism as an ideal form of life and as a modus vivendi for coexistence among rival ways of living, see T. H. McLaughlin, "Parental Rights and the Religious Upbringing of Children," *Journal of Philosophy of Education* 18, no. 1 (1984): 75–83, and Chapter Ten.
55 Scheffler, *Conditions of Knowledge*.
56 Buber, *I and Thou*; F. Rosenzweig, "The Builders: Concerning the Law," in *On Jewish Learning*, ed. N. Glazer, 72–92 (New York, NY: Schocken, 1955).
57 Taylor, "What Is Human Agency?" in *Human Agency and Language*, 15–44.
58 Levinson, *Demands of Liberal Education*, 51–57.
59 Brighouse, *On Education*, 13.
60 Brighouse, *On Education*, 14.
61 D. Johnston, *The Idea of a Liberal Theory: A Critique and a Reconstruction* (Princeton, NJ: Princeton University Press, 1996).
62 Alexander, *Reclaiming Goodness*, 44–48.
63 See Chapter Five.
64 Brighouse, *On Education*, 77–94.
65 See Chapter Nine.

CHAPTER EIGHT

1   Plato, *Republic*; Peters, "Education as Initiation."
2   H. Spencer, *Education: Intellectual, Moral, Physical* (London: Watts, 1945); B. Bode, *Modern Educational Theories* (New York, NY: Macmillan, 1927).
3   Williams, *Ethics and the Limits of Philosophy*; Murdoch, *Sovereignty of Good*.
4   This may be one reason why every few years someone declares the curriculum field moribund or in crisis, see Schwab, *Science, Curriculum, and Liberal Education*, 287–321; Huebner, *Lure of the Transcendent*.
5   There is of course no one right way to conceptualize the curriculum field. John McNeil has divided it into four traditions that more or less correspond to examples I have chosen to examine here. He calls them the technological curriculum, academic rationalism, the humanistic curriculum, and social reconstructionism. J. D. McNeil, *Curriculum: A Comprehensive Introduction* (Boston: Little Brown, 1984), 1–81. Elliot Eisner divided the curriculum field into similar categories in his *Conflicting Conceptions of Curriculum*—E. W. Eisner and E. Valance, eds, *Conflicting Conceptions of Curriculum* (Berkeley: McCutchan, 1974)—and in the first edition of Eisner, *The Educational Imagination*, 1979. In the third edition of that book (Eisner, *The Educational Imagination*, 2001), he adopted the term "curriculum ideologies" in place of "conceptions of curriculum" to describe a slightly different organization of the field.
6   The point here is not, of course, that all beliefs, desires, or actions of human agents are entirely volitional. Clearly we embrace many beliefs, experience numerous desires, and engage in much behavior without due consideration or exercise of will. Nor, as Harry Frankfurt points out, are human beings "alone in having desires and motives, or in making choices." See H. Frankfurt, "Freedom of Will and the Concept of a Person," *Journal of Philosophy* 67, no. 1 (1971): 6. The point rather is that human agents have the capacity to subject their beliefs, desires, and actions to particular sorts of evaluative judgment and to choose whether or not to believe, desire, or enact them based on those judgments. This view may share certain features in common with what philosophers have lately come to call "epistemic voluntarism," which is roughly the view that one's stance is always underdetermined by evidence or argument. Rationality does not compel one to adopt a particular position, therefore, and we are free to choose among a variety of equally compelling alternatives. However, epistemic voluntarism is notoriously difficult to pin down, and in all events my point here is about free will, not epistemology, which entails not only the possibility that people have the capacity to choose beliefs, desires, and actions on the basis of considered judgment, but also that they can choose to ignore those judgments and opt for irrationality as well. See B. von Fraasen, *The Empirical Stance* (New Haven: Yale University Press, 2004); P. Lipton, "Epistemic Options," *Philosophical Studies* 12 (2004): 147–58.
7   Alexander, *Reclaiming Goodness*, 44–48. It is useful to recall that I use the term "fallible" in a broader sense than that commonly associated with the work of Karl Popper. It includes the possibility of moral as well as cognitive mistakes; see Chapter Five n. 37.
8   Frankena, *Ethics*, 72–76; see Chapters Five and Nine.

9   Taylor, *Ethics of Authenticity*; Smith, *Charles Taylor*, 65–66; Walzer, *Thick and Thin*, xi; Alexander, *Reclaiming Goodness*, 145–50.

10 Hegel referred to this kind of transcendental ideal as absolute (see Hegel, *Reason in History*). Kant called them regulative principles (see Kant, *Prolegomena*). They articulate the ends toward which pure and practical reason strive. This guarantees the possibility of truth, since advocates of different intellectual or moral traditions may disagree, but are assumed nonetheless to aspire to common ends. Regulative principles also motivate inquiry, since without the possibility of achieving a desirable end, there would be no reason to inquire altogether. Both Hegel and Kant have been criticized for understanding these ideals as dogmatic and unchanging, whereas a more compelling reading would see them as dynamic concepts, suggesting infinite growth, evolution, or fermentation (see Alexander, *Reclaiming Goodness*, 112; Phenix, "Transcendence and the Curriculum").

11 Frankfurt, "Freedom of Will."

12 Taylor, "What is Human Agency?" in *Human Agency and Language*.

13 Cf. H. A. Alexander, "Ethics, Ideology, and Curriculum," *Jewish Educational Leadership* 2(2004): 4–11.

14 R. Tyler, *Basic Principles of Curriculum and Instruction* (Chicago: University of Chicago Press, 1949).

15 Bobbitt, *How to Make a Curriculum*.

16 W. W. Charters, *Curriculum Construction* (New York, NY: Macmillan, 1923).

17 Bode, *Modern Educational Theories*.

18 D. Hume, *An Enquiry Concerning the Principles of Morals* (La Salle, IL: Open Court, 1953).

19 G. E. Moore, *Principa Ethica* (Cambridge: Cambridge University Press.1993).

20 Of course, not all ethical theorists accept Hume's logical critique or Moore's argument that goodness is not identical with any natural quality; see, A. N. Prior, *Logic and the Basis of Ethics* (Oxford: Oxford University Press, 1949). Critical social theorists would argue, for example, that facts and values are both socially determined and, so, intimately intertwined with one another. Yet, despite these important admonitions to conceive the relations between Is and Ought as less dichotomous than Hume or Moore may have allowed, many critics of this distinction nevertheless admit that there exists a moral or political *telos*, or end in view, or horizon of significance that can be distinguished from our efforts to describe the world in which we live or theorize about how it works; see, Bernstein, *Beyond Objectivism and Relativism*.

21 H. Kliebard, "The Tyler Rationale," in *Curriculum Theorizing*, ed. W. Pinar, 70–83 (Berkeley, CA: McCutchan, 1975).

22 It could be argued that this assumes with the behaviorists that notions such as freedom and dignity are unscientific, ineffective, and meaningless. According to behaviorism, human behavior is to be engineered, not educated, through a process that sidesteps the will altogether by determining outcomes in advance and controlling the environment in order to achieve them, whether or not students would choose these outcomes given the opportunity. See B. F. Skinner, *Beyond Freedom and Dignity* (New York, NY: Knopf, 1971).

23 See Counts, *Dare the Schools Build a New Social Order*.

24 Peters, "Education as Initiation."

25 Schwab, *Science, Curriculum, and Liberal Education*; also Hirst, *Knowledge and the Curriculum*; P. H. Hirst and R. S. Peters, *The Logic of Education* (London: Routledge and Kegan Paul, 1970).

26 L. Shulman and E. Keisler, eds, *Learning by Discovery: A Critical Appraisal* (Chicago: Rand McNally, 1966).

27 Aristotle, *Metaphysics*.

28 Schwab, *Science, Curriculum, and Liberal Education*, 322–83.

29 Shulman, "Those Who Understand."

30 Phillips and Burbules, *Postpositivism and Educational Research*; Bernstein, *Beyond Objectivism and Relativism*.

31 Alexander, "Liberal Education and Open Society."

32 Schwab, *Science, Curriculum, and Liberal Education*, 228.

33 Schwab, *Science, Curriculum, and Liberal Education*.

34 MacIntyre, *After Virtue*; MacIntyre, *Whose Justice, Which Rationality?*

35 See my discussion of the difference between moral and amoral ideologies in the curriculum in Chapter Five.

36 Eisner, *Educational Imagination*, 1st ed.; Eisner, *Educational Imagination*, 3rd ed.

37 Langer, *Problems of Art*.

38 Goodman, *Ways of Worldmaking*.

39 Eisner, *Cognition and Curriculum Reconsidered*; also Huebner, *Lure of the Transcendent*, 23–25.

40 Eisner, *Enlightened Eye*; see Chapter Three.

41 Schwab, *Science, Curriculum, and Liberal Education*, 105–32; also J. Garrison, *Dewey and Eros: Wisdom and Desire in the Art of Teaching* (New York, NY: Teachers College Press, 1997).

42 Eisner, *Educational Imagination*, 3rd ed., 97–107.

43 Alexander, "Liberal Education and Open Society."

44 Taylor, "What is Human Agency?" in *Human Agency and Language*; Taylor, *Ethics of Authenticity*.

45 Walzer, *Thick and Thin*.

46 Alexander, "Elliot Eisner's Aesthetic Theory of Evaluation"; Phenix, "Transcendence and the Curriculum."

47 Eisner, *Educational Imagination*, 3rd ed., 97–107.

48 Apple, *Ideology and Curriculum*; Apple, *Education and Power*.

49 Marx and Engels, *German Ideology*; Horkheimer and Adorno, *Dialectic of Enlightenment*; Foucault, *Order of Things*.

50 Marx and Engels, *German Ideology*.

51 Lyotard, *Postmodern Condition*; Foucault, *Order of Things*; Aronowitz and Giroux, *Postmodern Education*.

52 Watt, *Ideology, Objectivity, and Education*, 1–26.

53 Gur-Ze'ev, *Destroying the Other's Collective Memory*; McLaren, *Life in Schools*.

54 Counts, *Dare the Schools Build a New Social Order*.

55 This appears to be the view taken by O'Neil in *Educational Ideologies*, by John Goodlad in his discussion of ideology in *Curriculum Inquiry: The Study of Curriculum Practice* (New York, NY: McGraw-Hill, 1979), and by Eisner in the third edition of *The Educational Imagination* (47–86).

56 See Chapter Five, n. 17. As I pointed out there, some philosophers have found it useful to make a rather rigid distinction between the terms morals and ethics, reserving the former for the concern in modern philosophy since Kant

with deontological or duty-related questions and the latter for the premodern and post-MacIntyre interest in virtues and values. While I agree with this point in principle, and endorse it in Chapter Twelve, in everyday speech, especially among educators, the terms ethics and morality are used more or less interchangeably, and attempts to insist upon more restrictive uses of the terms may sometimes lead to confusion rather than to increased clarity.

57 Watt, *Ideology, Objectivity, and Education*, 1–26.
58 Alexander, *Reclaiming Goodness*, 94–107.
59 D. Finn, N. Grant, and R. Johnson, *Social Democracy, Education, and the Crisis* (Birmingham, UK: University of Birmingham Center for Contemporary Cultural Studies, 1978), 34, quoted in Apple, *Education and Power*, 150–51.
60 Apple, *Education and Power*.
61 Cf. E. Ellsworth, "Why Doesn't This Feel Empowering: Working Through the Repressive Myths of Critical Pedagogy," *Harvard Educational Review* 59, no. 3 (1989): 297–324.
62 Berlin, "Two Concepts of Liberty," in *Four Essays on Liberty*, 122.
63 Berlin, *Four Essays on Liberty*, 132–33.
64 Some authors go so far as to refer to all "normalizing" education as a form of violence, blurring substantial and important distinctions between the bullying tactics used by repressive rulers and what parents or teachers in particular traditions might do to encourage our traditionally oriented students to remain within the fold (Gur-Ze'ev, *Destroying the Other's Collective Memory*, 1–24).
65 One might respond, of course, that intolerance of this kind is found among all ideological positions, certainly within many of the religious traditions our young traditionalists might choose to embrace. But the whole point here is that we can distinguish between ideological traditions, religious and otherwise, that embrace agency and those that undermine it. Radical curriculum theorists tend to undermine it. For a classic view of political education rooted in rational moral traditions rather than narrow political ideologies, see Oakeshott, "Political Education," in *Rationalism in Politics*, 111–36.
66 Cf. H. A. Alexander, "The Frankfurt School and Post-Zionist Thought," in *Israel and the Post Zionists*, ed. S. Sharan, 71–86 (Brighton: Sussex Academic Press, 2003).
67 To be sure, I do embrace a substantive ethical position, which I call liberal communitarianism (see Chapter Nine). This view undoubtedly influences my criticism not only of the radical curriculum, but also of the traditions represented by Tyler, Schwab, and Eisner, upon which I have commented above. But Apple and other critical pedagogues cannot fault me for this, since they hold that all views, mine as well as theirs, are influenced, if not determined, by ideological, cultural, or class interests, and if my comments are but a mere reflection of my own arbitrary ideological orientation, their positions too must be counted as arbitrary and indefensible on other than narrow ideological grounds. My point, in all events, is not that the radical curriculum does not embrace my own brand of liberalism, but rather that without a conception of agency, its critique of oppression falters as a *moral* critique and the liberation it promises turns out to be a gateway to new forms of subjugation. For a very balanced presentation of additional related issues, see N. C. Burbules and R. Berk, "Critical Thinking and Critical Pedagogy: Relations, Differences, Limits," in *Critical Theories in Education: Changing*

Terrains of Knowledge and Politics, eds T. S. Popkewitz and L. Fendler, 45–65 (New York, NY: Routledge, 1999).

68 Postmodern critical pedagogues might respond that this is but a restatement of their critique of modern critical social theory, since it is never possible to overcome domination. But surely the point of engendering critical consciousness, even for the postmodernists, is to promote some relief from domination, however partial. A critical pedagogy that merely reinforces the inescapability of our current subjugation is a dismal educational theory indeed.

69 Cf. J. Dewey, "The Child and the Curriculum," in *The Child and the Curriculum and the School and the Society* (Chicago: University of Chicago Press, 1909).

70 J. Dewey, *Experience and Education* (New York, NY: Macmillan, 1938); Peters, *Ethics and Education*; I. Scheffler, *Reason and Teaching* (London: Routledge and Kegan Paul, 1973).

71 Berlin, "Two Concepts of Liberty," in *Four Essays on Liberty*, 194.

72 J. E. McPeck, *Teaching Critical Thinking: Dialogue and Dialectic* (New York, NY: Routledge, 1990).

73 R. H. Ennis, *Critical Thinking* (Upper Saddle River, NJ: Prentice-Hall, 1996); S. P. Norris, *The Generalizability of Critical Thinking* (New York, NY: Teachers College Press, 1992); R. Paul, *Critical Thinking: What Every Person Needs To Survive in a Rapidly Changing World* (Rhonert Park, CA: Center for Critical Thinking and Moral Critique, 1993); Siegel, *Educating Reason*.

74 Taylor, *Sources of the Self*.

75 Buber, *I and Thou*.

76 Rosenzweig, "Builders," in *On Jewish Learning*.

77 Cf. Dewey, *Experience and Education*.

78 Walzer, *Thick and Thin*, xi.

79 Alexander, *Reclaiming Goodness*, 92–93.

80 Walzer, *Thick and Thin*, 21.

81 Cf. Oakeshott, *Rationalism in Politics*.

82 Elsewhere I have described two aspects of this expressive dimension of the curriculum. Miriam Ben Peretz and I have called one of these "pedagogy of the sacred." This refers to one of the ways in which we initiate students into the values and virtues we cherish most. Often our most fundamental desires are so embedded in our emotional and cultural beings that it is difficult to be articulate about what makes them important to us. So we turn to nondiscursive forms to express our feelings, such as rituals, metaphors, stories, and symbols. Songs such as national anthems or public ceremonies such as sports rallies can sometimes serve these functions, see Alexander and Ben Peretz, "Pedagogy of the Sacred." I have called a second aspect of this expressive dimension "pedagogy of difference," which suggests that we teach students to celebrate the ways in which they are different, while respecting the differences of others (see Chapter Five).

83 Although justice dictates making every effort to equalize inequalities that are consequences of social conditions such as vast inequity in the distribution of wealth, some inequalities cannot be balanced, such as native intelligences, proclivities, or talents of one kind or another. No matter what we do, not every student will be a great scientist, athlete, or musician.

84   This conception of strong evaluation in the curriculum bears some resemblance to what Richard Paul has called critical thinking in the strong sense, see Paul, *Critical Thinking*; and R. Paul and L. Elder, *Critical Thinking: Tools for Taking Charge of Your Learning and Your Life* (Saddle River, NJ: Prentice-Hall, 2000).

85   The joy that emerges from the admission of one's fallibility suggests that this is a eudaimonian, not a perfectionist or utilitarian ethic; it recognizes the fragility of the human condition, on the one hand, and the satisfaction of learning from our mistakes, on the other. To recognize and learn from error we must accept and grow from criticism, which is not possible in a perfect society. See J. Steutel and D. Carr, eds, *Virtue Ethics and Moral Education* (London: Routledge, 1999), 12–16; and Chapter Nine, n. 40.

CHAPTER NINE

1   Alexander, *Reclaiming Goodness*, 3–24.

2   The term "learning community" is a popular phrase that refers to a particular sort of reflective and inquisitive environment in classrooms. L. Shulman, *Communities of Learning and Communities of Teaching*, Mandel Institute Monographs #3 (Jerusalem: The Mandel Institute, 1997). I use the term in a wider sense to denote communities in which studying a vision of the good is an integral part of their way of life. In traditional Jewish communities, for example, study of sacred texts is a form of worship and worship a form of study. M. Kadushin, *Worship and Ethics* (Westport, CT: Greenwood, 1978). Samuel Heilman draws on the Yiddish *Learnen* to depict the sort of learning and teaching that becomes a driving force of life in the traditional Talmudic academy. S. Heilman, *The People of the Book: Drama, Fellowship, and Religion* (Chicago: University of Chicago Press, 1987); also M. Halbertal and T. H. Halbertal, "The Yeshiva," in *Philosophers on Education*, ed. A. O. Rorty, 458–69 (London: Routledge, 1998); and following Martin Buber, Franz Rosenzweig discusses how *Learnstoff*, or learning of subject matter, can be transformed into *Lehre*, or teaching that transforms life (Rosenzweig, "Builders," in *On Jewish Learning*).

3   The term "liberal communitarian" can be confusing in that communitarians are often critical of political liberalism. The designation is intended to denote the sort of communitarianism that seeks to bolster liberal democracy by replacing extreme individualism with persons tied to expansive communities and should be contrasted with "conservative communitarianism" that supports nonexpansive communities that can undermine open society. Liberal communitarianism shares much with what McDonough and Feinberg have called "affiliated liberalism." K. McDonough and W. Feinberg, "Liberalism and the Dilemma of Public Education in Multicultural Societies," in *Citizenship Education in Liberal Democratic Societies: Teaching for Cosmopolitan Values and Collective Identities*, eds K. McDonough and W. Feinberg, 1–22 (Oxford: Oxford University Press, 2003). However, the former tends to emphasize the democratic need for robust authenticity grounded in affiliation and the latter the tensions between group and individual rights in liberal societies. Liberal

communitarians may authenticate fewer ethical affiliations than affiliated liberals, therefore, in line with the extent to which these affiliations embrace such notions as human agency and responsibility.

4 Geertz, "Blurred Genres," in *Local Knowledge*.

5 Frankena, *Ethics*, 4–9; see Chapter Five.

6 Williams, *Ethics and the Limits of Philosophy*, 1.

7 Frankena, *Ethics*, 9–10.

8 Carr and Steutel, "Introduction," in Steutel and Carr, *Virtue Ethics and Moral Education*, 7. Consequentialist theories like utilitarianism are not usually designated as deontological, since they justify duties on the basis of outcomes rather than the nature of duties themselves. Frankena calls utilitarianism a teleological theory, which moves it closer to the virtues ethics, although some would question whether the maximization of utility could be counted as a genuine purpose or good; it entails nothing other than an aggregate of individually chosen goods. Some refer to consequentialist theories as instrumental rather than teleological; the relation between means and ends in the former is mechanical and quantitative and in the latter qualitative or essential—having to do with the very meaning of values. However, it is not altogether clear that the distinction between instrumentalism and teleology can be maintained.

9 Mill, *On Liberty*, chap. 1, 226.

10 M. Sandel, "Introduction," in *Liberalism and its Critics*, ed. M. Sandel, 1 (Oxford: Basil Blackwell, 1984).

11 Sandel, *Liberalism and its Critics*, 2.

12 Sandel, *Liberalism and its Critics*, 3.

13 Sandel, *Liberalism and its Critics*, 4.

14 Rawls, *Theory of Justice*; Rawls, *Political Liberalism*; Rawls, *Justice as Fairness: A Restatement*.

15 Sandel, *Liberalism and Its Critics*, 5.

16 L. Trilling, *Sincerity and Authenticity* (Cambridge, MA: Harvard University Press, 1982), 3–5.

17 Taylor, *Ethics of Authenticity*, 28–29.

18 Taylor, *Ethics of Authenticity*, 40.

19 Taylor, *Ethics of Authenticity*, 41; also C. Taylor, *Varieties of Religion Today: William James Revisited* (Cambridge, MA: Harvard University Press, 2002).

20 Kenneth Strike raises a number of important questions about the price of "thick" identity in liberal democracy. His main concern seems to be that identity language privileges the demands of association to those of principle in the process of self-definition. This can lead to a new tribalism that subjugates freedom of conscience to the politics of group recognition, and does not adequately describe many people, including Strike himself, who define themselves according to a variety of principles and ideals drawn from many sources. I share Strike's concern that an overemphasis on group solidarity can undermine important democratic values, but am equally concerned that his version of individualism threatens democracy no less. This is one reason why goodness as intelligent spirituality tempers the subjective and collective strands of identity formation with a concern for ideals that transcend self and community. See K. A. Strike, "Pluralism, Personal Identity, and Freedom of Conscience," in *Citizenship and Education in Liberal Democratic Societies*,

eds K. McDonough and W. Feinberg, 76–95 (Oxford: Oxford University Press, 2003); and Alexander, *Reclaiming Goodness*, 139–69.

21 L. Kohlberg, *The Philosophy of Moral Development* (New York, NY: HarperCollins, 1981); S. B. Simon, L. W. Howe, and H. Kirschenbaum, *Values Clarification* (New York, NY: Hart Publishing, 1972); E. Durkheim, *Moral Education* (New York, NY: Free Press, 1961).

22 Reed is hesitant to view Kohlberg as so thoroughly Kantian, and understands Kohlberg's enduring contribution in the development of the notion of just community discussed briefly here. Given the heavy influence of Rawls and Piaget on the early Kohlberg, however, it is difficult to discount the concomitant impact of Kant. Nevertheless, I agree with Reed that the notion of democratic community in the later Kohlberg indicates his awareness of some of the difficulties with Kantian liberalism later raised by the communitarians. See D. R. C. Reed, *Following Kohlberg: Liberalism and the Practice of Democratic Community* (Notre Dame, IN: University of Notre Dame Press, 1998).

23 J. Piaget, *The Child and Reality* (New York, NY: Grossman Publishers, 1973).

24 S. Modgil and C. Modgil, eds, *Lawrence Kohlberg: Consensus and Controversy* (Philadelphia: Falmer, 1986); J. Habermas, *Moral Consciousness and Communicative Action* (Cambridge, MA: MIT Press, 1990), 116–94; D. C. Phillips and J. Nicolayev, "Kohlbergian Moral Development: A Progressing or Degenerating Research Program," *Educational Theory* 28, no. 4 (1978): 268–301.

25 C. Gilligan, *In a Different Voice* (Cambridge, MA: Harvard University Press, 1982); Noddings, *Caring*; Buber, *I and Thou*.

26 Noddings, *Caring*, 73–74; Buber, *I and Thou*, 59.

27 T. H. McLaughlin and M. J. Halstead, "Education in Character and Virtue," in *Education in Morality*, eds T. H. McLaughlin and M. J. Halstead, 132–63, 134–35 (London: Routledge, 1999).

28 N. Noddings, *Educating Moral People: An Alternative to Character Education* (New York, NY: Teachers College Press, 2002).

29 I. Gur-Ze'ev, *Philosophy, Politics, and Education in Israel* [in Hebrew] (Haifa: University of Haifa Press, 1999); Apple, *Ideology and Curriculum*; Apple, *Education and Power*; McLaren, *Life in Schools*.

30 Walzer, *Thick and Thin*.

31 For example, W. J. Bennett, "Moral Literacy and the Formation of Character," in *Moral Character and Civic Education in the Elementary School*, eds J. Benniga, 131–38 (New York, NY: Teachers College Press, 1991); W. J. Bennett, *The Book of Virtues: A Treasury of Great Moral Stories* (New York, NY: Simon and Schuster, 1993).

32 For example, D. Carr, *Educating the Virtues: An Essay on the Philosophical Psychology of Moral Development and Education* (London: Routledge, 1991); Gutmann, *Democratic Education*; Callan, *Creating Citizens*.

33 McLaughlin and Halstead, "Education in Character and Virtue," 137–38.

34 Rosenzweig, "Builders," in *On Jewish Learning*.

35 See Oakeshott, "Political Education," in *Rationalism in Politics*, 43–69.

36 Alexander, *Reclaiming Goodness*, 41–53; see Chapter Five.

37 Taylor, "What is Human Agency?" in *Human Agency and Language*; Taylor, *Sources of the Self*, 25–52.

38 Not all moral philosophers agree that fallibilism is a consequence of freedom and intelligence, see Frankena, *Ethics*, 72, 76.

39 Frankena, *Ethics*, 76.

40 Alexander, *Reclaiming Goodness*, 44–48; see Chapter Eight.

41 The admission of fallibility suggests that this is a eudaimonian, not a perfectionist ethic; it recognizes the fragility of the human condition, on the one hand, and the joy of learning from our mistakes, on the other. To recognize and learn from error, we must accept and grow from criticism, which is not possible in a perfect society. Moral education must engage students in criticism, therefore, from both within and without of particular and common perspectives. Liberal democracies are imperfect, which means that they can get better or worse based on the decisions of the citizens who govern them. See Steutel and Carr, *Virtues Ethics and Moral Education*, 12–16; n. 85 in Chapter Eight.

42 Williams, *Ethics and the Limits of Philosophy*, 4–5.

43 Alexander, *Reclaiming Goodness*, 141–50.

44 Walzer, *Thick and Thin*.

45 Alexander, *Reclaiming Goodness*, 198–201.

46 Tonnies, *Community and Society*; Durkheim, *Division of Labor in Society*.

47 Charles Taylor sums up the characteristics of these sorts of communities in his own interpretation of Hegel that charts a middle way between better-known readings of the left and the right. The German word *Sittlichkeit*, he explains, "refers to the moral obligations I have to an ongoing community of which I am a part." It might be roughly translated as ethics, goodness, and community, and Taylor contrasts them with *Moralitat*, which corresponds to a combination of morality and the notion of the Right. See C. Taylor, *Hegel* (Cambridge, NJ: Cambridge University Press, 1975), 376–77; also A.W. Wood, "Hegel on Education," in *Philosophers on Education*, ed. A. O. Rorty, 300–17 (London: Routledge, 1998).

48 Alasdair MacIntyre's argument for the demise of common schools does not follow from liberal democracy's principled inability to adjudicate between conflicting conceptions of the good; see A. MacIntyre, "How to Seem Virtuous without Actually Being So," in *Education in Morality*, eds T. H. McLaughlin and M. J. Halstead, 118–31 (London: Routledge, 1999). What follows is an increased emphasis in the common school on particularity as proposed by Macedo and enhanced emphases on the commons in separate schooling as suggested by Alexander; see Macedo, *Liberal Virtues*; Alexander, *Reclaiming Goodness*. On the burdens and dilemmas of common schooling in relation to spiritual, moral, and citizenship education, see T. H. McLaughlin, "Education, Spirituality, and the Common School," in *Spirituality, Philosophy and Education*, eds D. Carr and J. Haldane, 185–95 (London: Routledge Falmer, 2003); T. H. McLaughlin, "The Burdens and Dilemmas of Common Schooling," in *Citizenship and Education in Liberal-Democratic Societies*, eds K. McDonough and W. Feinberg, 121–56 (Oxford: Oxford University Press, 2003); and in relation to cultural diversity, see Feinberg, *Common Schools/ Uncommon Identities*.

49 In addition to the influence of William James mentioned here, this view also shares Dewey's commitment to such notions as communities of inquiry, the common faith of democratic societies, and the importance of balancing

tensions between communal and individual interests and between authority and freedom. It also shares Dewey's view that philosophy should address problems of everyday life and find concrete expression in how we live and educate.

50   Alexander, *Reclaiming Goodness*, 150–56.

51   Alexander, *Reclaiming Goodness*.

52   Alexander, *Reclaiming Goodness*, 191–92; Alexander and McLaughlin, "Education in Religion and Spirituality."

53   S. Rawidowicz, "On Interpretation," *Proceedings of the American Academy for Jewish Religion* 26(1957): 83–126; H. A. Alexander, "Science and Spirituality: Tradition and Interpretation in Liberal Education," *Curriculum Inquiry* 22, no. 4 (1992): 383–400; T. H. McLaughlin, "Nicholas Burbules on Jesus as Teacher," in *Spirituality and Ethics in Education*, ed. H. A. Alexander, 21–33 (Brighton: Sussex Academic Press, 2004). In *Creating Citizens*, Eamonn Callan suggests that the sort of juxtaposition of opposing positions required of liberal democracy and "reasonable pluralism" "shapes the self in profound and disturbing ways," because it requires "serious imaginative engagement with rival views about good and evil, right and wrong" (13, 40). I do not find this disturbing in the least. To reap the benefits of liberal society, traditions must engage in the sorts of ongoing reinterpretation that such a society requires. It is this dialectical process that tempers extremism by calling upon members of particular communities to consider their obligations as citizens in a common community that protects the right of all citizens to publicly celebrate distinctiveness. The traditions that are most threatened by this process are likely to be those that pose the greatest threat to liberal democracy, and so in greatest need of "interpretatio."

54   I mean "objective" in the sense developed by Paul Tillich, according to which there is an "object" of "ultimate concern." Faith, on this view, must be in something that has moral content and ontological substance. Tillich, *Dynamics of Faith*, 1–11; also R. Trigg, *Rationality and Religion* (Oxford: Blackwell, 1998), 59–69; Blackburn, *Essays in Quasi-Realism*, 3–11.

55   Phenix, "Transcendence and the Curriculum"; Huebner, *Lure of the Transcendent*.

56   R. M. Adams, *Finite and Infinate Goods: A Framework for Ethics* (Oxford: Oxford University Press,1999), 1.

57   Alexander, *Reclaiming Goodness*, 145–50.

58   It is valid to ask at this juncture what the language of spirituality adds to this discussion. First, it is descriptive. The increased concern for what people are calling spirituality today is a result of these modern dynamics, and intelligent spirituality offers a framework within which this thirst for a way of life can be quenched without damaging the democratic society that makes it possible. Spiritual education, in this view, is inexorably linked to moral and democratic education. Additionally, it constitutes a covering category that indicates how both religious and nonreligious ways of life can fulfill democracy's need for "thick" identity. This is especially important because people on both sides of this divide exclude one another from being considered legitimate responses to this need, e.g., J. White, *Education and Well-Being in a Secular Universe* (London: Institute of Education, University of London, 1995). Finally, it

emphasizes Noddings's point that intelligent believers and unbelievers often have more in common with one another than with unintelligent believers and unbelievers (Noddings, *Educating for Intelligent Belief and Unbelief*, xiii). Surely, the conditions of ethical discourse and the civic virtues of democracy are central ingredients of this commonality.

59 Green, *Voices*, 112–15; H. A. Alexander, "Thomas Green's Educational Formation of Conscience," *The Journal of Philosophy of Education* 34, no. 2 (2000): 395–400.

60 Alexander and McLaughlin, "Education in Religion and Spirituality."

61 However, psychological and sociological understanding is likely to be very useful in the cultivation of identity.

62 Eisner, *Cognition and Curriculum Reconsidered*.

63 In the original version of the essay on which this chapter is based, this section was entitled "The Study of Moral and Spiritual Education." I have changed it in this version to "The Practice of Moral and Spiritual Education" to differentiate this discussion from the chapters in Part Two of this volume that deal with the history and philosophy of educational research. Although I discuss the study of this sort of practice toward the end of the section, my main point here is that this study is a form of Phronesis, or wisdom gleaned from traditions of practice, which is sometimes to be found in the sacred texts of spiritual traditions. Although I have gone to some lengths in Part One to argue that all educational research, indeed all inquiry altogether, begins and ends with what Schwab called "the practical," it seems especially appropriate to emphasize that point in Part Four of this volume, which considers intelligent spirituality in the curriculum.

64 Peters, *Psychology and Ethical Development*.

65 J. Noel, "On Varieties of 'Phronesis,'" *Educational Philosophy and Theory* 31(1999): 273–89.

66 J. Schwab, "The Practical: Something for Curriculum Professors to Do," *Curriculum Inquiry* 13, no. 3 (1983): 239–56; Schwab, *Science, Curriculum, and Liberal Education*, 322–64.

67 Shulman, "Those Who Understand."

68 Jackson, *Life in Classrooms*.

69 P. W. Jackson, R. E. Boostrom, and D. T. Hansen, *The Moral Life of Schools* (San Francisco: Jossey-Bass, 1993).

70 Eisner, *Educational Imagination*, 3rd ed., 215–19; Eisner, *Enlightened Eye*.

71 I use the term "literature and the arts" here to refer to the creation as well as the study of symbolic representation, "history" to refer to the critical study of the past as well as narrative records of collective memory, "philosophy" in the analytic sense of clarifying the meaning of concepts and the logic of arguments and defending one's views on the basis of a prior reasoning, and "theology" as the systematic study of the nature and existence of higher goods, not only of God in the sense common to Western religion, but also the interpretation of traditions that embody those goods in narratives, rituals, symbols, and rules. By qualitative inquiry, I mean the interpretation of educational and communal practices expressed in thick description and grounded in participant observation, key informant interviews, and the examination of material culture.

72 Langer, *Problems of Art*.

73   *Genesis* 6:9. The translation is mine. The authoritative 2000 revision of the 1967 edition of the Jewish Publication Society *Hebrew-English Tanakh* translates the verse as follows: "Noah as a righteous man: he was blameless in his age."

74   D. T. Hansen, *The Call of Teaching* (New York, NY: Teachers College Press, 1995).

75   N. C. Burbules, "Jesus as Teacher," in *Spirituality and Ethics in Education*, ed. H. A. Alexander, 7–20 (Brighton: Sussex Academic Press, 2004); McLaughlin, "Nicholas Burbules on Jesus as Teacher"; H. A. Alexander and S. Glick, "The Judaic Tradition," in *The Blackwell Companion to Philosophy of Education*, ed. R. Curran, 33–49 (Oxford: Blackwell, 2003); H. A. Alexander, "A Jewish View of Human Learning," *The International Journal of Children's Spirituality* 4, no. 2 (1999): 155–64; H. A. Alexander, "God as Teacher: Jewish Reflection on a Theology of Pedagogy," *The Journal of Beliefs and Values* 22, no. 1 (2002): 5–17; H. A. Alexander, "Education," in *Etz Hayim: A Torah Commentary*, ed. D. L. Lieber, 1365–369 (Philadelphia and New York, NY: The Jewish Publication Society and The Rabbinical Assembly, 2002); Y. Waghid, *Conceptions of Islamic Education: Pedagogic Framings* (New York, NY: Peter Lang, 2011).

76   L. Cremin, *Public Education* (New York, NY: Basic Books, 1976), 27–53.

77   Shulman, "Those Who Understand."

78   My students at the University of Haifa, therefore, are examining topics such as the construction of Druze identity in Israeli junior high schools, the role of informal education in the cultivation of secular Jewish identity in Israel, the impact of music in school ceremonies on Israeli identity, and the tensions between religion and modernity in Israeli yeshiva high schools.

79   Glaser and Strauss, *Discovery of Grounded Theory*.

80   See Chapter Three.

81   See Rabbi Shlomo ben Yitzhak on *Genesis* 1:1 and Rabbi Shlomo ben Meir on *Genesis* 37:2.

82   Frankena, *Ethics*, 27; A. J. Heschel, *God in Search of Man* (New York, NY: Farrar, Straus and Cudahy Heschel, 1955), 336–37; D. Bridges, *Fiction Written Under Oath? Essays in Philosophy and Educational Research* (Dordrecht: Kluwer, 2003).

83   Eisner, *Art of Educational Evaluation*; Eisner, *Enlightened Eye*; J. Dewey, *Art as Experience* (New York, NY: Perigree, 1980).

CHAPTER TEN

1   Berlin, *Four Essays on Liberty*; Oakeshott, *Rationalism in Politics*; Gray, *Two Faces of Liberalism*.

2   Kant, *Groundwork*; Kant, *Critique of Practical Reason*; Locke, *Two Treaties of Government*; Rawls, *Theory of Justice*; Rawls, *Political Liberalism*.

3   Callan, "Why Bring the Kids into This?"

4   J. White, *The Aims of Education Re-Stated* (London: Routledge and Kegan Paul, 1982).

5   B. A. Ackerman, *Social Justice in the Liberal State* (New Haven, CT: Yale University Press, 1980); McLaughlin, "Parental Rights," 78.

6 Ackerman, *Social Justice in the Liberal State*, 79. Taylor referred to something like this in his discussion of human agency in which choices that define who we are require strong values that originate outside of us. See Taylor, "What is Human Agency?" in *Human Agency and Language*; Taylor, *Ethics of Authenticity*.
7 Callan, "McLaughlin on Parental Rights," 112–13.
8 Callan, "McLaughlin on Parental Rights," 115–16.
9 McLaughlin, "Religion, Upbringing and Liberal Values," 122.
10 Callan, "Why Bring the Kids into This?" 24.
11 Callan, "Why Bring the Kids into This?" 11.
12 J. Kvanvig, *The Value of Knowledge and the Pursuit of Understanding* (Cambridge: Cambridge University Press, 2003).
13 Callan, "Why Bring the Kids into This?" 24.
14 Callan, "Why Bring the Kids into This?" 10.
15 Callan, "Why Bring the Kids into This?" 12.
16 Callan, "Why Bring the Kids into This?" 10.
17 M. Buber, *Two Types of Faith* (New York, NY: HarperCollins, 1951).
18 H. H. Price, "Belief 'in' and Belief 'that,' " *Religious Studies* 1(1965): 5–28.
19 M. M. Kellner, *Must a Jew Believe Anything* (Oxford: Littman Library of Jewish Civilization, 1999).
20 Walzer, *Thick and Thin*.
21 Halevy, *Kuzari*, 35–49.
22 H. Wolfson, *From Philo to Spinoza: Two Studies in Religious Philosophy* (New York, NY: Behrman House, 1977).
23 Bacon, *New Organon*.
24 Hume, *Enquiry Concerning Human Understanding*; Kant, *Prolegomena*.
25 Kant, *Religion within the Limits of Reason*.
26 MacIntyre critiques Burke's closed form of traditionalism for this reason, MacIntyre, *After Virtue*, 244; E. Burke, *Reflections on the French Revolution* (Oxford: Oxford University Press, 1999).
27 Kuhn, *Structure of Scientific Revolutions*; Lakatos, *Methodology of Scientific Research Programs*.
28 Berlin, *Four Essays on Liberty*.
29 J-J Rousseau, *The Social Contract and Other Later Political Writings* (Cambridge, MA: Cambridge University Press, 1997); Marx, *Critique of Hegel's Philosophy of Right*.
30 Kant, *Groundwork*; Kant, *Critique of Practical Reason*; Locke, *Two Treaties of Government*; Rawls, *Theory of Justice*; Rawls, *Political Liberalism*.
31 Gray, *Two Faces of Liberalism*; Berlin, *Three Critics of Enlightenment*, 168–242; T. Hobbes, *Leviathan* (Peterborough, ON: Broadview Press, 2002); Burke, *Reflections on the French Revolution*; Oakeshott, *Rationalism in Politics*.
32 Callan, "Why Bring the Kids into This?"
33 Callan, "Why Bring the Kids into This?" 15–16.
34 Callan, "Why Bring the Kids into This?" 16; Kvanvig, *Value of Knowledge*, 191–93.
35 Callan, "Why Bring the Kids into This?" 17.
36 Callan, "Why Bring the Kids into This?" 22.
37 Quine, "Two Dogmas of Empiricism," in *From a Logical Point of View*, chap. 1; see Chapter Four.

38 *Quine, Ontological Relativity.*

39 Alexander, *Reclaiming Goodness*, 94–107.

40 Callan, *Creating Citizens*, 17.

41 Kuhn, *Structure of Scientific Revolutions*; Lakatos, *Methodology of Scientific Research Programs.*

42 Foucault, *Order of Things*; Oakeshott, *Rationalism in Politics.*

43 MacIntyre, *After Virtue.* Responding to Sandel's critique of the "unencumbered self" (Sandel, *Liberalism and the Limits of Justice*, 54–59), Callan argues that liberal autonomy requires only that we can revoke "ends currently constitutive of identity should we come to see them as worthless" (Callan, *Creating Citizens*, 54). This appears to presuppose that rational reflection detached from any tradition is the default position against which other attachments can be judged, rather than the more defensible view that one end can only be revoked from the perspective of another.

44 Alexander and McLaughlin, "Education in Religion and Spirituality," 363–64.

45 Callan, "Why Bring the Kids into This?" 19.

46 G. E. M. Anscombe, "On Transubstantiation," in *The Collected Papers of G.E.M. Anscombe*, Vol. 3, *Ethics, Religion, and Politics*, 107–12 (Minneapolis: University of Minnesota Press, 1981).

47 Anscombe, *The Collected Papers of G. E. M. Anscombe*, 107.

48 Anscombe, *The Collected Papers of G. E. M. Anscombe*, 108.

49 Anscombe, "Faith," in *The Collected Papers of G. E. M. Anscombe*,113–20.

50 Callan, *Creating Citizens*, 60, 38.

51 Callan, *Creating Citizens*, 30, 225.

52 Rawls, *Political Liberalism*, 54–58.

53 Callan, *Creating Citizens*, 37–38.

54 Callan, *Creating Citizens*, 65; C. Calhoun, "Standing for Something," *Journal of Philosophy* 68 (1995): 523–39.

55 I. B. Singer, *The Slave* (New York, NY: Farrar, Straus, and Giroux, 1988).

56 I. B. Singer, *Love and Exile* (New York, NY: Farrar, Straus and Giroux, 1986).

57 Callan, *Creating Citizens*, 63.

58 Callan, *Creating Citizens*, 67.

59 Callan, *Creating Citizens.*

60 Alexander, *Reclaiming Goodness*, 156–62. Callan's critique of Rawls's political liberalism in *Creating Citizens* rejects the neutrality of public reason, arguing that liberal values ought to be privileged; but in doing so, he presupposes the very liberal values in question.

61 Oakeshott, *Rationalism in Politics.*

62 Callan, *Creating Citizens*, 38.

63 Oakeshott, *Rationalism in Politics*, 31. The origins of this tendency may also be found in the marriage of religion to political power under the Emperor Constantine I in the fourth century and the so-called companions of Muhammad who became the first Caliphs beginning in the seventh century.

64 Oakeshott, *Rationalism in Politics*, 128.

65 See Chapter Five.

66 Buber, *I and Thou*, 59

67 Palmer, *To Know as We Are Known.*

68 Scheffler, *Conditions of Knowledge.*

69 Buber thought that ritual objectifies dialogue, but tradition can also be encountered as a subject, see Rosenzweig, "Builders," in *On Jewish Learning*.
70 *Genesis* 4:1 (JPS).
71 T. Merton, *New Seeds of Contemplation* (New York, NY: New Directions, 1972).
72 Noddings, *Caring*.
73 Noddings, *Caring*, 30.
74 R. Otto, *The Idea of the Holy* (Oxford: Oxford University Press, 1958); Tillich, *Dynamics of Faith*; Phenix, "Transcendence and the Curriculum"; Eliade, *The Sacred and the Profane*.
75 *Exodus* 5:1(JPS).
76 *Exodus* 32–33. Emphasizing the battle described after the incident of the golden calf in which some three thousand people were killed, Freud suggests that in accepting religion, the Hebrews exchanged one form of slavery for another. S. Freud, *Moses and Monotheism* (New York, NY: Vintage, 1955). Walzer (*Exodus and Revolution*) counters that freedom is often won at the cost of human life, though Moses may have gone overboard in this case.
77 H. A. Alexander, "Soul Searching: Prayer and the Process of Education," in *International Handbook of Religion and Values*, eds J. Arthur and T. Lovat, 146–57 (New York, NY: Routledge, 2013).
78 A. J. Heschel, *God in Search of Man*.
79 Langer, *Problems of Art*; see Chapters Three and Eight.
80 *Isaiah* 6:3 (JPS).
81 *Ezekiel* 3:12 (JPS).
82 Oakeshott, *Rationalism in Politics*.
83 Eisner, *Enlightened Eye*, 9–26.
84 A. J. Heschel, *Man's Quest for God: Studies in Prayer and Symbolism* (New York, NY: Charles Scribner's Sons, 1954), 26.
85 Heschel, *God in Search of Man*, 121.
86 Alexander, *Reclaiming Goodness*, 139–70.
87 *Deuteronomy* 6:5 (JPS).
88 The translation is mine. In his more formal English, Phillip Birnbaum translates this passage as follows: "With a great love hast thou loved us, Lord our God.... Enlighten our Eyes in Thy Torah; attach our hearts to thy commandments," P. Birnbaum, trans. *Daily Prayer Book* (New York, NY: Hebrew Publishing Company, 1997), 76.
89 Callan, *Creating Citizens*; also Macedo, *Liberal Virtues*.
90 Callan, *Creating Citizens*, 40.
91 Berlin, *Four Essays on Liberty*, 133.
92 McLaughlin, "Parental Rights," 76.
93 See Sacks, *Dignity of Difference*. This, perhaps, is what it means to possess "openness with roots." See A. S. Bryk, V. Lee, and P. B. Holland, *Catholic Schools and the Common Good* (Cambridge, MA: Harvard University Press, 1993); Alexander and McLaughlin, "Education in Religion and Spirituality," 363–64; T. H. McLaughlin, "Peter Gardner on Religious Upbringing and the Liberal Ideal of Religious Autonomy," *Journal of Philosophy of Education* 24, no. 2 (1990): 107–125; T. H. McLaughlin and W. Hare, "Four Anxieties about Open-Mindedness: Reassuring Peter Gardner," *Journal of Philosophy of Education* 32, no. 2 (1998): 239–44.
94 Noddings, *Educating for Intelligent Belief and Unbelief*, xiii.

CHAPTER ELEVEN

1   McLaughlin, "Parental Rights"; McLaughlin, "Religion, Upbringing, and Liberal Values"; Callan, "McLaughlin on Parental Rights"; Callan, "Why Bring the Kids into This?"
2   M. Hand, "Faith-Based Education and Upbringing: Some Concluding Remarks," in *Faith in Education: A Tribute to Terence McLaughlin*, ed. G. Haydon, 94–106 (London: Institute of Education, University of London, 2009), 98–99.
3   Eamonn Callan shared this concern with me in conversation, although the formulation is mine.
4   Alexander, "Autonomy, Faith, and Reason," 44; see Chapter Ten.
5   Popper, *Open Society and its Enemies, Vol. II*, 369–96; K. R. Popper, "The Myth of Framework," in *The Myth of the Framework: In Defence of Science and Rationality*, ed. M. A. Notturno (London: Routledge, 1996), chap. 2, 33–64.
6   McLaughlin, "Parental Rights."
7   Callan, "McLaughlin on Parental Rights."
8   McLaughlin, "Religion, Upbringing and Liberal Values," 122.
9   Callan, "Why Bring the Kids into This?" 24.
10   Oakeshott, *Rationalism in Politics*.
11   Quine, "Two Dogmas of Empiricism," in *From a Logical Point of View*, chap. 1; Quine follows in the venerable path of Hume's critique of Bacon, Hegel's critique of Kant, and Berlin's abandonment of the analytic philosophy of his day for the history of ideas.
12   Quine, *Ontological Relativity*.
13   I. Berlin, *Vico and Herder: Two Studies in the History of Ideas* (London: Hogarth Press, 1976); Gray, *Isaiah Berlin*, 38–75.
14   Hand, "Faith-Based Education and Upbringing."
15   Hand, "Faith-Based Education and Upbringing," 98; Callan, "Why Bring the Kids into This?" 19.
16   T. H. McLaughlin, "The Distinctiveness of Catholic Education," in *The Contemporary Catholic School: Context, Identity, and Diversity*, eds T. H. McLaughlin, J. O'Keefe, and B. O'Keefe, 136–54 (London: RoutedgeFalmer, 1996), 144.
17   T. H. McLaughlin, "Distinctiveness and the Catholic School: Balanced Judgment and the Temptations of Commonality," in *Catholic Education: Inside-Out Outside-In*, ed. J. Conroy, 65–87 (Dublin: Veritas, 1999); T. H. McLaughlin, *Liberalism, Education, and Schooling: Essays by T. H. McLaughlin*, St. Andrews Studies in Philosophy and Public Affairs, eds D. Carr, M. Halstead, and R. Pring (Charlottesville, VA: Imprint Academic, 2008), 207–208.
18   Hand, "Faith-Based Education and Upbringing," 99.
19   Alexander and McLaughlin, "Education in Religion and Spirituality," 359; McLaughlin, "Peter Gardner on Religious Upbringing"; T. H. McLaughlin, "The Scope of Parents' Educational Rights," in *Parental Choice and Education: Principles, Policy, and Practice*, ed. J. M. Halstead, 94–107 (London: Kogan Page, 1994); T. H. McLaughlin, "Sex Education, Moral

Controversy, and the Common School," in *Sex, Education, and Religion*, eds J. Reiss and A. Mabud, 186–224 (Cambridge: The Islamic Academy, 1998).

20 Alexander and McLaughlin, "Education in Religion and Spirituality," 361–62.

21 Alexander and McLaughlin, "Education in Religion and Spirituality," 361.

22 McLaughlin, "Education, Spirituality, and the Common School"; McLaughlin, *Liberalism, Education, and Schooling*, 239–52.

23 T. H. McLaughlin, "The Ethics of Separate Schools," in *Ethics, Ethnicity, and Education*, eds M. Leicester and M. J. Taylor, 114–36 (London: Kogan Page, 1992); McLaughlin, "Distinctiveness and the Catholic School"; McLaughlin, *Liberalism, Education, and Schooling*, 175–218.

24 T. H. McLaughlin, "Wittgenstein, Education, and Religion," *Studies in Philosophy of Education* 14, no. 2–3 (1995): 295–311; T. H. McLaughlin, "Israel Scheffler on Religion, Reason, and Education," *Studies in Philosophy of Education* 16, no. 1–2 (1997): 201–23; McLaughlin, *Liberalism, Education, and Schooling*, 282–331.

25 McLaughlin, "Wittgenstein, Education, and Religion"; McLaughlin, *Liberalism, Education, and Schooling*, 183–85.

26 McLaughlin, *Liberalism, Education, and Schooling*, 283.

27 McLaughlin, *Liberalism, Education, and Schooling*, 284

28 Kvanvig, *Value of Knowledge*, 192–93; Callan, "Why Bring the Kids into This?" 14–15.

29 Callan, "Why Bring the Kids into This?" 15–16.

30 McLaughlin, *Liberalism, Education, and Schooling*, 285.

31 McLaughlin, *Liberalism, Education, and Schooling*, 293–98.

32 McLaughlin, *Liberalism, Education, and Schooling*, 295–98.

33 McLaughlin, *Liberalism, Education, and Schooling*, 298; D. Z. Phillips, "Philosophy and Religious Education," *British Journal of Educational Studies* 18(1970): 5–17.

34 McLaughlin, *Liberalism, Education, and Schooling*, 299.

35 McLaughlin, *Liberalism, Education, and Schooling*, 299–301.

36 McLaughlin, "Israel Scheffler on Religion"; McLaughlin, *Liberalism, Education, and Schooling*, 304–31.

37 McLaughlin, "Israel Scheffler on Religion"; McLaughlin, *Liberalism, Education, and Schooling*, 311.

38 R. S. Peters, *Reason, Morality and Education: The Swarthmore Lecture 1972* (London: Friends Home Service Committee, 1972), 1; McLaughlin, *Liberalism, Education, and Schooling*, 305.

39 Peters, *Reason, Morality and Education*, 80; McLaughlin, *Liberalism, Education, and Schooling*, 306.

40 McLaughlin, *Liberalism, Education, and Schooling*, 306–307; Peters, *Reason, Morality and Education*, 81.

41 McLaughlin, *Liberalism, Education, and* Schooling, 308–309; Peters, *Reason, Morality and Education*, 94–98.

42 McLaughlin, *Liberalism, Education, and Schooling*, 311.

43 McLaughlin, *Liberalism, Education, and Schooling*, 312.

44 McLaughlin, *Liberalism, Education, and Schooling*, 304–31.

45 McLaughlin, *Liberalism, Education, and Schooling*, 325; Scheffler, *Reason and Teaching*, 139.

46 McLaughlin, *Liberalism, Education, and Schooling*, 313; I. Scheffler, *Teachers of My Youth: An American Jewish Experience* (Dordrecht: Kluwer, 1995), 14–15.

47 Alexander, "Autonomy, Faith, and Reason," 43; see Chapter Ten.

48 M. Kaplan, *Judaism as a Civilization* (Philadelphia: The Jewish Publication Society of America, 1994).

49 McLaughlin, *Liberalism, Education, and Schooling*, 319; Scheffler, *Teachers of My Youth*, 176.

50 Scheffler, *Reason and Teaching*, 142.

51 Scheffler, *Teachers of My Youth*, 178–82.

52 McLaughlin, *Liberalism, Education, and Schooling*, 320–25.

53 McLaughlin, *Liberalism, Education, and Schooling*, 328; Scheffler, *Teachers of My Youth*, 59.

54 J. Dewey, *Reconstruction in Philosophy* (Boston: Beacon, 1971); Kaplan, *Judaism as a Civilization*.

55 McLaughlin, *Liberalism, Education, and Schooling*, 327–28.

56 McLaughlin, *Liberalism, Education, and Schooling*, 329.

57 McLaughlin, *Liberalism, Education, and Schooling*, 330.

58 McLaughlin, *Liberalism, Education, and Schooling*, 330–31.

59 McLaughlin, *Liberalism, Education, and Schooling*, 204–14; McLaughlin, "Distinctiveness and the Catholic School."

60 Alexander, "Autonomy, Faith, and Reason," 44; see Chapter Ten.

61 Galston, *Liberal Purposes*.

62 In *Reclaiming Goodness*, I called the latter a "community of communities." Alexander, *Reclaiming Goodness*, 41.

63 Berlin, *Four Essays on Liberty*, 118–72.

64 H. A. Alexander, H. Pinson, and Y. Yonah, eds, Conclusion to *Citizenship, Education, and Social Conflict: Israeli Political Education in Global Perspective*, 256–68 (New York, Routledge, 2011).

65 McLaughlin, "Citizenship, Diversity, and Education," 235–50; McLaughlin, *Liberalism, Education, and Schooling*, 120–36.

66 McLaughlin, *Liberalism, Education, and Schooling*, 122.

67 McLaughlin, *Liberalism, Education, and Schooling*, 128.

68 McLaughlin, "Burdens and Dilemmas of Common Schooling"; McLaughlin, *Liberalism, Education, and Schooling*, 137–74.

69 McLaughlin, "Ethics of Separate Schools"; McLaughlin, "Burdens and Dilemmas of Common Schooling"; McLaughlin, *Liberalism, Education, and Schooling*, 137–98; Alexander, Pinson, and Yonah, Conclusion to *Citizenship, Education, and Social Conflict*.

70 Gray, *Two Faces of Liberalism*.

71 McLaughlin, *Liberalism, Education, and Schooling*, 129.

72 Galston, *Liberal Purposes*; McLaughlin, *Liberalism, Education, and Schooling*, 124, 129–30, 150–51.

73 McLaughlin, *Liberalism, Education, and Schooling*, 130.

74 McLaughlin, *Liberalism, Education, and Schooling*, 128, 161.

75 McLaughlin, *Liberalism, Education, and Schooling*, 153, 131.

76 McLaughlin, *Liberalism, Education, and Schooling*, 151–53.

77 McLaughlin, *Liberalism, Education, and Schooling*, 159.

78 McLaughlin, *Liberalism, Education, and Schooling*, 160.

79 McLaughlin, *Liberalism, Education, and Schooling*, 161.
80 Tomasi, *Liberalism Beyond Justice.*
81 McLaughlin, *Liberalism, Education, and Schooling*, 169–72.

CHAPTER TWELVE

1   K. Gary, "Spirituality, Critical Thinking, and the Desire for What is Infinite," *Studies in Philosophy of Education* 25, no. 4 (2006): 315–26.
2   K. Gary, *Studies in Philosophy of Education*, 322.
3   K. Gary, *Studies in Philosophy of Education*.
4   Alexander and McLaughlin, "Education in Religion and Spirituality."
5   Frankena, *Ethics*.
6   James, *Varieties of Religious Experience*.
7   Gary, "Spirituality, Critical Thinking," 323.
8   Gary, "Spirituality, Critical Thinking," 316.
9   Gary, "Spirituality, Critical Thinking," 325.
10 J. Pieper, *Leisure, The Basis of Culture* (South Bend, IN: St. Augustine's Press, 1998), 12.
11 Heschel, *God in Search of Man*.
12 Gary, "Spirituality, Critical Thinking," 326.
13 See Chapter Two; Aristotle, *Metaphysics*; Smith, *Charles Taylor*, 35–41.
14 Gary similarly confuses scholastic contemplation with spiritual exercise in his subsequent essay "Leisure, Freedom, and Liberal Education," *Educational Theory* 56, no. 2 (2006): 121–36. This said, his point is well taken that the current spiritual awakening is reacting against an account of critical thinking with a "penchant for fostering an aggressive, skeptical, questioning bent of mind" (122).
15 I. Twersky, *A Maimonides Reader* (New York, NY: Behrman House, 1972).
16 Heschel, *God in Search of Man*, 348–60.
17 Kellner, *Must a Jew Believe Anything?*
18 Berlin, "Two Concepts of Liberty," in *Four Essays on Liberty*, 118–72.
19 Kant, *Groundwork*.
20 Walzer, *Thick and Thin*.
21 MacIntyre, *After Virtue*.
22 W. James, *Talks to Teachers on Psychology: And to Students on Some of Life's Ideals* (New York, NY: Henry Holt, 1921).
23 Frankfurt, "Freedom of Will."
24 Taylor, "What is Human Agency?" in *Human Agency and Language*.

BIBLIOGRAPHY

Ackerman, B. A. *Social Justice in the Liberal State*. New Haven, CT: Yale University Press, 1980.

Adams, R. M. *Finite and Infinite Goods: A Framework for Ethics*. Oxford: Oxford University Press, 1999.

Alexander, H. A. "Schools without Faith." *Religious Education* 76, no. 3 (1981): 307–21.

———. "Cognitive Relativism in Evaluation." *Evaluation Review* 10, no. 3 (1986a): 259–80.

———. "Elliot Eisner's Aesthetic Theory of Evaluation." *Educational Theory* 36, no. 3 (1986b): 259–70.

———. "Is Phenomenology the Basis of Qualitative Inquiry?" In *Proceedings of the Philosophy of Education Society 1987*, edited by F. Margonis, 379–89. Champaign, IL: The Philosophy of Education Society, 1988.

———. "Liberal Education and Open Society: Absolutism and Relativism in Curriculum Theory." *Curriculum Inquiry* 19, no. 1 (1989): 11–32.

———. "Empathy and Evaluation: Understanding the Private Meanings of Behavior." *Studies in Philosophy of Education* 22, no. 4 (1991): 123–34.

———. "Science and Spirituality: Tradition and Interpretation in Liberal Education." *Curriculum Inquiry* 22, no. 4 (1992): 383–400.

———. "Rationality and Redemption: Ideology, Indoctrination, and Learning Communities." In *Philosophy of Education Yearbook 1996*, edited by F. Margonis, 65–73. Champaign, IL: The Philosophy of Education Society, 1997.

———. "A Jewish View of Human Learning." *The International Journal of Children's Spirituality* 4, no. 2 (1999): 155–64.

———. "Thomas Green's Educational Formation of Conscience." *The Journal of Philosophy of Education* 34, no. 2 (2000): 395–400.

———. *Reclaiming Goodness: Education and the Spiritual Quest*. Notre Dame, IN: University of Notre Dame Press, 2001.

———. "Education." In *Etz Hayim: A Torah Commentary*, edited by D. L. Lieber, 1365–69. Philadelphia and New York: The Jewish Publication Society and The Rabbinical Assembly, 2002a.

———. "God as Teacher: Jewish Reflection on a Theology of Pedagogy." *The Journal of Beliefs and Values* 22, no. 1 (2002b): 5–17.

———. "Aesthetic Inquiry in Education: Community, Transcendence, and the Meaning of Pedagogy." *Journal of Aesthetic Education* 37, no. 2 (2003a): 1–18.

———. "The Frankfurt School and Post-Zionist Thought." In *Israel and the Post Zionists*, edited by S. Sharan, 71–86. Brighton: Sussex Academic Press, 2003b.

———. "Ethics, Ideology, and Curriculum." *Jewish Educational Leadership* 2 (2004a): 4–11.

————. "Moral Education and Liberal Democracy: Spirituality, Community, and Character in an Open Society." *Educational Theory* 53, no. 4 (2004b): 367–87.

————. "Education in Ideology." *The Journal of Moral Education* 34, no. 1 (2005a): 1–18.

————. "Human Agency and the Curriculum." *Theory and Research in Education* 3, no. 3 (2005b): 343–69.

————. "A View from Somewhere: Explaining the Paradigms of Educational Research." *Journal of Philosophy of Education* 40, no. 2 (2006a): 205–22.

————. "Spirituality, Morality, and Criticism in Education: A Response to Kevin Gary." *Studies in Philosophy and Education* 25, no. 4 (2006b): 327–34.

————. "What Is Common about Common Schooling: Rational Autonomy and Moral Agency in Liberal Democratic Education." *Journal of Philosophy of Education* 41, no. 4 (2007): 609–24.

————. "Engaging Tradition: Michael Oakeshott on Liberal Learning." In *Learning to Live with the Future*, edited by A. Stables and S. Gough, 113–27. New York, NY: Routledge, 2008.

————. "Autonomy, Faith, and Reason: McLaughlin and Callan on Religious Initiation." In *Faith in Education: A Tribute to Terence McLaughlin*, edited by G. Haydon, 27–45. London: Institute of Education, University of London, 2009a.

————. "Educating Identity: Toward a Pedagogy of Difference." In *Religious Education as Encounter: A Tribute to John Hull*, edited by S. Miedema, 45–52. Münster: Waxmann, 2009b.

————. "Literacy and Citizenship: Tradition, Reason, and Critique in Democratic Education." In *Philosophy of Education in the Era of Globalization*, edited by Y. Raley, and G. Preyer, 30–50. New York, NY: Routledge, 2010.

————. "Soul Searching: Prayer and the Process of Education." In *International Handbook of Religion and Values*, edited by J. Arthur and T. Lovat, 146–57. New York, NY: Routledge, 2013.

————. "Traditions of Inquiry in Education: Engaging the Paradigms of Educational Research." In *A Companion to Research in Education*, edited by A. D. Reid, E. P. Hart, and M. A. Peters, 13–25. Dordrecht: Springer, 2014.

Alexander, H. A., and M. Ben Peretz. "Toward a Pedagogy of the Sacred: Transcendence, Ethics, and the Curriculum." In *Spiritual Education, Cultural, Religious, and Social Differences: New Perspectives for the 21st Century*, edited by J. Erricker, C. Ota and C. Erricker, 34–47. Brighton: Sussex Academic Press, 2001.

Alexander, H. A., and A. Bursztein. "The Concept of Translation in the Philosophy of Education." [In Hebrew.] In *Studies in Jewish Education*. Vol. 11, edited by J. Cohen, E. Holtzer and A. Isaaacs, 337–54. Jerusalem: The Magnes Press of the Hebrew University of Jerusalem, 2007.

————. "Normative Deliberation in Education." [In Hebrew.] In *Educational Eclectics: Essays in Memory of Shlomo (Seymour) Fox*, edited by S. Wygoda and I. Sorek, 149–69. Jerusalem: Mandel Foundation and Keter Publisher, 2009.

Alexander, H. A., and S. Glick. "The Judaic Tradition." In *The Blackwell Companion to Philosophy of Education*, edited by R. Curran, 33–49. Oxford: Blackwell, 2003.

Alexander, H. A., and T. H. McLaughlin. "Education in Religion and Spirituality." In *The Blackwell Guide to Philosophy of Education*, edited by N. Blake, P. Smeyers, R. Smith and P. Standish, 356–73. Oxford: Blackwell Publishing, 2003.

Alexander, H. A., H. Pinson, and Y. Yonah, eds. Conclusion to *Citizenship, Education, and Social Conflict: Israeli Political Education in Global Perspective*, 256–68. New York, NY: Routledge, 2011.

Althusser, L. *Writings on Psychoanalysis*. New York, NY: Columbia University Press, 1999.

Anscombe, G. E. M. "Faith." In *The Collected Papers of G. E. M. Anscombe*. Vol. 3, *Ethics, Religion, and Politics*, 113–20. Minneapolis: University of Minnesota Press, 1981a.

———. "On Transubstantiation." In *The Collected Papers of G.E.M. Anscombe*. Vol. 3, *Ethics, Religion, and Politics*, 107–112. Minneapolis: University of Minnesota Press, 1981b.

Appiah, K. A. *The Ethics of Identity*. Princeton, NJ: Princeton University Press, 2005.

Apple, M. W. *Ideology and Curriculum*. New York, NY: Routledge, 1979.

———. *Education and Power*. New York, NY: Routledge, 1985.

Aquinas, T. *On the Truth of the Catholic Faith*. Translated by A. Regis. New York, NY: Doubleday, 1955.

Aristotle. *Politics*, edited by T. J. Saunders. Translated by T. A. Sinclair. London: Penguin Classics, 1981.

———. *Metaphysics*. Translated by D. Bostock. Oxford: Clarendon Press, 1994.

Aronowitz, S., and H. Giroux. *Postmodern Education: Politics, Culture and Criticism*. Minneapolis: University of Minnesota Press, 1993.

Bacon, F. *The New Organon*, edited by L. Jardine and M. Silverthorne. Cambridge: Cambridge University Press, 2002.

Bellah, R. N., R. Madsen, W. M. Sullivan, A. Swindler, and S. M. Tipton. *Habits of the Heart: Individualism and Commitment in American Life*. Berkeley: University of California Press, 1986.

Benn, S. *A Theory of Freedom*. Cambridge: Cambridge University Press, 1988.

Bennett, W. J. "Moral Literacy and the Formation of Character." In *Moral Character and Civic Education in the Elementary School*, edited by J. Benniga, 131–38. New York, NY: Teachers College Press, 1991.

———. *The Book of Virtues: A Treasury of Great Moral Stories*. New York, NY: Simon and Schuster, 1993.

Ben-Porath, S. R. *Citizenship under Fire: Democratic Education in Times of Conflict*. Princeton, NJ: Princeton University Press, 2006.

Berger, P., and T. Luckmann. *The Social Construction of Reality*. New York, NY: Penguin, 1969.

Berlin, I. *The Hedgehog and the Fox: An Essay on Tolstoy's View of History*. New York, NY: Simon and Schuster, 1953.

———. *Four Essays on Liberty*. Oxford: Oxford University Press, 1969.

———. *Vico and Herder: Two Studies in the History of Ideas*. London: Hogarth Press, 1976.

———. *Against the Current: Essays in the History of Ideas*. Princeton, NJ: Princeton University Press, 1997.

———. *The Proper Study of Mankind*, edited by H. Hardy and R. Hausheer. London: Random House, 1998.

———. *Three Critics of Enlightenment: Vico, Hamann, and Herder*. Princeton, NJ: Princeton University Press, 2001.

Bernard, H. R. *Research Methods in Anthropology*, Lanham, MA: Rowman and Littlefield, 1995.

Bernstein, R. J. *Beyond Objectivism and Relativism: Science, Hermeneutics, and Praxis*. Philadelphia: University of Pennsylvania Press, 1983.

Biesta, G., and N. C. Burbules. *Pragmatism and Educational Research*. Lanham, MD: Rowman and Littlefield, 2003.

Birnbaum, P., ed. *Daily Prayer Book*. Translated by P. Birnbaum. New York, NY: Hebrew Publishing Company, 1997.

Blackburn, S. *Essays in Quasi-Realism*. Oxford: Oxford University Press, 1993.

Bobbitt, F. *How to Make a Curriculum*. Boston, MA: Houghton Mifflin, 1924.

Bode, B. *Modern Educational Theories*. New York, NY: Macmillan, 1927.

Bodgan, R., and S. K. Bilken. *Qualitative Research for Education*. 5th ed. Boston, MA: Allyn and Bacon, 2006.

Bolle, K. W. *The Freedom of Man in Myth*. Nashville, TN: Vanderbilt University Press, 1968.

Bourdieu, P. *The Logic of Practice*. Translated by R. Nice. Cambridge: Polity Press, 1990.

Bridges, D. *Fiction Written under Oath: Essays in Philosophy and Educational Research*. The Hague: Springer, 2005.

Brighouse, H. *On Education*. New York, NY: Routledge, 2005.

Bruner, J. S. *Actual Minds, Possible Worlds*. Cambridge, MA: Harvard University Press, 1986.

Bryk, A. S., V. Lee, and P. B. Holland. *Catholic Schools and the Common Good*. Cambridge, MA: Harvard University Press, 1993.

Buber, M. *Two Types of Faith*. New York, NY: HarperCollins, 1951.

———. *I and Thou*, New York, NY: Touchstone, 1996.

Burbules, N. C. "Jesus as Teacher." In *Spirituality and Ethics in Education*, edited by H. A. Alexander, 7–20. Brighton: Sussex Academic Press, 2004.

Burbules, N. C., and R. Berk. "Critical Thinking and Critical Pedagogy: Relations, Differences, Limits." In *Critical Theories in Education: Changing Terrains of Knowledge and Politics*, edited by T. S. Popkewitz and L. Fendler, 45–65. New York, NY: Routledge, 1999.

Burke, E. *Reflections on the French Revolution*. Oxford: Oxford University Press, 1999.

Calhoun, C. "Standing for Something." *Journal of Philosophy* 68 (1995): 523–39.

Callahan, R. E. *Education and the Cult of Efficiency*. Chicago, IL: University of Chicago Press, 1962.

Callan, E. "McLaughlin on Parental Rights." *Journal of Philosophy of Education* 19, no. 1 (1985): 111–18.

———. *Autonomy and Schooling*. Kingston and Montreal: McGill-Queen's University Press, 1988.

———. *Creating Citizens: Political Education and Liberal Democracy*. Oxford: Clarendon Press, 2004.

———. "Why Bring the Kids into This? McLaughlin and Anscombe on Religious Understanding." In *Faith in Education: A Tribute to Terence McLaughlin*, edited by G. Haydon, 9–26. London: Institute of Education, University of London, 2009.

Campbell, D. T., and J. Stanley. *Experimental and Quasi-Experimental Design for Research*. Chicago, IL: Rand McNally, 1963.

Carr, D. *Educating the Virtues: An Essay on the Philosophical Psychology of Moral Development and Education*. London: Routledge, 1991.

Carr, D., and J. Steutel. Introduction to *Virtue Ethics and Moral Education*. London: Routledge, 1999.

Cassirer, E. "The Educational Value of Art." In *Symbol, Myth, and Culture*, edited by D. P. Verne, 196–215. New Haven, CT: Yale University Press, 1979.

Charters, W. W. *Curriculum Construction*. New York, NY: Macmillan, 1923.

Chatterji, M. "Evidence on 'What Works': An Argument for Extended-Term Mixed-Method (etmm) Evaluation Designs." *Educational Researcher* 34, no. 5 (2005): 25–31.

Chesterton, G. K. *Orthodoxy*. New York, NY: Dodd, Mead, & Co., 1952.

Cicero, M. T. *The Republic and the Laws*. Translated by N. Rudd. Oxford: Oxford University Press, 2009.

Clandinin, D. J., and M. F. Connelly. *Narrative Inquiry: Experience and Story in Qualitative Research*. San Francisco, CA: Jossey-Bass, 2000.

Coleman, J. S. *The Adolescent Society*. Glencoe, IL: The Free Press, 1962.

Collingwood, R. G. *The Principles of Art*. Oxford: Clarendon, 1964.

Comte, A. *Introduction to Positive Philosophy*. London: Hackett, 1988.

Counts, G. S. *Dare the Schools Build a New Social Order*. Chicago, IL: University of Chicago Press, 1981.

Covers, R. "Nomos and Narrative." *Harvard Law Review* 97, no. 4 (1983): 1–68.

Cremin, L. *Public Education*. New York, NY: Basic Books, 1976.

Creswell, J. W. *Research Design: Qualitative, Quantitative, and Mixed Approaches*. Thousand Oaks, CA: Sage, 2003.

Cronbach, L. J. "Beyond the Two Disciplines of Scientific Psychology." *American Psychologist* 30 (1975): 116–26.

Denzin, N. *The Research Act*. 3rd ed. Englewood Cliffs, NJ: Prentice Hall, 1989.

Descartes, R. *Meditations on First Philosophy*. Translated by J. Cottingham. Cambridge: Cambridge University Press, 1996.

———. *Discourse on Method and Related Writings*. Translated by D. M. Clark. London: Penguin, 1999.

Dewey, J. *The Child and the Curriculum and the School and the Society*. Chicago, IL: University of Chicago Press, 1909.

———. *How We Think*. Boston, MA: Heath, 1910.

———. *Democracy and Education*. New York, NY: Macmillan, 1916.

———. *Experience and Education*. New York, NY: Macmillan, 1938a.

———. *Logic: A Theory of Inquiry*. New York, NY: Henry Holt, 1938b.

———. *Reconstruction in Philosophy*. Boston, MA: Beacon, 1971.

———. *Art as Experience*. New York, NY: Perigee Books, 1980.

Durkheim, E. *Moral Education*. New York, NY: Free Press, 1961.

———. *The Division of Labor in Society*. Translated by W. D. Hall. New York, NY: Macmillan, 1984.

Dworkin, G. *The Theory and Practice of Autonomy*. Cambridge: Cambridge University Press, 1988.

Egan, K. *Getting It Wrong from the Beginning: Our Progressivist Inheritance from Herbert Spencer, John Dewey, and John Piaget*. New Haven, CT: Yale University Press, 2004.

Eisenhart, M. "Hammers and Saws for the Improvement of Educational Research." *Educational Theory* 55, no. 3 (2005): 245–61.

Eisenstadt, S. N. *From Generation to Generation*. Glencoe, IL: The Free Press, 1956.

Eisner, E. W. "Educational Connoisseurship and Educational Criticism: Their Forms and Uses in Educational Evaluation." *Journal of Aesthetic Education* 10, no. 3/4 (1976): 135–50.

———. "The Impoverished Mind." *Educational Leadership* 35, no. 8 (May 1978): 615–23.

———. *The Educational Imagination: On the Design and Evaluation of School Programs*. 1st ed. New York, NY: Macmillan, 1979.

———. "Aesthetic Modes of Knowing." *Learning and Teaching the Ways of Knowing, NSSE Yearbook* 48, no. 2 (1985): 23–36.

———. *The Art of Educational Evaluation: A Personal View*. London: Falmer, 1988.

———. *Cognition and Curriculum Reconsidered*. New York, NY: Teachers College Press, 1994a.

———. *The Educational Imagination: On the Design and Evaluation of School Programs*. 3rd ed. Saddle River, NJ: Prentice-Hall, 1994b.

———. *The Enlightened Eye: Qualitative Inquiry and the Enhancement of Educational Practice*. 2nd ed. Upper Saddle River, NJ: Prentice-Hall, 1998.

Eisner, E. W., and E. Valance, eds. *Conflicting Conceptions of Curriculum*. Berkeley, CA: McCutchan, 1974.

Eliade, M. *Myths, Dreams, and Realities*. New York, NY: Harper and Row, 1957.

———. *Myth and Reality*. New York, NY: Harper and Row, 1963.

———. *The Sacred and the Profane*. New York, NY: Harcourt, Brace, and Javanovich, 1987.

Ellsworth, E. "Why Doesn't This Feel Empowering: Working through the Repressive Myths of Critical Pedagogy." *Harvard Educational Review* 59, no. 3 (1989): 297–324.

Ennis, R.H. *Critical Thinking*. Upper Saddle River, NJ: Prentice-Hall, 1996.

Erickson, F., and K. Gutierrez, "Culture, Rigor, and Science in Educational Research." *Educational Researcher* 31, no. 8 (2002): 21–25.

Feinberg, W. *Understanding Education: Toward a Reconstruction of Educational Inquiry*. Cambridge: Cambridge University Press, 1983.

———. *Common Schools/Uncommon Identities: National Unity and Cultural Difference*. New Haven, CT: Yale University Press, 2000.

———. *For Goodness Sake: Religious Schools and Education for Democratic Citizenry*. New York, NY: Routledge, 2006.

Feuer, M. J., L. Towne, and R. J. Shavelson. "Scientific Culture and Educational Research." *Educational Researcher* 31, no. 8 (2002): 4–14.

Feyerabend, P. K. *Science in a Free Society*. London: Verso, 1982.

———. *Against Method*. London: Verso, 1996.

Finn, D., N. Grant, and R. Johnson. *Social Democracy, Education, and the Crisis*. Birmingham: University of Birmingham Center for Contemporary Cultural Studies, 1978.

Foucault, M. *The Archeology of Knowledge and Discourse on Language*. London: Pantheon, 1982.

———. *The Order of Things: An Archeology of the Human Sciences*. New York, NY: Routledge, 2001.

Frankena, W. K. *Ethics*. 2nd ed. Englewood Cliffs, NJ: Prentice Hall, 1973.

Frankfurt, H. "Freedom of Will and the Concept of a Person." *Journal of Philosophy* 67, no. 1 (1971): 5–20.

Frankl, V. *The Doctor and the Soul*. New York, NY: Random House, 1973.

Freire, P. *Pedagogy of the Oppressed*. London: Continuum, 2000.

———. *Education for Critical Consciousness*. London: Continuum, 2005.

Freud, S. *Moses and Monotheism*. New York, NY: Vintage, 1955.

Gadamer, H. G. *Truth and Method*. New York, NY: Crossroad, 1989.

Galston, W. A. "Civic Education in the Liberal State." In *Liberalism and the Moral Life*, edited by N. L. Rosenblum, 89–101. Cambridge, MA: Harvard University Press, 1989.

———. *Liberal Purposes: Goods, Virtues, and Diversity in the Liberal State*. Cambridge: Cambridge University Press, 1991.

———. *Liberal Pluralism: The Implications of Value Pluralism for Political Theory and Practice*. Cambridge: Cambridge University Press, 2002.

Gange, R. "Educational Technology as Technique." *Educational Technology* 8 (Nov. 1968): 5–18.

Garrison, J. *Dewey and Eros: Wisdom and Desire in the Art of Teaching*. New York, NY: Teachers College Press, 1997.

———. "John Dewey's Theory of Practical Reason." *Educational Philosophy and Theory* 31, no. 3 (1999): 291–312.

Gary, K. "Leisure, Freedom, and Liberal Education." *Educational Theory* 56, no. 2 (2006a): 121–36.

———. "Spirituality, Critical Thinking, and the Desire for What Is Infinite." *Studies in Philosophy of Education* 25, no. 4 (2006b): 315–26.

Geertz, C. *The Interpretation of Cultures*. New York, NY: Basic Books, 1973.

———. *Local Knowledge: Further Essays in Interpretative Anthropology*. New York, NY: Basic Books, 1983.

———. "The Strange Estrangement: Taylor and the Natural Sciences." In *Philosophy in an Age of Pluralism*, edited by J. Tulley, 83–95. Cambridge: Cambridge University Press, 1994.

Gilligan, C. *In a Different Voice*. Cambridge, MA: Harvard University Press, 1982.

Giroux, H. *Border Crossings: Cultural Work and the Politics of Education*. New York, NY: Routledge, 2005.

Glaser, B. G., and A. Strauss. *The Discovery of Grounded Theory*. Chicago, IL: Aldine, 1974.

Goodlad, J. I. *Curriculum Inquiry: The Study of Curriculum Practice*. New York, NY: McGraw-Hill, 1979.

Goodman, N. *Languages of Art*. Indianapolis, IN: Bobbs-Merrill, 1968.

———. *Ways of Worldmaking*. Hassocks: Harvest Press, 1978.

———. "Art as Inquiry." In *Aesthetics Today*, edited by M. Philipson and P. Gudel, 301–21. New York, NY: Meridian, 1990.

Gramsci, A. *Selections from the Prison Notebooks*. New York, NY: International Publishers, 2008.

Gray, J. *Isaiah Berlin*. Princeton, NJ: Princeton University Press, 1996.

———. *The Two Faces of Liberalism*. London: New Press, 2002.

Green, T. F. "Teaching, Acting, and Behaving." *Harvard Educational Review* 34, no. 4 (1964): 507–24.

———. *The Activities of Teaching*. New York, NY: McGraw-Hill, 1971.

———. *Voices: The Educational Formation of Conscience*. Notre Dame, IN: University of Notre Dame Press, 1999.

Guba, E. G. *Toward a Methodology of Naturalistic Inquiry in Education*. Los Angeles, CA: UCLA Center for the Study of Evaluation, 1978.

———. "The Alternative Paradigm Dialogue." In *The Paradigm Dialogue*, edited by E. Guba, 17–27. Newbury Park, CA: Sage, 1990.

Guba, E. G., and Y. S. Lincoln, *Effective Evaluation*. San Francisco, CA: Jossey-Bass, 1981.

———. *Naturalistic Inquiry*. Beverly Hills, CA: Sage, 1985.

———. *Fourth Generation Evaluation*. Newbury Park, CA: Sage, 1989.

Gur-Ze'ev, I. *Philosophy, Politics, and Education in Israel*. [In Hebrew.] Haifa: Haifa University Press, 1999.

———. *Destroying the Other's Collective Memory*. New York, NY: Peter Lang, 2003.

———. *Beyond the Modern-Postmodern Struggle in Education*. Rotterdam: Sense, 2008.

Gutmann, A. *Democratic Education*. Princeton, NJ: Princeton University Press, 1987.

Gutmann, A., and D. Thompson. *Democracy and Disagreement*. Cambridge, MA: Harvard University Press, 1998.

Habermas, J. *Knowledge and Human Interests*. Boston, MA: Beacon, 1972.

———. *Moral Consciousness and Communicative Action*. Cambridge, MA: MIT Press, 1990.

Halbertal, M., and T. H. Halbertal. "The Yeshiva." In *Philosophers on Education*, edited by A. O. Rorty, 458–69. London: Routledge, 1998.

Halevy, Y. *Kuzari: An Argument for the Faith of Israel*. New York, NY: Schocken Books, 1964.

Hand, M. "Faith-Based Education and Upbringing: Some Concluding Remarks." In *Faith in Education: A Tribute to Terence McLaughlin*, edited by G. Haydon, 94–106. London: Institute of Education, University of London, 2009.

Hansen, D. T. *The Call of Teaching*. New York, NY: Teachers College Press, 1995.

Harvey, L. *Critical Social Research*. New York, NY: Routledge, 1990.

Hegel, G. W. F. *Reason in History*. Translated by R. S. Hartman. Minneapolis, MN: Bobbs-Merrill, 1953.

———. *Philosophy of Right*. Oxford: Oxford University Press, 1967.

———. *The Phenomenology of Spirit*. Translated by A. V. Miller. Oxford: Clarendon Press, 1978.

Heidegger, M. *Being and Time*. Translated by J. Stambaugh. New York, NY: SUNY Press, 1996.

Heilman, S. *The People of the Book: Drama, Fellowship, and Religion*. Chicago, IL: University of Chicago Press, 1987.

Hempel, C. G. *The Philosophy of Natural Science*. Englewood Cliffs, NJ: Prentice-Hall, 1966.

Heschel, A. J. *Man's Quest for God: Studies in Prayer and Symbolism*. New York, NY: Charles Scribner's Sons, 1954.

———. *God in Search of Man*. New York, NY: Farrar, Straus and Cudahy, 1955.

Higgins, C. "Teaching and the Good Life." *Educational Theory* 53, no. 2 (2003): 131–54.

Hill, B. V. "Do Religious Studies Belong in the Public School?" *Religious Education* 75, no. 6 (1980): 659–66.

Hirsch, E. D. *Validity in Interpretation*. New Haven, CT: Yale University Press, 1971.

Hirst, P. H. *Knowledge and the Curriculum*. London: Routledge and Kegan Paul, 1974.

Hirst, P. H., and R. S. Peters. *The Logic of Education*. London: Routledge and Kegan Paul, 1970.

Hobbes, T. *Leviathan*. Peterborough, ON: Broadview Press, 2002.

Horkheimer, M., and T. Adorno. *Dialectic of Enlightenment*. Palo Alto, CA: Stanford University Press, 2007.

House, E. R. *The Logic of Evaluative Argument*. Los Angeles, CA: UCLA Center for the Study of Evaluation, 1977.

Howe, K. R. "Against the Quantitative-Qualitative Incompatibility Thesis, or, Dogmas Die Hard." *Educational Researcher* 17 (1988): 10–16.

———. "Getting Over the Quantitative-Qualitative Debate." *American Journal of Education* 100 (1992): 236–56.

———. "The Question of Educational Science: Experimentism vs. Experimentalism." *Educational Theory* 55, no. 3 (2005): 307–21.

Huebner, D. *The Lure of the Transcendent*, edited by V. Hillis. New York, NY: Routledge, 1999.

Hume, D. *An Enquiry Concerning the Principles of Morals*. La Salle, IL: Open Court, 1953.

———. *An Enquiry Concerning Human Understanding*. Oxford: Oxford University Press, 2007.

Husserl, E. *Cartesian Meditations: An Introduction to Phenomenology*. Translated by D. Cairns. The Hague: M. Nijhoff, 1960.

———. *Ideas: A General Introduction to Pure Phenomenology*. Translated by W. R. Boyce Gribson. London: Allen and Unwin, 1967.

———. *The Crisis of the European Science and Transcendental Phenomenology*. Translated by D. Carr. Evanston, IL: Northwestern University Press, 1970.

Jackson, P. W. *Life in Classrooms*. New York, NY: Holt, Rinehart and Winston, 1968.

———. *The Practice of Teaching*. New York, NY: Teachers College Press, 1986.

Jackson, P. W., R. E. Boostrom, and D. T. Hansen. *The Moral Life of Schools*. San Francisco, CA: Jossey-Bass, 1993.

James, W. *The Meaning of Truth*. New York, NY: Longman, Green, 1909.

———. *Talks to Teachers on Psychology: And to Students on Some of Life's Ideals*. New York, NY: Henry Holt, 1921.

———. *The Will to Believe and Other Essays*. New York, NY: Dover, 1956.

———. *The Varieties of Religious Experience*. New York, NY: Signet Classics, 1958.

———. *A Pluralistic Universe*. Lincoln, NE: University of Nebraska Press, 1996.

———. *Pragmatism and Other Writings*. New York, NY: Penguin Classics, 2000.

Johnson, R. B., and A. J. Onwuegbuzie. "Mixed Method Research: A Research Paradigm Whose Time Has Come." *Educational Researcher* 33, no. 7 (2005): 14–26.

Johnston, D. *The Idea of a Liberal Theory: A Critique and a Reconstruction*. Princeton, NJ: Princeton University Press, 1996.

Kadushin, M. *Worship and Ethics*. Westport, CT: Greenwood, 1978.

Kaplan, M. *Judaism as a Civilization*. Philadelphia, PA: The Jewish Publication Society of America, 1994.

Kant, I. *Religion within the Limits of Reason Alone*. New York, NY: Harper Torchbook, 1960.

———. *Critique of Pure Reason* New York, NY: Macmillan, 1970.

———. *The Critique of Judgment*. Oxford: Oxford University Press, 1988.

———. *Critique of Practical Reason*. Translated by M. Gregor. Cambridge: Cambridge University Press, 1997.

———. *Groundwork for the Metaphysics of Morals*. Translated by A. Zweig. Oxford: Oxford University Press, 2002.

———. *Prolegomena to Any Future Metaphysics*. Translated by G. Hatfield. Cambridge: Cambridge University Press, 2004.

Keats, J. "Ode on a Grecian Urn." In *The Complete Poems*, edited by J. Barbard, 344. New York, NY: Viking Press, 1977.

Kellner, M. M. *Must a Jew Believe Anything*. Oxford: Littman Library of Jewish Civilization, 1999.

Kenniston, K. *The Uncommitted: Alienated Youth in American Society*. 1st ed. New York, NY: Harcourt, Brace, and World, 1965.

Kincheloe, J. L., and P. L. McLaren. "Rethinking Critical Theory and Qualitative Research." In *Handbook of Qualitative Research*, edited by N. K. Denzin and Y. S. Lincoln, 138–57. Thousand Oaks, CA: Sage, 1994.

Kliebard, H. "The Tyler Rationale," In *Curriculum Theorizing*, edited by W. Pinar, 70–83. Berkeley, CA: McCutchan, 1975.

———. *The Struggle for the American Curriculum, 1893–1958*. 3rd ed. New York, NY: Routledge, 2004.

Kohlberg, L. "Moral Education in the Schools: A Developmental Approach." *School Review* 74, no. 1 (1966): 1–30.

———. *The Philosophy of Moral Development*. New York, NY: HarperCollins, 1981.

Kuhn, T. S. *The Structure of Scientific Revolutions*. Chicago, IL: University of Chicago Press, 1962.

Kvanvig, J. *The Value of Knowledge and the Pursuit of Understanding*. Cambridge: Cambridge University Press, 2003.

Lakatos, I. *The Methodology of Scientific Research Programs*. Cambridge: Cambridge University Press, 1978.

Lakatos, I., and A. Musgrave, eds. *Criticism and the Growth of Knowledge*. Cambridge: Cambridge University Press, 1970.

Langer, S. *Problems of Art*. New York, NY: Scribners, 1957.

Larkin, R. *Suburban Youth in Cultural Crisis*. New York, NY: Oxford University Press, 1979.

Lesnoff, M. H. *The Structure of Social Science*. London: Allen and Unwin, 1974.

Levin, H. M. *Workplace Democracy and Educational Planning*. Paris: Paris Institute of International Education, UNESCO, 1978.

Levinas, E. *Humanism of the Other*. Translated by N. Poller. Urbana-Champaign, IL: University of Illinois Press, 2005.

Levinson, M. *The Demands of Liberal Education*. Oxford: Oxford University Press, 1999.

Lewin, K. *Field Theory in Social Science*. New York, NY: Harper and Row, 1951.

Lightfoot, S. L. *The Good High School.* New York, NY: Basic Books, 1983.

Lincoln, Y. S., and E. G. Guba. *Naturalistic Inquiry.* Newbury Park, CA: Sage, 1985.

———. "But Is It Rigorous? Trustworthiness and Authenticity in Naturalistic Evaluation." In *Naturalistic Evaluation,* edited by D. D. Williams, 73–84. San Francisco, CA: Jossey-Bass, 1986.

Lipton, P. *Inference to the Best Explanation.* London: Routledge, 1991.

———. "Epistemic Options." *Philosophical Studies* 121 (2004): 147–58.

Locke, J. *An Essay Concerning Human Understanding.* New York, NY: Oxford University Press, 1979.

———. *Two Treaties of Government.* Cambridge: Cambridge University Press, 1988.

Lorrain, J. *The Concept of Ideology.* London: Hutchinson, 1979.

Lucas, G. *Critical Anthropology.* New York, NY: New School for Social Research, 1972.

Lyotard, J. F. *The Postmodern Condition.* Minneapolis: University of Minnesota Press, 1979.

Macedo, S. *Liberal Virtues: Citizenship, Virtue, and Community in Liberal Constitutionalism.* Oxford: Oxford University Press, 1990.

———. *Diversity and Distrust: Civic Education in a Multicultural Democracy.* Cambridge, MA: Harvard University Press, 2000.

Machiavelli, N. *The Prince.* New York, NY: Bantam, 1984.

MacIntyre, A. *After Virtue: A Study in Moral Theory.* Notre Dame, IN: University of Notre Dame Press, 1984.

———. *Whose Justice, Which Rationality?* Notre Dame, IN: University of Notre Dame Press, 1989.

———. "How to Seem Virtuous without Actually Being So." In *Education in Morality,* edited by T. H. McLaughlin and M. J. Halstead, chap. 7, 118–31. London: Routledge, 1999.

Maimonides, M. *Guide to the Perplexed.* Translated by M. Friedlander. New York, NY: Dover, 1956.

Mannheim, K. *Ideology and Utopia.* London: Routledge and Kegan Paul, 1936.

Marx, K. *Critique of Hegel's Philosophy of Right.* Cambridge: Cambridge University Press, 1970.

Marx, K., and F. Engels. *Collected Works.* New York, NY: International Publishers, 1998.

———. *The German Ideology.* New York, NY: Prometheus, 1998.

Maxcy, S. J. "Pragmatic Threads in Mixed Methods Research in the Social Sciences: The Search for Multiple Modes of Inquiry and the End of Philosophical Formalism." In *Handbook of Mixed Methods in Social and Behavioral Research,* edited by A. Tashakkori and C. Teddlie, 51–90. Thousand Oaks: CA, Sage, 2003.

McDonough, K., and W. Feinberg. "Liberalism and the Dilemma of Public Education in Multicultural Societies." In *Citizenship Education in Liberal Democratic Societies: Teaching for Cosmopolitan Values and Collective Identities,* edited by K. McDonough and W. Feinberg, 1–22. Oxford: Oxford University Press, 2003.

McLaren, P. *Life in Schools: An Introduction to Critical Pedagogy in the Foundations of Education.* 2nd ed. White Plains, NY: Longman, 1994.

McLaughlin, T. H. "Parental Rights and the Religious Upbringing of Children."
  Journal of Philosophy of Education 18, no. 1 (1984): 75–83.
———. "Religion, Upbringing and Liberal Values: A Rejoinder to Eamonn Callan."
  Journal of Philosophy of Education 19, no. 1 (1985): 119–27.
———. "Peter Gardner on Religious Upbringing and the Liberal Ideal of Religious
  Autonomy." *Journal of Philosophy of Education* 24, no. 2 (1990): 107–25.
———. "Citizenship, Diversity, and Education: A Philosophical Perspective."
  Journal of Moral Education 21, no. 3 (1992a): 235–50.
———. "The Ethics of Separate Schools." In *Ethics, Ethnicity, and Education*,
  edited by M. Leicester, and M. J. Taylor, 114–36. London: Kogan Page, 1992b.
———. "The Scope of Parents' Educational Rights." In *Parental Choice and
  Education: Principles, Policy, and Practice*, edited by J. M. Halstead, 94–107.
  London: Kogan Page, 1994.
———. "Wittgenstein, Education, and Religion." *Studies in Philosophy of
  Education* 14, no. 2–3 (1995): 295–311.
———. "The Distinctiveness of Catholic Education." In *The Contemporary
  Catholic School: Context, Identity, and Diversity*, edited by T. H. McLaughlin,
  J. O'Keefe, and B. O'Keefe, 136–54. London: RoutedgeFalmer, 1996.
———. "Israel Scheffler on Religion, Reason, and Education." *Studies in
  Philosophy of Education* 16, no. 1–2 (1997): 201–23.
———. "Sex Education, Moral Controversy, and the Common School." In
  Sex, Education, and Religion, edited by J. Reiss and A. Mabud, 186–224.
  Cambridge: The Islamic Academy, 1998.
———. "Distinctiveness and the Catholic School: Balanced Judgment and the
  Temptations of Commonality." In *Catholic Education: Inside-Out Outside-In*,
  edited by J. Conroy, 65–87. Dublin: Veritas, 1999.
———. "The Burdens and Dilemmas of Common Schooling." In *Citizenship and
  Education in Liberal-Democratic Societies*, edited by K. McDonough and
  W. Feinberg, 121–56. Oxford: Oxford University Press, 2003a.
———. "Education, Spirituality, and the Common School." In *Spirituality,
  Philosophy and Education*, edited by D. Carr and J. Haldane, 185–95. London:
  Routledge Falmer, 2003b.
———. "Nicholas Burbules on Jesus as Teacher." In *Spirituality and Ethics in
  Education*, edited by H. A. Alexander, 21–33. Brighton: Sussex Academic Press,
  2004.
———. *Liberalism, Education, and Schooling: Essays by T. H. McLaughlin*.
  St. Andrews Studies in Philosophy and Public Affairs, edited by D. Carr, M.
  Halstead, and R. Pring. Charlottesville, VA: Imprint Academic, 2008.
McLaughlin, T. H., and M. J. Halstead. "Education in Character and Virtue." In
  Education in Morality, edited by T. H. McLaughlin and M. J. Halstead, 132–63.
  London: Routledge, 1999.
McLaughlin, T. H., and W. Hare. "Four Anxieties about Open-Mindedness:
  Reassuring Peter Gardner." *Journal of Philosophy of Education* 32, no. 2
  (1998): 239–44.
McNeil, J. D. *Curriculum: A Comprehensive Introduction*. Boston, MA: Little
  Brown, 1984.
McPeck, J. E. *Teaching Critical Thinking: Dialogue and Dialectic*. New York, NY:
  Routledge, 1990.
Merton, R. K. *Social Theory and Social Structure*. New York, NY: Free Press, 1968.

Merton, T. *New Seeds of Contemplation*. New York, NY: New Directions, 1972.

Mill, J. S. *On Liberty and Other Essays*. In *Collected Works of John Stuart Mill*. Vol. 18, edited by J. M. Robson, 213–310. Toronto, ON: University of Toronto Press, London, Routledge and Kegan Paul, 1977a.

———. *The Logic of the Moral Sciences*. In *Collected Works of John Stuart Mill*. Vol. 18, edited by J. M. Robson, 832–952. Toronto, ON: University of Toronto Press, London: Routledge and Kegan Paul, 1977b.

Mills, C. W. *The Sociological Imagination*. Oxford: Oxford University Press, 2000.

Modgil, S., and C. Modgil, eds. *Lawrence Kohlberg: Consensus and Controversy*. Philadelphia, PA: Falmer, 1986.

Moore, G. E. *Principa Ethica*. Cambridge: Cambridge University Press, 1993.

Moss, P. A. "Understanding the Other/Understanding Ourselves: Toward a Constructive Dialogue about 'Principles' in Educational Research." *Educational Theory 55*, no. 3 (2005): 268–83.

Murdoch, I. *The Sovereignty of Good*. London: Routledge and Kegan Paul, 1970.

Musgrave, F. *Youth and the Social Order*. Bloomington: Indiana University Press, 1964.

———. *Ecstasy and Holiness*. Bloomington: Indiana University Press, 1974.

Nagel, E. *The Structure of Science: Problems in the Logic of Scientific Explanation*. London: Routledge and Kegan Paul, 1961.

Nagel, T. *The View from Nowhere*. Oxford: Oxford University Press, 1986.

Nash, R. J. *Faith, Hype, and Clarity: Teaching about Religion in American Schools and Colleges*. New York, NY: Teachers College Press, 1999.

Nietzsche, F. *The Birth of Tragedy, The Gay Science, Thus Spoke Zarathustra, and On the Genealogy of Morals*, edited by D. B. Allison. Lanham, MD: Rowman and Littlefield, 2001.

Noddings, N. *Caring: A Feminine Approach to Ethics and Moral Education*. Berkeley, CA: University of California Press, 1984.

———. *Educating for Intelligent Belief and Unbelief*. New York, NY: Teachers College Press, 1993.

———. *Educating Moral People: A Caring Alternative to Character Education*. New York, NY: Teachers College Press, 2002.

Noel, J. "On Varieties of 'Phronesis.'" *Educational Philosophy and Theory 31* (1999): 273–89.

Norris, C. *Against Relativism: Philosophy of Science, Deconstruction, and Critical Theory*. Oxford: Blackwell, 1997.

Norris, S. P. *The Generalizability of Critical Thinking*. New York, NY: Teachers College Press, 1992.

Nozick, R. *Philosophical Explanations*. Cambridge, MA: Harvard University Press, 1981.

Oakeshott, M. *Rationalism in Politics and Other Essays*. London: Methuen, 1962.

———. *On Human Conduct*. Oxford: Clarendon Press, 1975.

———. *The Voice of Liberal Learning*. New Haven, CT: Yale University Press, 1989.

———. "Religion and the Moral Life." In *Religion, Politics, and the Moral Life*, edited by T. Fuller, 39–45. New Haven, CT: Yale University Press, 1993.

O'Neill, W. F. *Educational Ideologies: Contemporary Expressions of Educational Philosophy*. Santa Monica, CA: Goodyear Publishing, 1981.

Onwuegbuzie, A. J. "Positivists, Post-Positivists, Post-Structuralists, and Post-Moderns: Why Can't We All Get Along: Towards a Framework for Unifying Research Paradigms." *Education 122*, no. 3 (2002): 518–30.

Otto, R. *The Idea of the Holy*. Oxford: Oxford Press, 1958.

Palmer, P. *To Know As We Are Known: Education as Spiritual Journey*. San Francisco, CA: Harper and Row, 1983.

Parsons, T. *The Social System*. Glencoe, IL: The Free Press, 1951.

Pascal, B. *Pensees*. London: Penguin, 2000.

Patton, M. Q. *Utilization Focused Evaluation*. Thousand Oaks, CA: Sage, 1978.

———. *Qualitative Evaluation Methods*. Thousand Oaks, CA: Sage, 1980.

———. *Qualitative Evaluation and Research Methods*. Newbury Park, CA: Sage, 1990.

Paul, R. *Critical Thinking: What Every Person Needs to Survive in a Rapidly Changing World*. Rhonert Park, CA: Center for Critical Thinking and Moral Critique, 1993.

Paul, R., and L. Elder. *Critical Thinking: Tools for Taking Charge of Your Learning and Your Life*. Saddle River, NJ: Prentice-Hall, 2000.

Pelto, P. J., and G. H. Pelto. *Anthropological Research: The Structure of Inquiry*. Cambridge: Cambridge University Press, 1978.

Peshkin, A. "The Researcher and Subjective Reflections of Ethnography of Schooling." In *Doing Ethnography of Schooling: Educational Ethnography in Action*, edited by G. Spindler, 48–67. New York, NY: Holt, Reinhart, and Winston, 1982.

Peters, R. S. *Education as Initiation*. London: Evans, 1965.

———. *Ethics and Education*. London: George Allen, and Unwin, 1966.

———. *The Concept of Education*. London: Routledge and Kegan Paul, 1967.

———. "Education as Initiation." In *Philosophical Analysis and Education*, edited by R. D. Archambault, 87–112. London: Routledge and Kegan Paul, 1972a.

———. *Reason, Morality and Education: The Swarthmore Lecture 1972*. London: Friends Home Service Committee, 1972b.

———. *Psychology and Ethical Development*. London: George Allen and Unwin, 1974.

Phenix, P. H. *Realms of Meaning*, New York, NY: McGraw-Hill, 1964.

———. "Transcendence and the Curriculum." *Teachers College Record* 73, no. 2 (1971): 271–83.

Phillips, D. C. "A Guide for the Perplexed: Scientific Educational Research, Methodolatry, and the Gold versus Platinum Standards." In *A Companion to Research in Education*, edited by A. D. Reid, E. P. Hart and M. A. Peters, 129–40. Dordrecht: Springer, 2014.

Phillips, D. C., and N. C. Burbules. *Postpositivism and Educational Research*. Lanham, MD: Rowman and Littlefield, 2000.

Phillips, D. C., and J. Nicolayev, "Kohlbergian Moral Development: A Progressing or Degenerating Research Program," *Educational Theory* 28, no. 4 (1978): 268–301.

Phillips, D. Z. "Philosophy and Religious Education." *British Journal of Educational Studies* 18 (1970): 5–17.

Piaget, J. *The Child and Reality*. New York, NY: Grossman Publishers, 1973.

Pieper, J. *Leisure, The Basis of Culture*. South Bend, IN: St. Augustine's Press, 1998.

Plato. *Phaedrus*. Translated by R. Waterfield. Oxford: Oxford University Press, 2002.

———. *The Republic*. Translated by R. Waterfield. Oxford: Oxford University Press, 2008.

Popkewitz, T. *Paradigm and Ideology in Educational Research: The Social Functions of the Intellectual*. London: Falmer, 1984.

Popper, K. R. *The Open Society and Its Enemies*. London: Routledge and Kegan Paul, 1963.

———. *Objective Knowledge*. Oxford: Clarendon Press, 1972.

———. *The Logic of Scientific Discovery*. London: Routledge, 1992.

———. *The Myth of the Framework: In Defence of Science and Rationality*, edited by M. A. Notturno. London: Routledge, 1996.

Price, H. H. "Belief 'in' and Belief 'that.' " *Religious Studies* 1 (1965): 5–28.

Prior, A. N. *Logic and the Basis of Ethics*. Oxford: Oxford University Press, 1949.

Purpel, D. E. *The Moral and Spiritual Crisis in Education*. Granby, MA: Bergin and Garvey, 1988.

Quine, W. V. O. *Ontological Relativity and Other Essays*. New York, NY: Columbia University Press, 1969.

———. *From a Logical Point of View*. Cambridge, MA: Harvard University Press, 1999.

Quine, W. V. O., and J. S. Ullian. *The Web of Belief*. 2nd ed. New York, NY: Random House, 1978.

Ramirez, M., and A. Castaneda. *Cultural Democracy, Bicognitive Development and Education*. New York, NY: Academic Press, 1974.

Raths, L., M. Harmin, and S. Simon. *Values and Teaching*. Columbus, OH: Merrill, 1966.

Rawidowicz, S. "On Interpretation." *Proceedings of the American Academy for Jewish Religion* 26 (1957): 83–126.

Rawls, J. *A Theory of Justice*. Cambridge, MA: Harvard University Press, 1971.

———. *Political Liberalism*. New York, NY: Columbia University Press, 1993.

———. *Justice as Fairness: A Restatement*. Cambridge, MA: Harvard University Press, 2001.

Raz, J. *The Morality of Freedom*. Oxford: Clarendon Press, 1986.

———. *Engaging Reason: On the Theory of Value and Action*. Oxford: Oxford University Press, 2002.

Reed, D. R. C. *Following Kohlberg: Liberalism and the Practice of Democratic Community*. Notre Dame, IN: University of Notre Dame Press, 1998.

Reisman, D. "Al-Farabi and the Philosophical Curriculum." In *The Cambridge Companion to Arabic Philosophy*, edited by P. Adamson and R. Taylor, 52–71. Cambridge: Cambridge University Press, 2005.

Richardson, L. "Writing: A Method of Inquiry." In *Handbook of Qualitative Research*, edited by N. K. Denzin and Y. S. Lincoln, 923–48. Thousand Oaks, CA: Sage, 1994.

Ricoeur, P. *Freud and Philosophy*. Translated by D. Savage. New Haven, CT: Yale University Press, 1970.

———. *The Conflict of Interpretations*. Translated by D. Ihde. Evanston, IL: Northwestern University Press, 1974.

———. *Hermeneutics and the Human Sciences*. Translated by J. B. Thompson. Cambridge: Cambridge University Press, 1981.

Rist, R. "On the Relation among Educational Research Paradigms." *Anthropology and Education Quarterly* 8, no. 2 (1977): 37–57.

Rorty, R. *The Consequences of Pragmatism*. Minneapolis: University of Minnesota Press, 1982.

———. *Contingency, Irony, and Solidarity*. Cambridge: Cambridge University Press, 1989.

Rosenak, M. *Commandments and Concerns: Jewish Religious Education in a Secular Age.* Philadelphia, PA: Jewish Publication Society, 1987.

Rosenfeld, G. *Shut Those Thick Lips: A Study of School Failure.* New York, NY: Holt, Rinehart, and Winston, 1971.

Rosenzweig, F. *On Jewish Learning,* edited by N. Glazer. New York, NY: Schocken, 1955.

Rousseau, J-J. *The Social Contract and Other Later Political Writings.* Cambridge: Cambridge University Press, 1997.

———. *Emile, or Treatise on Education.* Amherst, NY: Prometheus Books, 2003.

Royce, J. *The Basic Writings of Josiah Royce.* Vol. 1 and Vol. 2, edited by J. J. McDermott. New York, NY: Fordham University Press, 2005.

Rozak, T. *The Making of a Counter Culture.* Garden City, NY: Doubleday, 1968.

Rubenstein, R. *The Religious Imagination.* New York, NY: Bobbs and Merrill, 1968.

Ryle, G. *The Concept of Mind.* New York, NY: Harper and Row, 1949.

Sacks, J. *The Dignity of Difference.* Rev. ed. London: Continuum, 2003.

Said, E. *Orientalism.* New York, NY: Vintage Books, 1979.

Sandel, M., ed. *Liberalism and Its Critics.* Oxford: Basil Blackwell, 1984.

———. *Liberalism and the Limits of Justice.* Cambridge: Cambridge University Press, 1998.

Scheffler, I. *Reason and Teaching.* London: Routledge and Kegan Paul, 1973.

———. *Conditions of Knowledge.* Chicago, IL: University of Chicago Press, 1983.

———. *In Praise of the Cognitive Emotions and Other Essays.* New York, NY: Routledge, 1991.

———. *Teachers of My Youth: An American Jewish Experience.* Dordrecht: Kluwer, 1995.

Schutz, A. *On Phenomenology and Human Relations.* Chicago, IL: University of Chicago Press, 1970.

———. *Life Forms and Meaning Structure.* Translated by H. R. Wagner. London: Routledge and Kegan Paul, 1982.

Schutz, A., and T. Luckmann. *The Structures of the Life World.* Translated by R. M. Zaner and J. Tristram Engelhardt. Evanston, IL: Northwestern University Press, 1983.

Schwab, J. *Science, Curriculum, and Liberal Education,* edited by I. Westbury and N. Wilkof. Chicago, IL: University of Chicago Press, 1978.

———. "The Practical: Something for Curriculum Professors to Do." *Curriculum Inquiry* 13, no. 3 (1983): 239–56.

Schwandt, T. A. "Constructivist, Interpretivist Approaches to Human Inquiry." In *Handbook of Qualitative Research,* edited by N. Denzin and Y. S. Lincoln, 118–37. Thousand Oaks, CA: Sage, 1994.

———. "A Diagnostic Reading of Scientifically-Based Educational Research." *Educational Theory* 55, no. 3 (2005): 285–305.

Searle, J. *The Construction of Social Reality.* New York, NY: The Free Press, 1995.

Shaddish, W. R., T. D. Cook, and D. T. Campbell. *Experimental and Quasi-Experimental Designs for Generalized Causal Inference.* Boston, MA: Houghton Mifflin, 2002.

Shulman, L. "Those Who Understand: Knowledge Growth in Teaching." *Educational Researcher* 15, no. 2 (Feb. 1986): 4–14.

———. *Communities of Learning and Communities of Teaching.* Mandel Institute Monographs No. 3. Jerusalem: The Mandel Institute, 1997.

Shulman, L., and E. Keisler, eds. *Learning by Discovery: A Critical Appraisal.* Chicago, IL: Rand McNally, 1966.

Sieber, S. D. "The Integration of Fieldwork and Survey Methods." *American Journal of Sociology* 73 (1973): 1335–59.

Siegel, H. *Relativism Refuted.* The Hague: Reidel, 1987.

———. *Educating Reason.* New York, NY: Routledge, 1988.

———. "Can Rationality Be Redeemed?" In *Philosophy of Education Yearbook 1996*, edited by F. Margonis, 74–76. Champaign, IL: Philosophy of Education Society, 1997.

Simon, S. B., L. W. Howe, and H. Kirschenbaum. *Values Clarification.* New York, NY: Hart Publishing, 1972.

Singer, I. B. *Love and Exile.* New York, NY: Farrar, Straus, and Giroux, 1986.

———. *The Slave.* New York, NY: Farrar, Straus, and Giroux, 1988.

Skinner, B.F. *Beyond Freedom and Dignity.* New York, NY: Knopf, 1971.

Smart, J. C. C. *Ethics, Persuasion, and Truth.* London: Routledge and Kegan Paul, 1984.

Smith, N. H. *Charles Taylor: Meaning, Morals, and Modernity.* Cambridge: Polity, 2002.

Snook, I. A. *Indoctrination and Education.* London: Routledge and Kegan Paul, 1972.

Snow, C. P. *The Two Cultures.* Cambridge: Cambridge University Press, 1990.

Spencer, H. *Education: Intellectual, Moral, Physical.* London: Watts, 1945.

Spindler, G. *Education and Cultural Process.* New York, NY: Holt, Rinehart, and Winston, 1974.

Spradley, J. *The Ethnographic Interview.* New York, NY: Holt, Reinhart, and Winston, 1979.

———. *Participant Observation.* New York, NY: Holt, Reinhart, and Winston, 1980.

Stake, R. E. *The Art of Case Study Research.* Thousand Oaks, CA: Sage, 1995.

Steiner, G. *After Babel: Aspects of Language and Translation.* Oxford: Oxford University Press, 1998.

Steutel, J., and D. Carr, eds. *Virtue Ethics and Moral Education.* London: Routledge, 1999.

St. Peter, E. "'Science' Rejects Postmodernism." *Educational Researcher* 31, no. 8 (2002): 25–28.

Strauss, A., ed. *George Herbert Mead on Social Psychology.* Chicago, IL: University of Chicago Press, 1977.

Strike, K. A. "Pluralism, Personal Identity, and Freedom of Conscience." In *Citizenship and Education in Liberal Democratic Societies*, edited by K. McDonough and W. Feinberg, 76–95. Oxford: Oxford University Press, 2003.

Tamir, Y. *Liberal Nationalism.* Princeton, NJ: Princeton University Press, 1995.

Tarski, A. "The Semantic Conception of Truth." *Philosophy and Phenomenological Research* 4, no. 3 (1944): 341–76.

Tashakkori, A., and C. Teddloe. *Mixed Methodology: Combining Qualitative and Quantitative Approaches.* Thousand Oaks, CA: Sage, 1998.

Taylor, C. *The Explanation of Behavior.* London: Routledge and Kegan Paul, 1964.

———. *Hegel.* Cambridge: Cambridge University Press, 1975.

———. *Philosophy and the Human Sciences.* Cambridge: Cambridge University Press, 1985a.

———. *Human Agency and Language*. Cambridge: Cambridge University Press, 1985b.

———. *Sources of the Self: The Making of Modern Identity*. Cambridge, MA: Harvard University Press, 1989.

———. *The Ethics of Authenticity*. Cambridge, MA: Harvard University Press, 1991.

———. *Varieties of Religion Today: William James Revisited*. Cambridge, MA: Harvard University Press, 2002.

Tillich, P. *The Dynamics of Faith*. New York, NY: HarperCollins, 1986.

Tocqueville, A. de. *Democracy in America*. Translated by G. Lawrence, edited by J. P. Mayer. New York, NY: Harper and Row, 1996.

Tomasi, J. *Liberalism beyond Justice: Citizens, Society, and the Boundaries of Political Theory*. Princeton, NJ: Princeton University Press, 2001.

Tonnies, F. *Community and Society*. Translated by C. P. Loomis. New York, NY: Harper and Row, 1957.

Trigg, R. *Rationality and Religion*. Oxford: Blackwell, 1998.

Trilling, L. *Sincerity and Authenticity*. Cambridge, MA: Harvard University Press, 1982.

Twersky, I. *A Maimonides Reader*. New York, NY: Behrman House, 1972.

Tyack, D. *The One Best System: A History of American Urban Education*. Cambridge, MA: Harvard University Press, 2007.

Tyler, R. *Basic Principles of Curriculum and Instruction*. Chicago, IL: University of Chicago Press, 1949.

von Fraasen, B. *The Empirical Stance*. New Haven, CT: Yale University Press, 2004.

von Wright, G. H. *Explanation and Understanding*. Ithaca, NY: Cornell University Press, 1981.

Vygotsky, L. S. *Mind in Society*. Cambridge, MA: Harvard University Press, 1978.

Waghid, Y. *Conceptions of Islamic Education: Pedagogic Framings*. New York, NY: Peter Lang, 2011.

Walzer, M. *Thick and Thin, Moral Argument at Home and Abroad*. Notre Dame, IN: University of Notre Dame Press, 1985.

———. *Exodus and Revolution*. New York, NY: Basic Books, 1986.

Watt, J. *Ideology, Objectivity, and Education*. New York, NY: Teachers College Press, 1994.

Weber, M. "Science as a Vocation." In *From Max Weber*, edited by H. H. Gerth and C. W. Mills, 129–58. New York, NY: Oxford University Press, 1946.

Weiss, C. *Evaluation Research*. Englewood Cliffs, NJ: Prentice Hall, 1972.

Wexler, P. *Holy Sparks: Social Theory, Education, and Religion*. New York, NY: Macmillan, 1997.

White, J. *The Aims of Education Re-Stated*. London: Routledge and Kegan Paul, 1982.

———. *Education and the Good Life: Autonomy, Altruism, and the National Curriculum*. New York, NY: Teachers College Press, 1991.

———. *Education and Well-Being in a Secular Universe*. London: Institute of Education, University of London, 1995.

Williams, B. *Ethics and the Limits of Philosophy*. Cambridge, MA: Harvard University Press, 1985.

Williams, D. D., ed. *Naturalistic Evaluation*. San Francisco, CA: Jossey-Bass, 1986.

Winch, P. *The Idea of Social Science and Its Relation to Philosophy*. London: Routledge and Kegan Paul, 1958.

Wolfson, H. *From Philo to Spinoza: Two Studies in Religious Philosophy*. New York, NY: Behrman House, 1977.

Wood, A. W. "Hegel on Education." In *Philosophers on Education*, edited by A. O. Rorty, 300–17. London: Routledge, 1998.

Young, I. M. *Inclusion and Democracy*. Oxford: Oxford University Press, 2002.

INDEX

Note: The letter 'n' following locators refers to notes